AUTHOR	CLASS
MACINTYRE, D.	940·545

TITLE The naval war against Hitler.

THE NAVAL WAR AGAINST HITLER

THE NAVAL WAR
AGAINST HITLER

Donald Macintyre

B. T. Batsford Ltd *London*

First published 1971
© Donald Macintyre, 1971
7134 1172 4

Printed in Great Britain by Willmer Brothers Limited, Birkenhead, Cheshire
and bound by C. Tinling and Co. Ltd., Prescot, Lancs., for the publishers
B. T. Batsford Ltd., 4 Fitzhardinge Street, London W1

Contents

Acknowledgment

The author wishes to thank Evans Bros. for permission to use passages from his book *Narvik* (1959) in chapters 1 and 2. Thanks are also due to the respective authors and publishers for permission to quote from the following books: *Brassey's Annual* (1953), William Clowes and Sons Limited for p. 316; Admiral of the Fleet Viscount Cunningham, *A Sailor's Odyssey*, Hutchinson & Co. (Publishers) Limited for pp. 119, 135 and 136; *The Memoirs of Admiral Dönitz*, George Weidenfeld and Nicolson Limited for pp. 110, 261, 262, 327 and 329; Wolfgang Frank, *Sea Wolves*, George Weidenfeld and Nicolson Limited for p. 260; Vice-Admiral Sir Peter Gretton, *Convoy Escort Commander*, Cassell & Co. Limited for p. 322; Professor S. E. Morison, *History of the US Navy in World War II*, Little, Brown & Company and Oxford University Press for pp. 257–9; Admiral W. S. Sims, *The Victory At Sea*, John Murray Publishers for p. 255.

The Author and Publishers also wish to thank the following for permission to reproduce the illustrations which appear in this book: Associated Press for fig. 25; Imperial War Museum for figs 2–9, 11–16, 18–21, 26–31, 34–36, 42–44, 46–50, 52–55, 58–60, and 62–70; Ministero della Difesa Marina, Rome for figs. 33 and 38–41; Ministry of Defence (Royal Navy) for fig. 61, Suddeutscher Verlag, Munich for figs. 22, 37, 51, 56 and 57; Ullstein Verlag; Berlin for figs. 1, 10, 17, 23, 24, 32 and 45.

The Illustrations

Maps and Diagrams

Prologue:
Sea Power's Classic Role

When Hitler, having secured his eastern frontier by the lightning elimination of Poland, turned west to pursue his ambition to dominate Europe, one principal factor stood between him and its achievement; British sea power and the German lack of it.

The narrow failure of the Luftwaffe to overcome the air defence of the British Isles may have prevented the invasion of England, though even if the air assault had succeeded it is by no means certain that invasion would have been feasible without control of the sea. On the other hand, given control of the sea, Germany could have brought about the defeat of Britain without recourse to invasion.

The outcome of the five-year war which followed, so far as it directly concerned Germany and her Italian ally on the one hand and Britain and the USA on the other, depended absolutely upon control of the sea. This firstly allowed Britain to recover her defeated continental army and re-equip it to defy any attempted invasion. It then permitted her to despatch land forces by sea in the traditional style of a maritime power to strike at any chosen part of the enemy's perimeter and withdraw again when the inferiority of the numbers she could muster made this necessary. In this way she was able to hold the enemy in check until the vast resources of the United States came to the rescue to even the odds; following which it was sea power again which enabled the Allies to assault the enemy wherever they chose and to supply their armies after they had been put ashore.

Sea power, which, for most of the time, functions inconspicuously, ponderously and undramatically, depends of course firstly upon a superior strength of warships and the maintenance and supply of such ships, either in suitably situated and defensible bases or by means of a massive, sea-borne logistic complex of auxiliary vessels. But it depends also upon the correct equipment and deployment of this armed strength, the skilful strategic and tactical handling of the fleets, squadrons and units of which it is composed, and the skill and courage of those manning them.

From time to time the weaker power challenges the stronger or defies the latter to prevent her from using the sea for her own purposes. There then comes one of the intermittent flares-up in the war at sea; perhaps a full-scale encounter between major units on either side, perhaps an operation spread over a week or more aimed at securing or preventing the passage of an important military convoy, or perhaps the highlights of a continuous campaign of months or years to secure or prevent the safe passage of the vital sea traffic of one side or the other. Conveniently, if inaccurately, such episodes can be called naval battles; for example the Churchill-designated 'Battle of the Atlantic'.

If the stronger maritime power, so challenged, has failed to keep pace technically with its opponent, if the expertise of its higher command is found defective or if the personnel of its navy has deteriorated in skill or courage, it will lose the battle and lose control of the sea either locally or more widely: in the latter case, it is likely to lose the war.

In September 1939 the German Navy found itself launched into war when its planned massive expansion had hardly been begun. The only heavy ships commissioned and worked up were the so-called pocket-battleships, *Deutschland, Admiral Scheer* and *Admiral Graf Spee,* the two battleships *Scharnhorst* and *Gneisenau* and the cruiser *Admiral Hipper.* In the face of the greatly superior British and French naval strength, therefore, the only challenge they could offer was that of attacking the Allies' merchant shipping. And it was for the role of commerce raiders in distant seas that the pocket battleships had been brilliantly designed. On displacement of some 12,000 tons (ostensibly 10,000 in accordance with the Versailles Treaty) they mounted six 11-inch guns, they had side armour $5\frac{1}{2}$ inches thick and had a top speed of 28 knots, so that the only Allied ships which could successfully engage them were the three British battle-cruisers *Hood, Renown* and *Repulse* and the French *Dunkerque* and *Strasbourg.*

Prior to the outbreak of war the *Deutschland* and *Admiral Graf Spee* had been secretly sailed to waiting positions in the North and South Atlantic, respectively, and on 26 September they began operations. The *Deutschland* found herself foiled by the convoy system which had been quickly established on the transatlantic routes; after an almost fruitless cruise she was recalled to Germany on 1 November. In the South Atlantic, however, where merchant ships continued to sail independently along well-defined routes, the *Graf Spee,* under the command of Captain Langsdorff, soon began to reap a rich harvest; by frequent shifts of ground she was able to evade the numerous Allied hunting groups, which included the carriers *Hermes* and *Ark Royal.*

Had Langsdorff remained content to hunt in the wide, mid-ocean spaces, it is possible he would have been able to continue cruising and

Battle of the River Plate, 13 December 1939

Legend:
- Combined tracks of Ajax and Achilles
- Track of Exeter
- Track of Graf Spee
- Smoke screens

Sea Miles
0 1 2 3

0644
Range 17,000 yards.
31 knots
0700
0708
Range 11,000 yards
Range 13,000 yards
Ajax flies off aircraft 28 knots
Achilles damaged by splinters
0630
Ajax opens fire 25 knots
Achilles opens fire
Range 19,200 yards
0614 Smoke sighted to N.W.
Opens fire
Range 19,400 yards
Hit
2 hits
Hit
2 hits
Fires torpedoes
Exeter, Ajax and Achilles.
Fires torpedoes
Hit
COURSE UNCERTAIN
Firing one turret in local control
Sea slight from S.E.
Visibility extreme
N
Wind moderate

0636
0646
0700
0614
0615
OPENS FIRE ON AJAX & EXETER
0722
Range 11,000 yards
Ajax hit— 2 turrets lost
0730
Ajax fires torpedoes
0730
0800
To Montevideo
0730
To Montevideo

— ARTHUR BANKS —

raiding for many months (as the *Admiral Scheer* was to do from October 1940 to March 1941) and return safely via the Arctic to Germany. The valuable and thronging traffic off the River Plate lured him there, however; and there he was intercepted at 0608 on 13 December 1939 by a squadron composed of the 8-inch cruiser *Exeter* (Captain F. S. Bell) and the 6-inch cruisers *Achilles* (Captain W. E. Parry) of the Royal New Zealand Navy and *Ajax* (Captain C. H. L. Woodhouse) in which flew the broad pennant of Commodore Henry Harwood, who had anticipated Langsdorff's move.

Following tactics on which Harwood had earlier decided in such circumstances, the British force divided into two divisions, the *Exeter* engaging the enemy from the south, the two light cruisers from the east, forcing Langsdorff to divide his armament. Believing at first that he had to deal with only a cruiser and two destroyers, he concentrated his 11-inch guns on the *Exeter* while his secondary armament of eight 5.9-inch guns engaged the two light cruisers.

With the aid of radar (with which British ships were not at that time equipped), the *Graf Spee*'s turret guns quickly found the range of the *Exeter*. She was soon heavily damaged and, 35 minutes after the battle began, she had only one turret left in action and had flooded compartments which gave her a heavy list. By 0750 she had been forced to break off the action.

The *Graf Spee* had not had things all her own way, however. The *Exeter*'s 8-inch guns had hit with their fifth or sixth salvo and several times subsequently. The fire of the two light cruisers had been effective enough to cause Langsdorff to divide his main armament at 0630 and turn one of his turrets on to them; and at 0640 the *Achilles* received some damage, the most serious being the disruption of the radio link by means of which the fire of the two light cruisers was controlled in concentration. This threw out its accuracy for nearly half an hour; nevertheless when the *Graf Spee* turned at 0716 with the apparent intention of finishing off the crippled *Exeter*, the *Ajax* and *Achilles* turned after her, closing the range and scoring so many hits that even their armour-clad opponent was forced to turn back to shake off such a persistent onslaught.

The *Ajax* was twice hit by 11-inch shells; both her after turrets were put out of action and her topmast brought down; with the range by this time down to 8,000 yards, Harwood had to turn away and take cover behind a smoke screen. His bold tactics had been effective, however, and the *Graf Spee* with more than a score of damaging hits, 37 men killed and 57 wounded, now shaped course for the neutral waters of the River Plate and the harbour of Montevideo to seek repairs, turning at intervals to fire a few well-aimed salvos to force the shadowing British cruisers to keep their distance.

A concentration of British warships off the Plate, including the battle-cruiser *Renown*, and the aircraft carrier *Ark Royal* was now set in motion. But except for the 8-inch cruiser *Cumberland* which arrived on the evening of 14 December to replace the *Exeter*, none could arrive until the 19th. Langsdorff obtained permission from the Uruguayan Government for a three-day extension of the normal 24 hours' stay in a neutral port allowed to a belligerent warship, in order to repair damage.

Radio news reports inspired by the British bluffed Langsdorff into believing that the *Ark Royal* and *Renown* were waiting for him when he finally got under way on the evening of the 17th; rather than expose his crew to a hopeless fight against such odds, he scuttled his ship in the estuary after transferring the crew to an attendant German merchant ship. Three days later Langsdorff shot himself.

The first challenge by Hitler's Navy to Allied control of the distant ocean, one which was bound to be of short duration or of insignificant importance so long as the Allies were free to deploy their whole naval strength in opposition, thus ended in failure. The lack of incident elsewhere in the first few months of the war upgraded the engagement into the Battle of the River Plate. It was, in fact one of innumerable episodes in the war against Allied merchant ships, the *guerre de course*, the traditional role of the weaker side in a maritime war.

The *Graf Spee*'s brief career was an attempt to deprive the Allies of an untrammelled use of the ocean. The next challenge to Allied sea power was, conversely, a defiance of Allied ability to prevent German use of the North Sea, the Skagerrak and the Norwegian Sea to launch an invasion of Norway.

1 The Rape of Norway

Through the bitter cold winter of 1939/40, Britain and France, goaded
into a war for which neither felt any universal enthusiasm and for which
neither had been prepared, seemed to be passively awaiting the blow they
knew must fall but which they hoped to postpone by avoiding
provocation. The French, with a false belief in the impregnability of the
Maginot Line, adopted a defensive attitude of mind which was surely
corroding the morale of their fighting forces. Caught in a condition of
military weakness which was the inevitable outcome of a decade during
which it was still believed that the Kaiser's War had been a 'War to end
Wars', followed by a decade in which the Peace Pledge campaign was the
outward sign of a rooted unwillingness to pay for defence, the British
were belatedly adapting their industry to armaments production.

Meanwhile, the absence of the expected air raids on Allied cities
granted a breathing space which neither of the Allies wished to jeopardize
by taking the offensive. Royal Air Force aircraft flew into enemy territory
armed with nothing more lethal than pamphlets which had a negligible
effect on the will to fight of the German people, their powers of reasoning
deadened by the brassy propaganda of their Nazi rulers.

The anticlimactic overture to Armageddon was to be known as the
'phoney war'. Except at sea, indeed, it was 'phoney'. There in home
waters, warships and merchantmen alike were being assailed by mine,
torpedo and bomb; in September the aircraft carrier *Courageous* was
sunk by a U-boat in the South Western Approaches; in the following
month Gunther Prien in *U47* penetrated the defences of Scapa Flow to
sink the battleship *Royal Oak*. Further afield, where merchant ships were
being intercepted by disguised commerce raiders as well as the *Graf Spee*,
the Battle of the River Plate made a nine days' wonder in a Britain bored
by the black-out, irked by rationing and war-time restrictions and hoping
for some evidence that the enemy was being injured.

The events at home relapsed into their previous leisurely pace. Almost
alone in pressing for some offensive action by the Allies was Winston

Churchill, First Lord of the Admiralty. From the beginning of the war his eyes had been fixed on neutral Norway where Germany's most important supply route for high-grade iron ore from the Swedish mines at Lulea was able to run in safety from the port of Narvik, through the channels known as the Leads between the off-shore islands and the coast. He repeatedly pressed the British Government to permit the mining of the Leads to force the traffic out into the open sea where the Royal Navy could get at it.

In Germany, too, Grand Admiral Raeder, C-in-C of the German Navy, was at the same time pointing out to Hitler the desirability of gaining bases on the Norwegian coast and by 10 October 1939 he had already made definite proposals for the occupation of that country.

Neither side took any firm steps to turn proposals into action during the winter 1939–40, though a plan had been drawn up by the Allies for sending volunteers and equipment through Norway and Sweden to the aid of Finland which was courageously fighting off an unprovoked Russian attack. At the same time it was planned to land troops to occupy Narvik and Lulea in the north, Trondheim, Bergen and Stavanger in southern Norway, troops which, it was believed, would be welcomed by the Norwegians.

Before this plan could be implemented, the Finns were forced to surrender; but the possibility of it had led the Germans to complete preparations for their own invasion plan—Operation *Weserübung*—and by 10 March 1940 only four days' notice was required to launch it.

With the collapse of the Finnish plan, Churchill at once began pressing again for his long-desired mine-laying operation, in which he received support from Paul Reynaud, the newly elected French Premier. The Supreme Council at last decided in favour of the plan, the operation being finally fixed for 8 April. That this would be likely to spark off action by the Germans against Norway was foreseen and an invasion force was assembled to occupy the ports of Stavanger, Bergen, Trondheim and Narvik, though only if and when 'the Germans had violated Norwegian neutrality, or there was clear evidence that they intended to do so'. This plan was known as 'R-4'.

Information of Allied activity reaching Germany convinced Hitler that the Allies were planning to occupy Norway and on 1 April 1940 he signed the order setting *Weserübung* on foot, naming 0515 on 9 April as zero hour for the simultaneous assault of all the major Norwegian ports. Thus each of the antagonists, in ignorance of the other's intentions, was, by a remarkable coincidence, simultaneously preparing to operate in Norwegian waters, the British with much hesitation and reluctance, the Germans with ruthless determination, *blitzkrieg* tactics and treachery.

For the German plan, which Raeder frankly admitted to be 'contrary to all principles in the theory of naval warfare' and only feasible 'provided surprise is complete', the whole available German fleet was to be used, divided into six groups, as follows:—

Group I for Narvik—Ten destroyers under Commodore Bonte, carrying 2,000 troops, supported by the battle-cruisers *Scharnhorst* and *Gneisenau* which would make a diversionary cruise in the Arctic after escorting the destroyers to Vestfiord.

Group II for Trondheim—Heavy cruiser *Hipper* and four destroyers carrying 1,700 troops.

These two groups were to sail in company, commanded by Vice-Admiral Lütjens, his flag in the *Gneisenau*.

Group III for Bergen—The light cruisers *Köln* and *Königsberg*, the old training cruiser *Bremse* and a number of small craft, carrying altogether 1,900 troops.

Group IV for Kristiansand and Arendal—The light cruiser *Karlsruhe*, three torpedo boats, a flotilla of MTBs and their parent ship *Tsingtau*.

Group V for Oslo—The heavy cruiser *Blücher*, the pocket battleship *Lützow*, the light cruiser *Emden* and some smaller craft, carrying 2,000 troops.

Group VI for Egersund—Four minesweepers taking 150 men to occupy the Cable Station.

The transports for the initial assaults were similarly organized in groups though they were to sail singly and inconspicuously. In the role of Trojan horses, seven ships would leave Hamburg well in advance, joining the normal traffic to Murmansk, but remaining in wait at Narvik, Trondheim and Stavanger.

Another 15 merchantmen would carry 3,761 troops, 672 horses, 1,377 vehicles and 5,935 tons of Army stores, divided among the various ports. Finally there was the all-important question of oil fuel for the destroyers, particularly those at Narvik, which could not carry sufficient for the return voyage. Two tankers *Kattegat* and *Skagerrak* from Wilhelms-haven would make for Narvik and Trondheim respectively. Another, the *Jan Wellen*, would leave Murmansk for Narvik.*

The whole plan was a model of Teutonic thoroughness and care. As Raeder had said, provided secrecy and surprise were achieved it should succeed, at least so far as delivering the troops to their assault points.

Even as the first assault group slipped out of Wilhemshaven and steered north, British troops for Narvik and Trondheim were filing aboard transports in the Clyde where Admiral Evans had hoisted his flag in the cruiser *Aurora*. Others for Bergen and Stavanger were aboard the ships of the First Cruiser Squadron, *Devonshire*, *Berwick*, *York* and *Glasgow* at Rosyth. Far to the north four destroyers were thrusting through heavy seas and snowstorms towards the Vestfiord at the entrance

---

*At the same time three Groups were to land troops at Copenhagen and two other ports for the occupation of Denmark.

to which they were to lay their mines. In support of them were the battle-cruiser *Renown* and eight destroyers. Further south the minelayer *Teviot Bank* and four destroyers were heading for an area off Stadtlandet.

It might seem that the Fates were setting the stage for a head-on clash as the forces of each side converged on the same chosen areas, ignorant of the other's movements. The facts were to prove far otherwise.

The secrecy which Grand Admiral Raeder had laid down as essential for the success of Operation *Weserübung* was never fully maintained. From various sources indications of something afoot reached the Admiralty, some of them specifically mentioning an impending German invasion of Norway. The C-in-C Home Fleet, Admiral Sir Charles Forbes, was kept informed, but cautioned against accepting the truth of the reports which might well be 'only a further move in the war of nerves'.

When therefore, the German Groups I and II were sighted and reported by RAF reconnaissance aircraft early on 7 April, Forbes took no action beyond bringing the fleet to one hour's notice for steam, pending further information expected from a force of RAF bombers sent to attack. Unfortunately confirmation of the German heavy units' northward progress was not signalled by this force until they returned to base in the afternoon after their unsuccessful attack. Thus it was 2015 that evening before the C-in-C in the battleship *Rodney* led the battleship *Valiant*, the battle-cruiser *Repulse*, the cruisers *Sheffield* and *Penelope* and ten destroyers to sea from Scapa Flow and steered to the north-eastward at high speed. At the same time the Second Cruiser Squadron—*Galatea*, *Arethusa* and 11 destroyers—was ordered to sea from Rosyth to reach a position 80 miles west of Stavanger by 1700 on the 8th and then sweep northwards.

Too late to intercept the two most powerful German Groups—I and II—these moves were to be equally unsuccessful in catching Group III owing to the British forces being kept well out in the North Sea to guard against the possibility of the German moves being directed towards a break-out into the Atlantic. The only encounter during 8 April took place in low visibility at dawn between units of Groups I and II and the solitary British destroyer *Glowworm*, which had lost touch with the *Renown* the previous day in the wild weather. Taken under fire by the *Hipper* at close range, the *Glowworm* was quickly damaged; unable to escape she tried to torpedo her much superior foe and, when that failed, her shattered frame was steered to ram, causing the cruiser serious but not crippling damage before she herself was sunk by gunfire.

During the 8th, the German Groups I and II parted company according to plan, the former carrying on northwards for the Vestfiord while the latter waited at sea until it was time to steer for Trondheim. The remaining Groups duly sailed in time to arrive off their allotted destinations at dawn on the 9th. Group V, for Oslo, was reported passing

Copenhagen and again reported and attacked, unsuccessfully, by a British submarine.

In face of the widespread enemy naval movements which thus became known during the day, the Admiralty immediately abandoned the plan R4, freeing the First Cruiser Squadron from their troop-carrying task. They and other ships on detached duty were ordered to join the C-in-C; but preoccupation with the possibility of an enemy break-out kept all forces except the *Renown*, flying the flag of Vice-Admiral Whitworth, and his accompanying destroyers, well out from the coast, and so uninvolved.

In the far north, indeed, Admiral Whitworth, having collected his nine destroyers off the Vestfiord, following their detachment to lay the minefield called for by the Wilfred plan, had also felt it necessary to steer to seawards to guard against the break-out. In the furious Arctic gale raging he could not get very far; but it was sufficient to uncover the entrance to Vestfiord where at 2000 Commodore Bonte's ten destroyers parted company with the *Scharnhorst* and *Gneisenau* to steam through the snow-swept fiords to Narvik, while the two battle-cruisers turned to punch their way through the northerly gale into the Arctic. And, early on 9 April, while at Narvik, Trondheim, Bergen, Kristiansand and Oslofiord the German invasion forces were about to turn their guns on the meagre defences of neutral Norway, the *Scharnhorst* and *Gneisenau* were sighted from the *Renown*, silhouetted against the dawn light.

In the long-range exchange of fire which followed, both the *Renown* and the *Gneisenau* were hit more than once but without suffering serious damage; but when the German ships increased speed to 28 knots into the teeth of the northerly gale to escape, the forward turrets of both *Scharnhorst* and *Gneisenau* were put out of action by the steep Arctic seas. Unable to accept similar damage, the *Renown* lost touch and turned south-eastward for the Vestfiord to patrol the mouth of which Whitworth had already, belatedly, sent his destroyers.

There, during the forenoon of the 9th, Captain Warburton-Lee, the senior officer in the *Hardy*, received a signal from the C-in-C ordering him 'to send some destroyers up to Narvik to make certain that no enemy troops land'. Then at midday the Admiralty intervened by signalling directly to Warburton-Lee: 'Press reports state one German ship has arrived Narvik and landed a small force. Proceed Narvik and sink or capture enemy ship. It is at your discretion to land forces if you think you can recapture Narvik from number of enemy present.'

With only this scanty and, of course, very erroneous intelligence to go upon, Warburton-Lee was left to decide with what proportion of his destroyer force he should act. Previous orders had called for a patrol to be maintained in the vicinity of the newly-laid minefield and, furthermore, Admiral Whitworth would need destroyers for a screen. Warburton-Lee, therefore, leaving the remainder, set off with the *Hardy*, *Hotspur*,

Havock and *Hunter* of his own Second Flotilla, to feel his way through snow squalls and mist up the fiord, intending to arrive off Narvik at 2000 that evening.

Although, as a result of information coming in from various sources, it was by this time clear to the British Government and Admiralty that a German invasion of Norway was under way, details were lacking. Everywhere, in fact, the Norwegian defences had been taken by surprise; such resistance as was met had been, in accordance with Admiral Raeder's orders, 'broken ruthlessly'.

At Bergen and Trondheim the invaders bluffed their way past the defending batteries which were left to be overrun after the two ports had been occupied almost without a shot fired. At Kristiansand, Group IV was repulsed for a while, only to be finally allowed past the gun defences owing to mistaken identification in poor visibility. In the approaches to Oslo, Group V, having quickly overwhelmed a patrol boat which challenged them, slipped past the outer defences where the battery commanders, lacking orders from headquarters, refused the responsibility of opening fire. In the Drobak Narrows, however, they encountered a resolute defence: the heavy cruiser *Blücher*, leading the line, was knocked out by the guns of the fortress of Oscarsborg and sent to the bottom by two torpedoes with the loss of more than 1,000 troops and sailors.

It was at Narvik that German ruthlessness was most blatantly demonstrated. The ten German destroyers under Commodore Bonte,* carrying 2,000 troops of a mountain division under General Dietl, had little difficulty in navigating the twisting fiords; many of the lights and beacons on shore were still burning in spite of an order from the government to extinguish them. The pilot station at Tranöy was passed at 0300. At 0410 he passed Baröy and entered the long Ofotfiord. Two small patrol boats at the entrance signalled the alarm and for some reason—perhaps in the hope of delaying the Germans—informed them that there were eight warships in Ofotfiord.

At the Narrows of Ramnes, fortifications were reputed to exist but there was no sign of them as the flotilla sailed past. Bonte, however, detached three of his ships to land troops to locate and occupy them. They did not, in fact, exist, though both British and Germans believed them to do so. With the remainder of his ships Bonte led on. Coming abreast Herjangsfiord he detached others to proceed up it and send troops to the little township of Elvegaard where the regimental depot for the area, holding important stocks of equipment, was occupied without resistance. Then with his flotilla leader, *Heidkamp*, the *Arnim* and *Thiele*, he made for the harbour of Narvik itself.

Almost to the minute, at the allotted time of 0515, a snowstorm parted

*Wilhelm Heidkamp (flagship), *Anton Schmitt, Wolfgang Zenker, Hans Lüdemann, Hermann Künne, Dieter von Roeder, Erich Giese, Erich Köllner, Georg Thiele* and *Bernd von Arnim.*

its veil to reveal the harbour crowded with ships of all nationalities loaded with iron ore or awaiting cargoes. In the entrance lay a warship quickly identified as the 4,000-ton coastal defence ship *Eidsvold* of the Royal Norwegian Navy, an ancient vessel dating from 1900 but mounting an armament of two 8.2-inch and six 5.9-inch guns. A signal lamp winked agitatedly, ordering the German ships to stop. A shot was fired across the *Heidkamp*'s bow.

Remembering Raeder's demand for ruthlessness, the Commodore stopped his ships and planned black treachery. A boat was sent to the *Eidsvold* with an officer to demand free passage. If negotiations failed, as they were almost certain to do, the officer was instructed to fire a red Verey light as soon as he left the Norwegian ship.

While he waited for the signal, Bonte surreptitiously manoeuvred his ship to keep his torpedo tubes trained on the *Eidsvold*. As the red light soared into the sky, two torpedoes leapt away on their short run to the target. Before the Norwegians realized what was happening their ship had been blown up, broken in half and sunk with the loss of all but a handful of her company.

The roar of the explosion told the *Eidsvold*'s sister ship *Norge*, flagship of the Senior Naval Officer, Commodore Askim, at anchor inside the harbour, what she could expect. The *Arnim* was already going alongside the wharf, her decks plainly crowded with troops. On to her the *Norge* turned her guns, though ineffectively. The reply was instantaneous as a storm of shots from the quick-firing 5-inch guns of the destroyers fell on her, followed by two torpedoes. The *Norge* rolled over and sank, leaving some 50–60 survivors only.

In sharp contrast to the devoted, if unskilled defence by the *Norge* and the uncompromising attitude of the captain of the *Eidsvold* in the face of hopeless odds, the commandant of the garrison, Colonel Sundlo, proved to be a traitor. A follower of Quisling, he ordered the garrison not to resist. By the time orders came from Divisional headquarters removing him from his post, it was too late and General Dietl was in firm control.

So, during that fatal 9 April, every key position on the coast of Norway fell into German hands in accordance with the plans for *Weserübung*. Boldness, speed and ruthlessness had achieved their object as Raeder had forecast, in the face of Norwegian hesitancy and ill-conceived British naval strategy. So far the loss of the *Blücher* had been the only serious casualty to the German fleet, and Grand Admiral Raeder had cause to be satisfied.

The most dangerous phase of *Weserübung* was still to come, however. Although lack of fighter protection forced the British Home Fleet away from the Norwegian coast during the 9th, unbarring the return routes from Trondheim and Bergen, British submarines were patrolling the Skagerrak and Kattegat. Off Kristiansand was the *Truant* (Lieutenant-

Commander C. H. Hutchinson); after a long day submerged to evade the numerous hunters scurrying to and fro above, a chance came at 1830 for a brief sweep of the horizon through the periscope. It was rewarded with the sight of the *Karlsruhe* making a high-speed, homeward dash. At 1856 Hutchinson gave the order to fire a full salvo of torpedoes. Their tracks were seen and the cruiser swerved to avoid them; but in vain; hit right aft she was stopped, fatally damaged, her end being hastened by torpedoes from an escorting torpedo boat when her crew had been taken off. The *Truant* was meanwhile hunted and attacked remorselessly; she was at the end of her endurance, damaged by depth charges, batteries exhausted and air almost too foul to breath when at last at 2325, 19 hours since she had dived, she broke free of the pursuit and surfaced to head for home and urgent repairs.

Off the Skaw, the submarine *Spearfish* (Lieutenant-Commander J. H. Forbes) had been suffering a similar experience, surfacing damaged half an hour before midnight, after 20 hours submerged. An hour later the pale gleam of what was taken for the tumbling bow-wave of a destroyer was suddenly sighted on the starboard beam. Unwilling to dive with his batteries so low, Forbes put his wheel over to port to get away from this fresh menace. While *Spearfish* was swinging round, he kept his binoculars on the white streak and then realized that what he was looking at was not a bow wave but the stern wash of a ship travelling at high speed—and a big ship, too. It was a worthy target for his torpedoes. Remaining on the surface, he manoeuvred to bring his tubes to bear.

The pocket-battleship *Lützow**—for such was the *Spearfish*'s target—had sailed from Oslo at 1440 that afternoon, 10 April. She was urgently required at Kiel to be prepared for a foray into the Atlantic. Thus, although no suitable fast escorts were available for her, it was decided that high speed and darkness would be sufficient protection from prowling British submarines.

To avoid those reported in the Kattegat, her commanding officer, Captain Thiele, had taken a wide sweep to the westward to avoid the danger area and so fell foul of the *Spearfish*. Unlike British ships at the time, the *Lützow* was equipped with an early version of radar, intended primarily for gunnery ranging. On this, when ten miles north of the Skaw, she detected some object fine on her starboard bow. As the range came down, Thiele ordered an alteration of course to port to avoid it. The swinging stern of the great ship at high speed raised a tall, white stern wave. It was this which had betrayed her to Forbes.

It was this alteration, too, which just gave time for the *Spearfish*'s crew to bring her torpedo tubes to the ready. When, three minutes later, the *Lützow* was brought back to her original course, Forbes was able to launch a salvo of six torpedoes, aiming them hastily by eye at the great ship racing by. One found its mark right aft in the pocket-battleship,

*The *Deutschland* re-named

wrecking her propellers and rudder and causing heavy flooding. She lay, a helpless hulk, drifting on the current towards the Skaw.

So parlous was her condition that Thiele nearly decided to beach her before she should sink. The knowledge that salvage tugs with powerful pumps were on their way held his hand. Carrying on, lying deep in the water, the *Lützow* did indeed ground involuntarily for a time but was hauled off. At a crawl the passage through the Belt to Kiel was made, where she finally arrived on the evening of the 13th, so damaged that it was to be a full year before she went again to sea.

Though the escape route for Group III at Bergen had been uncovered, the light cruiser *Königsberg*, damaged by shore batteries had not been able to take advantage of this to escape. She was reported by air reconnaissance during 9 April and before daylight on the 10th two squadrons of naval Skua dive-bombers took off from the Orkneys for Bergen which was at the extreme limit of their radius of action. Led by Captain R. T. Partridge, Royal Marines, and Lieutenant W. P. Lucy, RN, and navigated by Partridge's senior observer, Lieutenant Geoffrey Hare, they made a perfect landfall to locate the *Königsberg* alongside a jetty in the harbour. Three direct bomb hits and several near misses sent her to the bottom in a few minutes, the first major warship ever to be sunk by an air attack.

At Narvik a fatal flaw in the German plan for withdrawal of their warships had already revealed itself in the non-arrival of one of the two tankers to refuel Bonte's squadron. Only the converted whaleship *Jan Wellen* from Murmansk was found in the harbour. Not until late on the 10th could refuelling be completed; until then the German destroyers were trapped.

The harbour to which they had penetrated lay far from the open sea, being reached by travelling first up the wide Vestfiord, formed by the sea area enclosed between the long line of the Lofoten Islands thrusting south-westward into the Arctic Ocean and the deeply indented mountainous mainland. Where the Vestfiord begins to narrow, the island of Tranöy juts out from the eastern shore and here pilots for the remainder of the journey were normally embarked. A few miles further and the Vestfiord abruptly narrows at the island of Baröy and becomes the Ofotfiord. From here to Narvik the Ofotfiord runs eastward, a narrow waterway between precipitous mountain sides falling sheer into the sea and at that season mantled in deep snow to the water's edge. The steep cliffs break back at intervals to form a number of side fiords. The first of these, on the southern shore, is Ballangenfiord in which there is room to berth one or two small ships, though the little town of Ballangen has no harbour. Then on the same side comes a steep, narrow cleft, Skjomenfiord.

The head of the Ofotfiord has now been reached and here three deep indentations push in between the hills. To the north lies Herjangsfiord with the hamlet of Bjerkvik at its head and the Norwegian regimental depot of

Elvegaard a mile or so from the sea. Eastward runs Rombaksfiord, deep and narrow; south-eastward, Beisfiord. On the hilly promontory between these last two is the town of Narvik, facing down the Ofotfiord, with the harbour formed by the bay just inside the narrow entrance of the Beisfiord. The long, restricted approach to the iron-ore port could easily be defended against an attacker; but exit from it could similarly be blocked.

Nine hundred miles from his base, and with the British fleet at sea in strength to intercept him, the German commander's only hope of breaking out was to sail at the earliest possible moment before the advantage of surprise had been lost. This he had been unable to do, for one of the two tankers which should have been at Narvik to refuel his ships had not arrived, and only the converted whaleship *Jan Wellen* from Murmansk was available. The destroyers each required between 500 and 600 tons of fuel. Not only was this far beyond the capacity of the tanker but her pumping arrangements were such that transfer of oil was very slow and only two destroyers at a time could be served.

Commodore Friedrich Bonte, however, was not unduly worried. He would sail on the night of the 10th when he was confident of evading enemy patrols by a high-speed dash through the night. The naval command would then arrange for tankers to meet his ships at sea. Meanwhile, U-boats were on patrol in the Vestfiord which would give him ample warning of any hostile forces and perhaps be able to damage them also. His powerfully armed ships could then be got ready to give a good account of themselves in the narrow waters of the Ofotfiord. It was unfortunate that the batteries commanding the Narrows did not exist; but to back up the U-boat pickets, one destroyer at a time would be stationed in the Ofotfiord, being relieved as necessary for the refuelling programme.

While waiting their turn to fuel, two destroyers would be berthed off Ballangen, ten miles to the westward of Narvik; others would be in the Herjangsfiord, running north from the main fiord. The remainder, except the one on patrol, would be in the harbour of Narvik itself where the tanker lay.

To the Senior Officer of the Third Flotilla—one of the three flotillas of which the German force was composed—the duty was delegated of ensuring that these arrangements were carried out. Commodore Bonte was thus able to face the night—it was to be his last on earth—with a quiet mind, particularly as at 2022 there came in a signal from *U51* reporting five British destroyers in Vestfiord steering south-west—away from Narvik. There was evidently no immediate attack to be expected, so the German flotilla settled down for the night. In the bitter cold and the falling snow, look-outs huddled in their thick clothing, cursing the fate which put them on watch on such a night when in any case they could see nothing but drifting snowflakes.

The ships which *U51* had glimpsed heading westwards between the snow squalls had been Captain Warburton-Lee's flotilla which we last saw heading up Vestfiord and intending to arrive off Narvik at 2000 on 9 April. On his way, Warburton-Lee pondered the inadequacy of the information in his possession and its doubtful source. A press report on the situation in a remote, minor port beyond the Arctic Circle, that 'one German ship had arrived and landed a small force', was neither dependable nor easily credible.

He bethought himself, therefore, of the pilot station at Tranöy in the Vestfiord. Arriving off it at 1600, he sent ashore to learn what the pilots could tell him. As he had suspected, the Germans were in greater strength than had been reported. Six warships, larger than those of the British flotilla, as well as a submarine had gone up the fiord, the pilots said, adding that the entrance to Ofotfiord was probably mined. The Germans also held the town of Narvik in considerable strength, and the English would need twice as many ships as they had, the Norwegians gloomily estimated.

The Germans were not the only ones, however, who knew the value of surprise. Signalling this fresh intelligence to the Admiralty, Warburton-Lee added: 'Intend attacking at dawn, high water!' High water would allow his ships to float over the moored mines, if they existed; dawn was the ideal moment for achieving surprise.

While off Tranöy, Warburton-Lee had a welcome reinforcement in the shape of the *Hostile*, commanded by Commander J. P. Wright. He had been on detached service with the cruiser *Birmingham*; but when that ship was sent home, he had hurried to join his flotilla leader. With his five ships, Warburton-Lee now turned seawards to await the hour at which he calculated he must turn back to arrive off Narvik at first light. Thus it was that *U51* had sighted him on a course away from Narvik which gave a false sense of security to Commodore Bonte.

At 2100, in reply to Warburton-Lee's signal, the Admiralty gave him orders which would have had most unfortunate results had they been obeyed. The flotilla was to patrol during the night in the entrance to Ofotfiord, lest the enemy should leave Narvik and by turning off through Tjelsundert, a channel leading north to Vaagsfiord, escape without encountering the British force. Fortunately, Warburton-Lee ignored this message. Otherwise he would certainly have run against the German destroyer on patrol, surprise would have been lost and calamity might have followed.

The message ended, 'Attack at dawn: all good luck'. This was sufficient for *Hardy*'s captain. Thereafter he had no doubt as to what he must do, even when the Admiralty in midnight session thought the operation was so hazardous that they began to have second thoughts and signalled: 'Norwegian coast defence ships *Eidsvold* and *Norge* may be in German hands: you alone can judge whether in these circumstances attack should be made. We shall support whatever decision you take'. By the time this reached him, the flotilla was already past Tranöy and, in continuous snowstorms, was feeling its way into Ofotfiord.

Out at sea, Admiral Whitworth in the *Renown* had followed this interchange of signals and from the moment he had received Warburton-Lee's first signal at 1800 had pondered whether he should send reinforcements to the Second Flotilla. He had the cruiser *Penelope* and destroyers under his command. By the time they could make their way up the Vestfiord through the blinding curtain of falling snow and join forces with the Second Flotilla delay would have been imposed on the operation.* He decided to leave well alone. In the light of later events it seems unfortunate that the *Penelope* was not sent after the Second Flotilla even if she did not join it until after the attack had been delivered.†

At 0100 on 10 April they had groped their way past Tranöy. Following the *Hardy* was the *Hunter* commanded by Lieutenant-Commander L. de Villiers. In her wake came the *Havock*, Lieutenant-Commander Rafe Courage. The *Hotspur* was next, the ship of the second-in-command of the force, Commander H. F. N. Layman, and finally, the *Hostile*.

The shoreline was invisible behind the curtain of snow for long stretches of the tortuous passage. One nearly disastrous moment came when a white hillside loomed dimly out of the mists directly ahead of the *Hardy*, which swerved hastily away to avoid running aground. Astern of her, the others also only sensed their danger at the last moment and saved themselves by emergency manoeuvres which threw the line into temporary confusion.

Then the bright lights of a local passenger steamer suddenly appeared as it steamed right through the line of darkened ships. Unaware of her narrow escape as wheels were put hastily over, engine-room telegraphs clanged and turbines screamed in reverse to claw the destroyers clear of collision, the steamer passed on and vanished in the snowfall.

The first grey light was growing as the flotilla passed through the Narrows into Ofotfiord—15 miles to go. It was here that Commodore Bonte must have believed that one of his ships was on guard in accordance with his instruction. The commanding officer of the German Third Flotilla must have thought so also; he was later to state that the *Roeder* had been told to remain on patrol until relieved by the *Lüdemann*. But in the *Roeder*'s diary there was the entry 'Am relieving

---

*The control of the operations of ships of his own force taken out of his hands by the Admiralty's direct orders to Warburton-Lee, Whitworth felt he might only confuse the issue by interfering.

†The Germans, working to a carefully prepared plan, were implementing it with speed and vigour, at Narvik as elsewhere. The British, 'caught on the wrong foot', groped blindly and irresolutely. Boldness might have brought them glittering success at Bergen and Trondheim. At Narvik it was left to Warburton-Lee and his little force to gather the laurels but their triumph would have been more complete and less costly if they had been in greater strength.

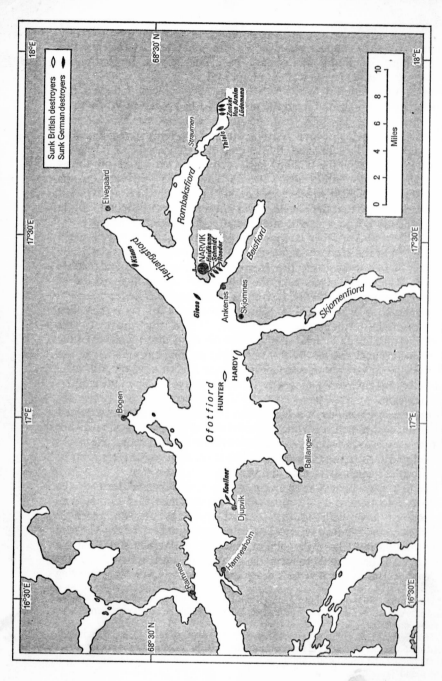

Scene of the Battles of Narvik, 10 and 13 April 1940

Sunk British destroyers
Sunk German destroyers

Miles
0 2 4 6 8 10

68°30' N
18°E
17°30'E
17°E
16°30'E

Elvegaard

Straumen

Zenker
Von Arnim
Lüdemann

Thiele

Rombaksfiord

Herjangsfiord

Kjeldn

NARVIK
Heidkamp
Schmidt
Roeder

Beisfiord

Giese

Ankenes

Skjomnes

Skjomenfiord

HUNTER

HARDY

Ofotfiord

Bogen

Ballangen

Koellner

Djupvik

Hammesholm

Rammes

Schmitt from 0400 as anti-submarine patrol until dawn.' (German times were an hour ahead of the British which are used throughout this book.)

So at 0400 British time, as dawn was breaking, the *Roeder* turned towards harbour, leaving the patrol position empty. A bare mile or so behind her, hidden in the snow and mist, the British destroyers were following. As the *Roeder* came to anchor at 0420 the snowfall was beginning to clear and visibility was increasing as daylight grew.

Nothing had been seen of the British ships when at 0430 the harbour suddenly erupted in shattering explosions and shell splashes. The sleeping crews came clattering on deck to action stations, shocked and dazed, unable to distinguish any enemy and believing at first that they were under air attack.

Commodore Bonte's flagship, *Heidkamp*, at anchor in the harbour, was the first to suffer as a torpedo exploded in her after magazine, blowing it up, causing fearful casualties, including the death of the Commodore himself. Then the *Schmitt* seemed to leap bodily in the water as a torpedo burst in her engine room and another in her boiler-room, breaking her in two pieces which sank at once. Other torpedoes were bursting against merchant ships in the harbour and against the shore, while salvoes of shells rained on the *Roeder*, starting fires and wreaking heavy damage.

There came a brief lull. Not a shot had been fired as yet from the German ships, taken completely by surprise. Then gun flashes were seen in the harbour entrance and at last the German gun crews came into action; but with no clear targets in sight their shooting was wild and inaccurate, whereas they themselves were repeatedly hit. The two ships which had been alongside the *Jan Wellen* taking in fuel had slipped their wires at once, but one of them, the *Lüdemann*, had a gun knocked out and a fire started which necessitated flooding the after magazine. The other, the *Künne*, escaped being hit but the concussion of the torpedoes which sank the *Schmitt* had put her engines temporarily out of action.

It was the *Roeder*, however, which bore the brunt of the attack. One of the first hits had wrecked her cable gear so that her anchors could be neither weighed nor slipped. With fires raging and heavy damage she was moved astern, dragging her anchors behind her, to the pier, where her condition seemed so perilous that her captain gave the order to abandon ship.

Most of this damage had been caused by three of Warburton-Lee's destroyers. Going in alone in the *Hardy* at the outset, he had been able calmly to manoeuvre among the tightly packed merchant ships in the harbour and bring his torpedo tubes to bear before his first gun salvoes woke the sleeping enemy to action. Of the seven torpedoes fired, two had hit and sunk the *Schmitt*, another had blown off the stern of the *Heidkamp*, and others had hit merchant ships. He had then withdrawn to let *Hunter* and *Havock* take his place. Both fired torpedoes, though it does not seem that any of the German destroyers were hit by them, and both continued the gun action in which the *Roeder* was so severely damaged.

In reply the *Roeder* also fired torpedoes in the direction of the harbour entrance, but those which found their target were seen to run under the British destroyers without exploding. They were either set too deep, or like the torpedoes supplied to German U-boats at the beginning of the war, they were fitted with magnetic pistols which failed to function in high latitudes.

The two remaining ships of Warburton-Lee's flotilla, *Hotspur* and *Hostile*, had been left on guard outside the harbour to neutralize batteries believed to be mounted on the north shore of the Narvik peninsula. Finding that these were not in fact in existence, the *Hostile* had joined in the gun action and had seen her 4.7-inch shells plunge home in the boiler room of the *Roeder* to start a devastating fire. As the others withdrew, *Hotspur* and *Hostile* covered them with a smokescreen from the German fire which was at last becoming more effective. At the same time the *Hotspur* took the opportunity to send four torpedoes into the mass of shipping in the harbour.

In the low visibility, it had not been possible for any examination to be made of the side fiords. But this did not seem of any great importance as five out of the total of six German destroyers reported by the pilots of Tranöy had been located and engaged. Warburton-Lee therefore now led all five of his ships to the harbour entrance for a further bombardment as they steamed past. They were greeted with fairly intense fire but it was still ineffective and they had suffered little damage when they withdrew two or three miles down the fiord.

There Warburton-Lee surveyed the situation and called for reports of the number of torpedoes each ship still had aboard. Though *Hardy* had only one and the *Hunter* none, *Hotspur* had four, *Havock* three and the *Hostile* had her full outfit of eight. Most of the enemy destroyers had apparently been located in the harbour and were sunk or damaged. The British flotilla having spent more than an hour in the vicinity without meeting any serious opposition, there seemed nothing to prevent a final attack before withdrawing. Once more, therefore, he signalled for single line ahead and, at 15 knots, led the way back to the harbour entrance. Mist had thickened over Narvik but occasional targets showed up and were engaged as the destroyers turned to port in each other's wakes. The *Hostile* sent four of her torpedoes shorewards and saw another enemy torpedo pass harmlessly under her.

Well satisfied with the success achieved by daring and surprise, the British commander prepared to withdraw. But the luck which had attended him so far had run out. As he turned away from Narvik to head seawards, three fresh enemy ships suddenly appeared out of the mist to the northwards.

The three German ships, *Zenker*, *Giese* and *Köllner*, which had been berthed for the night in Herjangsfiord, had heard and seen nothing of the action until 0515 when the alarm was finally got through to them. Fifteen minutes later they had got under way and now arrived in time to engage the British flotilla as it turned to retire. Considerably larger than the British ships and each armed with five 5-inch guns as compared to the four 4.7-inch guns of the *Hardy* class, they were at first identified as a cruiser and three destroyers. As such, Warburton-Lee reported them to his C-in-C, adding 'Am withdrawing to westward.' Signalling for 30 knots, he led the flotilla seaward.

A running fight developed, but in the low visibility neither side achieved any success. The German destroyers were among those which had not refuelled. Their tanks were all but empty so that they could not stay long in chase. The British flotilla was about to escape almost unscathed, when suddenly out of the mist ahead there loomed a further two German destroyers across their path. The British were trapped.

The two ships in Ballangenfiord, *Thiele* and *Von Arnim*, had not sighted the British destroyers on their way in, but they had received the alarm signal. Thick fog had delayed their getting under way until 0540, so that only by the narrowest margin did they finally appear on the scene to turn the tables.

At first sight of them, Warburton-Lee hoped they might be reinforcements coming to him—as well they might have been had Admiral Whitworth's decision gone the other way. A signalled challenge from the *Hardy*, however, was answered by an accurately placed salvo of 5-inch shells. With only their forward guns available to engage the enemy, the leading British ships were at first seriously outgunned. The signal 'Keep on engaging the enemy', had just broken out at the *Hardy*'s yardarm when a shell hit squarely on her bridge with devastating effect.

Warburton-Lee was mortally wounded and every man on the bridge with him was either killed or wounded. From the *Havock*, third ship of the line, Lieutenant-Commander Courage, who was manoeuvring his ship to avoid a shoal of German torpedoes, which were fortunately seen in good time running on the surface, thought that one of them had hit the leader as a great explosion and a huge column of smoke broke out amidships in her. It was in fact a salvo of shells which had hit and started a raging boiler-room fire.

On the *Hardy*'s bridge with his captain was the secretary, Paymaster-Lieutenant G. H. Stanning. At the explosion of the first shell he was lifted clean off his feet to fall asprawl the gyro compass binnacle. Gathering himself together he found his left foot hanging lifeless; but he had otherwise escaped serious injury—a miracle it seemed as he surveyed the shambles around him, his captain terribly wounded and the navigator lying kicking on the deck, apparently dying.

From the wheelhouse below the bridge there came no sound and no reply to orders. The ship was careering along at high speed with no one in control, the rock-bound shore close on the port side. Paymasters were neither trained nor expected to take part in fighting or control of the ship. Their duties in action were to cipher and decipher messages and perhaps keep a record of events. They were non-executive officers. The secretary was usually given the expressive sobriquet of 'Scratch'.

In the absence of any executive officer, Stanning, with great initiative, at once took action. Dragging his wounded leg behind him, he struggled down from the bridge, took the wheel from the lifeless hands of the coxswain and steered down the fiord until a seaman arrived to relieve him, when he again made his painful way to the bridge to resume control.

The second salvo of shells had cut the steam pipes to the engines and now the *Hardy* was rapidly losing way. It seemed that she must soon come to a standstill, a blazing hulk to be hammered to a wreck by the concentrated fire of the enemy. The torpedo officer, Lieutenant G. R. Heppel, assuming that the bridge steering position had been put out of action, had made his way aft to connect up the auxiliary steering position, but finding the ship answering to the wheel, returned to the bridge in time to approve an order which Stanning had just given, to run the dying ship ashore before she sank.

Meanwhile, as the crippled *Hardy* steered away, the *Hunter*, now leading the line, drew the enemy's fire and was almost at once set on fire and disabled. Astern of her, Commander Layman in the *Hotspur*, his telegraphs set to Full Speed Ahead, saw the *Hunter* swerve across his path as her speed fell away. He called an order to the coxswain at the wheel which would take his racing ship clear.

At that moment a shell burst below his bridge, cutting not only the controls between the wheel and the steering gear, but twisting and jamming the engine-room telegraph connection. Unable either to steer or to give orders to stop engines, Layman saw his bow cleave deep into the *Hunter*'s hull.

The two ships were locked together, the *Hotspur*'s forward way spinning them slowly round. To get control of his ship again, Layman left the bridge to run aft to where he could give verbal orders to the engines and the auxiliary steering position right aft. Hardly had he left when a shell hit on the bridge, bursting against the pedestal of the gun director, killed every soul left on the bridge and in the director tower.

The German destroyers were now pouring a devastating fire into the two crippled ships. Reaching the after superstructure where 'X' gun was mounted and whence the two after guns were being kept in action and controlled by the wounded Sub-Lieutenant L. J. Tillie, Layman was able to control his engines by verbal orders passed down the engine-room hatch. He managed to disengage his ship from the now sinking *Hunter*, then, by the cumbrous method of passing messages down to the tiller flat in the extreme stern, he was able to shape a wavering course down the fiord and away from the hail of shells which was rapidly reducing the *Hotspur* to a wreck.

Of the British flotilla, two ships only, *Havock* and *Hostile*, had avoided serious damage. Swerving past the interlocked *Hunter* and *Hotspur*, they had found themselves running clear of the action to the westward after engaging the *Thiele* and *Arnim* at point blank range as the Germans ran past on an opposite course to join the three ships from Herjangsfiord. *Havock*, now at the head of the line, turned back to bring support to the two injured ships, but finding both his forward guns out of action, Courage turned westward again, screening the *Hotspur* with smoke and continuing to engage the enemy with his aft guns.

Then, his forward guns repaired, he followed the *Hostile* round as the two ships boldly steered towards the greatly superior enemy force so as to cover the escape of the *Hotspur*. The enemy showed no enthusiasm to continue the fight. The three ships from Herjangsfiord were so short of fuel that they could not chase the *Hotspur*, while the *Thiele* and *Arnim* had both suffered so heavily in the gun action that they left the fight and made hastily for harbour. The *Thiele* had been repeatedly hit, had two guns out of action, was on fire and had a magazine flooded. The *Arnim* had been five times hit and had a boiler-room out of action.

The fight had ended with three out of the five British ships escaping seawards. The *Hardy* was aground and on fire, and last seen with one gun still in action while her crew scrambled ashore. The majority escaped and were rescued a few days later as will be related elsewhere. The *Hunter* had sunk in mid-fiord, the bitter cold of the ice-flecked water claiming all but fifty of her crew who were picked up by the Germans, ten of them dying later.

Warburton-Lee's gallant leadership earned his memory a posthumous Victoria Cross, the first to be awarded in the War.

As for the ten ships of the German flotilla, two had been sunk—*Heidkamp* and *Schmitt*—three had been so damaged as to make them unseaworthy or nearly so—*Roeder*, *Thiele* and *Arnim*—and another, the *Lüdemann*, had a flooded magazine and other damage. The *Künne* had her engines temporarily disabled and had suffered damage from shell splinters. Only the *Zenker*, *Köllner* and *Giese* were undamaged and they had shot away more than half their ammunition.

A further German calamity was to make this latter handicap all the more serious. As the three surviving British ships were passing through the Narrows on their way to sea, a large merchant ship was sighted making up the fiord. Commander Layman, his ship much damaged, being controlled from aft and with no means of signalling, had delegated command of the flotilla to Commander Wright of the *Hostile* who now brought the merchant ship to with a shot across her bows. When another shot from the *Havock* hit her in the bow and set her on fire, the crew were seen to abandon ship. They were picked up by the *Havock* whence an armed boats' crew was sent to examine the ship, now identified as the German supply ship *Rauenfels*. She was burning so furiously, however, that the boat was recalled. Getting under way again, Lieutenant-Commander Courage ordered two rounds of high explosive shell to be fired into her.

The result was spectacular and left no doubt of the German ship's cargo as she blew up with a shattering explosion, sending a column of flame and débris up to a height of 3,000 feet. The *Havock* was indeed fortunate to escape with slight damage to her hull and no casualties.

Thus ended the first Battle of Narvik. That it was a material victory for the British flotilla must be conceded. Out of the ten destroyers of Commodore Bonte's squadron, only four remained fully battleworthy and the damage to the four others surviving could not be made good, cut off as they were from repair facilities.

Warburton-Lee's initiative and dash were to have wider repercussions. The Norwegians, hitherto dazed by the sudden, unprovoked German attack on their country, took heart to resist. The detailed plans of the Germans for Narvik were completely disrupted. The morale of their destroyer crews was so shaken by the suddenness and surprise of the assault that they were bereft of the skill and resolution which might have enabled them to extricate and save the seaworthy survivors of the battle. While they fumbled and hesitated, nemesis approached.

2 Withdrawal from Europe: Sea Power the Rescuer

News of the Second Flotilla's gallant exploit, arriving at about the same time that the success of the Fleet Air Arm aircraft from Hatston became known, seemed a bright gleam in an otherwise black horizon. In spite of its superior strength the Home Fleet had failed to prevent the German naval forces from reaching any of the key ports on the Norwegian west coast, even though information which should have enabled them to do so had been available in time.

Except for the achievement of the submarines related above and at Narvik, they also failed to make the German Navy pay the proper price for their rash defiance of their greatly superior opponents. The C-in-C Home Fleet, after hesitating until nearly noon on 9 April, detached a cruiser squadron and destroyer to attack at Bergen, only to have his orders annulled by the Admiralty who feared the shore defences might by then have been taken over by the enemy.

Trondheim was the next target considered. It was politically and stategically even more important than Bergen and not yet so strongly dominated by German air power. Had the port been invested by the main body of the Home Fleet and a force sent up the fiords on the following day, 10 April, the valuable cruiser *Hipper* would have been trapped. Instead, it was decided to employ the torpedo bombers from the *Furious*, and a whole day was wasted waiting for her to join the fleet. In the interval the *Hipper* escaped to join the *Scharnhorst* and *Gneisenau* as they returned undetected down the middle of the North Sea. When the Swordfish aircraft from the *Furious* finally arrived over the Trondheim fiord only two German destroyers were found, anchored in such shallow water that the aerial torpedoes aimed at them struck the bottom and exploded on launching.

What a different approach had been that of Warburton-Lee—'intend attacking at dawn!' His initiative and daring had turned Narvik into a mortal trap for nearly half the total German destroyer strength. Yet even now the harvest which Warburton-Lee's sowing had prepared was nearly lost to the British through indecision and hesitation.

Although Admiral Whitworth, on receiving *Hardy*'s last signal, had at once ordered the cruiser *Penelope* with four large, Tribal-class destroyers forward to 'support the retirement of the Second Destroyer Flotilla, counter-attacking the enemy as necessary', their objective was laid down, not to storm into the Narvik fiord and finish off the shaken German flotilla, but to 'prevent reinforcements reaching Narvik' and to 'allow no force from Narvik to escape'. When Captain Yates of the *Penelope* was at last given freedom by the Admiralty to attack, he delayed a day in order to gather in his destroyers on patrol and distribute written operation orders to them.

Before Yates' leisurely hour for action had come (dawn on the 12th), his chance to strike a spectacular blow had vanished. Sent on a wild-goose chase after a reported enemy tanker down the coast on the 11th, the *Penelope* struck a rock and was severely damaged. Fortunately for the British, Captain Bey, senior surviving officer of the German flotilla had also failed in resolution. By the evening of the 10th he had managed to get two of his ships seaworthy and refuelled. With these he had set off soon after dark, but the sight of the *Penelope* and two destroyers silhouetted against the glow of the Arctic night sky had sent him scuttling back to harbour. Nor would he risk attempting a break-out on the 11th, though by that time seven ships were reasonably seaworthy. And when two of them were severely damaged through running aground he was further, and fatally, delayed.

For by now an assault had been organized for the 13th; Admiral Whitworth, flying his flag in the battleship *Warspite*, was to lead the four Tribal-class destroyers, *Bedouin*, *Cossack*, *Eskimo* and *Punjabi* and five smaller destroyers *Hero*, *Icarus*, *Kimberley*, *Forester* and *Foxhound*. At 0730 that morning they made rendezvous inside the Vestfiord, some 100 miles from Narvik and headed up the fiord, the destroyers going ahead, some screening the battleship, others with sweeps out against a suspected minefield.

The Germans' ability to decipher many of the British naval messages at this time brought ample warning to Captain Bey that a formidable attack using a battleship, destroyers and aircraft was planned for the afternoon of 13 April. He at once gave orders for the best possible disposition of his force which would at least make the enemy pay heavily for any success. The battleworthy ships would disperse into the side fiords—Ballangen and Herjangs—where they might hope to encircle the British force, as by good fortune they had managed to do at the last on the 10th. The *Köllner* was to be moved at once to Taarstadt where she could lie in ambush.

Such were Bey's orders, but his own fatalistic, even despairing attitude would seem to have spread to the force under his command. When, at

1300, the *Köllner*, escorted by the *Künne*, on her way to Taarstadt, sighted the British force approaching through the Narrows, the remainder of the German destroyers had not yet raised steam for their move from Narvik harbour where all six of them lay concentrated. On receipt of the alarm from the *Künne*, all but the immobilized *Roeder* were ordered out by Bey; one by one, as sufficient steam became available, they got under way—first the *Lüdemann*, followed by *Zenker* and *Arnim*. The *Thiele* and *Giese* were still more unprepared and did not follow them for some time.

Meanwhile, the *Künne* had retired in face of so greatly superior a force, exchanging ineffective fire at the limit of visibility, some six miles. The *Köllner*, patently unable to offer battle in her damaged state, had headed for Djupvik Bay on the south side of the fiord where she could lie unsighted until the British ships passed at close range when her captain hoped to be able to use his torpedoes to good effect before himself being overwhelmed. His hopes were doomed to be shattered. From the *Warspite* had been launched the Swordfish floatplane she carried, and now it was scouting ahead. Its observer, Lieutenant-Commander W. L. M. Brown, was to send back invaluable information.

Having reported the two enemy ships, the Swordfish had flown on up the fiord, reported the enemy dispositions and turned for a reconnaissance of Herjangsfiord. There the delighted airmen saw a submarine *U64*, lying fully surfaced. Putting his clumsy machine into the nearest approach to a dive of which it was capable, the pilot, Petty Officer F. R. Price, released his two 350-lb anti-submarine bombs. A direct hit sent the U-boat to the bottom within half a minute.

Returning down the fiord, the crew of the aircraft were just in time to see the *Köllner*'s retirement into ambush and signal a warning to the *Warspite*. Thus, when the leading British destroyers, *Bedouin* and *Eskimo*, rounded the point of Djupvik Bay it was with torpedo tubes and guns trained to starboard and ready to open fire. Torpedoes splashed into the water from both British and German ships and at the same moment guns on either side flamed into action. It was a hopeless fight for the *Köllner*. She had got only one salvo away when the combined fire of the *Bedouin* and *Eskimo* smashed her into silence. Then the first torpedo arrived, blowing off the *Köllner*'s bow. As the *Warspite* nosed round the corner the monstrous blast of her 15-inch guns split the air and went bellowing away, the thunder tossed back and forth from mountainside to mountainside. In a few minutes, the *Köllner* rolled over and sank. Her own torpedoes had missed.

The British squadron swept on, all eyes peering into the mist for a first sight of the enemy. The *Künne*, retiring, met the *Lüdemann* and *Zenker*. She turned into line with them and the three ships together awaited the coming fight. As the first British ships came dimly into sight, the Germans, now joined also by the *Arnim*, turned to bring all their guns to bear and to fire torpedoes; but with ships of both sides firing independently, the German destroyers weaving back and forth in a confusing pattern, and the British swerving to avoid the flights of torpedoes whose tracks could be seen streaking past or under them, spotting the fall of shot was impossible. As the Germans retired before the advancing British, keeping at the limit of visibility, the shooting on both sides became wild and quite ineffective. Frost and snow blurred gun and director telescopes. The gunfire echoed and rolled round the steep sides of the fiord, an occasional shattering blast as the 15-inch guns of the *Warspite* found a target adding to the sound and fury. The concussions dislodged clouds of snow from the hillsides which blew blindingly across the scene.

As Narvik was approached and the German destroyers stood for a time to fight, the range came down and ships came into clearer view of each other. The Germans began to take heavy punishment while they themselves were coming to the end of the meagre supply of ammunition left to them after the battle of three days before. At the same time, to add to the confusion of the scene of smoke and gun flashes from the weaving destroyers, the force of ten Swordfish led by Captain Burch, Royal Marines, arrived from the *Furious* to deliver their attack.

They had had a frightening flight through the fiords, under low clouds streaming down the mountainsides and through snowstorms. At the scene of action the cloud base had lifted sufficiently for them to climb to 2,000 feet before diving down on their targets. But it was a wasted effort. As the Luftwaffe, equipped with properly designed dive-bombers as they were, had already discovered, ships free to manoeuvre were difficult targets. For the slow-moving and highly vulnerable Swordfish, whose proper weapon was the torpedo, this form of attack was even more ineffective. Though bombs fell close to the *Künne* and *Arnim* they did little damage and there were no direct hits, while two aircraft were shot down.

By now the German ships were suffering heavily from the gunfire of the British ships. *Zenker*, *Arnim* and *Künne* had expended all their ammunition when Bey gave the order to retire up Rombaksfiord, the narrow inlet stretching eastward past the town of Narvik. The *Künne* had already retired up Herjangsfiord, pursued by the *Eskimo*, and her captain now beached his ship and ordered his crew to escape ashore. A torpedo from the *Eskimo* completed her destruction.

The British destroyers had not escaped unscathed. The *Punjabi* repeatedly hit amidst a rain of 5-inch shells, had suffered numerous casualties and much damage, including crippling hits in the engine room which forced her temporarily out of action, immobilized, just after she had succeeded in manoeuvring clear of several enemy torpedoes. Heroic efforts put out her numerous fires and repaired the damage and within an hour she was again steaming into action, though a jagged hole in her bow restricted her to 15 knots. In the meantime, while the other German destroyers were retreating up the fiord, the *Giese*, with steam on her engines at last, came alone out of the harbour to be quickly smothered by the fire of six British destroyers and abandoned, drifting.

Another British ship which now suffered severely was Commander R. St V. Sherbrooke's *Cossack*. Going into the harbour she was met by heavy fire from the *Roeder* at her berth alongside the wharf which, amongst other damage, severed all leads from the bridge to the steering engine and wrecked the engine-room telegraphs. Before emergency repairs could be made, the ship swung away out of control to run hard aground on the south shore of the fiord opposite the harbour. There she remained for the next 12 hours, sniped at by troops ashore and exchanging shots from time to time with field guns, until finally towed off, stern first, by the *Kimberley* when the battle was over.

The *Roeder*, hammered into silence and set ablaze, was abandoned by her crew and blew up just as the *Foxhound* was about to go alongside to take possession. Of the remainder of the British destroyers, Commander Micklethwait's *Eskimo* was the first to follow the retreating enemy up the Rombaks fiord. She was followed by the *Forester* and *Hero* and then by *Bedouin* and *Icarus*. As they steered through the neck of the fiord where it narrows to barely 500 yards wide, they were engaged by the *Lüdemann* and *Thiele*. The two German ships were quickly battered out of action, the *Lüdemann* escaping up the fiord to join the *Zenker* and *Arnim* where they were scuttling themselves, while the *Thiele* with the last of her steam was run aground, capsized and sank. Before this, however, both had succeeded in launching their remaining torpedoes. The *Eskimo*, which had turned across the narrow fiord to fire her own torpedoes, narrowly escaped the first flight by some smart manoeuvring. The *Forester* and *Hero* escaped by retreating at full speed astern and so outrunning the speeding 'tin fish'. When the second flight of torpedoes—from the *Thiele*—arrived, however, Micklethwait was unable to avoid them all; one shattered in a fierce blast of high explosive the whole fore part of the ship as far aft as the superstructure. As she retreated down the fiord the anchors and cables swinging below the mass of wreckage hanging down took the ground in 90 fathoms bringing her effectively to a halt.

The Second Battle of Narvik came thus to an end. The last of the ten German destroyers had been sunk or become total losses on the rocky shore. The *Eskimo* and *Cossack* were got painfully away to the anchorage at Skjelfiord where they received temporary repairs to get them home. A light seen winking from the shore by the *Ivanhoe* proved to be a message from the survivors of the *Hardy* who, soon after their ship had gone aground, had set off to the little township of Ballangen where there was a hospital and no Germans.

As soon as these had all been gathered in, the *Warspite* and her destroyers withdrew from Narvikfiord, going back to the open waters of the Vestfiord. There they were to await the arrival of the military expedition that was on its way under Admiral of the Fleet, the Earl of Cork and Orrery—with his flag in the cruiser *Aurora* followed by the *Southampton* carrying the military commander, General Mackesy, and two brigades of troops in five troopships.

Controversy was to rumble for a long time as to whether Narvik could have been captured by naval landing parties immediately after this Second Battle. One side maintained that naval landing parties from Whitworth's squadron could have achieved it, a view encouraged by a description made later by Theodor Bach, the Mayor of Narvik, of the German troops filing despondently up the mountainside from the town and asking the way to Sweden. What is more certain is that but for the vacillations of the British High Command which had first discarded plan R4 and then taken three days to re-embark the troops in conditions of great confusion, Lord Cork's expedition could have arrived in time to step ashore unopposed on the evening of 13 April in sufficient strength to hold Narvik against any counter-attacks by the Germans.

The two days which were to pass, however, before the troopships arrived, enabled General Dietl and his men to recover their morale and return, after which an Allied capture of Narvik would have taken a costly assault through deep snow, accompanied by a naval bombardment in which many Norwegians must have lost lives and property.

For Germany, the Norwegian campaign had ceased for the time being to be a naval affair, except for maintenance of supplies to their occupying army through the Kattegat and the Leads. Audacity and speed on the part of the Kriegsmarine, hesitation and doubt on that of the British Admiralty had enabled the former successfully to defy the greatly superior forces poised for action against it and to fulfil its part of the invasion plan. The cost had been heavy, nevertheless, with one heavy cruiser, two light cruisers and ten destroyers sunk, a pocket-battleship out of action for a year and the only two battleships in commission both damaged. The German Navy had, indeed, been temporarily eliminated as a fighting force.

The Royal Navy's losses, though far from negligible, represented a far smaller proportion of its total strength. The Home Fleet still had ample strength to fulfil its continuing task of escorting and supporting the Allied ground forces sent to Norway in a vain attempt to stem the German northward advance, and eventually to evacuate them when the lack of air support made this in a short time inevitable.

For Germany, the Norwegian campaign had ceased for the time being and south of Trondheim respectively, and intended to converge in a pincer movement on that important naval base, and at Narvik. In spite of a total absence of fighter cover against the German bombers by that time established on Norwegian airfields, the first two of these were safely put ashore between 16 and 19 April. For the next eight days anti-aircraft light cruisers and frigates were stationed in the two narrow fiords to give air defence to Namsos and Aandalsnes, a procedure which, later in the war, would have rightly been judged suicidal. Nevertheless for the next eight days they held their station in the face of repeated dive-bombing attacks; a frigate and four anti-submarine trawlers had been sunk and an AA cruiser and a frigate crippled by the 28th, when the decision was taken to withdraw both expeditionary forces.

This was brilliantly achieved during three nights, 29 April–1 May by British and French warships and troopships. At Aandalsnes not a ship was lost, while at Namsos it was not until all had cleared the fiords that a final effort by the Luftwaffe succeeded in sinking the French destroyer *Bison* and the British *Afridi*.

At Narvik, once the possible opportunity to seize the town following the destruction of the German flotilla had been allowed to slip away, General Dietl's troops, recovering their morale, had returned. Winter conditions, with deep snow in which the British troops were neither equipped nor trained to operate, combined with a reluctance to support a direct assault on the town with naval gunfire which would have cost many Norwegian lives, led to long delays. Not until 27 May, by which time an Anglo-French-Polish force of more than 24,000 soldiers had been assembled, were conditions judged suitable for an assault. By the end of the 28th Narvik had fallen: three days earlier, as German Panzer armies swept irresistibly across France towards the Channel ports, the Allied Governments had decided that all Norway must be abandoned.

On 6 June the withdrawal from Narvik began, the troops embarking in a number of passenger liners which sailed in two Groups on the 7th and 8th, escorted by cruisers and destroyers of the Home Fleet and the carrier *Ark Royal*, while the carrier *Glorious* embarked the RAF fighter squadrons which had been operating ashore at Bardufoss.

Sea power was again conferring on its possessors the priceless ability to withdraw from as well as strike at distant points of the enemy's perimeter at will. The risk run by such operations, apart from the ever-present one of submarine attack, is that of a surprise raid by the enemy's concentrated force on the vulnerable troop convoy. Prudence calls for a powerful escort; but for various reasons, the Home Fleet which should have provided it was widely scattered at the crucial time. And, all unknown to the British, the *Scharnhorst* and *Gneisenau*, their earlier damage repaired, had sailed from Kiel on 4 June and by the 8th were cruising right in the path of the second troop convoy, escorted only by the light cruiser *Southampton*, an AA cruiser, five destroyers and the *Ark Royal*.

What might have occurred had these two forces met is conjectural; but it was not to be. For on the afternoon of the 8th, from the German flagship's bridge was sighted the unmistakable outline of an aircraft carrier rising over the horizon. It was the *Glorious*, which, her deck and hangars cluttered with the evacuated fighters, had been detached with an escort of two destroyers, *Ardent* and *Acasta*, to return home independently. With no scouting planes in the air, she was taken by surprise and, though her destroyers screened her with smoke, the German guns, radar directed, soon hit and crippled and finally sank her.

The two destroyers had meanwhile gone gallantly out to attack with their torpedoes, a forlorn hope which inevitably led to their destruction; but the *Acasta*, before sinking, managed to launch four torpedoes, one of which hit the *Scharnhorst*, so severely damaging her that she and her sister were forced to bring their operation to a close and return to Trondheim.

Though the *Scharnhorst* was to be out of action for many vital months to come, this final episode of the Norwegian campaign with its tragic loss of 1,474 officers and men from the three sunken British ships and of so valuable a ship as the *Glorious*, was a calamitous end to a campaign made hopeless for the Allies from the start by their lack of an adequate air element for either their expeditionary forces or their fleet. A similar shortcoming was to cripple the British war effort for more than two years more.

While up in the Arctic, the Royal Navy and British, French and Polish troops were investing Narvik and preparing to storm the port, the Germans had launched on 10 May their *blitzkrieg* in the west with an invasion of Holland, meeting little effective resistance. There at once began for the Allied navies and merchant navies what was to become a seven-week stretch of operations to evacuate from the European mainland remnants of defeated armies as well as a large number of civilian refugees.

The Royal Navy's first task was to land demolition parties to put the Dutch ports and port facilities out of action, to bring out all merchant ships found there and to embark in cruisers and destroyers the Netherlands Royal Family and Government and the gold reserves. Eight days of operating under continuous air attack, during which the old destroyer *Valentine* was sunk and two others damaged, before the ports were finally abandoned, gave a foretaste of what was to be suffered when the German Stuka squadrons could give their whole attention to shipping strikes.

On the 19th, bombers sank the destroyer *Whitley* off the Belgian coast, during operations to bring refugees home from Ostend. As the German Panzer tanks cut through northern France to send the British Expeditionary Force and a portion of the French Army reeling back towards the channel ports, Vice-Admiral Bertram Ramsay (Flag Officer, Dover) began to organize shipping for evacuation if this should be ordered. Meanwhile, the movement was still the other way, with reinforcements being transported to Calais and Boulogne under destroyer escort on 22 and 23 May. The decision to evacuate the 20th Guards Brigade from the latter was, however, taken the following day.

Destroyers went alongside the quays, their guns engaging enemy batteries and machine-gun posts and doing what they could to deter the otherwise unmolested enemy bombers overhead, while wounded and exhausted troops filed on board. Two of them, the *Keith* and the *Vimy*, were caught in a concentration of artillery, mortar and machine-gun fire, suffering numerous casualties including their captains killed on the bridge. Of the seven destroyers engaged, however, only one, the *Venetia*, was seriously damaged before they sailed, loaded down with troops for Dover, at 2130 on the 24th. During the night two more destroyers embarked as many as they could, the little *Vimiera* taking no less than 1,400 Guardsmen, before the enemy overran the port. Some 300 Welsh Guards had to be left behind, but 4,360 soldiers had been rescued.

At Calais, where the garrison was ordered to fight to the last to hold up the enemy's advance on Dunkirk, destroyers supported them with gunfire, brought ammunition for the soldiers and evacuated non-fighting troops. Bombers sent the *Wessex* to the bottom and damaged the *Vimierà* and Polish *Burza*. During the night of 25–26 May and during the 26th a number of unarmed small craft made trips into the harbour to embark wounded and such troops as could be spared—the first example of the gallantry shown by the crews of a myriad miscellaneous small craft that was to play a large part in the 'miracle' of Dunkirk during the following nine days.

That same day, the 26th, the Dunkirk bridgehead was established; the three British Army Corps began to withdraw inside it, to be joined on the 29th by more than 26,000 French troops; and Operation 'Dynamo' was ordered to be carried out under the direction of Admiral Ramsay. Captain W. G. Tennant, RN, was appointed Senior Naval Officer, Dunkirk. For this operation, which initially envisaged a limit of 45,000 as the number which could be evacuated with the means available, the cross-Channel packets—up to now employed as personnel ships in the opposite direction—and destroyers were the main rescue ships. The Admiralty, however, had already arranged for all spare ships' boats from the home ports to be assembled and placed at Ramsay's disposal. As the operation progressed and the full meaning of the situation was borne in on the seamen, professional and amateur, of England, there streamed in to join these a huge fleet of drifters, schuyts, coasting steamers, tugs, lifeboats and yachts.

These, as well as destroyers and minesweepers gathered from other commands, operated off the open beaches of Malo, Bray and La Panne, whence many thousands were embarked by improvised means. Had this been the only means of rescue Dunkirk could never have become the miracle it did. Fortunately, although Dunkirk and its inner harbour had been reduced to rubble, two breakwaters running seaward on each side of the entrance were found to have deep enough water for destroyers and

personnel ships; and it was from them that the greatest number were
taken off.

The personnel ships, invaluable for their large carrying capacity and
high speed, were restricted to night runs after one had been sunk and
several damaged by gunfire in the almost continuous air attacks of
daylight hours. The remainder, their crews exhausted and shaken,
suffering many casualties, under attack by dive-bombers and motor
torpedo boats and in constant peril from mines, operated unceasingly.
When 'Dynamo' ended on 4 June, 308,888 men had been evacuated in
British ships and craft and 29,238 in Allied vessels. The total included
26,175 French troops. These figures should perhaps be taken into
account when measuring the price the Germans paid for the bold gamble
with their fleet in the occupation of Norway. Had they still had available
the cruisers and destroyers sunk or crippled there, the situation off
Dunkirk could have been far worse. As it was, six British and three
French destroyers and eight personnel ships had been sunk, 19 British
destroyers and nine personnel ships had been put out of action.

Nevertheless sea power had performed one of its classic roles in saving
a large, defeated Allied force, making its men available to fight another
day. Its efforts to do the same for the 51st (Highland) Division, cut off
under French command and driven to the coast at St Valery-en-Caux,
were frustrated by the descent of fog over the 67 merchant ships and
some 140 small craft despatched for the purpose. The 24-hour delay
imposed permitted only 2,137 British and 1,184 French troops to be
embarked before the remainder, including 6,000 of the Highland Division,
were forced to surrender on 11 June.

This was the only failure to rescue any large body of British troops
which had reached the coast. At Le Havre, meanwhile, British and
Canadian destroyers covering a swarm of small craft and personnel ships
were taking off 11,059 British troops, of whom 9,000 were taken to
Cherbourg before the decision was taken on the 15th to bring home the
remainder of the BEF. This evacuation cost the personnel ship *Bruges*
and damage to three more British destroyers by air attack.

The above evacuations had been planned as Operation 'Cycle'.
Operation 'Aerial' which now followed was on a much larger scale, with
evacuations from Cherbourg and St Malo directed by the C-in-C
Portsmouth and from Brest, St Nazaire and La Pallice on the French
Atlantic coast by the C-in-C Plymouth. Cherbourg was the first, when the
52nd Division, which, with the 1st Canadian Division, had been sent to
reinforce the French following Dunkirk, and a large miscellaneous body
known as 'Norman Force' were embarked between 15 and 18 June.
When the rearguard embarked under cover of destroyers on the 18th, a
total of 30,630, including the 9,000 from Havre had been rescued.
Meanwhile from St Malo another 21,474 including the Canadian Division,

had been safely lifted. Good fighter cover at both ports had prevented any losses.

From Brest during 16 and 17 June a total of 32,584 British and Allied troops were lifted in personnel ships and several ocean liners. On the following day, as a result of great efforts by the French dockyard, the uncompleted French battleship *Richelieu* sailed with the remainder of the French fleet, most of them steering south for African ports, a few to Plymouth and Portsmouth. As in the Channel ports, British naval demolition parties did as much damage as possible to port facilities before embarking—the last to leave—in destroyers.

Six ocean liners formed the bulk of the shipping sent to evacuate St Nazaire and Nantes. They anchored in Quiberon Bay where, during the 16th some 13,000 troops with stores and transport were embarked in the *Georgic, Duchess of York* and the Polish *Batory* and *Sobieski* which then sailed for home. Destroyers and small craft continued to ferry troops to the other big ships throughout the 17th. Fighter cover prevented losses until the afternoon when, during a heavy raid, the liner *Lancastria* with 5,800 troops on board was hit, caught fire and sank in 15 minutes. For reasons never fully explained, 3,000 lives were lost in spite of the swarm of small craft in the Roads.

The following day, the transports sailed in two convoys with some 27,000 troops. Meanwhile the French were making strenuous efforts to get the uncompleted battleship *Jean Bart* to sea and, though she was even less seaworthy than the *Richelieu*, succeeded in doing so on the 19th, when she, too, made for Casablanca. As a result of information that 8,000 Polish troops had arrived at St Nazaire, seven transports and six destroyers were sent on the 19th, but found only 2,000. This brought the St Nazaire and Nantes total to 54,411 British and 2,764 Allied troops.

At La Pallice the British SNO had to improvise his evacuation plans as the transports expected on the 16th had been diverted to Brest or St Nazaire. Troops were embarked in requisitioned cargo ships and, when false information of the enemy's imminent arrival was received on the 18th, they sailed in convoy, abandoning their transport. The evacuation were resumed, however, on the next two days, in ships which had been only partially filled at Brest, which embarked 4,000 Polish troops.

This was the final phase of Operation 'Aerial' as originally planned. But as France collapsed in ruins and asked for an armistice, a flood of refugees as well as many Polish and Czech troops were streaming through south-west France for Bordeaux, Bayonne and St Jean-de-Luz. To the Gironde on the 16th went the cruiser *Arethusa* from Gibraltar, while the destroyer *Berkeley* went up to Bordeaux where the British Embassy had arrived and the First Lord of the Admiralty (Mr A. V. Alexander), the First Sea Lord and Lord Lloyd were negotiating with Admiral Darlan to prevent the French fleet from falling into enemy hands.

During the next two days embarkation of refugees and Allied troops, mostly Polish and Czech, was hurried on, the ships sailing during 18 and 19 June while the British Embassy and Consular staffs embarked in the *Arethusa* together with the President of Poland and a number of his Ministers. By the 23rd, when operations moved on to Bayonne, some 6,000 Poles, for whom transport was actually waiting at Bayonne, had been embarked. At Bayonne, meanwhile, another 9,000 Poles had been taken on board the Polish liners *Batory* and *Sobieski*, while the *Ettrick* and the *Arandora Star* embarked refugees. On the 21st evacuation operations were shifted to St Jean-de-Luz and continued until brought to an end on the 25th by orders of the French acting in accordance with the terms of their armistice.

The evacuation from the south coast of France of 10,000 Allied troops and civilians, mostly in small freighters, between 24 and 26 June and of 22,656 men of military age and women and children from the Channel Islands completed the vast operation. In all 144,171 British, 18,246 French, 24,352 Polish, 4,938 Czech and 163 Belgian troops had been preserved to be re-armed and renew the fight, making a total of 191,970 to be added to the 308,888 brought off from Dunkirk. Thus had sea power deprived Hitler of the total victory in the west to which, in his landsman's view, he was entitled as a result of his triumphant sweep through the Low Countries and France.

Like Napoleon before him, it was borne in on him that to gain his ends only a successful invasion of England would suffice.

3 *Assembly of the Wolf Packs*

With the withdrawal of her Expeditionary Force from Europe Britain took up the logical stance for a sea power engaged in war with continental enemies more powerful militarily than herself. She would now wage a maritime war, standing necessarily on the defensive at first, following the débâcle in her initial continental strategy; but with returning strength she would be able to use her sea power in the traditional way to strike at the enemy's perimeter at points of her own choosing. And, meanwhile, she must seek to gather new and powerful allies and strengthen those she already had, in order to gather in the fullness of time the manpower and equipment which she lacked for the necessary eventual return to the continent.

Until that time, however, she must ensure the free passage to the United Kingdom of the merchant ships which brought not only more than half the food for the people of her crowded islands, but essential raw material for the manufacture of arms, ammunition, transport and all the multifarious 'sinews of war', including petroleum products, without which her farming would be largely brought to a standstill, her navy immobilized, her air force grounded.

The threat to Allied merchant shipping could come from the enemy's surface fleet, from disguised merchant cruisers on the distant trade routes, from air attack and from submarines. The first of these, in June 1940, had been eliminated for the time being as a result of the operations off Norway; merchant raiders were soon to set out from Germany but, though they were to prove a thorn in the flesh, indeed, in the years ahead, their achievements could never be enough to be decisive; air attack was largely limited to the coastal waters of Great Britain where it could be to a great extent countered by the fighter defences of the Royal Air Force; out in the Atlantic Ocean, farther and for longer patrols now that French Atlantic ports were available to them, German and, perhaps, Italian U-boats would return to the campaign against Allied merchant ships that the Norwegian operations had interrupted.

It was the last of these various threats that, as in the First World War, but contrary to expectations, was once again to come near to defeating Britain and her allies. The apparent completeness of the defeat of the U-boat in 1918 had led to unjustified confidence that the under-water menace to our merchant shipping had been mastered. This confidence was enhanced by the invention at the end of the war of a submarine detecting device, the ASDIC—so-called from the initials of the Allied Submarine Detection Investigation Committee under whose auspices it was developed. In conjunction with the depth-charge, a means of detecting and destroying a submerged submarine had been at long last achieved. The asdic remained, throughout the war, the one device by which a surface ship could detect and locate a submerged submarine.

This development and a strange and unjustified belief that in any future war enemy submarines would once again allow their operations to be circumscribed by adherence to the Rules of War, led to the assumption that the principal threat to our merchant shipping would come from surface raiders. As late as 1937 the Naval Staff reported that in their opinion 'the submarine would never again be able to present us with the problem we were faced with in 1917'. Consequently, not only was the primary task of Coastal Command enunciated as that of reconnoitring the North Sea to watch for the break-out of surface raiders, but no provision was made for convoy escorts beyond the existing asdic-fitted force of some 150 destroyers, half of which were veterans of the First World War maintained in reserve, coastal patrol vessels and 24 sloops.

That the size of this force may be seen in proper perspective, the task which faced it may be judged by the fact that in 1939 there were 3,000 deep-sea dry cargo merchant ships and tankers and 1,000 coasters registered in Great Britain, totalling 21 million tons. The average number of ships at sea on any one day was 2,500. The 150 escort destroyers and an almost total absence of aircraft for escort duties can be compared with the 1918 figures of 257 warships employed solely on escort with a further 500 so employed intermittently, 190 aeroplanes, 300 seaplanes and flying boats, and 75 airships.

It was not until Hitler, in April 1939, denounced the naval treaty which had strictly limited the size of the German Navy that any thought was given to an increase in the number of our escort craft. In July and August of that year, 56 patrol vessels were ordered which were to be the first of the famous 'Flower'-class corvettes. These were originally designed for coastal escort duties only. Though they began to come to sea in numbers in May 1940 and soon became the mainstay of our convoy escorts, it was not until they had been considerably modified for ocean work that they were reasonably efficient. Even so, their maximum speed of 16 knots was inadequate for anti-submarine work, being less than that of a surfaced German U-boat. Not until April 1942 did the first frigate of the River class, essentially designed for ocean escort work, come to sea. Jellicoe's warning, made to an unheeding Government in 1929, that 'war experience showed that the fast vessels needed for anti-submarine convoy escort cannot be hurriedly improvised' was thus substantiated.

As for air escort, at the outbreak of war Coastal Command of the RAF had no aircraft designed and no aircrews trained for anti-submarine work. Such tasks were subordinate to those of reconnaissance against surface raiders.

Unfortunately the basis on which the complacency with regard to the submarine threat rested, the efficacy of the asdic, was thoroughly unsound. Peacetime exercises with it had been largely confined to hunting submarines whose initial positions were known within fairly narrow limits. Such practices were only carried out in calm or moderate weather conditions and in daylight. The anti-submarine teams engaged were highly-trained and well practised. Even so, there were at least as many unsuccessful hunts as there were 'kills'. For reasons not then understood, there were occasions when the asdic failed lamentably. Nevertheless the belief was held by all but those with considerable experience of the asdic that the submarine was mastered. It was not appreciated that the greatly increased endurance of submarines would permit them to operate far out in the Atlantic which, unlike the First World War, would mean escorting our merchant convoys for the whole of their ocean voyage. Nor was it taken into account that improved submarine capabilities and technique would enable submerged attacks to be delivered in conditions of rough weather in which the performance of the asdic was greatly reduced.

Perhaps the greatest miscalculation, caused by an incomplete study of the lessons of the First World War, was that which assumed that U-boat attacks would be confined to submerged attacks. During 1918 the U-boat commanders, one of the most successful of whom was Karl Dönitz, foiled by the surface and air escorts from attacking submerged by day, had taken to night attacks on the surface. The low silhouette of their craft enabled them to approach and deliver their attacks unseen. In an effort to combat this manoeuvre, aircraft were fitted with searchlights, a development which was not resumed in the Second World War until 1942.

All this was recorded in the RAF Official History. Furthermore, in a book which was published in Germany before the war and had been available to the general public, Dönitz, now commanding Hitler's U-boat fleet, had advocated the technique of the night attack on the surface.

Now the asdic suffered from certain limitations, one of which was its poor performance against small surface targets. Thus if the U-boat commanders employed the same tactics as in the First World War—and opposed by the asdic they were certain to do so—the escorts would be confined to the same means of detection as in 1918, the human eye. Thus the linch-pin of the Navy's confidence in its ability to combat the U-boat was knocked out.

So, when on 3 September 1939, Britain found herself once again at war with Germany, although there was no doubt that to defend our merchant ships from attack they must be sailed in convoy—and, in fact, the first such convoy, from Gibraltar to Cape Town, had sailed the day before—the means of protecting these convoys was sparse in the extreme. A great part of the force of destroyers available was absorbed in screening duties with the Fleet, escorting the Army to France and protecting the large volume of shipping always at sea off our vulnerable East Coast. Air escort was virtually non-existent. RAF Coastal Command consisted of a few squadrons of twin-engined Anson aircraft, whose range was limited to 510 miles and which were almost wholly absorbed by the task of North Sea reconnaissance, and two squadrons of Sunderland flying-boats, which had a radius of 850 miles. The few remaining surface escorts took the outward-bound Atlantic convoys only as far as $12\frac{1}{2}°$W longitude—some 100 miles west of Ireland. Thence the merchant ships continued in company for two more days before dispersing to sail independently to their destinations. The escorts would meanwhile have met the homeward convoy which, having assembled at Halifax, Nova Scotia, would have crossed the ocean under escort of an armed merchant cruiser.

Inadequate as these measures were to prove as the war developed, they were at first, so far as ships in convoy were concerned, very successful. The German Navy, plunged into war by Hitler's policies seven years before they had expected it, was still at the beginning of its planned expansion. It possessed only 57 operational U-boats of which 30 were short-range boats suitable only for the North Sea. Of the 27 ocean-going types, 17 had sailed for the Atlantic during August. On an average, however, the number on patrol at any one time was usually about one-third of the total available.

From the very start, the U-boat commanders shunned attacks on convoys so long as other targets presented themselves. Consequently by the end of 1939 they had only succeeded in sinking four ships in convoy. Convoy proved itself effective against air attack also, only eight ships being sunk by this method while in convoy. The convoy system was not, however, complete. Ships of over 15 knots and, at first, those whose maximum speed was less than 9 were excluded and sailed independently. History repeated itself. No less than 102 such ships were sunk in the same period.

Another lesson taught by the first few months of the war was the ineffectiveness of 'search and patrol' against submarines. Hunting patrols destroyed one U-boat in September 1939 and another in October. Awakened to the capabilities of the asdic, the Germans took greater care to evade the patrols which were, thereafter, uniformly unsuccessful. Indeed the U-boats turned the tables on their hunters. When hunting groups consisting of an aircraft carrier and a small destroyer screen were deployed against them, they narrowly failed to torpedo the *Ark Royal* on 14

September and three days later sank the *Courageous* with a heavy loss of life.

But though taught, the lesson was not always remembered. At various stages in the Battle of the Atlantic, the desire for offensive action led to the employment of warships and aircraft in this way; but the U-boat proved itself almost immune to them except in very special circumstances or in the vicinity of convoys where, if it wished to attack it was bound to expose itself to discovery.

During the first six months of the war, both sides were so limited in numbers that their encounters were no more than skirmishes as compared to the widespread battle which was later to develop. At the same time, while the U-boats learnt to respect the ability of asdic-fitted warships to detect and attack them submerged and therefore concentrated when possible on unescorted independents, the Allies reached a clearer understanding of the limitations of the asdic. Nevertheless belief in the efficacy of patrol and search persisted. Convoys were starved of escorts, too many of which were being used to sweep the empty ocean wastes.

In his hopes of avoiding war with Britain, Hitler at first instructed his U-boat commanders to act in accordance with the Hague Convention; the torpedoing of the liner *Athenia* without warning on the first day of the war was in disobedience to orders. By November 1939, however, all restrictions had been removed and the zone in which any ship steaming without lights was liable to attack was steadily extended farther out into the Atlantic.

This first, skirmishing period came to an end in March 1940 when Hitler, planning his invasion of Norway, recalled all U-boats to take part in it. Thus in the Western Approaches to the British Isles a lull in the fight ensued which was to last until June 1940; when it came to an end, in the renewed struggle in the Atlantic, Britain, now fighting alone, was to find herself labouring under disadvantages she had never visualized. During the Norwegian campaign and the evacuation of the army from Dunkirk, the Royal Navy had suffered loss or damage to a great many of the destroyers on which convoy escort depended. More serious still was the establishment of air and submarine bases by the Germans along the French Atlantic coast. There was no longer any room for easy complacency about the mortal threat to Britain's shipping and supplies on which her continuance in the war and her very life depended.

In July 1940 the first Atlantic U-boat base came into operation at Lorient on the Bay of Biscay coast. At once the submarines' route to their patrol area was reduced by 450 miles. Not only could they remain longer on patrol but a greater proportion of the total number available could be kept in action. In spite of having lost 25 boats since the beginning of the war, replacements, which were beginning to come forward at an ever increasing pace, had kept this total up to 51.

It was at this very time that escorts were so scarce that large convoys

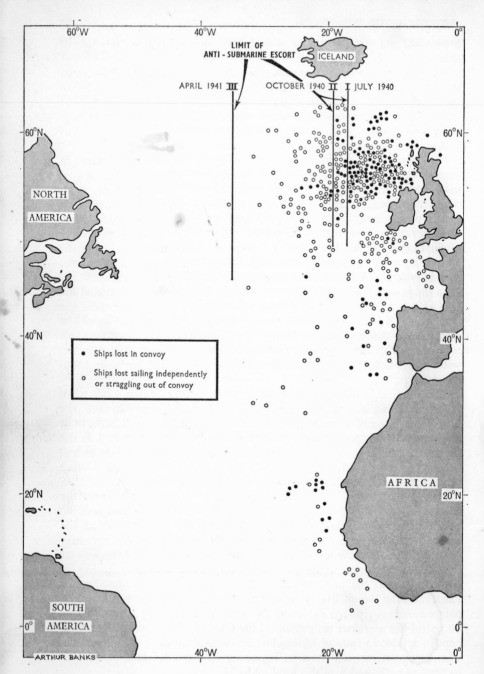

First 'Happy Time' of the U-Boats, July 1940 – April 1941

were sailing under protection of a single destroyer or sloop. Coastal Command's ability to help was similarly cut to the bone owing to the priority given to scouting in the North Sea to give early warning of the sailing of any invasion fleet. The Air Officer Commander-in-Chief, Air Marshal Sir F. W. Bowhill, pressed constantly for an increase in the strength of his Command and in particular for an allocation of the long-range, four-engine aircraft now becoming available. Ill-founded belief in the efficacy of strategic bombing led to priority being given to Bomber Command. A further handicap to the airmen of Coastal Command was the absence of an efficient weapon with which to attack U-boats. The anti-submarine bomb with which they were armed, which had a very short delay-action fuse, depended for success on a direct hit on the submarine still surfaced or a very near miss on one awash. Only a criminally unalert U-boat crew were likely to present themselves as such a target. It was not until 1941, as a result of impassioned pleas by Bowhill, that an airborne depth-charge was perfected.

Encouraged by the resounding success of his U-boat commanders, particularly as the claims of many of them were inevitably exaggerated, Hitler cast away the last restriction upon a total blockade of the British Isles. On 17 August he warned neutral shipping that they would be sunk at sight without warning.

To aid the U-boats, the first squadron of Focke-Wulf Condor four-engined, long-range aircraft had established itself in August at an airfield near Bordeaux. Adapted from a civil air-liner, the F-W 200, which was its short title, had a range far in excess of anything available to Coastal Command. Reconnoitring far out into the Atlantic, its primary task was to report the positions of convoys and to act as a radio beacon for U-boats in the vicinity. This task accomplished, it was free to expend its bomb-load on the almost defenceless merchant ships, opposed only by the quite inadequate and unsuitable armament of the few escorts spread at wide intervals round the convoys. Here was another opponent against whom, as yet, the convoys were helpless. In the first two months of its operations the F-W 200 sank 30 merchant ships totalling 110,000 tons. The outlook was indeed one of unrelieved gloom for the crews of the merchant ships, whose chances of being sunk were high and of being rescued thereafter were all too low. For the escorts, who were forced to watch in impotent despair their convoys being decimated, it was hardly less daunting. Victory at sea and, consequently, victory everywhere seemed in sight to the Germans.

By the late summer of 1940, all ships homeward bound across the Atlantic whose speeds were less than 15 knots were making the journey in convoys, fast (9—14.9 knots) or slow (7½—9 knots). The former, which assembled at Halifax, Nova Scotia, were designated HX; the latter, which began their passage at Sydney, Cape Breton, were SC. Outward-bound convoys were at first distinguished by their ports of origin, those gathered together from ports on the east coast of Britain being OA convoys, the remainder OB.

U-boats were not yet ranging across the Atlantic so these convoys were dispersed on crossing the fifteenth west meridian, their escorts then meeting homeward convoys which up to this point had sailed with an escort of an armed merchant cruiser or a solitary sloop. Little or no protection against U-boat attack was thus provided west of 15°W. As the number of escorts gradually increased and the density and efficiency of the air patrols of Coastal Command improved, so the U-boats shifted their operations westward. One of these westward extensions of activity had occurred during August and September 1940. Heavy losses were inflicted amongst ships after they had been dispersed from outward-bound convoys and on homeward-bound convoys before their local escort had joined. The dispersal point was shifted to 17°W. This was still not far enough out, but was the limit imposed by the shortage of escorts.

It was not only amongst unescorted ships that the U-boats were now achieving success. Appreciating by now that the asdic had greatly reduced a submarine's immunity when submerged, and harassed by the still sparse air patrols maintained in the vicinity of convoys by day, the U-boat commanders had reverted to the methods of the First World War which had been employed by Karl Dönitz, now chief of the U-boat arm. Approaching convoys by night on the surface, their low silhouettes were invisible from escorts quite close by. At the same time the asdic was unable to detect them. The sound beam became diffused near the surface and failed to send back a recognizable echo. Emboldened by this immunity, some of the U-boat commanders were penetrating to the middle of the convoys to loose their torpedoes at point-blank range. No wonder this was known amongst them as the 'Happy Time'.

Such was the situation in October 1940 when two convoys of heavily laden ships for Britain set out to cross the Atlantic. The first to sail was SC7 on the 5th of that month, 35 slow and elderly ships whose speed in convoy would not exceed 7 knots unless the weather was exceptionally favourable. Nevertheless they and the cargoes they carried were of inestimable value to Britain, still desperately striving to make up the losses suffered at Dunkirk. The formation in which convoys sailed, once they were out in the ocean, was a broad-fronted rectangle. Thus a convoy of 35 ships would be formed up in five columns of four ships and three columns of five ships each, the longer columns being in the centre. The columns would be five cables (half a mile) apart, the ships in column three cables (600 yards) apart. Allowing for ships not being always well closed up, the convoy thus covered a sea area of some five square miles.

Such a formation was necessary for several reasons. Long columns invariably become strung out. Whereas a column of five ships would probably be one and a half miles long, 15 ships would rarely be less than six or seven. Thus the broad-fronted formation was more compact from the point of view of escorting, while signals from the commodore, leading one of the centre columns, could be seen simultaneously from all ships. Furthermore, it offered a smaller target for submarines which normally attacked from the flank. Also the range of a torpedo being limited, ships in the middle columns were often immune from torpedoes fired from outside the screen of escorts. Convoys were manoeuvred by flag signals by day and coloured lights by night. They could alter course by wheeling, the normal, though protracted method of changing direction; or they could be ordered, in an emergency, to turn 45° to port or starboard, all ships turning together. Progress would then be in echelon, a formation which could not long be maintained without confusion arising.

The ocean escort for SC7 was the little sloop *Scarborough*, a lightly-armed warship designed for peacetime police work on distant foreign stations. In command of her was Commander N. V. Dickinson. *Scarborough* had reached Sydney a few days earlier, having carried on independently across the Atlantic after the dispersal of the outward OB216 at 17°W on 23 September. She brought with her a tale of havoc being wrought by the U-boats in the North Channel, between Iceland and Scotland. Out of a total of 19 ships, six had been sunk between nightfall and midnight of the 20th. No trace of the submarines had been picked up by the escort. The convoy was left in peace thereafter, the U-boats having fatter prey to seek in homeward-bound convoys. On the day before the convoy dispersed a solitary home-bound merchantman was spoken. She was the *Pacific Grove*, which had broken away from convoy HX72 during an attack the previous night when six ships had been torpedoed.

A deep sense of the futility of their efforts in the face of their skilful and elusive tormentors could not but weigh on the minds of Dickinson and his men. Now this one little sloop was the sole defence of 34 ships until a local escort should meet them in the Western Approaches.

There was little leisure for the senior officer of the escort to ponder what might be in store. A southerly gale which sprang up on the fourth day after sailing put the convoy in disarray. During the night four Great Lakes steamers, not designed for Atlantic rollers, lost touch and did not rejoin. Three of them were to suffer the fate of stragglers, being sunk by U-boats. For the next four days a speed of little better than 6 knots was the best that could be maintained.

On 16 October, as dusk was falling, two more escorts met the convoy—unusually far west, 21° 30'. They were the *Fowey*, a sister ship of the *Scarborough*, and the *Bluebell*, one of the new 'Flower'-class corvettes which were now beginning to come to sea. They were commanded by Merchant Navy officers belonging to the Royal Naval Reserve, fine professional seamen who were to form the backbone of the

Atlantic escorts for the rest of the war; but that at this stage of the war they and their young RNVR officers, and largely conscript seamen ratings, were untrained for and inexperienced in anti-submarine warfare would not be denied. These three ships, none of which had worked together before, and amongst which there was no common tactical doctrine or prepared plan of action in case of an attack, took station round the convoy, *Scarborough* on the port bow, *Fowey* to starboard and *Bluebell* astern. Visual communication between them was impossible by night. The radio link was tenuous and unreliable. The distance between them, some six miles, was more than enough for a surfaced U-boat to slink through undetected even though a full moon was shining down from a clear sky on a smooth, silver sea.

It was a peaceful enough scene to the casual observer. Nevertheless it was fraught with hidden menace. Away on the port side of the convoy, whence the serried array of black hulls stood out against the moonlight, Korvetten-Kapitän Hans Rösing, from the conning tower of *U48*, gazed through his excellent Zeiss binoculars. The course and speed of the convoy were estimated. Then to U-boat headquarters flashed the radio message giving this information. The response was soon chirruping in the earphones of *U48*'s radio operator as orders went out to six other boats, *U100, 28, 123, 101, 99* and *46*, on a patrol line to the east and north of Rockall, the little upthrust of bare seagull-haunted rock in the Atlantic lying between the thirteenth and fourteenth meridians. They were to make for the route reported by *U48* and cooperate with her. The fat, easy target in his binoculars was too tempting to Rösing to permit him to wait passively for his colleagues to join him. At daylight air patrols might be over, forcing him to submerge and perhaps lose touch. The opportunity might be missed. A curt order to the helmsman and *U48* turned in to the attack. Just before 0400 a salvo of torpedoes sped away towards the unsuspecting convoy.

Lieutenant-Commander Robert Aubrey, commanding the *Fowey*, stationed on the up-moon starboard side could be fairly sure when two distant explosions thudded under his feet and a distress rocket soared up from the convoy, that the attack must have come from the far side. He at once took his ship across to join the *Scarborough*. Together the two ships swept the area on the port side with their asdics, quartering the sea for some time but to no avail. Meanwhile Lieutenant-Commander R. E. Sherwood, RNR, of the *Bluebell*, had taken his ship to stand by the two torpedoed ships and eventually picked up the crews from their boats.

The convoy commodore, Vice-Admiral L. D. Mackinnon, his broad pendant in the freighter *Assyrian*, had at once ordered an emergency turn to starboard, away from the direction of the attack. Together the 30 remaining ships had swung 45° and steered thus in echelon until clear of the danger area before resuming their normal formation. With the escorts all occupied elsewhere, the convoy was now bereft of all protection. At daylight the *Scarborough* rejoined, having left *Fowey* to continue the hunt for the U-boat; but she had barely regained her station when from a Sunderland flying-boat on patrol came a signal that a U-boat had been sighted and attacked just beyond the horizon on the port quarter of the convoy. Dickinson immediately left to search for and attack it. So once again the 30 ships were left to chug slowly on unescorted. It was fortunate that *U48*, having been forced to dive by *Scarborough* and *Fowey* and later again put down by the Sunderland, had lost touch with the convoy.

Dickinson's zeal to hit back at the U-boats, and an over-estimate of the chances of a single ship being able to run down even a fairly recently located submarine, was to keep him vainly searching for more than 24 hours in the area reported by the Sunderland. By the time he decided to rejoin the convoy on the next day he had dropped so far astern that his maximum speed of 14 knots never enabled him to do so. Thus, losing sight of the primary object of an escort, 'the safe and timely arrival of the convoy', he was to play no active part in the events which were to follow.

When Aubrey realized the situation, he at once gave up his hunt for *U48* and took the *Fowey* hurrying after the convoy which he joined that afternoon, 17 October. When *Bluebell* also rejoined soon after dark he stationed her on the port side, while he again took up station to starboard. Two further escorts were on their way, the sloop *Leith* and the corvette *Heartsease*; but even when they arrived the escort would be sparse in the extreme. In the meantime *U48*'s loss of contact had left the German headquarters uncertain of SC7's position and route.

Another boat, *U38*, which had also reported the convoy, had given a position considerably farther to the north. Unable to decide which of the two U-boats was in error, the U-boat Command ordered a patrol line to be established, by daylight on the 18th, just to the eastward of Rockall, at a longitude which it was estimated the convoy would reach in daylight that day. This would increase the chances of interception.

While the six submarines were moving to their new positions, however, the convoy was again located. *U38* had passed the daylight hours of the 17th in hurrying, on the surface, in a wide curve beyond the horizon, to attain an attacking position by nightfall. Soon after midnight she was in position on the dark side of the convoy which was clearly silhouetted against the moonlight. Only the single little corvette *Bluebell* barred her way. Easily evading detection, *U38* moved in. Shortly after 0100 on the 18th a salvo of torpedoes was fired. Kapitän-Leutnant Liebe, captain of *U38*, was unlucky and unskilful. From this first salvo of torpedoes only one achieved a hit and this was on the freighter *Carsbreck*, third ship in the port column of the convoy. With a cargo of timber she was not easy to sink. Though she was brought to a standstill she remained afloat. The *Fowey* was at once taken to join *Bluebell* in a search for the U-boat on the port side of the convoy, but without result. Neither of these ships could do more than 14 knots, less than the U-boat's top speed on the surface, so that, unless the submarine could be forced to submerge, the chances of catching her were slim.

At this moment there came a welcome reinforcement, though still a meagre one, as the sloop *Leith* (Commander R. C. Allen, RN) and the corvette *Heartsease* (Lieutenant-Commander E. J. R. North, RNR) arrived on the scene. As senior officer of the escort, Allen now ordered *Fowey* back to the convoy while he himself with the two corvettes searched the area astern of the convoy. There he came across the damaged *Carsbreck*. Some of her crew had taken to the boats, but the master was still aboard with others. Learning that the ship was not likely to founder and could steam at 6 knots, Allen left *Heartsease* to pick up the men in the lifeboat and escort the *Carsbreck*. He then set course to rejoin the convoy with the *Bluebell*.

All these movements had left the convoy without any close escort until *Fowey* rejoined. In the meantime *U38* had been left undisturbed to reload her tubes and come in again to the attack. Soon after 0130 Liebe again fired a salvo. He was again unsuccessful. Admiral Mackinnon, from the bridge of the *Assyrian*, saw the track of a torpedo as it streaked across from port to starboard close ahead of his flagship. He at once switched on the green light signals ordering an emergency turn of 45° to starboard. No ship in the convoy was hit. The convoy was then ordered back to its original course.

There were no further alarms that night and at daylight *Leith* and *Bluebell* rejoined as escort. During the day there was a grim sign of the enemy's activities as rafts with men clinging to them were sighted near the convoy's route. From the rafts the master and crew of 18 of the Estonian steamer *Nora* were rescued by the *Leith*. The *Nora* had been sunk five days earlier. Meanwhile, as the convoy ploughed slowly on, a deadly ambush was being prepared for it. On completion of his attack, Liebe had signalled the position, course and speed of the convoy to U-boat headquarters. By noon on the 18th, the U-boat patrol line had sighted nothing. From *U38*'s report it seemed that the convoy might pass too far to the north for the others to intercept it. Headquarters decided to rely upon *U38*'s position and fresh instructions were sent out.

Amongst the pack of wolves which were thus closing on SC7 were two of the most successful U-boat commanders of that time. Commanding *U100* was Joachim Schepke whose record of tonnage sunk was only exceeded by Günther Prien, destroyer of the *Royal Oak* in Scapa Flow, and by Otto Kretschmer whose *U99* was now in the same pack. The last of these, contemptuous of the opposition he had so far encountered, planned to take his boat in amongst the columns of the convoy where he could pick his targets at point-blank range. As the sun was sinking low over the sea, ruffled only by a light breeze from the south-east, the U-boats gathered just beyond the horizon, out of sight. To the north of him,

Kretschmer could see the conning-tower of *U101*. A light winked from her. It was the long-awaited message 'Enemy in sight to port'. Soon afterwards the masts and funnels of a warship came into sight, then a cloud of smoke and finally the forest of masts of the convoy.

All unaware of the ambush waiting ahead, the convoy settled down for the night. Ahead of it the *Leith* weaved to and fro across the front. On the starboard bow was the *Bluebell*. At dusk the *Fowey* had been ordered to sweep for five miles astern to shake off any shadowers before resuming her station on the convoy's port side. As darkness fell, the commodore altered the convoy's course 40° to starboard which it was hoped might be unobserved by any U-boat in the vicinity. Nothing could save it from its fate, however. At 2015 the first explosion was heard as a torpedo blew a hole in the Swedish ship *Convallaria*, second ship of the second column in from the port side. That side of the convoy was devoid of any escort as the *Fowey* had not yet returned from her abortive sweep astern. Commander Allen therefore took the *Leith* on a search in that direction, continuing outwards for ten minutes, firing starshells.

Nothing was sighted. *Leith* then turned back to comb the area astern of the convoy and round the torpedoed ship. There the *Fowey*, which had picked up the crew of the *Convallaria*, was met and in company the two ships searched vainly up the convoy wake. Meanwhile the convoy had once again been left with only the *Bluebell* as close escort. The wolves closed in. Soon after 2200 a series of explosions told the tale of destruction. The log-book of *U99* gives an impression of the ease with which it was achieved.

18 October. 2124. Exchange recognition signals with *U123*. Convoy again in sight. I am ahead of it, so allow my boat to drop back, avoiding leading destroyers. Destroyers are constantly firing starshells.* From outside, I attack the right flank of the first formation.

2202. Weather, visibility moderate, bright moonlight. Fire bow torpedo by director. Miss.

2206. Fire stern tube by director. At 700 metres, hit forward of amidships. Vessel of some 6,500 tons sinks within 20 seconds. *I now proceed head-on into the convoy.*

2230. Fire bow tube by director. Miss because of error in calculation of gyro-angle. I therefore decide to fire rest of torpedoes without director, especially as the installation has still not been accepted and adjusted by the Torpedo Testing Department. Boat is soon sighted by a ship which fires a white star and turns towards us at full speed continuing even after we alter course.

---

*No doubt, unable to believe that convoy escorts could be as weak as, in fact, they were at this time, the numbers present are exaggerated and the slow sloops and corvettes are always called destroyers.

I have to make off with engines all out. Eventually the ship turns off, fires one of her guns and again takes her place in the convoy.

2330. Fire bow torpedo at a large freighter. As the ship turns towards us, the torpedo passes ahead of her and hits an even larger ship after a run of 1,740 metres. This ship of 7,000 tons is hit abreast the foremast and the bow quickly sinks below the surface, as two holds are apparently flooded.

2355. Fire a bow torpedo at a large freighter of 6,000 tons at a range of 750 metres. Hit abreast foremast. Immediately after the torpedo explosion there is another explosion, with a high column of flame from bow to bridge. Smoke rises 200 metres. Bow apparently shattered. Ship continues to burn with green flame.

19 October. 0015. Three destroyers approach the ship and search area in line abreast. I take off at full speed to the south-west and again make contact with the convoy. Torpedoes from other boats are constantly heard exploding. The destroyers do not know how to help and occupy themselves by constantly firing starshells which are of little effect in the bright moonlight. I now start attacking the convoy from astern.

And so it went on. At 0138 and 0155 Kretschmer torpedoed two ships which both sank, the latter in 40 seconds. Two shots at another ship missed but a third struck forward of the ship's bridge, sinking her. Just before 0400 *U99*'s last torpedo hit but failed to sink another ship from the convoy. By this time all cohesion had been lost and Kretschmer was able to stand by to see if his victim would sink, before bringing his gun into action to finish her off. Before he could do so another of the pack, *U123*, opened fire on the helpless merchantman. Some of the shells falling close to *U99*—'so that I have to leave the area quickly'— Kretschmer set course for his base at Lorient, after a night of unprecedented destruction which put his record far above that of his nearest competitor.

In the convoy it had been an appalling night. As ship after ship went down or hauled out and lay slowly sinking, torpedo tracks real and imaginary set the survivors jinking this way and that to avoid them. The risk of collision was added to that from the enemy. The ships opened the distance for their neighbours more and more until all formation and order was dissolved. By daylight the convoy was virtually scattered.

For the escorts it had been a night of shame and frustration as their vain efforts to get to grips with their elusive opponents were repeatedly interrupted by the necessity to rescue the crews of sunken ships. While the *Leith* was searching up the wake of the convoy with the *Fowey*, explosions were heard in the convoy. Soon a derelict ship was sighted, the freighter *Shekatika* from which Aubrey took off the crew before hurrying on towards the convoy. Then he came across a pathetic jumble of lifeboats and drifting wreckage from which he rescued the crew of the

Dutch *Boekolo*, whose master said his ship had been sunk while stopped, picking up survivors from another ship, the *Beatus*. The *Leith* meanwhile had pressed on and had come up with a group of four ships lying crippled and sinking close to one another—*Empire Miniver, Gunborg, Niritos* and *Beatus*—with the *Bluebell* standing by.

At this moment there came the first—and only—sight of the enemy, as a submarine was sighted ahead of the *Leith*, steering away on a similar course. Allen set off at full speed, illuminating his quarry with starshells while calling *Bluebell* to join him. Though the U-boat had the legs of her pursuers, her captain was bluffed into submerging. It should have been the end of her. As *Leith*'s asdic team went into operation, contact was gained. But *Leith*, like most of the ships which at this time were on escort duty, had old, out-dated equipment and a crew sorely lacking practice in the use of it. Before an effective attack could be delivered, the U-boat had given her the slip. The hunt could not be long protracted. The sea was littered with sinking ships, lifeboats and rafts. A tanker had been seen to blow up on the horizon.

Sending *Bluebell* to stand by the four crippled ships which were seen to be still afloat, Allen once more set off at 1150 at full speed to rejoin his defenceless convoy. Half an hour later he sighted the *Fowey* which had just embarked the survivors from *Shekatika* and *Boekolo*. *Fowey* was ordered to join and to get back to the convoy as fast as possible. Then yet another solitary ship was sighted. She was the *Blairspey*, another lumber ship, which had been torpedoed but was able to proceed at slow speed. She had, perforce, to be left to make the best of her way to port alone, and in fact, did so unmolested further. The disastrous count was not yet complete. Hurrying on down the track of the convoy, Allen came across another sinking ship surrounded by wreckage. It was the *Assyrian*, the flagship of the commodore, which had been torpedoed soon after midnight at the same time as the Dutch freighter *Soesterborg*, and the *Empire Brigade*. Crews from all three, including Admiral Mackinnon, the much-tried commodore, were taken on board before the *Leith* began a vain effort for the rest of the night to round up the scattered survivors of the convoy. Dawn revealed an empty sea to the dismayed escort commander.

Aubrey had had somewhat better luck. At daybreak eight ships were in sight and he soon had them gathered together with the master of one of them, the *Somersby*, appointed as commodore. As the day wore on, the fair weather broke. The night settled down in pelting rain, reducing visibility to a few hundred yards. The little convoy again became scattered; at daylight Aubrey found that the ship with which he had kept contact was the only one in sight.

By then, however, they were well into the North Channel where the U-boats forbore to follow them. A fresh target had been located for those with any torpedoes remaining. Shaken and tired by their ordeal, the remnants of SC7 made their way individually to port, while the escorts returned sorrowfully to their base with their crowd of survivors from sunken ships.* The disastrous count of 20 ships sunk and two more damaged, out of 34 which had started, was enough to mark October 1940 as one of the black months of the war at sea. But even as the surviving ships were entering the North Channel another convoy was suffering a similar fate.

The fast convoy HX79 had left Halifax some days after SC7 had set out from Sydney. By 18 October it was two days' steaming behind SC7 and making for the North Channel. It had an escort of two armed merchant cruisers, *Montclare* and *Alaunia*, and as yet no anti-submarine defence, when it was sighted and reported by Günther Prien whose boat, *U47*, having expended its torpedoes in previous attacks, had been retained at sea to send weather reports to headquarters. *U47* was instructed to shadow the convoy and 'home' all other boats in the area to it, including those which had been attacking SC7 and still had any torpedoes remaining.

During the 18th an escort of ostensibly considerable strength had met HX79. The senior officer was Lieutenant-Commander A. B. Russell, RN, commanding the destroyer *Whitehall*. In addition there were the minesweeper *Jason*, the corvettes *Hibiscus*, *Heliotrope*, *Coreopsis* and *Arabis*, the destroyer *Sturdy* and three trawlers, *Lady Elsa*, *Black Fly* and *Angle*. On paper a formidable force; but the ships of which it was composed had been got together at random; the Flower-class corvettes were newly commissioned and mostly straight from the shipyards which were now turning them out in a steady stream. Their crews lacked training and experience. None of the commanding officers of the ships of the escort had had any opportunity of meeting to discuss and determine a common plan in the event of an attack. Lieutenant-Commander G. T. Cooper of the *Sturdy* was subsequently to comment:

> With the exception of HGF33 which I escorted from Gibraltar to the latitude of Finisterre last June, this was our first experience of ocean convoy work in submarine areas. I had no details of this convoy, nor did I know the nature of the escort and I had never met any of the commanding officers of the other ships. No plan of action in the event of attack had therefore been discussed between us.

Lieutenant-Commander Russell had never before escorted a convoy in the Western Approaches, though he had escorted numerous convoys in

---

*Two of the escort commanders, Aubrey of the *Fowey* and Sherwood of the *Bluebell*, were to profit from their harsh experience to become veterans of the Battle of the Atlantic and to have their revenge on the U-boats. Aubrey was to command a ship in the famous group of U-boat killers led by Captain 'Johnny' Walker. Sherwood was to command the escort of a convoy in May 1943, the fight round which was to mark the turning-point of the Battle of the Atlantic.

the Channel and on the East Coast. His ship having been out of circulation for some time past, undergoing refit, he was out of touch with events and not aware how conditions had changed since the U-boats adopted the surface attack. Later he was to admit that 'there was an entire lack of coordination and teamwork to meet this form of attack'. Perhaps the most experienced of the escorts was the *Jason*, though her experience was not such as to breed confidence. Lieutenant-Commander R. E. Terry, her captain, ruefully commented that 'in the past six weeks he had picked up no less than 720 survivors from sunken merchantmen'.

Such was the force which settled down in their stations round HX79 on the evening of 19 October as it steered eastwards for the North Channel at 8½ knots. The convoy consisted of 49 ships. Sailing with it, and stationed in the centre was the Dutch submarine *O21*, an arrangement which was being tried out at this time as a possible defence against surface raiders.

It was a dark, overcast and drizzling night, with visibility varying between half a mile and three miles, and the moon had not yet risen, when at 2120 the attack opened with two ships on the starboard side of the convoy being torpedoed. In the absence of any prearranged plan the various escorts took individual, unco-ordinated action. The *Whitehall* crossed the front of the convoy and made an asdic search of the area on the starboard flank. Reaching the rear, she made contact with the *Arabis*. For half an hour the two ships swept up and down and across the wake of the convoy. Nothing was sighted. The *Jason* then joined them and a further search was made round the two torpedoed ships which were still floating.

In spite of the presence of three trawlers, ships well suited to the work of rescue, one of the convoy, *Loch Lomond*, had been detailed to act as rescue ship. With great courage her master had at once turned to carry out this duty. Nevertheless when three men on a raft made a frenzied appeal to be picked up, Russell felt compelled to comply, though a boat-load of other survivors were instructed to row over to the *Loch Lomond* near by. Then, as starshells blossoming to the eastward indicated further happenings in the convoy, Russell sped away to investigate, leaving *Jason* to stand by the torpedoed ships.

At 2315 there were two vivid explosions ahead. As he was making for them there was an enormous flash with flames reaching high up into the sky at a considerable distance in another quarter. Assuming it to be a tanker laden with petrol which had just been torpedoed, he turned off towards it. In fact it was a ship which had been torpedoed some days beforehand and had been burning ever since. It was an unfortunate diversion which gives some indication of how littered with burning, sinking or crippled ships were the North-Western Approaches at that time.

Finding nothing and coming to the correct conclusion that what he had seen had taken place some distance beyond the horizon, Russell resumed his course to overtake the convoy. He soon came across the trawlers *Angle* and *Lady Elsa* standing by four torpedoed ships, one of which was a burning tanker. Leaving the trawlers to do what they could, *Whitehall* hurried on, only to find yet another disabled ship with a number of lifeboats near her. Hardening his heart, Russell ignored them for the time being, though this meant leaving men in the water who were whistling and shouting for rescue. Joined now by the *Sturdy*, the *Whitehall* had barely reached the convoy when there were two more explosions. The tanker *Athel Monarch* and a freighter *Whitford Point* had been hit. The former was damaged only and eventually reached port; but the freighter went down in ten seconds.

Though the moon had risen some two hours earlier and visibility was now as much as five miles, a frantic search by *Whitehall* and *Sturdy* failed to get a sight of the enemy. There seemed nothing for Russell to do but to send *Sturdy* to rescue the struggling survivors of the *Whitford Point* while he himself took the *Whitehall* back to the help of the men he had been forced previously to abandon. Thereafter he quartered to and fro across the rear of the convoy. For a time there were no further incidents. Then at 0420 an explosion in the far distance to port of the convoy occurred. Moving over in that direction, Russell found the *Hibiscus* in station there. This was the first time that Russell had any information as to the whereabouts of the *Hibiscus*, which in fact had remained in the vicinity of the convoy throughout the night, without catching a glimpse of the enemy who were wreaking the havoc. Her captain confirmed that the explosion had been a long way off and so presumably unconnected with the convoy. In fact it was the Swedish steamer *Janus* whose master, at his crew's insistence, had broken convoy when the attacks started and had paid the inevitable penalty. He and his men were lucky to be picked up later when, during the following morning, *Hibiscus* was directed to the position by a patrolling Sunderland. Russell therefore took the *Whitehall* across the convoy to try to find out which escorts were still in company. On the starboard side he found *Heliotrope* which had also remained with the convoy throughout. Though she had circled the convoy continuously, she, too, had had no sight of an enemy. In deep despair, Russell returned to cover the rear of the convoy and to await the dawn.

There was to be yet one more calamity. Shortly before 0500 the *Jason* picked up a signal from the *Loch Lomond*, left on her own after rescuing survivors, that she was being chased by a submarine. Terry at once went to her aid; but he had not yet located her when at 0725, a white rocket soaring up into the air told him he was too late to save her. *Loch Lomond* had been torpedoed five minutes before. Though she was still afloat when *Jason* came up with her, she was beyond hope of salvage and her crew were in their boats from which *Jason* embarked them.

It was the final loss suffered by HX79. That there would have been

5–6 Admirals Pound and Raeder—opposing Navy Chiefs

7–9 Admirals Noble and Horton and their Atlantic opponent Admiral Dönitz

10 Black Swan-Class frigate   11 River-class frigate

TYPES OF ATLANTIC ESCORT

12 Convoy rescue ship   13 Anti-submarine trawler

14 Destroyer *Hesperus* (bow damaged after   15 Sloop
    ramming and sinking U-boat).

more on the following night, but for the fact that the U-boats had expended their torpedoes, seems certain. But it was bad enough. Twelve ships had been sunk and two more damaged, 24.5 per cent of the convoy. In SC7 the percentage had been 58.8. These two catastrophic encounters perhaps mark the very nadir of British fortunes in the Battle of the Atlantic. They were made harder to bear by the inability of the powerful escort of HX79 either to protect the convoy or exact a penalty from the U-boats. On the German side they represented the first occasion when pack tactics were employed. Their success greatly encouraged Admiral Dönitz, who had long wished to put them into use but had until then been frustrated by a shortage of operational boats. From then onwards they would be the standard tactics, to be used whenever the opportunity presented itself.

C

4 *German Surface and Submarine Concentration*

The convoy battles of October 1940 had been so complete a defeat for the escorts that the need for a strict examination of the causes for an all-out effort to stave off catastrophe, was brought home. The new German tactics of surface attack in packs by night posed a problem to which there seemed to be no answer readily available. The losses of SC7 could be explained by the swamping of the weak escort. HX79, on the other hand, had, on paper, a very strong one; yet its losses were nearly as great and, but for the expenditure of the U-boats' torpedoes, might have been worse. Furthermore, the submarines had been able to roam at will amongst the escorts and even inside the columns of the convoy, only one being detected and forced to dive. The concentrated loss from these two convoys within a period of three days brought home the seriousness of the situation in a way that more dispersed, yet equally severe losses might not have done. Something was evidently wrong with the methods—or the means—of protecting convoys. The school of thought which had never been convinced by the arguments for a convoy system began to make itself heard again.

Indeed, they had never been entirely silenced. Their views had prevailed sufficiently to lead to a number of the desperately needed destroyer escorts being wastefully employed on futile 'offensive' search and patrol, instead of as close escorts to convoys where they could be sure of encountering the enemy. This school, in defiance of the lessons of the past—chiefly, one must think, because they had never been studied—now advocated the sailing of our convoys along patrolled shipping lanes. They backed their arguments with the insidious siren song which promised an economy thereby in the use of escorts and aircraft. Fortunately, although this recommendation was approved by the Defence Committee when it sat under the Prime Minister's chairmanship to consider the convoy situation soon after the attacks on SC7 and HX79, the ever-increasing westerly spreads of the area of the U-boat operations made its implementation impossible.

The Defence Committee took the important decision that the time had come to release to trade protection duties many of the destroyers which up to then had been held on the east and south coasts against any invasion attempts by the enemy. This had the important result of leavening the slow, ill-trained sloops and corvettes which had hitherto formed the majority of the escorts with speedy vessels manned by experienced crews. Not only were these ships better equipped and trained to hunt any U-boats detected, but their high speed enabled them to cover greater areas of water round the convoy and so make the penetration of the screen by U-boats more hazardous. Furthermore they could rejoin the convoy quickly after being thrown out to aid a damaged ship or exhort a laggard, whereas, as has been seen, a corvette or sloop which once dropped behind was out of the picture for many hours. Before November was out the strengthening of the convoy escorts in this way had paid an encouraging dividend in the destruction of *U32* by the destroyers *Harvester* and *Highlander*, of *U31* by the *Antelope* and of *U104* by the corvette *Rhododendron*.

There were, however, many other duties for which destroyers were required elsewhere. Few could be spared for convoy duty. It was for this reason that Winston Churchill had been striving to persuade the Americans to release to us, in barter for base facilities in British possessions in the west, 50 over-age destroyers which were lying idle in reserve. In September 1940 he had succeeded and an agreement was signed. Though these ships were antique in armament and machinery and had to be fitted with asdics before they could be of use, they were to prove a valuable stop-gap at the height of the Battle of the Atlantic when every warship that could float and steam was beyond price.

Nevertheless it was obvious that there were many other requirements if the pack attacks were to be defeated. Development of an effective radar for ships and aircraft was given a high priority. To take advantage of the radio transmissions which U-boats had to make on high frequency to their headquarters, reporting the location of convoys, etc., if the wolf pack was to concentrate, a ship-borne high-frequency direction-finder (H/F D/F) was being developed. This would enable escorts to pinpoint U-boats locally, just as the shore-sited D/F stations were able to locate them more approximately. First steps were taken towards equipping escorts with the radio telephone so essential for teamwork amongst the escort groups which was required to defeat the obviously well-developed teamwork of the enemy. And, to make effective use of the new equipment, the escorts had to be formed into regularly constituted groups which would train together.

To develop, produce and supply all these technical aids to escort vessels would take time. Until then the U-boats were in a position of clear advantage. Yet the prime antidote to the U-boat was immediately to hand, if it had been appreciated. Already the U-boats were moving their patrol area farther westward to avoid the occasional Sunderland flying-boat which was all that Coastal Command could spare to quarter the sea area off the North-Western Approaches.

Aircraft were, indeed, coming from the factories in ever-increasing numbers, but a lack of appreciation of the crucial part they had to play in the defeat of the U-boats, on which all other operations of war ultimately depended, was still keeping Coastal Command the Cinderella of the RAF. Multi-engined aircraft went first to satisfy the demands of Bomber Command and the strategic bombing offensive on which such hopes were pinned—hopes which post-war research has shown to have been set far too high. As their contribution to the war at sea, aircraft of Bomber Command were sent out to bomb the U-boat yards and bases. Though it could not be known at the time, the effect of these raids on the U-boat offensive was negligible. Production was not slowed up nor was a single U-boat destroyed. Thus none of the means whereby the U-boats were eventually to be mastered was available in the winter of 1940.

It was indeed fortunate, therefore, that the nature of the problem facing the convoy escorts was so clearly revealed at a time when the enemy was still too weak in numbers to exploit to the full the technique he had re-discovered. With less than 30 operational U-boats, large-scale pack operations were inevitably followed by periods of replenishment and rest for a large proportion of his available force. During November and December 1940, no more than six U-boats operated simultaneously. Combined with winter weather and low visibility, this made interception of convoys and pack-attacks more difficult. One such attack, which took place on 1 December on HX90, was sufficient to banish any complacency. *U99*, the boat of the ace-commander, Otto Kretschmer, his reputation enhanced by the sinking in November of the armed merchant cruisers *Laurentic* and *Patroclus*, was among the pack of four boats which got amongst the ships of the convoy and sank 11 of them, including the armed merchant cruiser *Forfar*.

Winter weather, which handicapped the U-boats in their search for victims, operated to assist the surface units of the German fleet in breaking out past the British northern patrols into the Atlantic to take their share of the attack on the merchant convoys. The first to break out had been the pocket-battleship *Admiral Scheer*, which passed undetected through the Denmark Strait at the end of October 1940.

The comparative ineffectiveness of this form of operation by a single ship was demonstrated when on 5 November the homeward-bound convoy HX84 in mid-Atlantic saw her fighting-tops rise over the horizon. Captain E. S. F. Fegen, commanding the solitary escort, the armed merchant cruiser *Jervis Bay*, signalled the order to the convoy to scatter and took his ship out to the unequal combat. Before his ancient guns were silenced and his ship sunk the convoy had had time to scatter so widely that out of the 37 ships of which it was composed the *Scheer* could round up and sink only five.

The German then steered south to begin a cruise lasting five months, during which she roamed far and wide in the South Atlantic and Indian Ocean, capturing or sinking single, unescorted merchantmen before finally returning to Germany. Her total achievements were the sinking of the *Jervis Bay* and 16 merchantmen totalling 99,059 tons. It was a mere pin-prick compared to the destruction wrought by the U-boats; so, too, were the achievements of the heavy cruiser *Hipper*, which followed her into the Atlantic on 7 December with orders to attack convoys. Not until Christmas Eve did she locate one, a troop convoy bound for the Middle East, some 700 miles west of Finisterre. When she moved into the attack at dawn on Christmas Day, she found the escort of the cruisers *Berwick*, *Bonaventure* and *Dunedin* too much for her and she was driven off. Though her damage was only slight, combined with machinery defects it was enough to force her to make for Brest for repairs.

On 1 February the *Hipper* sailed to try again: this time she was luckier and on the 12th she intercepted a convoy of 19 ships homeward-bound from Freetown which had not yet been met by its escort. She sank seven of them before her captain, his fuel running low, decided he must return to Brest before opposition could arrive.

This brief success could not hide the unsuitability of single cruisers for operations against convoys and Grand-Admiral Raeder had already set on foot a plan for the two fast and powerful battle-cruisers *Scharnhorst* and *Gneisenau* to cruise in the North Atlantic in company. Their first attempt to break out had been foiled by the British Home Fleet: the C-in-C, Admiral Tovey, had been warned in good time and, at dawn on 28 January 1941, one of his cruisers, the *Naiad*, had located them to the south of Iceland. Superior radar in the German ships, however, had enabled them to avoid being brought to action; turning back at high speed they had given the *Naiad* the slip and disappeared into the Arctic gloom to refuel and await a more favourable opportunity. This had come about on 4 February when the Home Fleet's return to Scapa Flow to refuel left the Denmark Strait unwatched.

The arrival of this powerful squadron, under Vice-Admiral Lütjens, on the convoy routes was potentially disastrous. All that the Admiralty could spare in reply was one of the old, slow battleships of the *Royal Sovereign* or *Queen Elizabeth* classes to accompany a proportion of the convoys. Nevertheless, the inherent difficulties under which commerce raiders laboured in waters basically dominated by a superior enemy fleet were quickly revealed when the German squadron intercepted their first convoy on 8 February only to turn away empty handed when the fighting top of the convoy's sole escort, the *Ramillies*, was sighted. Lütjens could not afford to risk damage to his ships 3,000 miles from the nearest dockyard at Brest.

Moving further west after waiting for a few days for the alarm to die down, Lütjens next approached the convoy routes at a point beyond which westbound convoys were dispersed and on 22 February he was able to snap up five ships before bearing away south to shift his hunting ground to the Sierra Leone convoy route. Here again, it was the sight of the battleship *Malaya* which forced him to leave alone the one convoy he intercepted; whereupon, after sinking one independently-routed ship, Lütjens steered back to the transatlantic route, where, on 15 and 16 March he at last achieved the sort of success expected. Getting once again amongst a number of ships recently dispersed from convoy, he sank or captured 16 of them.

Lütjens now set course for Brest where he arrived on 22 March to receive congratulatory messages from Raeder. The cruise had certainly been a most successful one. Apart from the not inconsiderable total of 115,622 tons of shipping destroyed, the presence of the two battle-cruisers in the Atlantic had for a time completely disrupted the whole complex cycle of convoys with a consequent serious drop in vital imports to Britain.

Raeder was now planning an even more ambitious operation in which the *Bismarck*, the most powerful battleship in the world at that time, and the cruiser *Prinz Eugen*, both nearing completion, would break out to make, with the *Scharnhorst* and *Gneisenau*, a squadron which could defy the whole British Home Fleet.

It was never to be, however. From the moment the *Scharnhorst* and *Gneisenau* secured in the harbour of Brest they came under the constant surveillance and repeated attacks of the Royal Air Force. Both ships were hit by bombs and severely, though never fatally damaged. The *Gneisenau* was also torpedoed and severely damaged by a Coastal Command aircraft as she lay at a buoy in the harbour. In addition an intensive minelaying campaign by aircraft of Coastal and Bomber Command and by the minelayer *Abdiel* blocked the exit from Brest for long periods. Thus Grand-Admiral Raeder's dream of a simultaneous foray by the battle-cruisers and the *Bismarck* and *Prinz Eugen* was shattered.

Nevertheless, impatient for his beautiful great ship to prove her worth and perhaps blind, as were many seamen of his generation, to the changing nature of naval strategy with the advance of air power, Raeder determined to press on with the operation, using only *Bismarck* and *Prinz Eugen*. After a delay until the third week of May, occasioned by an engine-room defect in the *Prinz Eugen*, the two ships sailed in secrecy from Gdynia in the Baltic.

Raeder's hope of his ships' getting away undetected was not fulfilled; they were sighted as they steamed through the Kattegat, and air reconnaissance located them on the morning of 21 May 1941 at anchor in Korsfiord near Bergen. In thick weather with clouds hanging low on the Norwegian hillsides, defeating the Royal Air Force reconnaissance aircraft entrusted with the task of watching them, they slipped away to sea; but a naval aircraft braving fog and intense anti-aircraft fire penetrated to the Bergen fiords to gain the certain information that the *Bismarck* was out.

This was enough to set into motion the plans of Admiral Tovey, C-in-C, Home Fleet. His task was to intercept the enemy ships and prevent them reaching the Atlantic or, if that failed, to hunt them down in the wide ocean wastes. Already cruisers were patrolling the two most likely passages into the Atlantic—the Denmark Strait between Iceland and Greenland, and the strait between Iceland and the Faroes. The battle-cruiser *Hood*, flagship of Vice-Admiral L. E. Holland, and the new battleship *Prince of Wales* were on their way to Iceland. Now the C-in-C himself sailed in his flagship *King George V* with the aircraft carrier *Victorious*. From the Clyde the battle-cruiser *Repulse* would come to join him on passage to the northwest.

The *Hood* was more than 20 years old and was lightly armoured after the fashion of battle-cruisers of her generation; the *Prince of Wales* was only recently out of the builder's yard, her machinery still being cleared of 'teething troubles' and her ship's company inexperienced. The aircrews of the *Victorious* were so untrained that many of them had not yet landed on a carrier's deck. Nevertheless the forces immediately available to Admiral Tovey could be looked on as adequate if the *Bismarck* could be intercepted before breaking clear into the open ocean.

However, any one of a number of unpredictable chances might enable the enemy to evade the British forces in the smoky northern sea, foggy, snow-laden and storm-tossed even in May. In that event, only a great preponderance of force could ensure the necessary concentration being brought to bear to engage the *Bismarck* successfully, even though air reconnaissance might succeed in locating her. Had foresight given the British Navy aircraft carriers in sufficient numbers first to ensure the location of an enemy vessel and then to deliver overwhelming massed air attacks, as demonstrated soon after by the Japanese, the problem would have not been difficult to solve. But as it was, the only two carriers available between Gibraltar and Iceland were the *Victorious* and the *Ark Royal*, the latter in Force 'H' based on Gibraltar. Each carried only a handful of slow-flying, obsolescent Swordfish aircraft which combined the rôle of reconnaissance and torpedo attack aircraft. Yet it was to be the aircraft from the *Ark Royal* which were to bring eventual success.

During the night of 22 May, as *King George V*, *Repulse* and *Victorious* punched their way north-westward into a moderate sea, there was no certainty with regard to the *Bismarck*'s intended movements. The C-in-C had deduced that a break-out into the Atlantic was the enemy's most probable intention, and he was making his plans to intercept with the forces immediately available. The 23rd dawned grey and wet, with low cloud covering the sky. Air patrols between Iceland and the Faroes were just possible, and were relied upon for that area; but in the Denmark Strait, the most likely route for the enemy, two cruisers, *Suffolk* and *Norfolk*, shared the task of interception in that fog-smothered channel between the ice-barrier to the north-west and the inhospitable coast of Iceland.

Two factors were to operate in favour of the British. The *Suffolk* was fitted with a modern surface-warning radar set, a device still in its primitive stage of development but still good enough to enable detection and shadowing of a large target in fog or snowstorms. Secondly, the German Admiral Lütjens in the *Bismarck*, had chosen to pass through the Denmark Strait close in to the ice-barrier; and whereas on that side of the strait the weather was clear, towards Iceland dense fog covered the sea.

So on the evening of the 23rd the two German ships were sighted first by the *Suffolk* and soon afterwards by the *Norfolk*, and were then successfully shadowed through a night studded with snowstorms and fog patches. The reports coming regularly in from the cruisers brought the *Hood* and the *Prince of Wales* accurately on to the scene at dawn; and when at 0335 as the distant shapes of two large enemy ships came into sight against the north-western horizon, Admiral Holland knew that he had made a perfect interception.

Holland's original intention had been to concentrate the four British ships, so that the fire of his two capital ships could be combined against the *Bismarck* while his cruisers engaged the *Prinz Eugen*. On sighting the enemy, however, he decided not to wait for *Norfolk* and *Suffolk* to come up, but immediately turned *Hood* and *Prince of Wales* 40° together and steered to close the range. To all appearances he could well afford to do so. Against the *Bismarck*'s eight 15-inch guns, Holland could bring to bear the same number from the *Hood* and ten 14-inch from the *Prince of Wales*.

Unfortunately there were several adverse factors. The enemy ships were steaming with the cruiser leading the battleship. The similarity of their silhouettes led to the *Prinz Eugen* being taken for the *Bismarck* by the gun controllers in the *Hood*. A signal to concentrate the fire of both British ships on the leading enemy was made; and though it was corrected just before the first salvoes from the *Hood* crashed out, and in the *Prince of Wales* the mistake had been realized and the order ignored, it seems certain from German reports of the action that the *Hood* did in fact engage the *Prinz Eugen*.

Secondly, Holland's turn towards the enemy allowed only the forward turrets to bear, reducing the number of guns in action to four 15-inch and six 14-inch. This would not have been so serious had the British ships steered directly for the enemy while closing the range, thus presenting difficult end-on targets; but the course selected was only a partially converging one, so that neither was the target reduced nor the full fire-power brought to bear.

Finally, the teething troubles in the *Prince of Wales*'s turret machinery were to make themselves evident at her very first salvo. One gun was known to have a defect which would prevent it being reloaded after the first round. Of the remainder, first one and then another would miss a salvo; and though the contractor's workmen, still on board, strove manfully to keep the guns in action, it was only rarely that a full salvo was fired.

The action opened at 0352 when the *Hood* fired her first salvo at a range of 25,000 yards, the *Prince of Wales* joining in 30 seconds later. Two minutes later the *Bismarck* replied. The German battleship's shooting was of remarkable accuracy, as well it might be, fresh as she was from intensive practice in the sheltered waters of the Baltic. The *Hood* was at once racing through the tall leaping columns of 15-inch shell splashes. A shell from one of the first salvoes scored a hit at the foot of her mainmast, and started a serious fire. Eight minutes after the action started another plunged down through her armour and penetrated to one of her after magazines, which blew up. The great ship was torn asunder by a violent explosion, broke in half, and in less than three minutes had vanished, leaving only a pall of smoke and three survivors.

Meanwhile the *Prince of Wales* had been left undisturbed to engage the *Bismarck*—a fortunate circumstance, as in her untrained state it had taken six salvoes to find the range and straddle the target. Now the full fury of the enemy's fire descended on her. The range being down to 14,500 yards, the 8-inch guns of the *Prinz Eugen* joined those of the *Bismarck* to bring a continuous hail of fire accurately to bear. Shell after shell crashed home, and spray from near misses fell from masthead height as the water columns dissolved.

Then a 15-inch shell plunged full on to the bridge, smashing through it and exploding as it emerged. Everyone there except the captain and his chief yeoman of signals was either killed or wounded. With his guns firing more and more spasmodically as breakdowns occurred, it was time for Captain Leach to withdraw and await the support he knew must be hurrying to the scene. Under shelter of a smoke-screen he turned his ship away.

Indeed, had Captain Leach realized it, he was fortunate to have escaped so lightly. One of the four 15-inch shells which had hit his ship had pierced her side well below the water-line, and had come to rest deep in her bowels without exploding. The damage had not all been one-sided, however. Three times the *Bismarck* too had been struck by the *Prince of Wales*'s 14-inch shells. One of these hits was to be of crucial significance. Plunging right through the ship it had holed two oil tanks and flooded a compartment in which were situated the suction valves for further oil tanks forward of it. At one blow Admiral Lütjens had been deprived of more than a thousand tons of precious, irreplaceable oil fuel.

At once all hope of carrying on with his commerce-raiding operation had vanished. Furthermore Lütjens had to make up his mind immediately whether to turn back for the North Sea and make for his home waters, or to head for a French Biscay port. He chose the latter, and his fate was sealed. For unknown to him, from the moment he was sighted by the *Norfolk* the British Admiralty had begun to gather forces from all over the Atlantic, out of which a net was to be woven in which the enemy must become entangled whichever way he shaped his course. Force 'H' under Vice-Admiral Sir James Somerville, with his flag in the battle-cruiser *Renown*, and comprising in addition the aircraft carrier *Ark Royal*, the cruiser *Sheffield* and six destroyers, left Gibraltar and hurried north. The battleships *Rodney* and *Ramillies* were ordered to leave the convoy they were escorting, and to converge on the area south of Iceland. The *Revenge* sailed from Halifax to meet the *Bismarck* should she break westward. The cruisers *London* and *Edinburgh* were drawn in to make further strands of the net.

The C-in-C himself, in possession only of the news from the shadowing force that the *Hood* had been sunk and that the *Bismarck* was steering southward at undiminished speed into the Atlantic, was pushing ahead at his best speed to intercept. However, he could not hope to come up with the enemy before the next morning. During the night the cruisers might lose touch in the steadily deteriorating weather. A rising gale from the north-west with rain and low cloud was making ideal conditions for evasion. Admiral Tovey had one chance of damaging the enemy before dark: a torpedo attack by the *Victorious*'s aircraft. He accordingly detached the carrier to steer directly for the *Bismarck* and so gain a position within the range of her Swordfish aircraft, which it was estimated she could do by 1900.

Meanwhile, the *Prince of Wales*, *Norfolk* and *Suffolk* had been shadowing the *Bismarck*, the *Suffolk*'s radar enabling contact to be maintained in spite of the increasingly foggy conditions. At about 1630 Admiral Lütjens took advantage of a fog patch to turn briefly on the *Suffolk* to create a diversion during which the *Prinz Eugen* was detached to make her own way to safety, which she eventually succeeded in doing. The *Bismarck* then turned away westward.

This seriously upset the plans for the *Victorious*'s air strike. At 2000 the carrier was still 120 miles from the target, and closing with it only slowly. Though darkness was not due for more than three hours, the increasing wind and sea, accompanied by ever more frequent rain squalls, persuaded Captain Bovell to delay no longer. The meagre handful of torpedo aircraft, nine Swordfish in three sub-flights of three each, lumbered heavily into the air from the heaving deck and droned away into the grey smother.

For all their old-fashioned appearance, the Swordfish had one important up-to-date piece of equipment in the shape of an early type of radar set. An hour later, using this radar, they detected a ship beneath them which was presumed to be the *Bismarck*. Breaking from their cloud cover, the pilots were dismayed to find that it was the *Norfolk* which they had located. The cruiser, however, was able to set them on their right course, and once more the aircraft flew off on their search.

Again their radar picked up a target. Again as they broke cloud they found that it was not the *Bismarck* beneath them, but an American coastguard cutter on weather-reporting duties. The *Bismarck* too was indeed in sight some way farther on, but the premature descent from their cloud cover robbed the British aircraft of all possibility of achieving surprise. It was into a storm of anti-aircraft fire that they flew to deliver their torpedoes. In spite of it they pressed their attacks well home, so that for all her turning and twisting the *Bismarck* took one torpedo in her side.

That only one torpedo from this small number of aircraft should have hit, and that it happened to find a well-protected part of the battleship's hull and therefore achieved no more than a severe shaking, was not at all to the discredit of the airmen. Advocates of the air-borne torpedo for attack on surface ships had always visualized coordinated attacks by more than one squadron of aircraft. Now, as at Matapan, shortage of aircraft carriers in the British fleet had forced the use of the slow, vulnerable Swordfish aircraft, a few at a time. That only one torpedo found a billet was far less surprising than that none of the aircraft was shot down.

As the nine Swordfish landed again on the *Victorious'* deck in darkness and rain, bringing with them news of one certain torpedo hit, hopes rose high of the *Bismarck* being brought to action at daylight. They were to be sharply disappointed. Reliance had been concentrated on the *Suffolk*'s radar to hold contact during the night. As she zig-zagged to and fro, contact had inevitably been intermittently lost on her outward legs and regained when she turned and closed the range again. At 0115 the usual restoration of contact failed to materialize at the expected moment. As minute after minute slipped by with no report from the radar operator, the *Suffolk*'s captain realized that the *Bismarck* had given them the slip.

Reporting this unwelcome news to his admiral, he had to make a quick decision as to how best to set about regaining touch. There were two alternatives. Lütjens had either piled on speed and made off to the westward, or else he had circled round through north, crossed astern of the shadowers and gone east or south-east. Captain Ellis of the *Suffolk* unluckily plumped quickly for the former, and at full speed shaped course to the south-west. He was followed by the *Norfolk*, and at daylight the

Victorious's aircraft flew in search to the north-west. All drew a blank. At this vital moment the *Bismarck* had been lost.

The problem now facing the C-in-C and the Admiralty was an extremely complex one. Apparently the enemy had the choice of a number of different courses—assuming that the *Bismarck* had not been seriously damaged.

Lütjens might be making for the west coast of Greenland where he might meet an oiler in some desolate inlet and then head out into the western Atlantic to attack merchant convoys; or he might have planned a rendezvous with an oiler in mid-ocean far to the south. He might have decided to return to Germany through the Denmark Strait or between Iceland and the Faroes; or he could be making for a French Biscay port.

Though the probability that *Bismarck* had suffered at least some damage made the last two alternatives the most likely, her most menacing course was a westerly one. Once there she would be able to wreak havoc amongst the Atlantic shipping, which had of course been her main object in coming to sea. In the absence of any other indications, Admiral Tovey felt bound to guard against this possibility, and for the next few hours his forces continued westerly on their various searches.

Thus they were actually opening the distance between themselves and the *Bismarck*. For Lütjens was in fact steering for Brest. Except for Admiral Somerville's Force 'H' coming up from Gibraltar, and the battleship *Rodney*, where Captain Dalrymple-Hamilton had decided on his own initiative to remain to bar the way to a French port, Lütjens' escape route was clear. But then the German admiral cast away the advantage which his adroit manoeuvre had given him. He transmitted a long wireless message to German naval headquarters.

At once the operators in the chain of radio direction-finding stations in the British Isles tuned in and took bearings of the transmission. By 0830 on the morning of the 25th the Admiralty had enough information to appreciate that the *Bismarck* had gone south-eastward since last seen. Unfortunately, the bearings when received in *King George V* and plotted on an ordinary navigational chart which introduced errors, gave a different picture. To the C-in-C it appeared that the enemy was going north-eastward—back towards the North Sea. The search by his forces was adjusted accordingly, and he himself turned north-eastward in chase.

Force 'H' had not as yet been placed under the C-in-C's orders. Admiral Somerville therefore had the benefit of the Admiralty's own opinion, and was instructed to act on the assumption that the *Bismarck* was making for a French port. But throughout the forenoon the *King George V* was steering north-eastward and no word came from the Admiralty to suggest that this was wrong. Admiral Tovey was therefore highly puzzled when at 1330 he received from Whitehall a message giving the latest estimated position of the Bismarck which clearly indicated a course for the Bay of Biscay.

Unable to reconcile this latest information with the Admiralty's previous silence, it was not until 1430, after fresh calculations had thrown doubts on his previously plotted position of the enemy, that Tovey signalled for the Admiralty's conclusions. Still no reply came, and at 1610 he waited no longer, but turned back on what was in fact the right course to take. An hour later, to his infinite relief, a signal reached him which showed the Admiralty appreciation to be the same as his.

Even so, the long search in the wrong direction had reduced the force under Tovey's command to one ship, the King George V, and her stock of fuel remaining was now so low that economy was forcing a reduction of speed to 25 knots. The Repulse had already reached the end of her fuel endurance, and had been detached that morning to Newfoundland. To the north all but one of the cruisers and the Prince of Wales were similarly running short of oil, and now had to make for Iceland, taking the Victorious with them. The exception was the Norfolk, where at the risk of running down to a standstill, Rear-Admiral Wake-Walker decided to turn to join in the hunt to the south-eastward.

The night of 25/26 May was one of grim anxiety for Admiral Tovey as his flagship pressed on in pursuit, her stern lifting to the steadily growing following seas. A falling glass gave the promise of continuous dirty weather on the morrow, weather to make air reconnaissance difficult. Unless the Bismarck's rapid progress could be checked, there was little hope of bringing her to action before she came under the protection of shore-based aircraft. Only Force 'H' lay between the enemy and safety. Somerville's flagship Renown, a battle-cruiser more than twenty years old and lightly armoured, was no match for the Bismarck. All British hopes now rested on the Ark Royal and her handful of Swordfish aircraft. Only if they could find the enemy and get a torpedo home to a vital spot could failure be turned into success.

But the enemy had first to be accurately located. Searches during the night by Catalina flying-boats of Coastal Command proved fruitless. By dawn the sands of Tovey's luck seemed to be running out fast. Yet in fact the agents which were to lead to the Bismarck's destruction were already in motion. Soon after midnight, a Catalina aircraft had taken off from its British base for yet another long search. Through the night it had droned its way south, and dawn had revealed a blank, angry sea beneath low ragged rain clouds in and out of which the aircraft flew. At 0830 on 26 May, breaking out of one such cloud which had hung like a curtain almost to water-level, the pilot heard the American passenger sitting beside him suddenly say, 'What the devil's that?' Peering in the direction to which the American was pointing, the pilot saw the black bulk of the Bismarck. As the signal was going out, giving vital news which the Admiralty and the C-in-C had been nearly despairing of receiving, anti-aircraft fire from the battleship forced the pilot to sheer away and lose touch, which he could not thereafter regain.

But fortune had at last settled firmly on the British side. Even as the wireless operator in the Catalina was tapping out his message, reconnaissance Swordfish from the wildly heaving deck of the *Ark Royal* some 100 miles ESE were rumbling away to search, all ignorant of the Catalina's sighting. Half an hour after the flying-boat lost touch, one of the Swordfish sighted the *Bismarck*. From then onwards she was never to be let out of sight again.

Somerville sent the *Sheffield* on to gain surface contact, and meanwhile in the *Ark Royal* torpedoes were being got ready to arm the Swordfish as soon as they were back from their search. Not until nearly 1300 could the 15 aircraft be refuelled, armed and sent off, but at last they were on their way. After roughly the correct time of flight a contact appeared on their radar sets. They dived down out of the clouds, saw a large warship ahead and went at once into the attack.

The first flights to attack got their torpedoes away, only to see many of them explode as they hit the water. But before the later flights had reached their attacking position the pilots suddenly realized that their target was not the *Bismarck* but the *Sheffield*, of whose presence in the area they had been unaware. Calamitous as the mistake was, it was retrieved from disaster by the successful manoeuvres of the *Sheffield* to avoid the few torpedoes which ran true. But the high hopes which had been placed on the air attack had collapsed in ruins.

The news was almost enough to cause Tovey to despair. With the *Rodney* now in company, he was still 130 miles behind the *Bismarck* and catching up only very slowly. *King George V*'s fuel was down to 30 per cent remaining, and Tovey was soon to be forced to tell Admiral Somerville that unless the enemy's speed could be reduced by midnight he would have to give up the chase. The only real hope was a second and more successful attack by the aircraft.

At this stage in the action Tovey's forces were joined by the 4th Destroyer Flotilla, commanded by Captain Vian in the *Cossack*. With the other ships of his flotilla, *Maori*, *Zulu*, *Sikh* and the Polish *Piorun*, Vian had been engaged on the more prosaic duty of escorting a troop convoy heading southward in the Atlantic when at midnight on the 25th he had been ordered to steer north to join the C-in-C. Tovey's own destroyers had been forced by shortage of fuel to drop out of the chase. The 4th Flotilla was to take their place.

As he came north, Vian had picked up the signal from the Catalina aircraft. In spite of his orders to join his C-in-C, and give him the anti-submarine screen without which a battleship felt perilously naked, Vian felt sure during the coming night Tovey would wish him to be near the German ship. There he would be able perhaps to use his torpedoes to reduce the *Bismarck*'s speed, and with his shadowing reports to deliver her to the guns of the *King George V* at daybreak. Vian at once swung his ships on to a course to intercept, spreading them out to ensure a meeting.

As Vian ploughed on into the gale at the best speed which his destroyers could manage in the towering seas, the returning Swordfish were hastily refuelled and rearmed for yet another sortie. The first abortive attack had not been valueless; for the premature torpedo explosions had exposed a defect in the magnetic pistols with which they had been armed. The well-tried and reliable contact pistols would be fitted this time. The crestfallen pilots, fully aware of the bitter disappointment their failure had caused, were filled with renewed resolution to succeed at their second attempt; and in this spirit they took off once more, soon after 1700.

This time they were ordered to make contact with the *Sheffield* first. Soon after 1800 they did so and, directed towards the enemy 12 miles farther on, they melted back into the cloud blanket. The low cloud and poor visibility made a coordinated attack impossible. Over a period of some 30 minutes from 1855 onwards the Swordfish swooped down separately. How each aircrew succeeded no one could say, but at some time during the attack two torpedoes found a target, one of them hitting the *Bismarck* right aft, damaging her propellers, jamming her two rudders and putting the steering gear out of action.

It was the crucial blow of the long-drawn contest. For, reduced to 8 knots and unable to steer, the *Bismarck* was caught in the grip of the north-westerly gale and swung helplessly round into it. Soon she was lying wallowing, her bows to the north.

But it was not for some time that this startling change of fortune was known to the British forces. Not until the returning airmen were interrogated on board the *Ark Royal* was a conservative estimate of one torpedo hit arrived at; even this was believed to be amidships, in which case it might not have caused serious damage. The *Sheffield* had indeed reported that the enemy had swerved round on to a northerly course, but at the same moment she had been driven off by a sudden burst of accurate fire from the *Bismarck*'s 15-inch guns, which put the *Sheffield*'s radar out of action. The alteration of course might well have been simply part of the enemy's manoeuvres to avoid torpedoes.

Then reports came in one after the other from the *Ark Royal*'s shadowing aircraft. Each gave the enemy's course as north. At last Admiral Tovey could allow himself to believe that the *Bismarck* had been brought to bay. When at a few minutes after 2100 a first sighting report from the *Zulu* of Vian's flotilla assured him that contact would be held during the night, all doubt was dispersed, and he disposed his forces so as to bring them into action at daylight.

The rest of the story is the always pitiable tale of the agonizing end of a splendid ship, be she friend or foe. In the darkness, wild wind and heavy seas, Vian's destroyers stationed themselves round the doomed giant to watch and report her every movement. As the night wore on, in spite of an accurate fire brought to bear on them whenever they closed, the destroyers crept in to launch torpedoes. *Maori*, *Cossack* and *Sikh* each scored hits, further ensuring the *Bismarck*'s complete disablement. At daybreak Vian's task was completed as the guns of the *King George V* and *Rodney* flashed out. Almost at once the 16-inch shells of the *Rodney* were hitting, and a minute later the 14-inch of the flagship also. For a few minutes the *Bismarck*'s return fire was fairly accurate, but as damage mounted it became ragged, and soon her big guns were knocked out of action one by one.

But the Germans had once again shown that they could build ships almost indestructible by gun-fire. Anxious to make an end, Tovey signalled for any ships still with torpedoes unexpended to close and sink the *Bismarck*. The task fell to a ship which up to then had taken no direct part in the great hunt and indeed, had no real right to be there at all unless it be by reason of the unwritten privilege of any warship's captain to steer 'for the sound of the guns' unless expressly forbidden to do so.

The cruiser *Dorsetshire* had been escorting a homeward-bound convoy from Freetown when she took in the Catalina's sighting report. Leaving the convoy to the care of an armed merchant cruiser, Captain Martin had headed immediately for the position, 600 miles to the northward. Driving her way through the heavy seas at her best speed, she arrived on the scene in time to add the fire of her 8-inch guns to that of the battleships. On receipt of Admiral Tovey's order she was in a position to go straight on to put a torpedo into each side of the *Bismarck*. This was the coup-de-grâce. At 0840 on 27 May 1941, the huge ship slowly capsized, and the fires blazing aboard her were extinguished as she plunged to the bottom. From the cold, rough seas 110 survivors were picked up by *Dorsetshire* and *Maori*. With barely enough fuel remaining to reach port, Tovey steered thankfully for home.

Meanwhile, the comparative lull in U-boat operations which the opening months of 1941 had seen—a lull caused largely by the severe winter weather which made very difficult the location and shadowing of convoys and the subsequent concentration of U-boats necessary for employment of pack-tactics—had been offset by the earlier successful sorties of Raeder's surface warships, and the increasing effectiveness of the F-W 200 (Condor) aircraft of Group 40.

It was still—and it would remain—the U-boat which was the most effective weapon in the armoury of the German Navy. Though January 1941 showed a drop in its destructive achievements to a total of 21 ships of 162,782 tons, of which only three were actually in convoy, and in February the score rose only to 39 ships (nine of them in convoy)—a little more than half that of the previous October—an ominous feature was the absence of any U-boat sinkings during those two months. The number which would be ready for the expected spring offensive was thus increasing rapidly.

Some of the steps being taken to counter it have been told. Few of them would be ready by March. Destroyers of the Western Approaches Command were, indeed, beginning to sprout weird metal structures at their mastheads resembling large wire mattresses. These first radar aerials were not rotatable. From them went out a steady radar beam. The return signal from a target in the vicinity could be expected, if all went well, to appear as a peak in the wavering, dancing band of grass-like green light running across the screen. The range of the target could be estimated to a fair degree of accuracy. Its direction could only be guessed from a consideration of the height of the 'peak', a guess which depended for accuracy on the experience of the operators and the correct adjustment of an instrument only partially understood by them. Such was the state of development of radar for small ships of the Royal Navy in 18 months after the outbreak of war; whereas ships of the German Navy had been equipped with an efficient gunnery ranging set from the beginning. The principal advantage conferred by this radar set was an ability to keep rough station in the convoy screen without being able to see any of the ships of the convoy. Previously the attention of the officer of the watch and of his look-outs on a dark night had been largely absorbed in keeping station on a dimly discernible black shape which was the nearest ship of the convoy, and in avoiding collisions. Now at least for some of the time it would be possible to concentrate on searching for U-boats on the surface.

The chance of detecting a surfaced U-boat with this first radar set was a slim one. It was still necessary to see it and then to try to ram it. This might be successful, in which case the hunt was over at once—at a cost of a crumpled bow and the ship out of action for several weeks. More likely it would force the submarine to dive, when the asdic came into its own and enabled depth-charges to be sent down towards the target. The first essential, however, was a sight of the U-boat. Star shells had proved ineffective. Not only did they give insufficient illumination but the flash of the gun firing them completely blinded the officers and look-outs on the bridge for a space and greatly reduced the efficiency of their night-vision for some time. While awaiting the development of an efficient radar set, it was therefore in the direction of a better illuminant that research was directed. Rockets seemed to give the required answer. A type which burst to leave a brilliant white light hanging in the sky, given the name 'Snowflake', was to be issued in May to merchant ships. At a given signal every ship would fire one of these, thus, it was hoped, turning night into day.

A better radar set for aircraft of Coastal Command was also now beginning to be fitted, enabling them to contribute by night as well as by day to convoy defence.

At the same time, radio-telephony was becoming available for communication between escorts and between escorts and aircraft. It was of limited reliability and, being on a wave in the high-frequency band and so, unlimited in range, had to be used with caution as its signals could be picked up by monitoring stations in enemy territory. Not until after the entry of the United States into the war, when the excellent VHF radio-telephone called TBS (Talk Between Ships) became a standard fitting in all escorts, was there the free, reliable and rapid inter-communication so essential to coordinated teamwork.

Finally, from the ever-increasing number of escorts in the Western Approaches Command organized groups were being formed. Usually these consisted of two destroyers, one of which would be commanded by the group leader, a commander, RN, and perhaps six Flower-class corvettes. On the convoy route to Gibraltar and Freetown, where the danger of air attack was greatest, anti-aircraft sloops of the Stork class were included and one of these was usually the ship of the commander. Allowing for refits and repairs from weather or action damage, it was hoped to have six ships from each group always in sea-going condition.

Though there was little opportunity, as yet, for these groups to exercise and practise together—the tempo of the convoy schedule gave insufficient breathing-space between operations—the very fact that the commanding officers got to know one another, that the group commander knew their respective abilities (or, indeed, lack of them) and was able to convey to them in general terms what he expected of them under varying circumstances, built up the essential team spirit. In the blackness of stormy nights, with the convoy becoming dispersed as each master handled his ship differently in the grip of heavy seas, the group commander could be satisfied that the little corvettes hanging round the flanks would keep in touch and do everything possible to keep the convoy together. When the thud of torpedo explosions and the soaring of distress rockets announced the opening of an attack, each ship of the group would know what was expected of them, brief messages over the radio telephone keeping all members of the team informed as to the situation.

The results of these several improvements were soon to be seen. Convoy battles had been few in January and February 1941, partly owing to the convoys being diverted far to the north, almost to Iceland, so as to by-pass the U-boat patrol lines. This soon became apparent to the U-boat Command. In the first days of March the submarine concentration was moved to the area south of Iceland.

When Günther Prien in *U47* located the outward bound OB293 and was joined by his fellow ace Otto Kretschmer in *U99, U70*, the ex-Turkish boat *UA* and others, events at first followed the familiar pattern, the thud of torpedoes and the soaring rockets telling the story. Without radar, the escorts had been unable to prevent the wolves slinking past them in the darkness. But thereafter it was different. There was a new sense of purpose and an evident increase of skill amongst the escorts. *UA* was forced to dive in a hurry, was detected by an escort's asdic and so damaged by depth-charges that her captain was forced to disengage and set course for his base. Then *U70* was caught by the corvettes *Camellia* and *Arbutus*. Heavy damage to his boat forced Korvetten-Kapitän Matz to surface and surrender with most of his crew before *U70* went down for the last time. *U99* was forced to dive and withdraw with half of her torpedoes unexpended, an unusual experience for Otto Kretschmer. The convoy steamed on after suffering the comparatively light loss of two ships sunk and two damaged.

Prien, as was his duty, continued to shadow the convoy. Overbold, he ventured too close. The destroyer *Wolverine*, commanded by Commander J. M. Rowland, came suddenly on him as a sheltering rain squall cleared. *U47* crash-dived but depth-charges damaged her propeller shafts. Surfacing after dark in the hope of escaping the destroyer, which had clung persistently to an intermittent asdic contact, the submarine's propellers emitted a rattle clearly to be heard on *Wolverine*'s asdic, leading her accurately to the target. Further depth-charge attacks shattered *U47*'s hull. A vivid flash and an explosion from the depths told of her end, confirmed as wooden debris floated to the surface. As Dönitz, in an obituary notice, was later to record: 'The hero of Scapa Flow has made his last patrol. We of the U-boat service proudly mourn and salute him and his men....'

That night the survivors of the wolf-pack heard the Command ordering all U-boats in the area to report their positions. One by one they replied, all except *U70* and *U47*. They feared for the fate of their comrades. They were not left long to contemplate it, however. On the evening of 12 March there came once again the signal reporting a homeward-bound convoy south of Iceland, a rich bait comprising nearly 50 fine, deeply laden freighters and tankers, which must surely draw every U-boat in the area towards it. The boat from which the signal came was *U110*, commanded by Korvetten-Kapitän Lemp, who had opened the U-boat war on 3 September 1937, by sinking the liner *Athenia*. 1939

Among the boats which acted on Lemp's report were *U99* and *U100*, the latter commanded by Joachim Schepke, Kretschmer's friendly rival for first place in the list of tonnage sunk. The escort with the convoy was unusually powerful in the quality of the ships of which it was composed—five destroyers and two corvettes. With five fast ships quartering to and fro, the problem of getting through the screen was made more difficult for the U-boats.

The first to go into the attack on the night of 15 March could deliver only a long-range attack from outside the screen before withdrawing, having sunk one ship, the only success during that night. Nothing further occurred during the day which followed to indicate to the escort commander that a wolf-pack was gathering until, shortly before dusk, a shadowing submarine was sighted on the horizon. This was *U100*. Three destroyers raced away to hunt it, to attack it if contact could be gained on their asdics and to keep it down while in the gathering darkness the convoy turned away to a fresh course, which it was hoped might throw the U-boats off the trail. For two hours the destroyers searched without result, before leaving to rejoin the convoy.

Meanwhile the reduced strength of the escort had enabled Kretschmer to move in undetected and employ his usual deadly technique from amongst the columns of merchant ships. When explosions, rockets and the ghastly glare from burning tankers resulted, the escorts searched in vain, on the outskirts, for a sight of their enemy. For all the speed of the destroyers, now coming up to full strength as the hunters of *U100* rejoined, for all the experience of the captains of the escorts, several of them veterans of the convoy war, it seemed that the U-boat's immunity was unshakeable. Five ships were torpedoed. No news of any U-boat sighting came to the distracted escort commander.

Yet the basic virtue of the convoy system was about to be demonstrated: that it is in the immediate vicinity of the convoy, the lure to which every U-boat must come if it is to achieve its purpose, that the submarines are in greatest peril. Resisting the temptation to cast wildly about, firing starshells, as had been the tactics in the past, the escorts kept doggedly to their stations and prayed for a gleam of fortune.

It came with the arrival of *U100*, pounding after the convoy at high speed, the brash, over-confident Schepke determined to have his share in yet another massacre such as that of SC7. His bow wave betrayed him to look-outs on the bridge of the destroyer *Walker*, ship of the escort commander. A crash-dive saved him from being rammed. But a long hunt by *Walker* and the destroyer *Vanoc* finally forced *U100* to the surface to be rammed and sunk by *Vanoc*. Another 'ace', a hero of the U-boat arm, had followed Prien. The sea-wolves' ill-luck had not yet exhausted itself, however—ill-luck combined in some degree with a lack of caution bred by repeated encounters with an ill-trained and inexperienced enemy.

U99's torpedoes expended, Kretschmer had safely disengaged from the convoy and was circling round on the surface astern of it to set course for his base. Kretschmer himself, well satisfied with his night's work, had gone below, leaving the bridge in the charge of a junior officer. Suddenly there were sighted ahead the black silhouettes of two destroyers, one of them evidently stopped. They were, in fact, the *Vanoc*, stopped and picking up a handful of survivors from *U100*, and *Walker*, circling her to give her protection. With the usual advantage of the first sighting, *U99* could have swung away and escaped unseen. Instead the officer of the watch ordered an immediate crash-dive. As the submarine submerged, the asdic beam from the *Walker* picked her up. An accurately delivered pattern of depth-charges wrecked her machinery and inflicted other vital damage. No alternative was left to Kretschmer but to surface while he could and surrender. He and all but two of his crew were soon prisoners aboard the *Walker*, and *U99* had followed her interminable succession of victims to the bottom.

The loss of these four boats within a week, coming after a long period of complete immunity, and of the three most successful commanders, gave Admiral Dönitz food for serious thought. Had some new anti-submarine device been developed, he wondered. Until the other boats of the pack returned and their commanders could be interrogated, he could not tell. It seemed prudent however to shift his boats from the area south of Iceland where all the losses had occurred. By shifting them in a south-westerly direction, he gave them the same length of passage to their operational area, while at the same time they would be working beyond the westerly limit to which escorts based in Britain could go without refuelling.

The move was at once successful. Encountering SC26 to the south-east of Greenland before its Western Approaches escort had met it, the U-boats sank 10 ships out of the total of 22 in convoy. To counter this move, the Admiralty based escort groups in Iceland which took over the escort of convoys (from the home-based escorts) from south of Iceland to 35°W, and brought homeward-bound convoys from 35°W to a rendezvous with home-based escorts for the last part of their journey.

Thus the battle spread ever westwards. It was soon apparent that the time was coming when continuous escort would have to be provided clear across the Atlantic. How to do this was a knotty problem. None of the destroyers used on escort duty had sufficient endurance to remain with a convoy even as far as Newfoundland. Refuelling at sea was a seaman-like art which had been regrettably neglected by the Royal Navy in the years of peace. Equipment suitable for North Atlantic weather was being devised, but it was not until June 1942 that it came to be used regularly, after which it became an essential feature of every escort problem. Nor were there sufficient escorts to permit groups to be based in Canada or Newfoundland to take care of the western portion of the transatlantic journey.

The Royal Canadian Navy had been only a token force comprising seven destroyers and five minesweepers at the beginning of the war. The destroyers had gone at once to swell the ranks of the Royal Navy during the early months of the war, while great efforts were made to expand the Canadian Navy so that it might take its part as soon as possible in the Atlantic battle. Corvettes built in Canadian shipyards were soon being commissioned. When 50 American over-age destroyers were released to Britain, seven of them were taken over and manned by Canadians. By the end of May 1941, enough Canadian escorts were in commission, based for the most part at St John's, Newfoundland, and comprising the Newfoundland Escort Force, for a weak escort to be provided between the Canadian coast and longitude 35°W, where a Mid-Ocean Meeting Point was allocated. There a group based in Iceland would take over the escort while the Canadian group would transfer to a west-bound convoy for the last part of its journey. At an Eastern Ocean Meeting Point, about 18°W, a home-based group would relieve the Iceland group. The first convoy to sail eastwards so escorted was HX129 on 27 May. In July the reverse process was inaugurated when west-bound transatlantic convoys were given escort throughout their journey. A new nomenclature for them came into being at the same time, the OB convoys becoming ONF (fast) and ONS (slow). The system was highly complicated and liable to disruption owing to delays to convoys on account of bad weather or wide diversions round danger areas. It was the best, however, which could at this time be devised.

A further measure of protection for convoys was at this time provided by the establishment in Iceland of a squadron of twin-engined Hudson aircraft of Coastal Command and a squadron of Sunderland flying-boats. This provided a welcome westward extension of air cover which the U-boats found distinctly irksome. Nevertheless the number of aircraft available to Coastal Command was still far below requirements. In an effort to use those they had more effectively it was decided to take advantage of the increasingly reliable signal intelligence, by concentrating them in the vicinity of convoys which were thought to be threatened, instead of trying to give every convoy some measure of air escort. This might have been more successful had the tendency not persisted to employ much of the available air strength on offensive sweeps and searches, never very effective and less so at this stage of the war than later owing to the lack of any lethal weapon with which to attack any U-boat sighted.

Thus in May, when the U-boats returned to the area south of Iceland, no less than seven U-boats were able to gather round convoy OB318—an impossibility if there had been an air escort to keep them down during daylight hours. The loss of nine ships sunk and two others damaged was barely made up for by the capture of Lemp's U110, which surrendered after being depth-charged to the surface by the destroyers Bulldog and Broadway, and the corvette Aubretia. Though U110 sank while in tow before she could be got to port, documents of such value and importance were recovered from her as to make the event one of the most significant of the Atlantic campaign.

Nevertheless the unusual strength of the escort encountered so far to the west as a consequence of the reinforcement from the Iceland base, and the air patrols in the area, led the U-boat Command to shift its North Atlantic concentration again. The steadily increasing size and efficiency of the escort forces, sea and air, and the growing effectiveness of the U-boat tracking organization in the Admiralty, which enabled the convoys to be diverted round danger areas, were indeed making the North Atlantic a less profitable area of operations. The first 'Happy Time' for the U-boat commanders was over. Though spectacular successes were still achieved from time to time against convoys intercepted far to the west, before an adequate escort had joined them, the submarines spent long, fruitless periods contemplating an empty ocean, while convoys passed clear of them to arrive at their destinations unscathed.

In May 1941, following the attack on OB318, the U-boats waited for a week, some 350 miles to the south-east of Cape Farewell, and sighted nothing. Moved another 240 miles south-west, towards Newfoundland, it was a further four days before convoy HX126 was intercepted, nine ships being lost from it. There followed several weeks of inactivity in the area off Newfoundland. It was not until 20 June that a wide sweep north-eastwards to the area between Iceland and Greenland enabled *U203* to intercept HX133. The widely spread U-boat patrol line of 10 boats was called in and they were able to sink six ships and damage two more before escort reinforcements from Iceland arrived, to sink two of them and drive off the remainder. More frequent convoy interceptions would have been possible had the U-boats been free to press farther west and south to the area south of Halifax. But this would have taken them into the 'Security Zone' declared by the United States Government. Hitler's anxiety to keep the Americans neutral barred this area to the U-boats.

On the whole, therefore, the westward shift had not given the success which had been expected. The U-boat Command sought for a reason. Though its strength had been increasing since February 1941, slowly at first and sharply from May onwards, sinkings had not increased correspondingly. In July, indeed, they actually decreased considerably, though by then Dönitz had at his disposal three or four times as many boats as in January 1941.

Dönitz was loath to admit that this was owing to his opponents' increased efficiency as compared to the 'Happy Time'. He sought for a purely technical explanation. But when in search of independents or poorly escorted convoys he dispatched boats to the Freetown area, success was immediate though only temporary. Eight submarines intercepted and sank 81 unescorted ships before a tightening up of convoy measures achieved the usual sharp reduction of sinkings. Furthermore, though sinkings per boat were greater there than in the north, the long passage out and home made it less profitable.

Until July 1941 this was to some extent offset by the deployment of supply ships, at first with the connivance of the Spanish authorities at Las Palmas in the Canary Islands. When strong protests by the British Government induced the Spaniards to withdraw these facilities, supply ships were stationed in mid-Atlantic until the interception and destruction of six of them in May and June 1941 brought this method of supplying submarines to an end.

Foiled in his efforts to find a soft spot in the convoy defences, Dönitz cast around for a solution to the problem. The limit of the U-boats probing westward had been set by German anxiety not to become involved with the US Navy patrolling the US Security Zone which, since March 1941 had been extended eastwards to 26°W longitude. Although Roosevelt's promise of 'all aid short of war' to Britain, the passage of the Lend-Lease Bill, relief of the British garrison in Iceland in July 1941, followed by the announcement that US naval forces would escort shipping of any nationality to and from Iceland, all made it clear that the United States were moving steadily towards active participation on the Allied side, orders restricting the U-boats in the western half of the Atlantic remained in force.

Thus the effort to redress the balance by going westwards and southwards proving unsuccessful, it seemed that only by fighting their way through the convoy defence—a thing which had usually been avoided up to now when possible—could the attack on Allied merchant shipping be carried on by submarines. In July, therefore, all boats were concentrated once again in the Western and South-Western Approaches to the British Isles where it was expected that the combination of the Focke-Wulf Condor aircraft and U-boats might enable the successes of 1940 to be renewed.

The eastward shift of the wolf-packs did not prove a success. The advantages gained by the U-boats were counterbalanced by the greater escort strength, surface and air, which could be given to the convoys. Furthermore the position had been reversed, in that the U-boats were manned by the young and inexperienced crews who had taken the place of the early professionals who had all been killed, taken prisoner or withdrawn from operational duty; whereas it was the escort crews who were now becoming the skilled veterans.

Thus something of a stalemate developed with few successful attacks being made on the convoys, but few U-boats being sunk. While this lull held, the forces on both sides were growing in strength. By the end of August the total number of U-boats in commission was 198, of which 80 were operational, figures which were steadily rising. On the Allied side, besides a steady growth in the number of escorts, there had occurred a number of developments which were to have a profound effect on the course of the campaign. The losses from bombing by the F-W 200 aircraft, against which the gunfire of the escorts was ineffective, had led to the fitting out of fighter catapult ships. Four of these naval auxiliaries—merchant ships fitted with a catapult from which a fighter aircraft could be launched—were commissioned by the Royal Navy in April 1941. After completing his mission the pilot had to return to a shore base if there was one within range; otherwise he had either to 'ditch' his aircraft alongside a ship or bale out and hope to be picked up. Though it was not until August 1941 that concrete success came their way, when the Hurricane from one of them, the *Maplin,* shot down a F-W 200—some 400 miles out in the Atlantic, the idea had been followed up by the fitting of catapults to a number of freighters which came to be known as Catapult Aircraft Merchantmen or CAM-ships, which were to render valuable service until the advent of escort aircraft-carriers made them redundant.

The first of these auxiliary carriers also joined the escort forces at this time. This was *Audacity,* captured from the Germans as the liner *Hanover,* and fitted with a flight-deck. Even before her brief career—in which we shall meet her shortly—had demonstrated the inestimable value of such ships, five more had been sent to British yards for conversion and six ordered from the United States under Lend-Lease arrangements. Unfortunately for the course of the Battle of the Atlantic, it was quickly appreciated that they could fill a vital gap in the air cover for other operations as well; so that, except for *Audacity*'s inclusion in the escort of Gibraltar convoys, where she was primarily used to provide fighter defence, it was not until the winter of 1942 that a carrier sailed with a convoy—on the Arctic run to Russia. The transatlantic convoys were to be left without this decisive addition to their escorts until the spring of 1943.

Meanwhile the shore-based aircraft of Coastal Command had at last been equipped with the depth-charge; the new centimetric radar for surface craft and aircraft was being perfected, with which a surfaced U-boat could be detected in the dark; in combination, then, with the Leigh-Light—an airborne spotlight—also being developed, the hitherto invisible, slinking enemy could be surprised and harried. The pendulum was swinging in favour of the convoy defence. Before its ascendancy was established, however, there were to be some fierce battles in which losses were suffered on both sides.

Unsuccessful in the Western Approaches during July and August 1941, the U-boats were sent once again westward towards Greenland, seeking as always for a weak spot where they need not be for ever searching the skies for enemy aircraft and where they need not face the increasingly well-organized escort groups. In September they found it. The end-to-end escort of trans-Atlantic convoys which had been adopted had been the principal cause for the U-boats eastward move which had proved so unprofitable. It had not, however, been the strength of the escort in the western part of the convoy route that had forced this move but the failure to locate the convoys themselves.

Dönitz now reconsidered the problem and concluded that his patrol lines had been wrongly stationed. To take the best advantage of the air and surface escorts stationed in Ireland, the convoys had been taking an extreme northerly route. A strong force of 17 boats was now spread between the coast of Iceland and Greenland. On 9 September they were rewarded by a signal from one of their number that a very large convoy weakly escorted was in sight. The widely spread patrol line was called in and one by one arrived on the scene, to find themselves confronted with the sort of rich prize they had been vainly seeking since the end of the 'Happy Time'.

Convoy SC42 had sailed from Sydney, Cape Breton, on 30 August 1941. Its 65 ships had been formed up in 12 columns under the local escort of three corvettes of the Royal Canadian Navy. The broad pendant of Commodore W. B. Mackenzie, RNR, flew from the masthead of the freighter *Everleigh*. A thirteenth column of five more ships from St John's, Newfoundland, joined off that port on 2 September. At the same time the local escort was replaced for the ocean passage by the 24th Escort Group, comprising the destroyer HMCS *Skeena* and three Canadian corvettes, *Alberni*, *Kenogami* and *Orillia*. The senior officer of the escort was Commander J. C. Hibbard, RCN, of the *Skeena*.

The Royal Canadian Navy had grown from the squadron of 12 little ships with which it had entered the war so that numerically it was now strong enough to take over the escort of convoys in the comparatively safe waters of the Western Atlantic. The Royal Navy, over-extended in every ocean, had gladly delegated these duties to its Canadian comrades. National pride had demanded that Canadian ships should be formed into wholly Canadian groups; but herein lay a weakness. Little warships of the corvette class could be built and equipped more rapidly than crews to man them could be properly trained. Though the lesson that ill-trained escorts were no match for U-boats had been learnt from harsh experience, the relative quiet on the western portion of the convoy route during the summer had made it seem a fair risk to employ newly commissioned ships and weak, newly formed groups in that area.

In the case of SC42 the group commander was an experienced and skilful destroyer captain. His ship *Skeena* was a well-equipped and fairly modern destroyer like the 'A-I' class of the Royal Navy. The three corvettes, on the other hand, had been recently commissioned, their crews hastily trained, and sent to sea lacking experience. As in the early days of the campaign on the other side of the Atlantic, though Commander Hibbard's flotilla had been given the title, 24th Escort Group, in truth it still only comprised four ships fortuitously thrown together. Reporting on the events about to be described, Hibbard was to comment on this fact and that 'a far greater volume of signals was necessary than would ordinarily be the case where ships of an escort group know and understand the senior officer of the escort's intentions'. It is against such a background that the battle around SC42 must be viewed.

For the first four days after the convoy rounded Cape Race and headed north-eastward towards distant Iceland, easterly gales and heavy seas buffeted the deeply laden freighters. The convoy's nominal speed of $7\frac{1}{2}$ knots could not be kept up. By 5 September it was hove-to, the ships barely keeping steerage way on them. So they remained for two days.

When the wind at last began to ease off a little on the 7th and the slow progress resumed, Hibbard was relieved to find that, but for a detached group of five ships being shepherded by the *Kenogami*, 10 miles to the northward, his convoy was still complete. On the other hand, when a break in the overcast sky enabled him to fix his position by sun-sights, he calculated that only 3 knots had been made good during the last four days. A signal, reporting that he would be 72 hours late at the Western Ocean Meeting Point, was sent off for the benefit of the escorts from Iceland which would be coming to meet him.

Meanwhile, in the U-boat tracking room in the Admiralty, intercepted signals from U-boats had betrayed the fact that a group of them was gathering, barring the direct route to the predetermined meeting point. A diversion of course, at sunset on 8 September, was ordered. The new route led due north up the coast of Greenland. It was hoped that this would take the convoy in a wide sweep round the submarine patrol line. It was of no avail. Early the following morning, 9 September, the *Jedmore*, straggling somewhat astern, raised the first alarm as a periscope was sighted and the tracks of two torpedoes passed close ahead of her. The escorts converged on the area and for 45 minutes probed unsuccessfully with their asdics. Then the *Orillia* was sent to search for five miles astern before rejoining. Kept down for a time by these manoeuvres, the U-boat dropped far behind. She could not get to an attacking position again without making a long circuitous advance beyond the horizon. But before attacking, the signal which reported the convoy's position had been made to U-boat Command and had been picked up by the 16 other boats on the patrol line. At once they turned to intercept, their tedious scanning of an empty and stormy ocean at an end.

By midnight several had gathered round. For the next 30 hours confusion and dismay reigned in the convoy. The first ship to be torpedoed was the *Muneric*, loaded with iron ore, fourth ship of the port column. With such a cargo, she went quickly to the bottom. Hibbard took *Skeena* racing round in a wide circle from her station ahead of the convoy to search down the port side of the convoy. By the light of her starshells, the *Kenogami* sighted the submarine responsible, reported it to the escort commander and turned in chase. The U-boat dived but the corvette could get no contact by asdic. Eager to bring his more experienced asdic team into action, but ignorant of *Kenogami*'s position, Hibbard, over the radio-telephone, ordered her to fire starshells to guide him or to show a light. He was unaware that the corvette carried no starshell. No guiding light had been seen when rockets soaring up from the convoy called for Hibbard's attention elsewhere. Instructing *Kenogami* to continue to search for ten minutes, and, if no contact was gained, to rejoin the convoy, picking up survivors on the way, he hurried back.

From the Commodore, Hibbard learnt that a second U-boat had been sighted. With his meagre force of slow escorts, his own, faster ship restricted in speed by a shortage of fuel consequent on the three days' delay caused by the storm, the problem of giving the convoy adequate cover was insoluble. Its front stretched across more than six sea-miles. It was over three miles in length. Hibbard could only pray for luck to bring him an enemy in his path, when perhaps he could avenge those he could not protect.

Shortly before 0300 from rockets, lights and machine-gun fire he learnt that a U-boat had been sighted amongst the columns of ships. Swinging his destroyer round he took her down between the seventh and eighth columns. As he did so, the commodore ordered an emergency turn of all ships together 45° to port. Nightmare manoeuvres followed as the *Skeena* weaved her way through the great concourse of darkened ships, constant calls for full speed ahead or astern being necessary to avoid collision. In the midst of it all, a ship blew up as a torpedo struck home. Four minutes later two other explosions occurred, one in a ship right alongside the *Skeena*. Tracer bullets streaming out from several ships guided Hibbard to the U-boat. As *Skeena* passed closely across the bow of a ship in the seventh column, he saw her. A tight turn round the stern of another ship, his turbines screaming and his bridge structure rattling as every ounce of power wrenched the destroyer round, brought him in position to ram.

It was too late. The U-boat had dived. In the confused water of the criss-crossing ships' wakes, and the rough seas, his asdic could distinguish no contact. Not until the merchant ships had drawn a safe distance away could he drop depth-charges, hopefully, at random and in vain.

As the convoy steamed slowly onward, Hibbard could do nothing but hasten after it himself, and detail the *Orillia* to sweep astern and, if no contact resulted, to pick up survivors, while he exhorted the other two corvettes, of whose position he was ignorant, to rejoin with all speed. That at least three U-boats were engaged was evident. It was perhaps as well that it was not realized that no less than 17 were closing in on the almost defenceless convoy. The temptation to order the ships to scatter might have been too strong. A worse disaster might then have occurred as ships were picked off one by one. It was to be bad enough.

Soon after 0400 *Skeena* was back in her screening position. A brief lull followed; but at 0510 the now familiar thud of an exploding torpedo signalled a renewal of the attack. While *Skeena* vainly fired her questing starshell, another ship was hit half an hour later. A ship on the starboard side signalling that a submarine was in sight, Commodore Mackenzie ordered once again an emergency turn away to port. It had little effect as torpedo after torpedo got home, distress rockets sending their despairing messages into the sky. As the alarm died away, *Kenogami* and *Alberni* dropped back to rescue the crews of the torpedoed ships. In so desperate a situation it is hard to say what else they could have done; but the convoy was bereft of all protection except *Skeena*. The *Orillia*, far astern of the convoy since the previous attack, had made a peculiar signal: 'Am complying with your orders. Request to remain until daylight. Have good reasons.' Distracted by the dire events going on around him, the escort commander replied, 'Approved. Report situation at daylight and then rejoin.' Thus a quarter of his force was dispensed with. And in fact Hibbard was to hear no more of *Orillia* until five days later when he learnt that she had arrived at Reykjavik, escorting a damaged tanker which she had towed part of the way.

Meanwhile 10 September had dawned to reveal the convoy still punching into heavy seas at a mere 5 knots. Only *Skeena* was in her station ahead. *Alberni* and *Kenogami* were coming up from astern, their ness-decks and cabins crowded with survivors, when the leading ship of the second column from port, the CAM-ship *Empire Hudson*, was torpedoed at 0800. Sweeping down the port side of the convoy, *Skeena* gained asdic contact with, apparently, a submarine, and attacked. The satisfaction of being able to hit back at his persistent and seemingly ubiquitous enemy was short lived as Hibbard received a signal from the Commodore that a periscope had been sighted passing ahead of his ship. *Skeena* hurried back to the convoy, to try to ward off yet another attack evidently impending.

It failed to materialize. For the next four hours no attack developed, though at 1300 a burst of machine-gun firing at a periscope by ships off the port column sent the convoy side-stepping in an emergency turn to starboard. *Skeena* raced to the spot and scattered depth-charges but could get no contact with the submarine. Barely had she got back to her station when at 1425 the leading ship of the ninth column was torpedoed. Calling his two corvettes to join him, Hibbard took the three ships spread out in a line to search round the probable position from which the submarine had fired. As they were doing so, ships in the rear of the convoy opened fire at some object in the water astern of them. The escorts swung back. Ahead of them was a periscope which remained impudently in view, surveying the scene for nearly a minute. A quick attack by eye made by the *Skeena* was followed by others on an asdic contact. A huge air bubble bursting on the surface after her last attack, followed by loss of all contact, convinced Hibbard that at last revenge had been taken on one of the enemy. The corvettes were sent back to the convoy while *Skeena* remained for an hour probing with her asdic. No further sign of the U-boat was picked up, though asdic conditions were seemingly excellent. By 1730 *Skeena* was back in her station, her crew soberly confident that a U-boat had been sent to the bottom. Post-war records, however, fail to confirm this. As was to be shown on many occasions, strange water disturbances and even explosions, believed to indicate the destruction of a submarine, proved not to do so. The Admiralty was very right to demand more concrete evidence before recording a 'kill'.

For the remainder of that day, 10 September, the convoy enjoyed a respite. At dusk Commodore Mackenzie wheeled the great rectangle of

ships round to a north-easterly course. Speed had picked up a little as th
seas gradually diminished, though it was still a mere 6 knots. Th
following day a strong escort force from Iceland was due to join. Anothe
small reinforcement of two Canadian corvettes which had been on
training cruise was also heading for the convoy and would arrive durin
the night.

Before this could happen, a few minutes after midnight, the now all to
familiar routine of explosions, rockets and starshells began again. As th
convoy swung away in an emergency turn a submarine on the surface wa
reported by the leader of Column Eight. Indeed by now the U-boats
having taken the measure of the weak opposition to be expected, wer
behaving with increasing boldness. During the next two hours, three wer
sighted in the convoy as they coolly picked their targets. The exhauste
escorts, which had been continuously in action for 24 hours, cast bac
and forth searching for their tormentors without result until, at 0215
from the *Kenogami* was seen a low, black silhouette barely 500 yards awa
on her port bow. It was so close that her single 4-inch gun could not b
depressed sufficiently to hit. Then the U-boat dived. The asdic picked u
the target and a pattern of 10 depth-charges was sent down towards i
But this submarine was able to escape. Three more ships had bee
torpedoed. The order to rejoin the convoy came through before furthe
depth-charge attacks could be made. The sea was littered with boats an
rafts from which survivors of two sunken ships were picked up on th
way.

While all this was taking place, however, yet another U-boat, waitin
ahead of the convoy as it approached, was paying the penalty of over
confidence. Unnoticed by the exultant look-outs, from another directio
two bluff, chunky little craft were drawing near at their best speed of 1
knots.

The Canadian corvettes *Chambly* and *Moosejaw* had not long been i
commission, but they were nearing the end of an intensive period c
training and 'work-up'. They were commanded by J. D. Prentice, a retire
commander of the Royal Navy, lent, with a team of Royal Navy asdi
operators, to the Royal Canadian Navy. On 5 September, they ha
been lying in the harbour of St John's, scheduled to sail on a trainin
cruise on the 9th. A study of the U-boat dispositions promulgated by th
Admiralty convinced Prentice that SC42 was likely to be intercepted. Hi
training might therefore be given a more practical slant if he took his tw
ships in support. Permission was sought and obtained. At noon *Chambl*
and *Moosejaw* passed between the iron-bound cliffs flanking the harbou
entrance and steered to the north-east.

Having got well ahead of SC42, Prentice spent the 7, 8 and 9 Septembe
putting his corvettes through simple exercises and manoeuvres, shapin
his predominantly landsmen crews into seamen. Then, at 0215 in th
morning of the 10th, the message he had been expecting was handed t

him. 'A ship of SC42 has been attacked. Proceed with dispatch to join and escort convoy to Iceland if fuel permits. Steer to reach position ahead of convoy.' Thus it was that at midnight that day, as he steered westwards at his best speed, rockets from SC42 to the southward told him that his little force was to have its first experience of real action. Turning southwards he saw more rockets at 13 minutes after midnight, and again 22 minutes later.

At that moment, on the bridge of the *Chambly*, Prentice heard the asdic operator, Leading Seaman A. H. Johnson of his training team, shout 'Contact-Red Nine-O'. The clear-cut echo he could hear coming from the loud-speaker and Johnson's confident assessment of it as a submarine, only 700 yards away, brooked of no delay in taking action. A spatter of orders went to the helmsman and to the depth-charge team on the quarter deck, as *Chambly* was brought round on to an attack course, with weapons at the ready. Directed by a young Canadian, Sub-Lieutenant Chenoweth, RCNVR, who had just joined the ship and was on his first trip to sea, a pattern of five depth-charges was fired. As the explosions set the *Chambly* shuddering and leaping in the water, Prentice turned her back to repeat the attack. *Moosejaw* was already running in to do so when, with a swirl and a cascade of white water frothing off its casings, *U501* rose to the surface close ahead of her. *Moosejaw*'s searchlight stabbed out and settled on the submarine's conning-tower. A single round from the corvette's 4-inch gun slammed a shell into it. Before more could be fired the *Moosejaw* had collided with the U-boat which was still going slowly ahead. Before the two vessels sheered apart again, a single figure made a wild leap from the U-boat's bridge on to the corvette's deck. It proved to be *U501*'s captain.

The remainder of the German crew had by now mustered on the deck of the submarine. Most of them leapt into the water and were picked up by *Moosejaw*. Meanwhile Prentice had taken *Chambly* alongside the U-boat with the intention of boarding and, if possible, capturing her. He found that the diesel engines were still running and sending her through the water at some three to four knots. Hailing the men on deck he ordered them to stop the engines or they would not be rescued. This had the desired effect and *Chambly*'s boarding party were soon on their way in the corvette's boat. Awkwardly they scrambled aboard. Before they could make their way down through the conning-tower hatch, however, it became clear that the submarine was sinking. As British and Germans abandoned her together, the first lieutenant of *Chambly*, in charge of the boarding party was sucked down, narrowly escaping drowning. His experience gave the clue to the disappearance of one man from *Chambly*, Stoker Brown, who must have lost his life in the same way.

The destruction of *U501* was a remarkable outcome of a 'training cruise'. It was a piece of beginner's luck, perhaps. It was certainly cause for envy by the disheartened escort of SC42, frustrated in their efforts to hit back at the enemy by the necessity to rescue the crews of torpedoed ships and the inability to devote much time to offensive action before hurrying back to the defenceless convoy. Careful and conscientious training must also be credited to Prentice's success. *Kenogami*, for example, had three times had U-boats in sight at close range, but her inexperienced team had been unable to take advantage of it. In contrast stood out the instant, sure classification of contact by *Chambly*'s asdic team, the prompt action by Prentice himself and the accurate attack which brought *U501* to the surface in surrender.

Meanwhile SC42's agony was by no means halted by this single success. Three ships had been torpedoed at about the time *Chambly* and *Moosejaw* joined the escort at 0330. An hour and a half later two more went to the bottom. No sight of the enemy was obtained. With only three escorts to cover the straggling convoy—*Kenogami* and *Alberni* were far astern picking up survivors—this was not to be wondered at. At daylight Hibbard counted his charges and found that no less than 20 were missing. Of these 15 had been sunk. It was with heartfelt relief, therefore, that during the forenoon of the 11th reinforcements joined—the corvettes *Wetaskiwin* (Canadian), *Mimosa* (Free French) and *Gladiolus* (British) and the trawler HMS *Buttermere*. Soon after midday a more substantial reinforcement arrived, the 2nd Escort Group from Iceland, comprising the destroyers *Douglas*, *Veteran*, *Saladin*, *Skate* and *Leamington*, the senior officer being Commander W. E. Banks in the *Douglas*.

Hibbard must have envied Banks his abundance of fast escorts as he thankfully and wearily vacated his position as senior officer. Banks was able to throw out a hunting force, comprising *Veteran* and *Leamington*, to search for and keep down any submarines hovering beyond the horizon. Furthermore SC42 was now within range of aircraft operating from Iceland. It was from one of them that the first report of the enemy came. A U-boat was sighted on the surface 15 miles ahead of the convoy. *Veteran* and *Leamington* were well placed and were sent scurrying away to hunt. Half an hour later *Veteran* reported a submarine in sight on the surface. Banks sent *Saladin* and *Skate* away in support. They were not needed, however. In *Veteran* and *Leamington*—the latter one of the ex-American 'four-stackers'—well-drilled anti-submarine teams went into action. At dusk the four ships rejoined bringing the welcome news that the U-boat had been certainly destroyed. It was in fact *U207*.

Through that night, for the first time since the attack had started on 9 September, the convoy steamed on unmolested. The watch below, in escorts and merchantmen alike, were able to sleep undisturbed by the clang of the alarm bell. As a quiet day followed and another undisturbed night, taut nerves relaxed, and the strain went out of eyes which for three nights and days had ceaselessly scanned the surface of the sea around them for the low, sinister shape of the lurking enemy, the sly prying eye of a periscope or the dreaded streak of an approaching torpedo.

German records say that but for foggy weather the attack would have been renewed. It is true that five of the U-boat pack continued to trail SC42 and that during the night of 16 September, the last night before the convoy reached safe waters in the Minches, one more ship straggling astern was torpedoed to bring the total score of losses to 16. But it is unlikely that any determined attack would have been made in the face of the strong sea and air escort provided. This included, for a few hours on 14 September, three United States Navy destroyers, an early instance of America's participation in the Battle of the Atlantic even before she was officially at war.

The long-drawn battle round SC42 had exposed a serious weakness in the Atlantic life-line. Though end-to-end escort of convoys had been instituted, the protection given in the western part of their voyages was inadequate in size and quality. In spite of the steady increase in the number of escorts available, this could not yet be overcome. It lacked, too, the essential air cover, as the existing gap was unbridgeable by the type of aircraft in use. Fortunately for the Allied cause, many of the U-boats which had intercepted SC42 had expended most of their torpedoes and were short of fuel by the end of the battle. They returned to base leaving only five to reform the patrol line off Greenland. These intercepted SC44. They sank four merchant ships and the Canadian corvette *Levis* before they, too, had to turn for home.

It seemed to the U-boat Command that at last a chance to renew earlier success was at hand, by striking before the western gap in the convoy defences could be bridged. It was not to be. For some time Hitler had been pressing his naval staff to send U-boats to the Mediterranean, which he considered was 'the decisive area for the future conduct of the war'. Admiral Dönitz, never wavering in his belief that by attack on her merchant shipping in the Atlantic his U-boats could bring Britain to her knees, had resisted this policy through the summer months. Now he was to be overborne. At the moment when a fresh chance to strike a crippling blow had come, the means with which to deal it was snatched from his hand.

D

5   *Attack on the Convoys Held*

The interdependence of the several theatres of war and the crucial effect of sea power in each was clearly demonstrated by the naval stategy forced on the Germans at this time. As will be told in a later chapter, the position of the German and Italian armies deployed in North Africa was being undermined by the severe losses being inflicted on their supply convoys running across the Mediterranean.

Since the Italian Navy and Air Force were unable to wrest control of the central basin of the Mediterranean from the British, it became necessary for the Germans to take a hand. When orders reached the U-boat Command for, first, six and, later, four more submarines to be sent through the Straits of Gibraltar, Admiral Dönitz accepted this reduction of his striking power in the Atlantic, concurring in the strategical necessity for it. The sinking of the *Ark Royal* and *Barham* in November 1941 and of the cruiser *Galatea* a month later seemed certainly a worthwhile dividend. But when, on 21 November 1941, Dönitz received orders for the transfer of the entire force of operational U-boats to the Mediterranean and the approaches to the Straits of Gibraltar, he clearly saw the strategic mistake being made. He protested, but in vain. In his official history, *The War at Sea*, Captain Roskill stated that 'Not only did the German U-boats suffer considerable losses in their new theatre—no less than seven were sunk in November and December—but their transfer from the Atlantic brought us a welcome easement in that vital theatre.'

It was, in truth, a 'welcome easement'. No means existed of repairing the weak link in the convoy defences in the Western Atlantic, betrayed by the disastrous passage of SC42 in September. For convoys on other routes had been under heavy attack also. In the same month a small convoy of 11 ships homeward-bound from Freetown—SL87—was located by a U-boat on the 23rd, far out in the Atlantic. Three other U-boats were called in to the attack. Owing to the length of this route, only escorts with considerable endurance could be employed on it. Few were available. Those there were sacrificed in speed what they gained in endurance. Thus,

SL87's escort comprised the old sloop *Bideford*, the *Gorleston*, one of the ex-American coastguard cutters acquired under lend-lease, the corvette *Gardenia* and a diminutive Free French vessel, *Commandant Duboc*. Once again, a mixed force, unused to working together. The result was a foregone conclusion. Attacked on three successive nights, only four ships of the convoy remained when daylight on the fourth day came.

The Gibraltar convoys were potentially the most vulnerable of all, passing as they did within easy reach of the German U-boat bases on the Biscay coast, and of the airfield near Bordeaux, whence the F-W Condors operated. Being made up for the most part of small freighters engaged in the Spanish trade, and escorted throughout their voyage, they had not up to now attracted the same attention as the more important and, at first, less well-protected trans-Atlantic traffic. But with the increase in the number of operational U-boats available, the improvement in efficiency of the Focke-Wulf aircraft cooperating with them and the stiff opposition encountered elsewhere, they were now to come under more frequent attack. Here, too, the route was a long one, and, though destroyers of the local flotilla at Gibraltar could be sent out to augment the escort for the last few days of the passage, it was not possible for the old destroyers of the Western Approaches Command to accompany them for the whole journey. Thus, as on the Freetown route, sloops and corvettes made up the escort.

Not only was their speed inadequate in opposition to the U-boats but they were virtually helpless in face of the bombing attacks of the F-W Condors. Against the latter, as has been mentioned in the previous chapter, fighter-catapult-ships and CAM-ships had been fitted out. They had a moderate success. But it was the auxiliary aircraft-carrier which was to provide convoys with the continuous air cover which was to be one of the decisive developments in the Battle of the Atlantic. The first of these was *Audacity*, commanded by Commander D. W. Mackendrick. Intended primarily to provide fighter cover, she was equipped only with Grumman 'Martlet' fighters. Successful as these were in keeping the Focke-Wulfs at a distance, they also quickly demonstrated their value in detecting shadowing submarines or those running on the surface, in order to attain attacking positions ahead of the convoy. They could then force them to submerge, meanwhile calling out escort craft to hunt them. On the other hand, until anti-submarine aircraft, capable of carrying their own under-water weapons, were embarked, the slow escorts allotted to the Gibraltar convoys could not be got to the scene with any good chance of gaining contact with the enemy.

The *Audacity* quickly proved her worth when she sailed on her first escort duty in September 1941 with Convoy OG74 for Gibraltar, weakly escorted by a sloop and five 'Flower'-class corvettes. U-boats attempting to shadow and report the convoy were pounced on by the carrier's Martlets and forced to dive and subsequently held submerged and harmless by the corvettes. Not all could be thus warded off; another U-boat succeeded in sinking three freighters. Nor could the F-W Condors be entirely kept at bay. One caught a straggler and left her bombed and sinking; but the airmen were not left long to savour their triumph before a Martlet swooped to shoot these planes down into the sea.

But for the *Audacity*'s fighters, there is no doubt that a concentration of U-boats on this otherwise meagerly protected convoy would have been achieved with a repetition of some of the earlier convoy disasters. As it was 22 out of the 27 ships arrived safely. In contrast the homeward-bound HG73 with an escort of a sloop and eight corvettes—but no planes—lost nine ships to U-boats in three successive night attacks.

Simultaneously with the arrival of the *Audacity* there now came on the scene a man who was to show once for all time that defeat of the U-boat night attacks depended, above all, on the formation of escorts in regular flotillas or groups under experienced group leaders and their intensive training together in counter-measures scientifically devised to ensure that any attacking U-boat would be swept over by the asdic beam of an escort. Commander F. J. Walker, RN, was an officer who had specialized in anti-submarine warfare in the years before the war. Something of a 'stormy petrel', his differences of opinion with those in authority over him had damaged his career. Passed over for promotion to captain, his talents had been wasted in uninspiring shore appointments during the first two years of the war. Now, however, he was given command of the sloop *Stork* and of the 36th Escort Group. The *Stork*, a product of the building programmes of the immediate pre-war years, was a considerable improvement on the older sloops on whom much of the burden of convoy escort had up to now rested. She could make $19\frac{1}{2}$ knots and, instead of the miserable armament of three or four 4-inch guns, she had six dual-purpose 4-inch guns in twin-mountings. The anti-aircraft capabilities of this class of ship had, up to this time, led to their employment in the North Sea. But now they were to join the Western Approaches Escort Force, where for the rest of the war they were to prove excellent anti-submarine ships.

Besides the *Stork*, the 36th Escort Group included the old sloop *Deptford* and seven Flower-class corvettes. Walker at once brought his long experience of anti-submarine warfare to improve the efficiency of his group, not only as individual ships but as a well-knit team. At the group's base at Liverpool the depth-charge handling crews were put through incessant drills at the depth-charge 'loader' which had been set up on shore, until they learnt to handle the awkward, swaying 500-lb cylinders on a rolling deck, so that a second 'pattern' of charges could be got ready within ten seconds of the first being fired. In the ingenious Attack Teacher, where synthetic submarine hunts and depth-charge attacks could be carried out, the control teams—captains, anti-submarine control officers and asdic operators—spent long hours perfecting their techniques.

None of this was of any use, however, unless the submarine could be got within the very limited range of the asdic. Study of past convoy battles made it clear to Walker that only by pre-arranged, concerted moves of the escorts could this be ensured. Otherwise it was only by pure luck that contact was made. He devised, therefore, an operation of this sort to which he gave the name 'Buttercup'. It was the forerunner of a number of such, varying only in detail, intended to deal with the various situations which might arise. At the simple order 'Buttercup Starboard' (or Port, Astern, etc, according to the position from which the U-boat was believed to have fired its torpedoes), the escorts would come round to a pre-arranged heading, which would ensure the whole of the probable area being swept by asdic. It took repeated practice to achieve the desired effect. Walker took every opportunity to put his team through their paces. His enthusiasm and the fighting spirit which animated him soon spread throughout his group. His captains became similarly inspired and were soon so in tune with their leader's notions that they were able to carry out his wishes unbidden.

This was the team which, early in December 1941, lay at Gibraltar, while in the Roads gathered the 32 ships which were to form Convoy HG76. By this time the re-development of Admiral Dönitz's U-boat fleet had been accomplished. The majority of his operational boats, withdrawn from the trans-Atlantic routes, were now in the Mediterranean or athwart the approaches to the Straits of Gibraltar. Of the latter, seven were on their station. This was known to the Admiralty. A heavy attack on HG76 was certain. The convoy's sailing was therefore delayed until reinforcements for the 36th Escort Group could be gathered. By 14 December, three destroyers, two sloops and three Flower-class corvettes became available to augment the normal escort during the first two days of the convoy's passage when it would be breaking through the U-boat patrol line. During this time the convoy would also have the benefit of air escort by naval Swordfish aircraft based ashore at Gibraltar. Thus for every two ships in the convoy there was an escort. In addition there was the auxiliary aircraft-carrier *Audacity*.

Though some of the reinforcements had left to return to Gibraltar before the ensuing convoy battle really began, it was certainly a most powerful escort, particularly when looked at in comparison with the meagre force of two or three sloops or corvettes which had often been expected to beat off wolf-pack attacks on other occasions. With the numbers available to him, Walker was able to station them in a double ring round the convoy, thus greatly increasing the difficulties of any U-boat trying to get through to attack the merchant ships. Nevertheless, numbers alone had been shown before to be not enough. Clear-sighted direction and trained crews were also needed. These the 36th Escort Group had. With them they were to achieve the outstanding success of this phase of the Battle of the Atlantic, before radar came to swing the pendulum to the side of the escorts.

On the afternoon of Sunday, 14 December, the ships of HG76 filed out of Gibraltar Roads in the wake of the flagship of Commodore Raymond Fitzmaurice, the freighter *Spero*. By dark they were clear of the Straits and heading westwards out into the Atlantic in the usual rectangle made up of nine columns. From then onwards, as the Commodore was to report, 'the convoy had few dull moments'.

The first news of the enemy's presence came from the escorting Swordfish shortly before midnight. Running down a radar contact, the pilot sighted a U-boat lying in wait ahead of the convoy. Diving to the attack, he dropped his three depth-charges as the U-boat was submerging and marked the position with flares. The attack failed to put the submarine out of action; nor was the pilot able at once to get through to the *Stork* by radio. But hearing the explosions and sighting the flares, Walker steered for them and, with the sloop *Deptford* and the corvette *Rhododendron*, searched for some time. Though they were unsuccessful, the combined action of ships and aircraft kept the U-boat down and prevented an attack. It was no doubt the same submarine which the Swordfish encountered again two hours later, by that time well astern of the convoy. The aircraft had no depth-charges left but the U-boat was not to know this. It prudently submerged. The convoy steamed safely on into the night.

By daylight on the 15th, HG76 was beyond the operational radius of the aircraft from Gibraltar, but aircraft from *Audacity* took their place. As the little single-seater Martlets circled, nothing but empty sea met their pilots' eyes. Walker congratulated himself that the U-boats had been given the slip and concurred in the suggestion of Commander Mackendrick of *Audacity*, that, during 16 December, the air patrols should be dispensed with, to conserve the flying hours of the four aircraft which were all that remained serviceable in the carrier. But in fact, though the U-boats had been temporarily shaken off, Dönitz's other arm, the F-W Condors, had regained contact with the convoy. One of them had been briefly sighted from the ex-American destroyer *Stanley* late on the 15th. The aircraft's signals set every U-boat in the area on to a course converging on the convoy.

They had a long way to come. Meanwhile the convoy steamed slowly on in fair, blue weather, at its best speed of $7\frac{1}{2}$ knots, while Commodore Fitzmaurice took advantage of the respite to drill his ships in making emergency turns (all ships turning together) and in wheels. In the afternoon of the 16th, five ships of the escort left to return to Gibraltar, but 12 remained. All was apparently quiet when darkness fell. But, unknown to the escort commander, a U-boat had arrived on the scene and, keeping out of sight beyond the horizon, had settled down to shadow while waiting for the wolf-pack to form up.

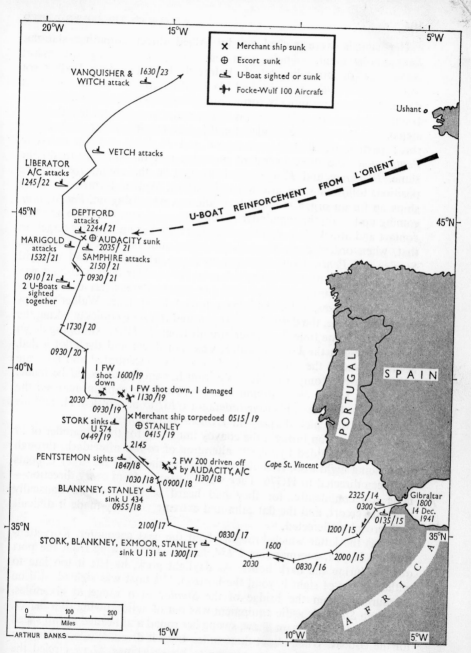

Battle round Convoy HG76, 14 – 23 December 1941

Her signals were picked up by Allied direction-finding stations. During the night, signals went out to *Stork* warning the escort commander of impending attack. Before daylight, therefore, Walker got in touch with *Audacity* and asked Mackendrick to send out air patrols at dawn. Results were quickly forthcoming. Twenty-two miles on the port beam of the convoy a U-boat was discovered. On receipt of the aircraft's signals, Walker at once headed for the position at full speed, directing three destroyers, *Blankney*, *Exmoor* and *Stanley*, and the corvette *Pentstemon*—the three fastest of his ships and the nearest—to do the same. *Blankney* and *Exmoor* arriving first in the submarine's diving position, followed soon afterwards by *Stork*, Walker formed the three ships up for an organized search. While this was going on, *Pentstemon*, coming up to join the remainder in company with *Stanley*, made an asdic contact and attacked. Touch was then lost with her underwater target, so that, when orders came from the *Stork* to join her unless in contact, *Stanley* and *Pentstemon* set course to do so. *Pentstemon* had wrought better than she knew, however, for some 90 minutes later a U-boat was sighted on the surface not far from her attack. Extensively damaged by the depth-charges, *U131* had been forced to surface. Walker's ships turned to engage, the destroyers *Exmoor* and *Blankney* quickly taking the lead. At the same time the fighter aircraft from *Audacity*, swooping down to machine-gun the U-boat bridge, was shot down and the pilot killed. Soon afterwards the submarine came under a concentrated and accurate gunfire to which only a feeble reply from her single gun could be made. With shells falling close around her, Baumann, her captain, realized the position was hopeless. He gave orders for *U131* to be scuttled. He and his whole crew were picked up by the *Exmoor* and *Stanley*.

This little action brought the convoy immunity for the remainder of 17 December and, aided by an 80° alteration of course after dark, through the ensuing night also. It could not continue, though. Five other U-boats had been directed to HG76. They were closing in from every direction— none too confidently, for they had heard of the convoy's unusually powerful escort, and the flat calm and extreme visibility made it difficult to approach undetected.

It was the latter which brought about the next encounter. Korvetten- Kapitän Heyda, commanding *U434*, had been shadowing from the port quarter during the dark hours. As daylight grew, he left it too late to withdraw out of sight beyond the horizon. His boat was sighted, still on the surface, from the bridge of the *Stanley* at a range of six miles. Although *Stanley*'s asdic equipment was out of action owing to a defect, her captain, David Byam Shaw, swung her round and headed at full speed for the U-boat. When about three miles away it dived. While waiting for the arrival of the *Blankney*, coming to his assistance, Shaw circled the submarine, its position betrayed by an oil slick, and dropped single depth-charges. Then *Blankney* arrived, gained asdic contact and directed

Stanley over the target to drop a pattern of 14 depth-charges. *Blankney* followed with another attack. Forty-nine minutes after being first sighted, *U434* came to the surface, her crew abandoned ship and she went to the bottom.

These two successes were cause for considerable satisfaction to Commander Walker in his first encounter with the U-boat packs. Before even reaching a position from which to attack the convoy, two of the enemy had been hunted down and destroyed. There could be no complacency, however. It was known that others were somewhere around seeking for a gap in the defences, while Focke-Wolf Condors made daily visits to reconnoitre the situation. But they were not able to linger, as was their wont, transmitting homing signals to the U-boats. Two that arrived during the forenoon of 18 December were set upon by *Audacity*'s fighters and damaged before the Martlets' guns jammed.

Nevertheless, in the calm, clear weather in which the tip of a masthead or the smallest wisp of smoke showed up clearly against the sharp-cut horizon, the U-boats could hardly fail to locate the convoy. On the other hand, these conditions cut both ways. As dusk was falling on the 18th, the conning-tower of a submarine, surfacing in the last of the light, was sighted from the *Pentstemon* against the sunset glow. With *Convolvulus* and *Stanley* she turned in chase. Gunfire from *Pentstemon* forced the submarine to dive, but no asdic contact could be made and at 2130, after two hours of fruitless search, the three ships set course to return to the convoy. With a persistence which, bearing in mind the strength of the opposition and the unfavourable conditions cannot but be admired, the submarine, *U574*, commanded by Korvetten-Kapitän Gentelbach, thereupon surfaced and followed the escorts towards the convoy. Thus it was that at 0345, from her station astern of the convoy on the outer screen, *Stanley*'s radio-telephone crackled into life with the message 'Submarine in sight'. Then came a second message, 'Torpedoes passing from astern'.

It was a pitch-black night. Walker in his station, also astern of the convoy, was uncertain of *Stanley*'s exact position. So that he could come to her aid, he ordered her to fire starshells to illuminate the submarine. Before she could do so, the two ships had come in sight of one another. They were exchanging indentities by flash light when, in a blinding sheet of flame reaching hundreds of feet into the air, *Stanley* blew up. At this the whole convoy sprang into brilliant light. The merchant ships had been supplied with the 'Snowflake' rockets, introduced to deal with the problem of U-boats penetrating to between the columns. Instructed to fire them as soon as a ship was torpedoed, they now did so. The resultant naked exposure of the convoy was an uncomfortable experience. As the commodore commented, 'One could not help being acutely aware that all ships of the convoy were vividly lighted up and shown to any other submarine that might be waiting to see their target. I do not know if "Snowflake" illumination by convoy ships helped the escort—I doubt it.' Indeed this device, designed to deal with a particular situation rarely experienced, proved a two-edged weapon in practice and one hard to control. The introduction of an efficient radar set was soon to make it redundant. In this case its use must have been of assistance to the U-boat which was at that moment approaching from the convoy's port bow to put a torpedo into the leading ship of the port column, the *Ruckinge*.

In the meantime dramatic events were occurring astern of the convoy. On seeing *Stanley* torpedoed, Walker had ordered 'Buttercup Astern'. The escorts had turned to comply but it was in *Stork* herself that the ping of the asdic had suddenly returned the sharp echo which signified contact with a submarine. The range was very short—700 yards. There was no time for deliberation or careful aim. Walker took the *Stork* straight in for a snap attack before settling down to a deliberate hunt. But only one more depth-charge attack had been made and *Stork* was running in for a third time when *U574* surfaced 200 yards ahead of her. Walker steered to ram; but the U-boat set off in a tight circle at high speed. The *Stork* followed, unable at first to get inside the submarine's turning circle. For 11 minutes the giddy chase continued. Walker himself wrote:

> I was surprised to find later by the plot that *Stork* had turned three complete circles.... I kept the U-boat illuminated with 'Snowflakes' which were quite invaluable in this unusual action. Some rounds of 4-inch were fired from the forward mountings until the guns could not be sufficiently depressed, after which the guns' crews were reduced to shaking fists and roaring curses at an enemy who several times seemed to be a matter of a few feet away rather than yards....
>
> Eventually at 0448 I managed to ram her just before the conning tower from an angle of about 20° on her starboard quarter and roll her over.
>
> She hung for a few seconds on the bow and again on the asdic dome and then scraped aft where she was greeted by a ten-charge pattern at shallowest settings.

Stork and the corvette *Samphire* picked up survivors from *Stanley* and from the U-boat, 28 British and 18 Germans, before shaping course to rejoin the convoy. On the way they came across the hulk of the *Ruckinge*, with the master, chief officer and 12 of her crew in a boat lying off. They were taken aboard *Stork*; *Samphire* was left to deal with *Ruckinge*—eventually to sink her as there could be no hope of salvaging her. The remainder of *Ruckinge*'s crew had been rescued by the *Finland* whose master had gallantly dropped back to do so, ignoring the risk involved. In the darkness the master's boat had not been found.

With daylight Walker was able to survey the results of the night's operations. Only one ship of the convoy, the *Ruckinge*, had been hit and a third U-boat destroyed had been added to the score, at the cost of a bent bow to the *Stork* and her asdic put out of action. The loss of *Stanley*, with her commanding officer and so many of her crew, was a harsh price to pay, nevertheless, and the battle was by no means over, as the familiar sight of two Condors on the horizon told. The blue weather had now gone. Two fighters from *Audacity* managed to intercept the Condors as they dodged in and out of the clouds, shooting down one and damaging the other. In the afternoon another put in an appearance and was also shot down. Then one of *Audacity*'s aircraft reported a submarine seven miles on the port beam of the convoy. Three escorts sped away and, though they made no contact, the U-boat was put down and discouraged from attempting any attack that night.

It was evident, however, that the heavy blows inflicted on the enemy had not brought the enemy's effort to an end. At U-boat headquarters there had been concern and even dismay as evidence of mounting losses came in. Besides the three boats sunk by the escort of HG76, another had been destroyed on 15 December by the Australian destroyer *Nestor* on patrol off Cape St Vincent. Dönitz had been faced with the alternatives of calling off the survivors of his pack, reduced now to three, or sending reinforcements to them. Ignorant as yet of the unusual strength of the escort, he chose the latter. Three U-boats, commanded by experienced captains were ordered to the scene—*U71*, *U751* (Korvetten-Kapitän Bigalk) and *U167*, whose captain was reigning 'ace' of the U-boat fleet, Korvetten-Kapitän Endrass.

While waiting for these reinforcements, the other U-boats hovered on the horizon but forebore to attack. Walker's last fast escorts, *Blankney* and *Exmoor*, had left on the 18th, so that reports from *Audacity*'s aircraft of submarines and sight of them from the *Stork*'s crow's nest could be met only by sending out his slow corvettes to keep them at a distance. By the afternoon of 21 December 'the net of U-boats seemed to be growing uncomfortably close in spite of *Audacity*'s heroic efforts to keep them at arm's length', Walker noted. He decided to try a ruse to shake them off. As soon as darkness fell the convoy was to alter sharply to a new course, while four of his escorts, pushed out in another direction, would stage a mock battle, firing starshell and 'Snowflakes' to draw the enemy away on a false scent. These moves were duly carried out but his plan was ruined through over-eager masters in the convoy who, ignorant of what was afoot, joined in the pyrotechnic display by firing their 'Snowflakes'. It was doubly unfortunate in that, for the sake of the plan, Walker had reduced the escorts round the convoy and the 'Snowflakes' in the convoy made it a perfect aiming mark. A few minutes later the *Annavore*, rear ship of the centre column, was torpedoed. This was the only casualty from amongst the merchant ships. But even while the escorts were performing their 'Buttercup' operation, a success which bid fair to even the scores in this long-drawn battle fell to the U-boats.

At dusk *Audacity*, in accordance with Mackendrick's usual custom, had moved out from the vicinity of the convoy. Before leaving Mackendrick had asked if a corvette could be spared to accompany him but Walker had been forced to refuse as only four escorts were at that time in close company with the convoy. Learning that Mackendrick was intending to manoeuvre to the starboard side of the convoy, Walker had suggested that the port side would be preferable, as it was from the starboard side that the U-boats were expected to approach. However, Mackendrick thought that the convoy's intended alteration of course to port soon after dark would inconvenience him, and eventually *Audacity* went off alone to starboard. Thus it was that, as *U751* was cautiously approaching on the surface, the illuminations and confusing criss-cross movements of escorts showing that the thoroughly alarmed convoy was an unhealthy place for him to be, Korvetten-Kapitän Bigalk suddenly found a long, dark shape silhouetted against the distant lights. He thought at first it was a tanker, but then realized it was a carrier—a heaven-sent target for any U-boat commander. Out of a salvo of torpedoes, one hit *Audacity* on the port side of her engine room, flooding it and bringing the ship to a standstill. Bigalk now boldly approached to point-blank range to put two more torpedoes into her. Within ten minutes *Audacity* had gone. Satisfied with this success, Bigalk turned away and made no further attempt to get at the convoy.

There, indeed, a highly confused situation existed. The messages coming over the radio-telephone to Walker reported widely scattered activity by his escorts. Operation 'Buttercup' had brought no contact to the *Stork*. Having no asdic since her ramming of *U574*, this could only have been from a sighting in any case. The operation completed, *Stork* resumed her station ahead of the convoy. In the meantime Walker had ordered the *Marigold* and *Convolvulus* to go to the aid of *Audacity*. *Marigold*, however, had not at first been able to comply as she was busy hunting a U-boat which she had sighted on the port side of the convoy. Then came a signal from *Samphire* that she was in asdic contact on the starboard side and was attacking, which she continued to do for some two hours. An hour later *Deptford*, on the other side, sighted a submarine evidently trying to get through to the convoy. Illuminating with starshell, at which the U-boat dived, *Deptford*, too, stuck doggedly to her asdic contact, delivering attack after attack until the contact was finally lost. Somewhere amongst the almost continuous thud and rumble of depth-charges, *U567*, the boat of Korvetten-Kapitän Endrass, had met its end. Which of the escorts was responsible is not known, for *U567* was lost without trace.

There was to be one other startling episode before the night was out. In pitch darkness, *Deptford* was rejoining after her long duel with *U567* (or

16 Focke-Wulf 200 (Kondor)

17 FW Kondor bombs ship in convoy

18 Sunderland flying boat on convoy escort duty

19 U-boat under machine-gun attack

AERIAL PARTICIPANTS IN THE ATLANTIC BATTLE

20 Captain 'Johnny' Walker   21 Lieutenant-Commander Peter Gretton

OPPONENTS IN THE ATLANTIC BATTLE

22 Otto Kretschmer   23 Joachim Schepke   24 Günther Prien

another). Officers and look-outs, weary after four days of unceasing action, failed to see the *Stork*. As Walker reported the incident:

> At 0517 on the 22nd I was aroused by an unusually ominous crash and came up to find *Deptford's* stem about one-third of the way into the port side of my quarterdeck. The damage was serious enough but not vital since the main engines and the steering gear (by an inch or two) had not been touched. The after cabin flat was wide open to the elements but the wardroom flat and the tiller flat were tight.
>
> *Deptford's* stem had walked straight into the temporary prison (of survivors of *U574*) and two of the five Boches were pulped, literally, into a bloody mess.

Dawn on 22 December, the sixth day of this memorable running fight, came at last to the escorts' weary crews. There had been little sleep for any of them since it had begun. They were reaching the end of their tether. Even the indomitable Walker confessed to finding the outlook gloomy. His own ship was badly damaged both fore and aft, reduced to a maximum speed of 10 knots and bereft of most of her offensive capabilities. *Deptford* had her asdic put out of action and was also reduced in speed. *Stanley* had gone with many of her crew. Above all the *Audacity* and her tireless aircraft were no longer throwing their protective umbrella over the convoy. Against this there was the satisfaction of knowing that in face of a concentrated and persistent attack only two ships of the convoy had been torpedoed, while three U-boats were known to have been destroyed. (The number was indeed four but this was not known till later.)

Relief was, in fact, at hand. For that morning there came the welcome sight of a friendly aircraft, one of the four-engined, long-range Liberators which had recently, at long last, been released to Coastal Command. It had come 800 miles from its base to provide air escort, a great advance on the capabilities of the aircraft available up to that time: an augury of developments which were eventually to play a leading part in the defeat of the U-boats. On this occasion the Liberator found U-boats still lingering disconsolately in the vicinity of the convoy and attacked them with depth-charges. The time had come for Dönitz to call off his hounds from this unexpectedly prickly hedgehog. The operation was finally abandoned.

The battle for HG76 was of importance for several reasons. In spite of painful losses on both sides, each classified it as a notable victory for the convoy escorts. The loss of four U-boats, including that of Dönitz's most experienced and skilful commander, and several Condor aircraft, was to some extent offset by the loss of Britain's first and at that time only auxiliary aircraft-carrier. But the fact remained that nine U-boats had been unable to deliver more than two hasty, tip-and-run attacks on a convoy with which they had been in touch for a full week. Though the strength of the escort was much in excess of anything which could as yet be provided on the trans-Atlantic routes, HG76 made it plain that the counter to the U-boat—trained escort groups and a combined sea-and-air escort—existed and, as Britain's resources grew, would eventually win. The writing was on the wall.

Dönitz's staff perceived it. In his *Memoirs* he writes, 'After this failure and in view of the unsatisfactory results of the preceding two months, my staff was inclined to voice the opinion that we were no longer in a position successfully to combat the convoy system because of recent experiences.' Dönitz did not agree:

> The weather and the exceptional strength of the escort had combined to create a situation more than usually unfavourable for a submarine attack. This one isolated case was no reason for making any fundamental change in my views with regard to attacks on convoys and I was proved right by subsequent events. Indeed it was to be in 1942 and the first months of 1943 that we were destined to fight our biggest convoy battles. The successes we achieved were enormous.

The German admiral was only justified in his views by the inability of the Allies, during the time he mentions, to profit by the old lessons re-learnt in the fight for HG76. Of these the greatest was the necessity for continuous air cover if the attacks of U-boat packs were to be defeated. Its eventual provision, at the very time that Dönitz was claiming 'enormous' success, was to force him, in May 1943, to concede victory to the Allies in the North Atlantic. Be that as it may, at the end of December 1941, both sides were poised for what might have been the decisive clash in the Atlantic. It would have been a clash which, with Dönitz's strength reduced by the dispersal of his U-boats in other theatres—the Mediter-ranean and the Arctic—and with Allied forces growing in strength and improved in performance by the addition of centimetric radar, high frequency direction finders and more efficient asdic equipment, might well have gone overwhelmingly in the Allied favour.

It was not to be. On 7 December 1941 the Japanese attack on Pearl Harbor, drawing the United States into the war, introduced an altogether new situation in the Atlantic as well as the Pacific. The effect on the U-boat war will be examined in a later chapter.

Before moving on to follow the application of sea power in other theatres, we should, perhaps, recount the final episode in the German effort to challenge Britain with her heavy surface units in the Atlantic.

By the end of 1941, Hitler had become obsessed with the belief that Britain was planning an invasion of Norway. This was to hamstring Admiral Dönitz's campaign by his insistence that a sizeable force of U-boats should be stationed in the north. Against the advice of his naval staff Hitler insisted in January 1942 that the *Scharnhorst, Gneisenau* and *Prinz Eugen* must also be transferred to Norway and that they should be brought home through the Channel which was not only the shortest route but one along which the ships could be given massive protection by escorting destroyers, motor torpedo boats, fighter and bomber aircraft.

That this was the German intention was appreciated both by the Admiralty and the Air Ministry by the beginning of February. A joint plan for the deployment of the forces available to them in opposition to this move had, in fact, been made as long ago as April 1941 under the code-name 'Fuller'. Though this might seem from a superficial view to be basically a maritime operation, the majority of the British forces to be engaged were aircraft. The naval units under the control of the naval commander concerned, Vice-Admiral Sir Bertram Ramsay at Dover, were confined to eight MTBs divided equally between Ramsgate and Dover, six old destroyers based on Harwich and six Swordfish torpedo-planes stationed at Manston RAF Station near the North Foreland which were to be controlled by the Admiral in coordination with the Air Officer Commanding No 11 (Fighter) Group.

The chances of so meagre a force by their own efforts stopping the passage through the Straits of the powerful German units were slim. Only in cooperation with the air forces available were they likely to achieve anything significant. These forces were very large, comprising three squadrons of Beaufort torpedo planes of RAF Coastal Command, more than 300 bombers of Bomber Command and five squadrons of RAF Spitfires. Coastal, Bomber and Fighter Commands each controlled the operations of their own aircraft.

Thus it must be established at the outset that the task of stopping the German squadron was primarily the responsibility of the Royal Air Force. The Flag Officer, Dover, controlled only his exiguous force of naval units while there was not even a single unified Air Command with which he could 'co-ordinate' his operations.

On 3 February, at the request of the Admiralty, the Air Ministry ordered its three operational commands to bring into force the arrangements for 'Fuller'. These divided themselves into two parts, a reconnaissance plan to ensure that the departure and subsequent movements of the German squadron from Brest would be reported and the readying of the strike aircraft of Coastal and Bomber Commands and fighter aircraft of Nos 10 and 11 Groups of Fighter Command.

The air reconnaissance plan organized by Coastal Command consisted of three radar-equipped night patrols, one off Brest, one between Ushant and the Isle de Brehat on the north Brittany coast, and one between Havre and Boulogne. The strike force of Coastal Command was widely dispersed with a squadron of Beauforts at Leuchars, Fife, for operations against the *Tirpitz* if she should come to sea, another squadron and a half at St Eval in Cornwall whence they could operate against the German

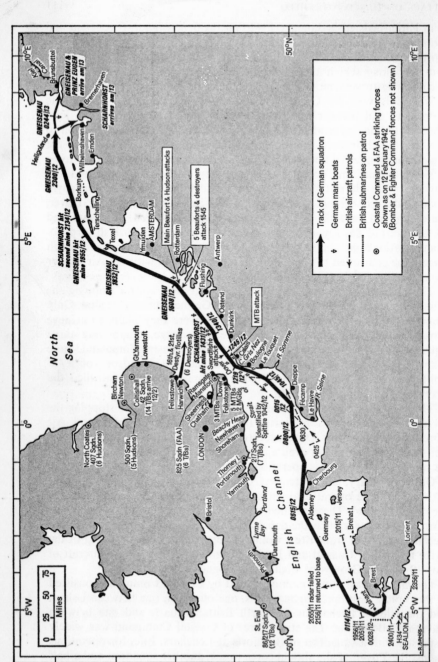

Escape of *Scharnhorst*, *Gneisenau* and *Prinz Eugen*, 12 February 1942

squadron in the western part of the Channel, and half a squadron at Thorney Island, near Portsmouth. When the C-in-C Coastal Command reached the conclusion on the 8th that the enemy would break out at any time from 10 February onwards, he gave orders for the squadron at Leuchars to move south calling at North Coates to pick up torpedoes for three of its planes. These orders could not be obeyed at once owing to airfields being snow-bound. Bomber Command, meanwhile, had 100 aircraft standing by from 10 February as a striking force.

At Dover, Admiral Ramsay, taking various factors including tidal conditions into consideration, had reached the conclusion that the enemy would aim to arrive in the Strait, at or before midnight. His forces were ordered to be at immediate notice each night. A further precaution taken by the Admiralty was an intensive mine-laying programme between 3 and 9 February when the fast minelayers *Manxman* and *Welshman* laid about 1,000 contact and magnetic mines in six fields between Ushant and Boulogne and Bomber Command laid 98 magnetic mines off the Frisian Islands.

Such were the British dispositions as darkness fell on 11 February 1942 over Brest where the German ships under the command of Vice Admiral Ciliax were preparing to get under way with an escort of six destroyers. Their intentions were to sail at 1930 and at 25 knots follow a route previously swept for mines and indicated by mark boats. This would bring them to the Straits of Dover by 1130 the next morning. From daylight, when 10 torpedo boats would join the escort, until dusk, fighter cover by never less than 16 aircraft would be provided, augmented from the time of passing Cap Gris Nez, when another torpedo boat flotilla and three flotillas of MTBs would also join.

The plan was a good one; it was also to be aided by much good luck. The first measure of this was heralded by the wail of air raid sirens at 1935 as a result of which departure was postponed until 2114. Thus the British submarine *Sealion* which had closed the entrance and remained near the Whistle Buoy, where she must otherwise have seen the big German ships sweep by, had seen nothing when she withdrew at 2035. At the same time the first of the three airborne radar patrols had failed. The radar set of the plane which should have been over the harbour entrance having broken down, the pilot had flown back to base for repair and did not return to his station until 2238 at which time the German squadron had cleared the entrance and was heading out to sea undetected.

By midnight they were rounding Ushant and should have been coming under the radar eye of the second patrol. But this too had suffered a defect, had been ordered to return and had not been replaced. The third patrol was maintained until dawn, but by that time the squadron had not advanced far enough to the eastward to come within range of the radar set. By 1100 they had successfully negotiated at slow speed a channel swept through a minefield which had been discovered only a few hours earlier off Etaples and, under a swarm of fighters and screened by more than 30 small craft, they had increased speed to 25 knots. And, though some alarm had been raised at Dover by some suspicious radar plots of shipping as well as some unusual jamming experienced by the British radar stations, as a result of which Ramsay's squadron of Swordfish aircraft had been brought to immediate readiness and both 16 Group of Coastal Command and 11 (Fighter) Group had been warned, the presence of this large concentration of shipping was still unreported.

It had, in fact, been identified at last at 1042 quite fortuitously by Group Captain F. V. Beamish, out on a fighter sweep in a Spitfire who, in the course of a dogfight with a Messerschmitt, had flown right over it. But it was not until he landed at 1109 that the momentous news began a roundabout journey through 11 Group, Fighter Command HQ and the Admiralty to Dover where it arrived at 1125.

By that time the squadron was already approaching the Straits. Any hopes of a combined attack by the widely dispersed force of torpedo planes being organized before the ships sped out of range had already gone. At St Eval, Thorney Island and Leuchars, all available Beauforts were got ready and despatched by various routes to attack as and when they could. At bomber stations 242 aircraft were similarly despatched. Nearest to the enemy and first to be launched, however, were the MTBs at Dover and Ramsgate and the six Swordfish of No 825 Squadron commanded by Lieutenant-Commander Eugene Esmonde.

The efforts of the MTBs can be briefly told. Essentially night-fighting craft, they were thrown in broad daylight against a vastly superior force. Nevertheless the five boats from Dover outpaced the powerful enemy screen to get their torpedoes away at the heavy ships soon after 1230. That they achieved no hits is not surprising; that they escaped almost unscathed was a miracle. The Ramsgate boats became involved with the rear of the enemy screen and failed to achieve a firing position before being forced to break off and return to base.

Almost simultaneously with the last of the attacks by the Dover boats, there was played out a bitter tragedy by the naval aircrews of 825 Squadron. The heavily laden biplanes had lumbered off the runway at Manston at 1220 to rendezvous with the large fighter escort of three squadrons of Spitfires from RAF Biggin Hill, to give top cover, and two more from Hornchurch, to engage the enemy's flank, which had been promised and which alone could give their attack the remotest chance of success. Only one squadron from Biggin Hill was at the rendezvous, but Esmonde could not delay if with his 80-knot planes he was to catch the enemy who were already ten miles past Calais. At 1230 he set off for the target, the aircraft formed in two sub-flights of three. His aircraft were very soon beset by enemy fighters whom the Sptifires of the escort were too few to hold off, though they did their best. With damage mounting in all the defenceless Swordfish and casualties among their crews, they flew dauntlessly on into the storm of flak from the enemy destroyers and small craft.

Esmonde's aircraft had lost most of its lower port main plane but was wallowing on when it was again hit by a burst of fire and crashed. The other two pressed on. Leading Airman A. L. Johnson, the air gunner in Sub-Lieutenant Rose's plane had been killed and Rose himself severely wounded in the back. In the other, the pilot, Sub-Lieutenant Kingsmill and his observer Sub-Lieutenant Samples had both been wounded and the aircraft was on fire. Nevertheless both succeeded in closing to within 3,000 yards to launch their torpedoes before turning back to crash just outside the destroyer screen.

Of the final moments of the second flight of Swordfish little is known. They were last seen pressing in to the attack and were probably the three seen from the *Scharnhorst* to be shot down by fighters. There were no survivors from them or from Esmonde's plane. From the others, Kingsmill, Samples and Leading Airman Bunce, and Rose and his observer, Sub-Lieutenant Lee, were rescued by British MTBs. No torpedoes from this truly foredoomed squadron, so selflessly sacrificed, found their target.

Meanwhile from Harwich, where the alarm had found them exercising at sea, the six old destroyers of the 21st and 16th Flotillas under Captain C. T. M. Pizey in the *Campbell* had set off to intercept. At the same time the Coastal Bomber Command air squadrons were being marshalled and despatched. The destroyers, reduced to five by the main engine failure of one of them, made radar contact with the enemy at 1517 and soon afterwards, in visibility down to four miles, sighted the big ships over which could be seen a wild mêlée of aircraft of every type, friendly and hostile. The scene was further confused by the fact that the *Scharnhorst* had, at 1431, detonated a mine and though not seriously damaged had stopped for a while.

Through a steadily increasing storm of gunfire the destroyers pressed on. The *Worcester* was heavily hit, set on fire and brought to a stop with 46 casualties, but not before she had managed to launch her torpedoes, as did the other four ships which remained unscathed by the enemy's gunfire and air attacks by friend and foe alike. Their torpedoes were all avoided by the enemy however. All returned to Harwich, the *Worcester* limping home at speeds varying from $3\frac{1}{2}$ to 8 knots.

While this last effort by Admiral Ramsay's meagre naval force was expending itself, the Royal Air Force's attacks had been developing. The first of these to reach the area was a wave of 73 bombers which took off at 1430. Weather conditions for the high-level type of attack on which the RAF relied were as bad as they could be, with rain clouds at 1,000 feet or less. In such conditions armour-piercing bombs were useless and the majority of the bombers were armed with general purpose bombs. Indeed, only a few succeeded in finding the target at all. Nor did the next two waves of 134 and 35 bombers respectively do any better. Out of the total of 242 only 39 claimed to have attacked naval units; they caused no damage; 15 aircraft were lost.

The Beaufort squadrons of Coastal Command had been caught woefully unprepared as a result of the failure of the reconnaissance arrangements. At Thorney Island, only four of the seven torpedo planes had been got ready by 1340. They set off to pick up a fighter escort at Manston but arrived too late, got split up and after much flying to and fro in the low visibility eventually attacked the enemy in ones and twos without success. The other three reached Manston at 1500 whence they set course and found the enemy without difficulty. One was shot down by enemy fighters, the other two attacked, again without success.

The Leuchars squadron, which had been under orders since the 8th to move south but had been prevented by snow-bound airfields, had fortunately started off early in the day. Three of the 14 Beauforts had no torpedoes and efforts to obtain them failed; two more had engine failures. Thus only nine arrived at Manston and left for the target at 1534. Seven of them launched their torpedoes which were all avoided by the enemy.

The 12 available Beauforts at St Eval, after moving first to Thorney Island and thence to Coltishall to pick up a fighter escort which did not materialize, did not reach the expected position of the enemy until 1741 and in the rain-filled dusk failed to find them, got split up and finally returned to base two short.

So the last chance of stopping the enemy's bold dash by direct attack had slipped away. Hitler had rightly assessed the capacity of the British to react to a sudden emergency under their existing, disunited command system; the German Navy and Air Force had carried out the operation with great skill and efficiency. They had had a good measure of luck, nevertheless. And now, just as Admiral Ciliax was congratulating himself, the luck ran out. At 1955 the *Gneisenau* struck a mine off Terschelling and though she was soon under way again at 25 knots the damage was to put her into dock on arrival and there she was to be so damaged in air raids that she never again put to sea. At 2134 the *Scharnhorst* struck her second mine, this time with serious consequences. She lay stopped for nearly an hour before limping away to Wilhelmshaven for lengthy repairs.

Today the episode is generally judged to have comprised a tactical victory for the Germans even though the abandonment of their hopes of offensive action by their surface fleet in the Atlantic was a clear admission of a strategic defeat. It is less than just, however, that blame for the tactical defeat suffered by the British has often been laid at the door of the Admiralty which, as we have seen, had only a minor share in the joint wielding of sea and air power on and over the Channel.

6 *Struggle for the Central Basin*

While in the Atlantic the challenge to Britain's sea power in the shape of attack on her vital merchant shipping from above, below and on the surface of the sea, had been steadily growing in intensity and scope, in the Mediterranean, war with more directly territorial objectives had developed. Italian armies from Libya, later to be joined by the German Afrika Korps under General Rommel, had opened the long campaign aimed at an Axis conquest of Egypt, a first step eastwards towards the oil-rich lands of the Middle East.

It was a war, however, in which both sides had to depend upon seaborne supplies for their armies. For the Italo-German forces the route was only a few hundred miles across the Central Mediterranean; for the British it ran some 2,000 miles east and west between Gibraltar and Egypt with its middle portion flanked on either side by enemy-held territory and airfields.

Thus the campaign in North Africa was to be decisively affected by the naval struggle to control the Central Basin. Roughly in the centre of it was the little island of Malta which, so long as it remained in British hands, could be a vital base from which to deploy sea and air forces in defence of the east-west supply route and to disrupt the supplies to the Axis armies in Africa.

Unfortunately for the British, however, no efforts had been made before the entry of Italy into the war to supply adequate defences for the island, either coastal or anti-aircraft artillery, or to construct airfields and station defensive fighters on them. The British Mediterranean Fleet, commanded by Admiral Sir Andrew Cunningham, had been forced to transfer its base to Alexandria, 1,000 miles to the eastward whence, unable to eliminate the Italian fleet which refused to accept its challenge to battle, it could only intermittently operate in the Central Basin. On the other hand, though Malta lay wide open to capture by an amphibious or airborne assault, the Italians failed to take advantage of the situation, and a small, but far from negligible force of naval torpedo planes, joined later by a few RAF bombers, continued to operate from the island against the Italian supply convoys.

In time to come, a build-up of air striking power on Malta and the basing of a submarine flotilla there were to make the island a key factor in control of the central basin. The naval campaign would then come to revolve largely round the ability of the British to build up and preserve Malta as an offensive base in the midst of waters otherwise dominated by enemy sea and air power. This involved, on the one hand, the supply and replenishment of the fortress; on the other, the efforts by the enemy to eliminate it. Some of the principal clashes by sea would result from it.

In the meantime, as Cunningham strove for control through the traditional British naval policy of seeking out and destroying the enemy fleet, he was confronted by an Italian refusal to let their fleet be drawn into battle while, at the same time, he could only operate in the central basin in the face of a huge preponderance of Italian submarine and air strength.

The Italians possessed more than 100 submarines—twice the number with which the Germans were wreaking havoc in the Atlantic. The Allied strength in destroyers, which roughly equalled that of the Italians, was divided between the two halves of the Mediterranean, leaving Cunningham with far less than the minimum required for screening his fleet as well as performing their multifarious duties of patrol and convoy. Italian submarines might thus make penetration of the central Mediterranean an unacceptable hazard.

For air support, each fleet was in the position of having to rely almost entirely upon the cooperation of an independent Air Force. Each found the situation less than satisfactory. The Italian Navy complained that the type of aircraft developed by the Air Force for reconnaissance—the single-engine Cant Z.501 seaplane, with a top speed of 100 knots—was woefully inefficient. More than 100 of them were available, nevertheless, and with this number it should have been possible to detect and shadow any large-scale movement of the enemy fleet. In striking power, the Italian Air Force was theoretically overwhelmingly powerful; but the heavy bombers in which it initially trusted, in opposition to the Navy's appeals for torpedo planes, were to prove largely ineffective.

Admiral Cunningham in comparison, so far as shore-based air support was concerned, had the services of only a handful of flying boats divided between Malta and Alexandria, too lightly armed to operate off the enemy's coasts within range of his shore-based aircraft. To be sure, he did have a carrier in his fleet, the 20-year-old *Eagle*, carrying 17 Swordfish torpedo-reconnaissance planes which provided the fleet with reconnaissance in its immediate vicinity while at sea. But this could not help him to bring the Italian fleet to action from his base 1,000 miles to the eastward of Malta. As for aerial striking power and defence, the *Eagle* represented his total resources. For the former about half of her complement of

Swordfish could be spared for attack purposes. The superior speed of Italian ships made it vitally important that they should be slowed down by air attack if the decisive naval action was to be brought about. In defence of the fleet, the *Eagle* had embarked just three Gloster 'Gladiator' biplane fighters, which Charles Keighley-Peach, her Commander (Flying) had extracted from a Fleet Air Arm store. Until he was able to instruct and give flying practice to a few volunteers from the Swordfish pilots, he constituted by himself the total fighter force of the fleet. In spite of a bullet through his thigh in one of his first combats, he had considerable success in shooting down the enemy reconnaissance machines which were shadowing the fleet.

On 20 May the First Sea Lord, Admiral of the Fleet Sir Dudley Pound, had written to Cunningham:

I am afraid you are terribly short of 'air', but . . . I do not see what can be done because, as you will realize, every available aircraft is wanted in home waters. The one lesson we have learnt here is that it is essential to have fighter protection over the fleet whenever they are within range of enemy bombers. You will be without such protection, which is a very serious matter, but I do not see any way of rectifying it.

In spite of this, Cunningham was mainly concerned with the problem of how to bring the Italian fleet to action.

'You may be sure that all in the fleet are imbued with a burning desire to get at the Italian Fleet', he had written on 6 June in reply to a message originating from the Prime Minister, Mr Churchill, criticizing his plans as 'purely defensive':

but you will appreciate that a policy of seeking and destroying his naval forces requires good and continuous air reconnaissance, and a means of fixing the enemy when located. I am far from well provided with either requirements, whereas the Italians have both. Indeed my chief fear is that we shall make contact with little or nothing except aircraft and submarines, and I must get the measure of these before attempting sustained operations in the Central Mediterranean.

The first two weeks of the campaign saw the opposing naval forces holding an uneasy balance. Though the Italian main fleet lay supine in its bases, Malta was repeatedly bombed, thus beginning its long ordeal which was to continue intermittently for more than two years. The Allied fleet, unable to draw its reluctant opponent to sea, turned its guns on to the Libyan port of Bardia and employed its light forces to good effect in hunting Italian submarines.

Then on 24 June, the whole situation was transformed by the collapse of France. The balance of naval power swung heavily in favour of Italy. In the western half of the Mediterranean, hitherto a French responsibility, there were virtually no British naval forces. In the other half, though

Cunningham's slight (and temporary) preponderance in battleship strength remained, he was now faced with an Italian superiority of seven heavy and 11 light cruisers and 61 destroyers over his own six light cruisers and 20 destroyers. The British advantage in battleships was more apparent than real, as, of Cunningham's four ships, three were unmodernized and so outranged by the two modernized enemy ships in service, and all were slower than the Italian ships. Furthermore, the Italian battleship strength was about to be increased by the addition of two more modernized ships and two splendid new battleships, *Vittorio Veneto* and *Littorio*.

Fortunately the situation in home waters following upon the campaign in Norway made it possible for the Admiralty to detach a powerful squadron, to be called Force 'H', to Gibraltar to fill the vacuum in the western Mediterranean. On 28 June Vice-Admiral Sir James Somerville hoisted his flag in the battle-cruiser *Hood* to take command of this force comprising, besides the *Hood*, the battleships *Valiant* and *Resolution*, the carrier *Ark Royal*, the light cruiser *Arethusa* and four destroyers.

The over-all situation at the end of June was, nevertheless, from the British point of view, a perilous one should the Italians take full advantage of their vastly improved position.

The elimination of France did, indeed, lead to greater activity by the Italian Navy. They now, for the first time, felt able to run convoys with urgent supplies of ammunition and equipment for their armies in Libya. With Malta untenable as a naval base and still almost devoid of strike aircraft,* there was little that could be done to prevent them. The onward transport of the supplies along the coast from Tripoli to Tobruk in destroyers, however, gave an opportunity to attack them by air. RAF bomber squadrons made repeated attacks on Tobruk but it was the Swordfish of No. 813 Squadron, disembarked from the *Eagle* while in harbour, which achieved the most concrete successes. Attacking on 5 July, they succeeded in torpedoing the destroyers *Zeffiro* and *Euro*, the former being sunk and the latter having her bow blown off. In the same attack a 4,000 ton transport was sunk and the liner *Liguria* damaged. In a further attack on 20 July two more destroyers, the *Ostro* and *Nembo*, were also sunk.

But it was the large force of Italian heavy warships which came to sea from time to time to cover their convoys that would have offered the possibility of a naval engagement if the necessary air reconnaissance had been available on the British side. Without it, chance alone could bring it about. Such a chance occurred during the early days of July 1940, though it was to result in no more than a 'brush'.

To give cover to convoys from Malta to Alexandria, Cunningham had taken his fleet to sea on the evening of 7 July. In the area south of Crete

*Nine Fleet Air Arm Swordfish of No. 830 Squadron had arrived in Malta from Toulon shortly before the French collapse.

which was soon deservedly to earn the name of 'Bomb Alley', it came under heavy and continuous air attacks by the high bombers of the Italian Air Force. The meagre high-angle batteries which, with the *Eagle*'s three Gladiators, comprised the fleet's air defences, were a feeble deterrent and the Italians flew in impeccable formation overhead to aim their bombs with remarkable precision. Time and again ships would be apparently smothered by the tall, black, leaping splashes from the carpet of bombs simultaneously released. Time and again they emerged unscathed, to give proof which was to be repeated in every theatre of war, that the chances of even accurate high-level bombing hitting a ship free to manoeuvre, if not negligible, were at least unacceptable. In the event, only the cruiser *Gloucester* was hit, her captain and 18 others being killed; the ship herself was able to remain with the fleet.

Meanwhile the Italian fleet under Admiral Campioni had also put to sea to give cover to a convoy for Libya and, at midday on 9 July, the skirmish off the coast of Calabria had opened with an unsuccessful torpedo attack by a small striking force of nine Swordfish flown off the *Eagle*. At 1500 the opposing cruisers—six Italian 8-inch 'heavies' and five British 6-inch 'light'—engaged at long range. A second torpedo attack by the *Eagle*'s Swordfish again failed to score. The *Warspite*, leaving her two slower, unmodernized sisters behind, hurried forward in support and at 1553 came within sight and extreme gun-range of Campioni's two modernized dreadnoughts, *Giulio Cesare* and *Conte di Cavour*, and opened fire.

It was just 1600 when Cunningham saw 'the great orange-coloured flash of a heavy explosion at the base of the enemy flagship's funnels'. The Italian fleet at once turned away under a heavy smoke screen and steered for the safety of its own protected waters in the Straits of Messina. Defying the massed strength of the Italian Air Force, Cunningham held on in chase to within 25 miles of the enemy coast before turning back.

The intermittent heavy air attacks which followed during the next four days as the British fleet returned to Alexandria, achieved no more than a number of near misses. On veterans like the *Eagle* they inflicted an accumulation of minor damage; nevertheless Cunningham, after his first encounters with air power, was inclined to belittle its effect on his freedom to operate. After the operation, he wrote:

It must have shown the Italians that their Air Force and submarines cannot stop our Fleet penetrating into the Central Mediterranean and that only their main Fleet can seriously interfere with our operating there. [The operation] produced throughout the Fleet a determination to overcome the air menace and not let it interfere with our freedom of manoeuvre and hence our control of the Mediterranean.

The truth of the matter was that it was only a matter of time, and the arrival on the scene of the Luftwaffe with its dive-bombers, for the central Mediterranean basin to be closed to naval forces that were without the benefit of a numerous fighter defence. In those narrow waters, such aircraft carriers as might become available could not provide sufficient strength. Only a large-scale deployment of fighters on Malta could do so.

On the basis of the lessons learnt in the action off Calabria, Cunningham asked for the addition to his force of one of the new armoured aircraft carriers to provide fighter-defence. The *Illustrious*, carrying 12 Fulmar two-seater fighters and 22 Swordfish, would be sent to him in the following month and would perform valiant service for a time.

Whatever might be the ability of 12 low-performance fighters to defend the fleet against assault by a properly equipped and trained air force, it was a fallacy to suppose that freedom of the Mediterranean Fleet to manoeuvre intermittently in the Central Mediterranean could achieve 'control' of that sea. 'Control', properly defined, had to mean ability to prevent the enemy from passing his convoys to and from Libya and to ensure the safe passage of convoys to the British Army of the Nile. Both of these depended upon the availability of Malta as a sea and air base, defensive and offensive, not for the main British Mediterranean Fleet but for the submarines and aircraft which had come to dominate naval warfare.

Though Cunningham had pressed, long prior to the outbreak of war, for Malta's air defence to be built up, the only fighter aircraft on the island at the end of July 1940 were three reserve Fleet Air Arm biplane Gladiators turned over to the RAF and flown by spare flying-boat pilots, which were to win fame as 'Faith, Hope and Charity'. Now, however, the vital importance of building up Malta's fighter strength was appreciated: 12 Hurricanes were loaded in the old carrier *Argus* and flown off to Malta from a position south of Sardinia. It was the first of many such operations by British ships and, on two memorable occasions the USS *Wasp*, by which the island was eventually to be given the means to defend herself.

By land as well as by sea the months of July and August 1940 were fraught with deep anxiety for the British commanders-in-chief. The Italian armies in Libya, greatly superior in number to the troops at the disposal of General Sir Archibald Wavell, were known to be preparing for an advance into Egypt. Reinforcements for the British Army had been withheld at first in favour of building up the army in France. Then, at Dunkirk, equipment had been lost in such quantity that nothing could be spared for the Middle East. The RAF had been similarly denied reinforcements; so that, at the end of May 1940, Air Marshal Longmore, responsible for air operations on the several fronts held by the Army in Egypt and for cooperation with the Navy in the Eastern Mediterranean and the Red Sea, including long-distance reconnaissance, had at his disposal only 96 bombers (Blenheim I) and bomber-transports (Bombay), 75 fighters (Gladiator), 24 Army Cooperation (Lysander) and 10 flying-boats (Sunderland)—a force manifestly incapable of meeting his minimum needs.

By mid-August, however, the vital needs of the Middle East had been partially acknowledged and strenuous efforts were being made to send reinforcements. A military convoy carrying troops, tanks and ammunition was despatched by the Cape route which was expected to reach Suez by 24 September. The heavy cruiser *York* and the light cruiser *Ajax* of the escort would join Cunningham's fleet. Twenty-four Hurricanes were on their way by the same route and a further 30 were being taken in the *Argus* to the Gold Coast port of Takoradi, thence to be flown to Egypt over a route organized across central Africa. In the next three years more than 5,000 aircraft were to use this route. In addition 24 Blenheims had reached Egypt via Malta, another 24 were being sent there by sea and six Wellingtons were being flown out.

A very useful addition to the maritime air component was a flight of three Glenn-Martin 'Maryland' long-range reconnaissance aircraft soon to be sent out to Malta, with which the Italian naval ports could be kept under observation—a task impossible for the slow and vulnerable flying-boats. On the other hand, the continued absence of any long-range fighters left the RAF still incapable of giving the fleet fighter cover except in the vicinity of its base. The arrival on 1 September of the *Illustrious* with her handful of Fulmars, together with the modernized and radar-fitted battleship *Valiant* and the anti-aircraft cruisers *Calcutta* and *Coventry*, was, therefore, most welcome.

Should the Italian battle-fleet accept action now, Cunningham would have two ships which could fire at long range, more than ever important as the enemy could by this time deploy a battle-squadron of five—the *Vittorio Veneto*, the *Littorio*, and three modernized older ships. Even so it soon became apparent that, even when everything was in their favour, the Italians would not seek a fight. Cunningham had taken his fleet to sea on 30 August to meet his reinforcements off Malta and at the same time to escort a convoy of two merchant ships and a tanker carrying supplies to the island. The Italian battle-fleet, comprising five battleships, 10 cruisers and 34 destroyers, ordered to sea to oppose Cunningham's two battleships, the *Eagle*, five light cruisers and nine destroyers, was located 90 miles away by a Swordfish from the carrier at dusk on 31 August.

Cunningham turned away and stationed himself in position to cover his convoy in expectation of battle the next day. Admiral Campioni, however, reversed course for the night. By morning the two fleets were so far apart that neither was able to locate the other until the Italians were finally found by a flying-boat that evening at the entrance to the Gulf of Taranto returning to base. His convoy safely delivered and his reinforcements met according to plan, Cunningham took his fleet back to Alexandria. The Italians' chance to strike while still commanding an overwhelming superiority had gone. From now onwards the air-striking force available to Cunningham would go a long way towards squaring the odds.

The apparently spiritless attitude of the Italian Navy had some justification if the policy of a weaker naval power to maintain a 'fleet in being' is accepted. When criticism of this policy arose the Chief of the Italian General Staff, Marshal Badoglio, was asked for his opinion. His judgment, summed up, was that, though battle should be accepted if necessary to further an ulterior object or to prevent the enemy from achieving his object, 'the conception of a naval battle as an end in itself is absurd'. (This policy, incidentally, is identical with that of the French during their naval wars with the British during the eighteenth century.)

From the point of view of morale, the apparent pusillanimity of the Italians inevitably reacted in favour of the British fleet, whose confidence was to be constantly heightened by repeated refusals of the Italians to stand and fight, so that eventually the British became ready and willing to undertake the seemingly impossible in order to get supplies through to Malta. On the other hand, the continued existence of a superior Italian fleet poised on the flank of the supply route to Malta was to play an important part in bringing the fortress within sight of starvation and capitulation, and was consequently to hamper severely the capacity of the British to interfere with the supply traffic to North Africa.

Italian freedom during the late summer of 1940 to pass their convoys to Libya unhindered across the short sea passage from Sicily to Cape Bon owing to continued British inability to use Malta led to hints from Churchill that Cunningham was being insufficiently offensive. To this he replied that only constant and complete air reconnaissance, which he was very far from enjoying, could enable him to force action on his unwilling enemy. When he steamed into the central basin in September and again in October to cover convoys, Campioni rejected the challenge.

The Italian fleet would not stand and fight at sea; but with the arrival of the *Illustrious*, bringing reinforcements of Swordfish torpedo planes and long-range petrol tanks for them, Cunningham had acquired the means to attack it in harbour. Another prerequisite of such an operation—up-to-date intelligence of the enemy's whereabouts—had also become available since the arrival in Malta of No 431 Flight of the RAF, (the three Glenn-Martin 'Maryland' reconnaissance aircraft mentioned above) with the speed and performance to keep a regular watch on the Italian naval bases. Plans were prepared and aircrews given intensive training for night operations; for any idea of sending the slow, lumbering Swordfish by day against the defences of a first-class naval base was out of the question.

When the Marylands provided evidence that the whole of the battle-fleet was concentrated at Taranto, 21 October was selected for the attack. A fire in the hangar of the *Illustrious* caused a postponement; defects in the petrol system of the *Eagle*, caused by the repeated shocks of near-miss bombs, forced her to be withdrawn; finally a number of the *Eagle*'s

Swordfish, transferred to the *Illustrious* for the operation, were lost owing to contaminated petrol in their tanks. In spite of these ominous setbacks, Operation 'Judgment' was fixed for 11 November, though only 21 aircraft instead of the originally planned 30 would be able to take part.

Meanwhile the preliminary operations were proceeding. In company with Admiral Somerville's Force 'H', reinforcements for Cunningham, comprising the battleship *Barham*, the cruisers *Glasgow* and *Berwick* and six destroyers carrying between them 2,150 troops for the Malta garrison, had sailed eastwards from Gibraltar on the evening of 7 November. Cunningham, with the *Warspite*, *Valiant*, *Malaya*, *Ramillies*, *Illustrious* and destroyers, was steering westwards from Alexandria to cover a convoy taking stores, fuel and ammunition to Greece and Crete, another of five store ships for Malta, and finally four empty store ships from Malta to Alexandria.

The Italian command knew at once of the movements of the two fleets. Admiral Campioni prepared to take his battle-fleet to sea on the 8th when he expected to have the necessary scouting reports from the Air Force. When no news reached him during the forenoon of the 8th he continued to wait in harbour. Though the shortage of oil fuel which the Italian Navy was to suffer may already have been having its influence, this delay was surely inexcusable if a desire to join action with the British fleet existed. When at last, during the afternoon, air reconnaissance reported the convoy for Malta, it was already beyond the point which the Italian fleet, sailing from Taranto, could intercept it. It must have been realized that Cunningham's fleet would be somewhere in the central basin to cover it, yet Campioni made no move.

For the next three days the British Mediterranean fleet was manoeuvring in the central basin less than 350 miles from Taranto, waiting for its reinforcements to join and for various ships to refuel at Malta. Though the Italian Air Force delivered some ineffectual bombing attacks on Cunningham's force as well as on Force 'H' to the southwards of Sardinia, its reconnaissance reports were so confused and conflicting that the Italian high command was completely baffled. Many of Campioni's ships carried scouting seaplanes on catapults. If his fleet had put to sea and used them for an organized search, he must soon have located his enemy; instead he remained in harbour waiting in vain for information. He was to suffer a bitter humiliation in consequence.

By the 11th Cunningham's reinforcements had joined him, the convoy was safely on its way from Malta to Alexandria and he was free to bear away for the selected flying-off position some 170 miles south-east of Taranto.

One of the *Illustrious*' aircraft had brought out from Malta the latest photographs of Taranto obtained by the Marylands. Five battleships could be seen in the anchorage. Later in the day a sixth battleship was sighted returning to harbour. All the Italian eggs were in one basket.

It was vitally important that the British force should be unobserved that day, a task in the hands of the fighter pilots of the *Illustrious* and the operators of the radar sets with which the fleet was now moderately well equipped. Italian reconnaissance planes which approached were pounced on with ruthless efficiency and shot down before they could make any report or driven off before they could catch sight of the fleet. So far as the Italian high command was concerned the Mediterranean fleet had vanished and was assumed to be on its way back to Alexandria.

At 1800, shortly before sunset, the *Illustrious*, with an escort of cruisers and destroyers, acknowledged the signal from the fleet flagship, 'Proceed in execution of previous orders for Operation "Judgment".' As she turned away to the north-westward a last signal winked out to her from Andrew Cunningham: 'Good luck then to your lads in their enterprise. Their success may well have a most important bearing on the course of the war in the Mediterranean.'

In the carrier's hangars final preparations were being made to the 21 'Stringbags' which were to take part. They were to be launched in two waves; the first, of 12 machines, would be led by Lieutenant-Commander Kenneth Williamson, commanding No 815 Squadron, with Lieutenant N. J. Scarlet as his observer. The remaining nine would be led by Lieutenant-Commander J. W. Hale, commanding officer of No 819 Squadron, whose observer was to be Lieutenant G. A. Carline. Not all even of this small force were to be armed with torpedoes. Six of the first wave and four of the second would carry bombs with which they would create a diversion by attacking cruisers and destroyers berthed in the inner harbour. Two of these bombers in each wave would also carry a number of magnesium flares and it would be their first duty to lay these in a line so placed as to show up in silhouette the Italian battleships in the harbour.

The torpedoes were something new and special. To detonate their warheads they had a new device known as a 'Duplex' pistol, so called because either a direct hit or the change of magnetic field as the torpedo passed underneath a ship would actuate it. The torpedoes would have to be set to run deep in case they were dropped outside the anti-torpedo nets known to exist. A small error in their depth-keeping would be enough to take them too deep for a direct hit. The magnetic device would then operate instead.

The prospect facing the 42 naval airmen was a daunting one. Photographic reconnaissance showed that torpedo planes would have to pass through a barrier of balloon cables to reach their dropping positions. Besides the massive volume of gunfire to be expected from the six battleships, nine cruisers and a great number of destroyers and auxiliaries present, the permanent defences of the port comprised 21 batteries of 4 inch HA guns, backed up by 200 automatic close-range weapons. Blinding illumination was to be expected from a large number of searchlights.

Unknown to the airmen, however, were two factors which were to go a small way towards reducing the hazards and difficulties. Recent storms had damaged a great many of the barrage balloons. Only 27 would be aloft this night. Then the anti-torpedo net defence was not fully extended, partly on account of a shortage of material and partly because Admiral Campioni was unwilling to hamper the movements of ships in and out of harbour by hedging them closely round with heavy, unwieldy lines of nets, particularly as, assuming that Cunningham was on his way back to Alexandria, he was intending to take his fleet to sea the following morning to bombard the forward base at Suda Bay.

At 2035 on 11 November, Kenneth Williamson led the first wave of Swordfish off the *Illustrious* deck. An hour later the second wave was airborne.

There is no space in a book of this nature and scope for details of the individual exploits and experiences of the various aircrews as, for the wild, brief minutes of their attacks, they dipped and weaved through an apparently impenetrable storm of tracer shells and bullets.* It will suffice to say that, as the last Swordfish droned away and the gunfire ceased, Italy's serviceable battleships had been reduced to two, the *Vittorio Veneto* and the *Cesare*. Of the remainder, the *Littorio* had suffered three torpedo hits, the *Duilio* one—to be out of action for five and six months respectively—the *Cavour* had been beached after being hit by a torpedo in a vital spot and was never again to be sea-worthy.†

The gallant leader of the attack, Kenneth Williamson, had been shot down and he and his observer taken prisoner. The crew of another plane destroyed were killed. By 0250 on the 12th all the remainder, some of their planes shot up and riddled with holes, had landed safely on board their ship.

The scene in Taranto harbour which greeted the eye at dawn on 12 November 1940 marked, for those who had eyes to see, the end of the battleship era in naval warfare. For five months two opposing battle-fleets had faced each other in the restricted waters of the Mediterranean, one unwilling to risk action though superior in strength, the other unable to force one. Neither had been able to wield sea power over the other in the fullest sense. The Italians had been unable to prevent supplies being sent to Malta by sea. The British had been unable to cut the Italian supply line to North Africa.

The relative strength of the two battle-fleets had now been reversed in favour of the British. Only two battleships remained available to the Italians against five in Cunningham's fleet. In his autobiography, Andrew Cunningham has said that: 'The crippling of half the Italian battle-fleet at a blow at Taranto had a profound effect on the naval strategical situation

*The attention of readers wishing to read of these is directed to a splendid account in *Taranto* by Don Newton and A. Cecil Hampshire.
†The *Andrea Doria*, which was undamaged, was not at this time ready for service.

in the Mediterranean.' This judgment is open to doubt. Certainly the dramatic success was a savage blow to Italian morale and confidence and a welcome boost to that of the British, at home as well as in the Mediterranean. It also removed for Cunningham the risk, previously accepted, of having to accept action with a greatly superior fleet. Furthermore, he could now dispense with his two older battleships *Malaya* and *Ramillies*, which in turn brought some relief to his overworked destroyer screen.

Basically, however, the naval situation in the Mediterranean remained virtually unchanged because battleships were no longer the linchpin of sea power. Each side lacked in some degree the element upon which control of the sea had come to depend—naval air strength, offensive and defensive.

The Italian Navy, forced to rely entirely upon an Independent Air Force, poorly trained and wrongly equipped for war over the sea, had, even prior to Taranto, been neutralized by the handful of aircraft carried by the *Illustrious* in the eastern half and by the *Ark Royal* of Force 'H' in the western half of the Mediterranean. The few, low-performance fighters in these two ships had been sufficient to take much of the sting out of the efforts of the Italian bombers; while the threat posed by the British naval torpedo planes had more than compensated for the Italian superiority in capital ships.

The British, on the other hand, though for the time being they could operate at will in the central basin and so run reinforcements safely through to Malta, could not take full advantage of it owing to an inability of the Royal Air Force to provide shore-based fighters and 'strike' aircraft—torpedo carriers or dive-bombers—upon which, based on Malta, the real control of the Central Mediterranean now depended. Thus were the British paying not only for their obstinate parsimony towards defence requirements in the years between the wars, but for the mistaken policy that placed responsibility for naval air requirements in the hands of an independent air force which inevitably gave priority to its independent rather than ancillary functions. For a maritime empire relying absolutely on sea power, it was disastrous.

For the time being, with the land campaign in North Africa hanging fire (though soon to swing temporarily in favour of the British), the inability of either side to control the central basin left each free to run their logistic convoys unmolested. The Italians were able to supply their armies in North Africa; on the other hand British supplies to Greece and Crete were being safely convoyed by Cunningham's forces and Crete was being put into a reasonable state of defence.

As for Malta, a convoy of two large fast merchant ships loaded with motor transport and stores for the island, together with a third ship destined for Alexandria, had assembled at Gibraltar. A further 1,400

30 Vice-Admiral Sir James Somerville of Force 'H'

31 Admiral Sir Andrew Cunningham, C-in-C Mediterranean

OPPOSING COMMANDERS IN THE MEDITERRANEAN

32 Admiral Angelo Iachino

33 Admiral Inigo Campioni

34 Italian battleship *Littorio*

35 Swordfish torpedo plane— the famous 'Stringbag'

36 Italian battleship *Duilio* crippled in air attack at Taranto

troops for the garrison were embarked in the cruisers *Manchester* and *Southampton*. Under cover of Admiral Somerville's Force 'H'—*Renown*, *Ark Royal*, the cruisers *Sheffield* and *Despatch* and five destroyers —they sailed eastwards on the evening of 25 November. At the same time the Mediterranean Fleet left Alexandria with a convoy of four more supply ships for Malta. On reaching the central basin, the *Ramillies* and the *Berwick* were to part company and carry on through the Sicilian Narrows to join Somerville.

It was now the turn of Somerville to try his hand at bringing an unwilling enemy to action. Both British moves were, as usual, known almost at once to the Italians. The Italian fleet, its battleship strength now reduced to the *Vittorio Veneto* and the *Cesare*, had been withdrawn to Naples since the disaster at Taranto. Force 'H' was thus the more convenient of the two possible objectives open to it. The High Command ordered Campioni to sail so as to be to the southward of Sardinia by the morning of the 27th. He had with him, besides the two battleships, six heavy cruisers and 14 destroyers. His orders were to seek battle only if he found himself faced by a decisively inferior force.

At about 1040 on the 27th it seemed that that moment had come when a scouting plane from the cruiser *Bolzano* reported a force of one battleship, two cruisers and four destroyers off Bone. Signalling for full speed, Campioni turned south-eastwards on a course to intercept. 'I had in mind that the English forces were inferior to the Italian', he reported later. 'Furthermore, an encounter would be brought about in waters closer to Sicily than Sardinia, that is, in conditions favourable to us.'

Meanwhile, from the Sicilian Narrows, the *Ramillies* and *Berwick* were coming west at the former's best speed of 20 knots to join Somerville who had at 1015 learnt of the presence of the Italian fleet. Sending his convoy away to the south-east, Somerville pushed ahead to make rendezvous with the *Ramillies* and *Berwick* and to interpose himself between the enemy and the convoy. The *Ark Royal* was ordered to prepare to launch a striking force of torpedo planes. When it became clear that the rendezvous would be made in time to engage the enemy with his whole force, Somerville was able to assess the relative strength of the two fleets. Reports from his scouting aircraft indicated that the enemy had either two or three battleships and at least six cruisers against his one modernized battle-cruiser, *Renown*, one old, slow and outranged battle-ship, *Ramillies*, and five cruisers, two of which were cluttered with their military passengers and only one of which had 8-inch guns. Furthermore, the impending action would be fought well inside the range of the Italian bomber forces based on Sardinia and Sicily.

This put the odds at first sight somewhat in favour of the enemy should he choose to stand and fight, as it would be difficult for the *Ramillies* to get into action effectively. But Somerville had in addition the uncertain asset of the *Ark Royal's* torpedo striking force. Unfortunately, many of

E

the pilots had only recently joined the ship. They lacked training and practice; and it must be remembered that at this stage of the war carrier striking forces, thrown in, as they were, in small numbers, had as yet failed to justify themselves in action against squadrons of warships at sea.

By now Campioni also had received more accurate information about his opponent's strength which, as far as could be judged from a number of conflicting reports, contained two or three battleships and an aircraft carrier. His appeals for intervention by the Air Force had as yet produced neither fighter defence nor bombers. The two admirals acted in accordance with the 'form' to be expected of them. Somerville decided that, 'Whatever the composition of the enemy force, it was clear to me that in order to achieve my object—the safe and timely arrival of the convoy at its destination—it was essential to show a bold front and attack the enemy as soon as possible'. Campioni, with Italy's only two serviceable battleships under his flag and hedged round by the high command's strict instructions, declined to take up the challenge. He signalled to his fleet to turn away for Naples. Though the opposing cruisers had by this time come within extreme range of each other, and the *Berwick* was damaged in the ensuing exchange of gunfire, the faster Italian ships soon drew out of range.

Somerville's only hope of catching the enemy now lay with the Fleet Air Arm's torpedo planes—a situation which was to be repeated many times during the war. Eleven Swordfish attacked but none was successful. The Italians, their superior speed unimpaired, drew steadily away to the north-eastward and under cover of their own Air Force which now arrived belatedly on the scene. The Italian airmen attacked with their customary accuracy, the *Ark Royal* at times being completely obscured in the midst of a forest of tall splashes from bursting bombs, only to emerge unharmed, her guns blazing furiously back at her attackers.

Nevertheless it was undoubtedly air power which had decided the course of events, the presence of the *Ark Royal* weighing most heavily on Campioni's mind as he made his decision to retire. The capital ships on either side again failed to come within range of each others' guns. Meanwhile, the convoys for Malta had been left undisturbed to reach harbour safely with their precious cargoes.

That the Italian Air Force was finding itself stretched beyond the limits of its resources as a result of Mussolini's ill-judged attack on Greece, was evident from the fact that for the first time Cunningham's fleet completed its cruise in the Central Mediterranean without a single gun being fired by any of his ships. For the time being the Italian ability to dispute control of the east-west route through the Mediterranean had vanished. On land, the Italian Army under Marshal Graziani was defeated by General

Wavell's Army of the Nile in a three-day battle occupying 9-11 December and expelled from Egypt with the loss of 38,300 prisoners.

British plans to take advantage of the new situation to run supply convoys through from Gibraltar to Malta and Greece, and from Alexandria to Malta, were at once put in hand. Already, however, movements were in train on the other side by which air power was to reverse the situation. The deteriorating situation in the Mediterranean was causing Hitler to cast a critical eye on his partner's efforts and to consider means of going to his assistance. His own failure to eliminate Britain by invasion was in any case leading him to turn his attention to the Mediterranean as an alternative theatre in which to strike at the British.

As yet Hitler had no intention of sending German troops to Africa. His aid to his ally was to be confined to air forces to strike at the British fleet and to neutralize Malta. Arrangements were pushed ahead, however, for the deployment on Sicilian airfields of Fliegerkorps X from Norway. This independent unit which included long-range bombers, dive-bombers, fighters and reconnaissance machines, in all some 450 aircraft, with its own defensive flak, transport, signals, bombs and fuel, had been specially trained and equipped for attacking ships. By mid-December it was on the move southwards through Italy. Early in January 1941 it was already established in some strength—some 300 aircraft of all types—under the command of General der Flieger Geister, spread between the airfields of Catania, Comiso, Trapani, Palermo and Reggio Calabria. It was to advertise its arrival in dramatic fashion.

Since mid-December the British Mediterranean Fleet had been able to establish ascendancy in the central basin. The C-in-C had been able to visit Malta in his flagship, the *Warspite*, while the remainder had operated to cover the passage of supply ships, to bombard Valona, the main supply port for the Italian armies fighting Greece and to attack Italian convoys and their terminal port of Tripoli.

On land the prospect seemed equally bright. The Greeks were having widespread successes against the Italian invaders. In North Africa the British Army of the Nile was preparing a further offensive which would drive the Italians out of Cyrenaica. Both on land and sea, however, it was to prove a false dawn. It had long been expected that Germany would feel impelled sooner or later to come south to aid and inspire her less enterprising ally. That Mussolini himself had not been satisfied with the higher direction of his navy was indicated by the dismissal, on 8 December, of Admiral Cavagnari as Chief of Staff. His successor was Admiral Arturo Riccardi who, since the beginning of the war, had held commands ashore and, with no experience of action, was in no position to advocate a more spirited policy for the Italian fleet. At the same time Admiral Campioni was replaced as C-in-C by Admiral Angelo Iachino, an officer of great repute in the Italian Navy who had previously commanded the Italian cruiser force which had acquitted itself well in the inconclusive action with Force 'H' south of Sardinia in November.

However, the situation was not one which could be improved by a change in the structure of the high command. The Italian Navy, not unreasonably, felt itself hamstrung by the inefficiency of the air reconnaissance at its disposal and the ineffectiveness of the striking power of the Air Force. It was very willing to accept the aid of Fliegerkorps X. The Italian Army, outclassed both in Africa and Greece, was equally in need of assistance from the Wehrmacht. Hitler was not yet contemplating a heavy involvement in either theatre; but early in January he was to give orders for the formation of an 'Afrika Korps' primarily equipped for defence, and which was intended to stiffen the Italian defence of Tripolitania. In Greece, the Italian failure was soon to imperil his plan to attack Russia and he would be forced to intervene to secure the flank of his line of advance. Thus, as 1940 came to an end, forces were already on the move which would dim the brighter prospects which seemed to be opening up for the British in the Mediterranean.

A convoy movement (Operation Excess) had meanwhile been planned. On the evening of 6 January 1942, a convoy of three ships with stores for Greece and one with ammunition and 12 crated Hurricanes as well as the crucial cargo of 3,000 tons of seed potatoes for Malta left Gibraltar and on the following day was joined by Force 'H', consisting of the battle-cruiser *Renown*, Admiral Somerville's flagship, the veteran battleship *Malaya*, the carrier *Ark Royal*, the cruisers *Sheffield* and *Bonaventure* and ten destroyers. At about the same time, to cover the passage of two laden supply ships for Malta from Alexandria and two groups of empty transports in the reverse direction, Admiral Cunningham put to sea with his flagship *Warspite*, the *Valiant* and the carrier *Illustrious*, while his cruisers *Gloucester* and *Southampton* transported troop reinforcements to Malta where they arrived on 8 January and sailed three-and-a-half hours later to join Somerville for the crucial day of the convoy's passage through the Sicilian Narrows.

Except for one attack by ten Savoia bombers, however, which achieved nothing and lost two of their numbers to the *Ark Royal*'s Fulmar fighters, that day, the 9th, passed surprisingly quietly; at sunset Force 'H' parted company and turned back for Gibraltar, leaving the *Bonaventure*, Cunningham's two cruisers and five destroyers to escort the convoy through the night and to meet the main body of the Mediterranean Fleet the next morning. The unwonted lack of enemy opposition was to instil a false confidence. Unknown to the British, on the airfields of Sicily, the dive-bombers of Fliegerkorps X had gathered.

Dawn on 10 January found the convoy and its escort still to the westward of Malta. Covering it was Cunningham's main force—*Warspite*, *Valiant*, *Illustrious* and five destroyers. His cruisers, *Gloucester*, *South-ampton* and *Bonaventure*, were escorting the destroyer *Gallant* which had struck a mine and was being towed into Malta by the *Mohawk*. The forenoon passed quietly. It seemed that the operation—the most ambitious and complex convoy operation so far attempted—was achieving complete success. An Italian reconnaissance plane was chopped out of the sky with deadly efficiency by Fulmars from the *Illustrious*. At 1330 two torpedo planes came in low to attack the battleship. Their torpedoes were avoided; but the attempt was nevertheless to have a fateful consequence. From their station high above the fleet the Fulmars on patrol came swooping down in chase of the two Savoias. Hardly had they done so when to the northward against the clear blue of the sky was seen a host of aircraft approaching in their squadrons. These were the Junkers 87s (Stukas), the true dive-bombers which could plummet vertically out of the sky to drop their 1,000-lb bombs with great accuracy and which were now making their début in the Mediterranean theatre. Behind them could be seen further formations of twin-engine Junkers 88s, more strictly 'glide' than 'dive' bombers, but carrying a heavier load of bombs and better able to defend themselves against fighters.

The slow-climbing Fulmars, recalled from their chase, clawed their way upwards to the defence, but neither they nor fresh fighters hastily flown off by the carrier could gain height quickly enough to intervene in good time. The Stukas were the first to attack. They concentrated principally upon the *Illustrious*. Every gun in the fleet opened on them but, as had been learnt earlier in the Norwegian campaign, in the absence of fighter defence only close-range automatic weapons in numbers far greater than those mounted in British warships could offer an effective defence.

To Admiral Cunningham it was a revelation of what efficiently used and properly equipped air power could achieve in sea warfare, as bomb after bomb struck the carrier.

> One was too interested in this new form of dive-bombing attack really to be frightened [he was to write later], and there was no doubt we were watching complete experts. Formed roughly in a large circle over the fleet they peeled off one by one when reaching the attacking position. We could not but admire the skill and precision of it all.

For ten minutes the *Illustrious* steamed through a hail of bombs raising their leaping brown columns of water as they exploded close alongside. Six times she shuddered under the impact of direct hits, some of which penetrated by means of the lift-wells to the hangars and lower deck spaces. Her steering gear was wrecked and, with her flight deck damaged and fires blazing fore and aft, she circled helplessly. But for her armoured flight deck which absorbed the shock of some of the hits, the *Illustrious* must have been sunk. As it was, though hit yet again in a later attack, she was able to limp away to reach Malta dockyard for temporary repairs. On the following day the dive-bombers struck again, this time at the

Gloucester and *Southampton* to the south-eastward of Malta where they had joined the escort of the slow convoy for Alexandria. Both ships were hit. The *Gloucester* was fortunate in that a bomb which plunged down through five decks failed to explode; but the *Southampton* was so heavily damaged that she had to be abandoned and sunk.

Thus, thunderously, the pilots of Fliegerkorps X advertised to the world their arrival on the Mediterranean scene and ushered in a new phase of the campaign. Benefiting from their none too brilliant experiences in the Norwegian campaign and perhaps inspired by the demonstration of what could be done by such properly trained dive-bombers as the Skuas of the Fleet Air Arm, which had sunk the *Königsberg* in a few minutes of dive-bombing, they had undergone special training for ship attack.

The consequences seemed likely to be decisive. The several convoys had, to be sure, reached their destinations unscathed; but the cost in ships of war had been prohibitive. Britain's few aircraft carriers were of incalculable importance to her prosecution of the war at sea. Though the *Illustrious* had reached the shelter of the Grand Harbour, Malta's still puny defences were unlikely to save her from further and probably fatal attacks. Carriers—by now established as the major units of the British fleet—could no longer be risked in the central basin of the Mediterranean. Thus the task of disputing the control of the vital convoy routes supplying the Italian and German forces in Africa would now rest upon Malta, the unsinkable but still poorly equipped carrier.

The Germans were alive to the importance of neutralizing the island, though except for a far-sighted few, of whom Rommel was one, they did not appreciate the absolute necessity to eliminate it permanently. Fliegerkorps X was given the task, but it was not until six days after the *Illustrious* entered the Grand Harbour that they were ready to attack in force. The breathing-space was made good use of to hasten temporary repairs to the carrier. The first massive raid by some 60 dive-bombers on 16 January was concentrated on the dockyard where she lay but she escaped with minor damage from a single bomb hit. On the 18th the attackers turned their attention to Malta's airfields and establishments. The carrier was almost ready to sail by the following day when another raid on the dockyard caused her further underwater damage. Nevertheless, in spite of all the enemy could do, as darkness was settling down over the harbour on the 23rd, the *Illustrious* crept slowly out between the heads of the breakwater unobserved by enemy planes and was soon making 20 knots towards Alexandria on the first leg of the long journey which was to take her to Norfolk, Virginia, for repairs.

Though the *Illustrious* had thus escaped the full consequences of the new turn of events, Malta was to continue to suffer under a succession of massive blows as Stukas and Me.110s streaked in for combined dive-bombing and low-level attacks, while Ju.88s and He.111 and Savoia bombers with fighter escort bombed from on high. It was little enough that the few fighters available on the island could do in reply. At any one time about six Hurricanes comprised the total force of high-performance fighters which could take the air. In addition there might be three of the Fulmars disembarked from the *Illustrious* and perhaps one of the surviving Gladiators. Between these fighters and the gun defences of the island 16 Axis aircraft were accounted for, but it was not enough to deter them. Through January, February and March the raids went on incessantly.

Yet, though the island's defences were almost negligible, its ability to strike back was far from paralysed. The Wellingtons of No 148 Squadron bombed the Sicilian airfields, destroying a number of aircraft and damaging hangars and facilities; while the Swordfish of 830 Squadron, in cooperation with the scouting Sunderlands, had notable successes against Italian convoys bound for Libya even while the air raids were at their height. Nor did the enemy raids prevent the re-establishment of a submarine base on Malta from which, in the months to come, the most deadly menace to the Libyan convoys was to operate. Had Fliegerkorps X been able to continue to throw their full weight of attack on Malta the outcome might have been different. But events elsewhere in the Mediterranean were to intervene and to mask the overriding importance of Malta from the Italian and German strategic viewpoint. They were also to demonstrate the closely woven interdependence of the various sectors of the Mediterranean theatre.

In North Africa the British Army of the Nile had advanced to capture Tobruk on 22 January, and by 6 February the Italian armies had been driven from Cyrenaica. German fears for their ally's ability to defend Tripolitania had already led to Hitler's order to form an Afrika Korps, the transport of which was begun at the beginning of February 1941. As a further stiffening of Italian defence, nearly half of Fliegerkorps X, mostly dive-bombers and fighters, was transferred to North Africa. Consequently, though the supply ships supporting the British Army, and their escorts, began to suffer painful losses, the intensity of the assault on Malta began to fall away just when the situation on the island was becoming critical.

Nevertheless, the situation during March seemed grim and foreboding owing to the air supremacy established by the Luftwaffe. Along the Libyan coast, warships of the Inshore Squadron were being lost or damaged almost daily. The naval C-in-C added his appeals to those of his Air Force colleague for reinforcements of fighter aircraft.

There seems to be some bad misunderstanding about the state of our Air Force out here [he wrote to the First Sea Lord on 11 March]. I feel the Chiefs of Staff are badly misinformed about the number of fighter squadrons available. Longmore is absolutely stretched to the limit and we seem to have far fewer than is supposed at home. We are getting sat on by the Germans in Cyrenaica. The figures there are over two hundred German and Italian fighters against thirty of our own.

[As for Malta], I have just seen the Air Vice Marshal who is here to report. He tells me that the Germans are right on top of them. He has only eight serviceable Hurricanes left. . . . He is being sent six from the shortage here; but that is no good. He ought to have two full squadrons and at once.

On hearing that he had been created a Knight Grand Cross of the Bath, Admiral Cunningham commented bitterly, 'I would sooner have had three squadrons of Hurricanes'. With a massive threat building up in the Balkans and in Libya, the air—and consequently the naval—situation was indeed desperate. Nevertheless, with the arrival on 10 March of the new carrier *Formidable* via the Suez Canal to replace the damaged *Illustrious*, Cunningham succeeded in running a convoy of four supply ships through to Malta without interference by the enemy.

On the other hand, beginning early in February, the Italians had been transporting to Tripoli the German Afrika Korps, an operation with which the British had been unable seriously to interfere. It had become possible during February to establish a few of the new small 'U' Class submarines at Malta, the nucleus of a flotilla which was to gain imperishable fame and to have in time a considerable effect on the campaign. The *Upright*, commanded by Lieutenant E. D. Norman, torpedoed and sank the Italian cruiser *Armando Diaz* on the night of 25 February; but it was not until well into March that the Malta flotilla was able to discover the best means of getting at the Libyan convoys. By that time most of the Afrika Korps, its original defensive structure transformed by the addition of a Panzer division, had reached its destination. The German high command sent one of its few congratulatory messages to the Italian Navy: 'Particularly gratifying is the fact that this operation could be carried out with so few losses, notwithstanding the great difficulties and the dangers of enemy action.' Before the impending storm broke in Libya and in Greece upon the British armies, outnumbered and almost without air support, the Italian Navy was to take a humiliating knock and lose this new found respect of its critical ally.

The Germans had been far from pleased with the efforts of the Italian Navy to interfere with the stream of supply ships and troop transports from Egypt reaching Greece, where their invasion was soon to be launched. As early as 14 February, at a meeting at Merano between Admiral Riccardi and Grand Admiral Raeder, the latter had urged that surface units of the Italian fleet should go over to the offensive by striking at this supply traffic. Riccardi's objections, based on the distances involved and the ability of the British, with their superior air reconnaissance, to evade any such threat, seemed at the time to have been accepted. But early in March the Germans again brought political pressure at the highest levels to spur the Italian Navy into action. From the *Comando Supremo* orders went out to the naval Chief of Staff, Riccardi, and thence to the C in-C, Iachino, that an offensive strike was to be mounted. To meet the Navy's objections, the Luftwaffe promised extensive cooperation by Fliegerkorps X—aerial reconnaissance over Alexandria and the Central and eastern Mediterranean and air cover for the fleet throughout daylight hours as far east as Cape Matapan. To ensure the efficiency of this operation, Fliegerkorps X was to carry out an escort and ship identification exercise for a large number of its aircraft over the Italian fleet on its first morning at sea, south of the Messina Straits. The Italian Air Force promised fighter cover from Rhodes while the fleet was in Cretan waters and air attacks on the airfields on Crete. All this had as its primary object the achievement of surprise on the part of the Italian fleet and assurance against it being itself surprised by the British Mediterranean Fleet. Finally, to calm Italian misgivings, the Luftwaffe claimed that their torpedo planes had crippled two of Cunningham's battleships on 16 March—a claim with no foundation in fact.

Fortified by these assurances, though far from convinced of their reliability or of the practical value of an operation which would make a heavy drain on Italy's diminishing stocks of oil fuel, Admiral Angelo Iachino sailed from Naples on the evening of 26 March, his flag flying in the *Vittorio Veneto*. At dawn the next day he passed through the Straits of Messina in company with the four destroyers of his screen and preceded by the 3rd Division of heavy cruisers—*Trieste, Trento, Bolzano* —and destroyers. From Taranto the 1st Division—*Zara, Pola* and *Fiume*—and from Brindisi the 8th Division—light cruisers *Abruzzi* and *Garibaldi*—had sailed with their attendant destroyers for a rendezvous with the C-in-C about 60 miles east of Augusta. The fleet then proceeded in company on a course which would take it to the vicinity of Gavdo Island to the southward of Crete.

Iachino's doubt of the efficiency of the air cooperation promised him were strengthened by the failure of any of Fliegerkorps X to appear for the exercise planned for the morning of the 27th, or to prevent a British Sunderland on reconnaissance from reporting him. Though from its report, which the Italians were able to decode, it was evident that only one division of cruisers had actually been sighted in the low visibility prevailing, Iachino knew from that moment that any prospect of achieving surprise had gone.

The flying-boat's report was correctly interpreted at Alexandria. The increased aerial reconnaissance activity by the enemy over the last few days had already suggested that some activity by the Italian fleet might be expected. Under cover of darkness that evening the Mediterranean Fleet slipped away to sea—*Warspite, Barham, Valiant, Formidable* and attendant destroyers—and steered to place itself between the enemy force and the convoy route to Greece, a course which would lead to roughly the same position south of Gavdo Island as that planned for the *Vittorio Veneto*. Vice-Admiral Pridham-Wippell, who, in *Orion*, with the *Ajax*, *Perth* and *Gloucester* and four destroyers, had been operating in the Aegean, was also given a rendezvous for dawn on the 28th to the south-west of Gavdo.

Thus, through the night of 27-28 March, the two fleets were hurrying towards a head-on clash the following morning, an encounter which was to develop into the Battle of Matapan. Full details of this action can be found in the book with that title by Captain S. W. C. Pack and need not be repeated here. It is sufficient to say that Admiral Iachino was justified in his mistrust of the air cooperation promised him, which left him unprotected against the air attacks mounted by the Royal Air Force bombers and the torpedo planes of the *Formidable*, and ignorant for much of the day of the position and composition of the forces opposing him. This mistrust led him, however, into a fatal error of judgment. Given the choice of believing either the information provided, late in the day, by a reconnaissance plane which made it clear that Cunningham's battle squadron was in close pursuit, or an estimate of Cunningham's position based on radio direction finding which placed him some 170 miles astern, he chose the latter. To the assistance of the cruiser *Pola*, hit and immobilized by a torpedo from one of the *Formidable*'s Swordfish and left behind as the remainder ran for base, he sent the cruisers *Zara* and *Fiume* and four destroyers. Running blindly athwart the course of the British battle-fleet during the night, both cruisers and two of the destroyers were blown out of the water. The *Pola* was then sunk at leisure. The *Vittorio Veneto*, also torpedoed by the Fleet Air Arm, and for a time in danger of being overtaken by the British battleships, escaped.

Once again an encounter between the two fleets had been dominated by the air element, the battleships on either side never coming within range of each others' guns. On this occasion the failure of the German and Italian Air Forces to fulfil their obligations to support the Italian fleet had permitted the handful of aircraft, RAF and Fleet Air Arm, firstly to give the British C-in-C the information necessary to bring his unwilling enemy into action, and then to cripple some of his fleeing units, delivering them to destruction by gun-fire. The Italians, in contrast, fighting blindly and without fighter protection, were perhaps lucky to escape greater losses.

Even while the Battle of Matapan was coming to its violent and bloody end, final preparations were being made by the Germans and Italians in Libya and the Balkans for massive assaults which, in the course of a few brief weeks, were drastically to alter the situation in the Mediterranean in their favour. On 31 March the Italo-German army attacked in Libya. By 3 April Benghazi had fallen and the British army was in full retreat. On the 6th the German 12th Army crossed the frontier from Bulgaria into

Greece and began the offensive which was, in less than three weeks, to give them possession of the whole of that country.

The former was to bring down on Admiral Cunningham's head unjustified exhortations, from a government not far from panic, to stop the Italian convoys carrying supplies to the German Afrika Korps. The latter was soon to involve the Mediterranean Fleet in hazardous and costly operations firstly to evacuate the Army from Greece and then to repel the enemy's efforts to invade Crete by sea, and finally to bring away the soldiers from Crete when it was captured by airborne invasion.

Cunningham always pointed out to the government that the interruption of the Libyan convoys was dependent upon the use of Malta as an air and sea base. Early in March the heavy losses on the ground amongst the Wellingtons of No 148 Squadron had necessitated the temporary withdrawal of the squadron to Egypt, leaving the handful of Swordfish as the only offensive air strength available. His appeals and those of his air colleague. Air Chief Marshal Longmore, for fighter reinforcements, had received scant satisfaction. A beginning was now made in building up the island's air defences by the despatch of a dozen Hurricanes to Gibraltar in the *Argus*. There they were transferred to the *Ark Royal* which, under cover of Force 'H', flew them off to Malta from a position south of Sardinia on 3 April. Though a further 23 Hurricanes were later sent by the same means on 27 April and 47 more on 21 May, for the time being Malta could do little to defend itself against the assaults of Fliegerkorps X, let alone strike at the Italian convoys in any strength.

In spite of the insecurity of the base, however, Cunningham, on 11 April, sent four destroyers of the 14th Flotilla—*Jervis, Janus, Mohawk* and *Nubian*—under Captain Philip Mack of the *Jervis*, to act as a raiding force. In an area so dominated by enemy air power, it could only operate by night. Lacking radar, interception of convoys reported by air reconnaissance was a chancy business. Nevertheless they were quickly successful.

A convoy of five transports escorted by three Italian destroyers had been located following the route along the Tunisian coast to Tripoli. As dusk was falling on 15 April, Mack led his force to sea and steered to intercept it off the Kerkenah Banks, some 30 miles to seaward of Sfax. By 0145 the flotilla had reached the estimated point of interception, and, in fact, was passing the enemy on an opposite course, all unawares, at a range of three miles. A quarter moon hung in a clear sky to the south-eastward, against which they should have been sighted by the Italian look-outs as they approached. Instead it was the British who were to enjoy the advantage of surprise when at 0158 having turned back, they saw the convoy silhouetted against the moonlight, six miles ahead.

Steering so as to keep the enemy between him and the moon, Mack brought his ships up from astern and on a parallel course to that of his unsuspecting prey. At 0220 the guns of the *Jervis* flashed out at the nearest Italian destroyer. This was the *Lampo*, where the startled captain had barely time to call for full speed and fire three salvoes from his guns before they were put out of action and his ship brought to a standstill. His torpedoes were launched but went wide.

The next escort to be engaged was the *Baleno*. The first salvo from the *Nubian* hit squarely on her bridge, wiping out at one blow the Italian captain and all his officers. Hammered to a wreck, the *Baleno* drifted helplessly out of the fight.

While the British destroyers were now turning their attention to the transports (one of which, the Italian ship *Sabaudia*, loaded with ammunition, blew up in a spectacular explosion), the escort commander, Commander Pietro de Cristoforo, in the destroyer *Tarigo*, turned back from his position ahead of the convoy and gallantly threw himself between the attackers and their prey. Mortally wounded by the first salvo aimed at his ship, his steering gear wrecked, a storm of shells tearing his ship apart, Cristoforo retained sufficient control of his ship, in its last moments before sinking, to launch three torpedoes at the *Mohawk*. Two of them found their mark, sinking the British destroyer, in which two officers and 39 ratings lost their lives.

These were the only British casualties. The remaining four transports, all German and loaded with troops and supplies for Rommel, were sunk as were the *Baleno* and *Tarigo*. The *Lampo* drifted on to the Kerkenah Bank and was eventually saved by the Italians. The 350 men, 300 vehicles and 3,500 tons of stores destroyed in the merchant ships represented the most serious loss suffered by the Afrika Korps during its initial transport to Libya. Except for one ship torpedoed and sunk by Swordfish of 830 Squadron, the only other losses inflicted on the Libyan traffic from the beginning of January to the end of April 1941 were the work of British submarines which sank ten ships totalling 27,168 tons during that period.

In time to come, as Malta's air strength was re-established, aircraft were to assume great importance in the struggle to cut Rommel's lifeline, and, though the submarines based on Malta were to have the greatest and most consistent successes, it is not too much to say that between them these two arms were to have a decisive influence on the battle for the Mediterranean. Details of their operations will be examined later.

Meanwhile, so far as the existing striking power of Malta-based forces allowed, everything possible was being done. The government at home, however, suffering the consequences of their failure to equip Malta in good time, were now so alarmed at the deteriorating situation in Libya and Greece, that they were demanding 'drastic measures to stabilize the position in the Middle East'. Suggestions were made that Cunningham should attempt a combined blocking and bombardment of the port of Tripoli, using the battleship *Barham* and a cruiser for block-ships. Examination of the proposal showed it to be completely impracticable.

Against his own judgment, and protesting that the elimination of Tripoli's port facilities was a task for air power, as he felt he knew well from the experiences at Greek ports under aerial bombardment by the Luftwaffe, Cunningham agreed to carry out instead a bombardment of Tripoli. Achieving complete surprise and coordination with air attack by Malta's Swordfish and Wellingtons, his fleet wreaked heavy damage on the city and withdrew without any interference by the enemy's air force based on the nearby airfield of Castel Benito.

Nevertheless the port itself suffered little and efforts by the government to induce Cunningham to repeat an operation which, in his opinion, was not worth the very heavy risks involved, petered out, overtaken by events elsewhere which absorbed all the fleet's resources. For on the same day as the bombardment the decision was taken by the government that British forces in Greece must be evacuated. An ordeal thus began which, with a brief interval, continued for soldiers and sailors alike, as they fought under a sky dominated by more than 500 aircraft of Fliegerkorps X and VIII, until 1 June when the last men were evacuated from Crete.

7 *Malta holds the Key*

Of the several periods of the Second World War during which Britain's hopes of avoiding defeat seemed to have sunk almost to vanishing point, few can have been more fraught with doom than the spring and early summer of 1941. In North Africa, General Wavell's Army of the Nile, its numbers and its exiguous air strength both greatly reduced by the despatch of assistance to Greece, had been unable to withstand the counter-attack of the enemy, now revitalized by General Erwin Rommel and his Afrika Korps. Cyrenaica, with the exception of Tobruk, was once again in enemy hands.

In Greece the British aid sent at such sacrifice had been insufficient to prevent the German 12th Army, covered by the overwhelming air superiority of Fliegerkorps VIII and part of Fliegerkorps X, from over-running the whole country in less than three weeks. By 21 April it was clear that the troops so arduously transported there would have to be evacuated. That it would have to be done by night and under conditions of daunting difficulty was stressed when, on the 21st and 22nd, the enemy's unopposed Air Force destroyed 23 ships, including a Greek destroyer and two hospital ships in Greek waters.

The general plan for Operation 'Demon', as it was named, was for the troops to make a fighting retreat to a number of beaches which could be reached by reasonably good roads. There, as soon as it was dark, the rescue ships would arrive, while a swarm of caiques, motor-boats and local craft would ferry the men off to them. These few sentences cover a complexity of organization, a degree of inspired improvisation in a constantly changing situation and an infinite variety of unpredictable events such as to require a book devoted entirely to the operation to give a full, detailed account.

Fifty-one thousand troops had to make their way under ceaseless attack by the Stukas to the various beaches allotted to them—Megara, Raphina and Raphtis near Athens, Nauplia, Tolon, Monemvasia and

Kalamata in Morea. From his headquarters at Suda Bay, Vice-Admiral Pridham-Wippell directed the movements of a great assortment of ships and craft. Of warships there were four cruisers—his flagship, *Orion*, the *Ajax*, *Phoebe*, and HM AS *Perth*; three anti-aircraft cruisers, *Calcutta*, *Coventry* and *Carlisle*; 20 destroyers; three frigates; and the infantry assault ships *Glenearn* and *Glengyle*. Under the Red Ensign were 19 medium-sized troop ships. Every available small craft was also sent to the beaches, including a number of 'A' lighters, forerunners of the LCTs.

By 24 April the various columns of troops had reached their allotted beaches. Exhausted, hungry and harried as they were, their morale remained high and Rear-Admiral Baillie Grohman, the naval liaison officer, later recorded that 'the Army organization in rear of the beaches and the discipline of the troops were magnificent; especially considering that they had been fighting a rearguard action for some weeks, from Salonika almost to Cape Matapan'.

That night the darkened ships crept shoreward to anchor as close in as possible, and soon the first small craft, loaded to the gunwales with troops, were bumping alongside.

So began the first of three major operations in which almost the entire British Mediterranean Fleet was engaged, succouring and supporting the Army in its struggle against impossible odds. During this phase, the bomber squadrons of the Luftwaffe had not yet had time to move their bases forward. Losses amongst the warships which could get well away from the coast were consequently comparatively light. Four troopships, however, were sunk, *Pennland*, *Slamat*, *Costa Rica* and *Ulster Prince*. At one or two of the embarkation points there were wharves and jetties at which the small craft could load or the smaller ships—destroyers and troop carriers—could themselves secure. But in general it was from open beaches that the evacuation took place, a process painfully slow. Each night at 0300 embarkation was halted and the ships hastened seawards to be away before the Luftwaffe's dive-bombers found them.

The fate awaiting any ship which lingered beyond this hour rather than abandon troops on the shore was shown in the case of the *Slamat* which did not clear from Nauplia until 0415 on the morning of the 27th. Soon after daylight the Stukas found her and quickly sent her to the bottom. The destroyers *Diamond* and *Wryneck* were sent to her aid and picked up 700 men, being dive-bombed all the while. Rescue operations completed, they steered at high speed for Suda Bay only to be set upon once again by dive-bombers who this time made no mistake, sending both ships to the bottom with the loss of all on board except one officer, 41 ratings and eight soldiers.

Nevertheless this was the only serious loss amongst the 50,732 troops embarked from Greece, about 80 per cent of the total originally sent to that country. The majority were transported back to Egypt, but 16,000 were left to form the garrison for Crete which, it was decided, must be held at all costs.

Before this phase of the campaign began there was a pause during which Cunningham might have expected a brief respite for his hard-driven cruisers and destroyers and rest for their crews. Bombed almost continuously during daylight hours whenever they had put to sea since the operation to reinforce Greece had begun on 5 March, the ships and their machinery were accumulating damage and defects. That officers and men were also showing signs of strain is not surprising. There was to be no respite, however, and little rest. Once again the situation in the campaign on land called for urgent, large-scale efforts by the Navy to rectify it. On 20 April General Wavell had reported to the Chiefs of Staff that a German Panzer division had been identified in North Africa. Tank reinforcements to enable him to cope with this large access of strength to the enemy were urgently required. The Prime Minister, declaring that 'the fate of the war in the Middle East, the loss of the Suez Canal, the frustration or confusion of the enormous forces we have built up in Egypt . . . all may turn on a few hundred armoured vehicles', brushed aside the Admiralty's previously expressed reluctance, since the arrival of the Luftwaffe in Sicily, to run convoys through the Central Mediterranean.

Even before the evacuation of Greece had been completed, a convoy of five transports carrying tanks for the Army of the Nile had sailed from England. It was to be run through the Mediterranean under cover, as usual, of Force 'H' as far as the Sicilian Narrows and of the Mediterranean Fleet from the Malta Channel onwards. At the same time Admiral Cunningham would seize the opportunity to throw supplies into beleaguered Malta by means of two convoys—a slow one of two tankers with oil fuel and a fast one of four supply ships. In addition there would be the special supply ship HMS *Breconshire* with oil fuel and munitions, which had already begun her long career of hazardous voyages to relieve Malta and where she was eventually to meet her heroic end. With Force 'H', too, were to come reinforcements for the Mediterranean Fleet in the shape of the battleship *Queen Elizabeth* and the cruisers *Naiad* and *Fiji*.

The operation, given the code-name 'Tiger', which had seemed to the Admiralty a hazardous gamble, went off with a smoothness exceeding all expectations. This was, no doubt, largely owing to the fact that the formidable Fliegerkorps X was at this time being transferred to take part in the impending German attack on Crete. It was further aided by the thick and cloudy weather encountered in the Central Mediterranean at a season when it was unprecedented. One ship of the 'Tiger' convoy, the transport *Empire Song*, was mined and sunk in the shallow, narrow Skerki Channel; another, the *New Zealand Star*, was only slightly damaged by another mine. Except for these two ships, there were no casualties; while, for good measure, the cruiser *Ajax* and three destroyers detached from the Mediterranean Fleet, bombarded Benghazi during the night of 7-8 May and sent two laden ammunition ships encountered in the offing, to the bottom. On the 12th, 238 tanks and 43 crated Hurricanes were unloaded in Alexandria harbour.

Fortune had indeed favoured the bold.

At home there was a tendency by the authorities to overlook this fact and to play down the hazards of operating within range of Luftwaffe bases. Neither Cunningham nor Somerville had any such illusions. As the former commented in his memoirs, 'Before long the dismal truth was painfully to be brought home to them'. It was to be indeed—in the waters surrounding Crete.

The capture of Crete was, from the strategic point of view, the logical sequel to the sweeping successes of the German Army in Greece. Such a prospect was clear enough to the German high command. A joint determination by the three armed services to achieve it in conjunction, which might have been expected to emerge, was, however, hindered partly by the division of strategic responsibilities between the two Axis partners and partly by the lack of cooperation between the services themselves, particularly between the Luftwaffe and the Kriegsmarine.

The German Navy fully appreciated the strategic importance of Crete in the struggle for control of the Mediterranean; but the arrangements between the Axis partners left naval matters in that theatre an Italian responsibility. In time to come the German Navy was to intervene, sending U-boats and light forces to the Mediterranean. At this stage the German Naval Staff confined itself to urging the Italian Navy into greater activity, but without notable success. The Luftwaffe, on the other hand, had been committed for the last five months to the major role in the campaign in the Mediterranean. The possession of Crete was of immense direct importance to it, both as a link in the most convenient air route to Cyrenaica and as a base from which to dominate the eastern Mediterranean, including Egypt.

It was natural, therefore, that the proposal to capture Crete, which was put to Hitler in the middle of April, should come from the Luftwaffe. The suggestion, however, was not for a combined operation by all three services, with the Navy transporting the assault forces under the umbrella of the overwhelming air power available, but for an airborne assault for which the Luftwaffe would be solely responsible. Only such heavy items as tanks, guns and reserve ammunition would go by sea, under escort of Italian warships.

The author of the scheme was General Kurt Student, at that time commanding Fliegerkorps XI (parachute and airborne troops) stationed in central Germany. On condition that the operation would be quickly accomplished and the troops released in time for the impending attack on Russia, Hitler gave his approval, without consulting either the Navy or the Army General Staff. Air support would be provided by Fliegerkorps

VIII—228 bombers, 205 dive-bombers 114 twin-engined and 119 single-engined fighters and 50 reconnaissance aircraft, a total of 716—as well as certain units of Fliegerkorps X, which were transferred from Sicily to Greece for the purpose. With such massive air strength, a combined operation on conventional lines would have been a more certain and less hazardous method of assault; but the Luftwaffe and its ambitious chief, Marshal Göring, had no wish to share the laurels with the sister services. The consequences were to be costly and to come within an ace of calamity.

With tremendous energy airfields in Greece and the Aegean islands were prepared to receive this huge force; the complex organization to overcome congestion on the airfields and to distribute the necessary fuel was set in motion. By 16 May the assembly was complete, including the 500 transport aircraft and 72 gliders of Fliegerkorps XI. In overall command of all Luftwaffe forces taking part was General Löhr, commanding Luftflotte 4. The date for the assault was fixed for the 20th.

The decision of the British government that Crete should be held must be accounted a notable example of the still prevalent lack of understanding of what could or could not be done in the face of an absolute enemy air superiority. General Maitland Wilson, while in Crete after evacuation from Greece, was asked by General Wavell for his opinion in the matter. He replied that 'unless all three Services are prepared to face the strain of maintaining adequate forces up to strength, the holding of the island is a dangerous commitment'. 'Adequate' air forces simply did not exist. It may be that the paper strength of three RAF and one Fleet Air Arm fighter squadrons on the airfields of Heraklion and Maleme deceived the authorities at home. In fact the survivors of these squadrons had been reduced before the end of April to half a dozen Hurricanes and a dozen obsolete Gladiators, their numbers diminishing as their pilots went aloft to fight against fantastic odds—especially after 14 May when the Germans began 'softening-up' attacks in preparation for the airborne assault. By 19 May they had been reduced to four Hurricanes and three Gladiators. With the concurrence of General Freyberg to whom had been entrusted the command in Crete, they were then sent away to Egypt. Thus, when the assault began at dawn on the 20th, the defenders were totally without fighter defence.

Nevertheless General Freyberg, though he had made no bones about expressing his opinion that to hold Crete his strength, particularly in the air, was inadequate, had also told the Prime Minister that he was not anxious about an airborne attack alone, an estimate which was to err only by a narrow margin. If, however, it were to be combined with a seaborne landing, he had no illusions about the difficulties which would face him.

Thus it appeared that the key to the defence of Crete was the prevention of seaborne landings. Implicit in the government's decision to hold the island was a belief in the ability of the fleet to operate without air support in waters dominated by an enemy air force of more than 500 bombers and dive-bombers. Cunningham knew better; his appeals for reinforcements of aircraft had gone unanswered; his only carrier, the *Formidable*, could not participate until her fighter strength, at this time reduced to four Fulmars, had been built up; but his duty was clear. On 20 May, when the assault on Crete opened, his cruisers and destroyers had for some days been committed, sweeping the sea approaches to Crete from the Aegean by night and withdrawing at daylight to the south of Crete when it was known that no enemy forces were at sea.

That morning, at 0600, the assault on Crete began with two hours of savage bombing of the area round Maleme airfield and Canea. Then at 0800, through the drifting clouds of smoke and dust, gliders were seen dropping down to land. Overhead the sky was full of German aircraft—bombers and fighters—ready to swoop on any British troops who left cover and exposed themselves. General Student's airborne troops nevertheless met an opposition far stiffer than anything expected. At the end of the first day's fighting, in which heavy casualties were suffered by both sides, Maleme airfield, which had been expected to fall quickly to a converging attack, remained a no-man's-land. The troops landed near Canea had made no progress whatever.

The airfields at Heraklion and Retimo were the German objectives for the afternoon of the first day; but here, too, the attacks were firmly held. The paratroopers suffered heavily and, in fact, Heraklion was not captured until it was abandoned on the night of 28 May as part of the general evacuation from Crete, while at Retimo two battalions of Australians under Colonel I. R. Campbell, cut off and isolated, resisted until the 30th, surrendering only when their food and ammunition were exhausted.

By noon on the second day, when no attempt had been made by the Germans to land the heavy equipment, artillery and tanks, which must come by sea, it seemed that Freyberg's belief in his ability to defeat a purely airborne assault was being justified. The Germans had thrown in their last available parachute troops and were being firmly held. So desperate was their situation and so slender seemed their hopes of success that General Student, held at Luftwaffe headquarters by General Löhr, suspected that this was to ensure his survival to answer to a Court of Inquiry. Possession of the disputed landing ground at Maleme, on which Student's Ju.52 transport planes, bringing reinforcements comprising the 5th Mountain Division, could alight, was the key to the situation. Two battalions of New Zealand infantry, with the aid of which the airfield could have been recaptured during the forenoon, were available in reserve near Canea. Had they been boldly thrown into the battle without delay,

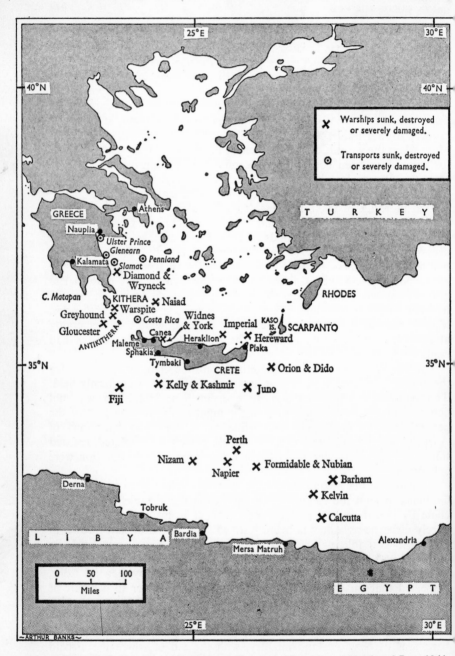

Legend:
- ✗ Warships sunk, destroyed or severely damaged.
- ⊙ Transports sunk, destroyed or severely damaged.

40°N · 25°E · 30°E · 40°N

T U R K E Y

GREECE

Athens

Nauplia ⊙ *Ulster Prince*

⊙ *Glenearn*

Kalamata ⊙ *Pennland*

⊙ *Slamat*

Diamond & Wryneck

C. Matapan

KITHERA ✗ *Naiad*

Greyhound ✗ *Warspite*

⊙ *Costa Rica*

Widnes & York

Imperial ✗ KASO IS. ✗ SCARPANTO

Gloucester ✗

ANTIKITHERA

Maleme Canea ✗ Heraklion ✗ *Hereward* ✗

Sphakia Plaka

RHODES

Tymbaki ✗ Orion & Dido

CRETE

✗ Kelly & Kashmir ✗ Juno

Fiji ✗

35°N · 35°N

Perth ✗

Nizam ✗ ✗ ✗ Formidable & Nubian

Napier

Derna

✗ Barham

Tobruk ✗ Kelvin

L I B Y A Bardia ✗ Calcutta

Mersa Matruh Alexandria

E G Y P T

0 50 100
Miles

~ARTHUR BANKS~

Naval losses in Evacuation of Greece and Crete, 24–27 April and 20 May–1 June 1941 the outcome of the airborne assault on Crete might have been different. Freyberg, with the knowledge of an impending seaborne attack in mind, decided that these troops could not be moved until relieved by an Australian battalion from Georgiopolis, some 20 miles along the coast to the eastward.

By the time this move had been completed it was too late. During the afternoon, disregarding artillery and mortar fire, Ju.52s landed. The 100th Mountain Regiment which they brought just turned the scales. By 1700 the airfield was firmly in German hands, available for a massive build-up by further airborne troops. The battle for Crete was lost from that moment.

Ironically enough, the seaborne assault, threat of which had played such an important part in these events, was repulsed that night by the Navy, their gunflashes visible to the Maori troops who were waiting to go, too late, into action to retake the airfield by a night attack.

Space cannot be devoted to any account of the further land fighting which continued, with great gallantry and heavy casualties on both sides, until the 27th when victory in the area around Maleme and Suda Bay was conceded to the Germans and the decision taken to evacuate from Crete as many troops as possible. The consequences to the Mediterranean Fleet of the ill-judged decision to try to hold Crete, however, must be recounted.

At dusk on the 20th two cruiser forces had returned to patrol to the northward of Crete, the *Dido*, *Ajax* and *Orion* with three destroyers under Rear-Admiral I. G. Glennie and the *Naiad*, *Perth*, the small anti-aircraft cruisers *Calcutta* and *Carlisle* and four destroyers under Rear Admiral E. L. S. King. During the night no invasion convoys were encountered and at daylight they once again withdrew to the southward of the island. By this time the enemy had evidently decided they could spare bombers from the land fighting, for throughout the day the ships were kept busy beating off attacks. With only their guns to rely upon, they yet succeeded in avoiding serious damage from the German dive-bombers, though the *Ajax* suffered some hurt from near misses. Italian high-level bombers, able to make deliberate practice without interference by fighters, scored an unusual success when a bomb which hit the destroyer *Juno* penetrated to a magazine, sending her to the bottom in two minutes with heavy loss of life.

During the 21st information came in from long-range air reconnaissance of gatherings of small craft, escorted by destroyers, making for Suda Bay from the island of Milos. These were clearly the expeditions to stop which was the fleet's primary duty. Admirals Glennie and King were told that, unless they had been located and dealt with during the night, they were to join forces at daylight and sweep northwards into the Aegean. Glennie's squadron, patrolling to the northward of Suda Bay at midnight, encountered the first convoy of 25 caiques and small steamers escorted by the Italian destroyer-escort *Lupo*. Brushing aside the gallant attempt at defence put up by the little Italian warship, the British cruisers and destroyers attacked the convoy in a mêlée lasting two and a half hours, the confusion of which was only partly resolved by the use of radar. Ten caiques were sunk, their troops killed or thrown into the sea. The remainder, with the damaged *Lupo*, turned back.

At 1530 Glennie called off his scattered pack and ordered them to rendezvous with him to the westward of Crete. His cruisers had expended much of their anti-aircraft ammunition during the previous day—his flagship, the *Dido*, as much as 70 per cent. He decided that under those conditions it would be folly to linger during daylight, a target for the full fury of the German dive-bombers.

Admiral King in the meantime had been patrolling during the night off Heraklion. Having encountered no enemy, at daylight he turned north-wards to search, in accordance with his orders. That air attack, heavy and continuous, would come was certain and at 0700 it started. Nevertheless, the squadron pressed on, fighting off the bombers with their guns and successfully avoiding the bombs by violent manoeuvres. The first signs of the prey they sought came at 0830, when the *Perth* fell in with a caique full of German troops and sank it. Then a small steamer was dealt with by the destroyers. It was not until 10 o'clock, however, that the escort of the second of the two convoys carrying reinforcements to the Germans in Crete was sighted. The convoy itself, carrying 4,000 troops to be landed at Heraklion, had already been recalled by orders of the German Admiral Schuster, commanding in the area, as a result of Glennie's action. Its escort, the destroyer-escort *Sagittario*, was rounding up stragglers when the British squadron hove in sight. She promptly laid a smoke screen and retired, but the destroyer *Kingston*, chasing after the *Sagittario*, came in sight of a large number of caiques.

A catastrophe of some magnitude might now have developed for the Germans. But at this moment Admiral King, his anti-aircraft ammunition running low after three hours of almost continuous attack and his speed limited to that of the *Carlisle* (20 knots), decided that to continue farther north, ever closer to the airfields of the Stukas and Ju.88s, was an unjustifiable risk to his whole force. He recalled his destroyers and turned westwards for the Kithera Channel. The convoy had been stopped and all movements of troops by sea cancelled. King's action nevertheless came in for criticism from his C-in-C. Had he gone in chase of the convoy, it is probable that, though the caiques would no doubt have scattered, a great many would have been sunk with a heavy loss of life amongst the troops of the Mountain Division embarked. It would not have had a direct influence upon the struggle for Crete, but the moral effect would have been far-reaching and relations between the Axis partners would hardly have been improved by the Italian Navy's failure to provide protection. What the cost to the Mediterranean Fleet would have been can only be guessed at by consideration of the subsequent events of that day.

Retiring at its best speed to the westward, King's squadron came under continuous air attack in which the *Naiad* was damaged, having two turrets put out of action, compartments flooded and her speed reduced to 16 knots. The *Carlisle* was also hit, Captain T. C. Hampton being amongst those killed. Admiral Rawlings, who, in company with Glennie's cruiser force, had been patrolling some 20-30 miles westward of the Kithera Channel and, as he put it, 'serving a useful purpose by attracting enemy aircraft', now moved in support. At 1330 the two forces were in sight of one another when the *Warspite* was hit by a heavy bomb which wrecked her starboard 4-inch and 6-inch batteries, so reducing her anti-aircraft armament by half.

Admiral King now assumed command of the combined fleet. He had not been able to gather information on the state of the various units when the destroyer *Greyhound*, returning after sinking a caique, was mortally hit by two bombs. Two other destroyers, *Kandahar* and *Kingston*, were sent to rescue her crew. The *Gloucester* and *Fiji* were left to stand by in support while the remainder of the fleet retired to the southwestward. This was a doubly unfortunate move. It again divided the fleet which, while concentrated, could put up a defence sufficient to daunt the dive-bombers; moreover, unknown to King, the two cruisers selected were the lowest in anti-aircraft ammunition, being 82 and 70 per cent short, respectively.

The *Kandahar* and *Kingston*, with devoted gallantry, had picked up the *Greyhound*'s survivors while beating off continuous low-flying bomb and machine-gun attacks when at 1500, orders were received for the four detached ships to withdraw: Admiral King had now been informed of the shortage of ammunition in the cruisers. Followed by a swarm of dive-bombers, they raced westwards to rejoin the fleet. It was already in sight when at last, at 1550 the *Gloucester*, which had survived so many bomb hits in the past, received a mortal blow from a number of bombs which disabled her and set her on fire.

Being barely clear of the Kithera Channel, within easy range of the enemy's air base, Captain William-Powlett of the *Fiji* was forced to take the agonizing decision to abandon his squadron-mate after dropping boats and life-saving rafts by her. Steaming away southward, the *Fiji* and the two destroyers beat off no less than 20 attacks in the next four hours, at the end of which the *Fiji* was reduced to firing practice shells at her tormentors. She deserved better luck than was to be her lot. At 1845 a lone Me.109 fighter-bomber dived out of a cloud to drop its bomb close alongside, holing her in the engine room and bringing her to a stop. Half an hour later another single aircraft found the almost defenceless ship and delivered the *coup de grâce* with three bombs. The destroyers dropped boats and rafts before withdrawing, and, returning after dark, they were able to rescue 523 of her crew.

So ended the calamitous day. The fleet's ordeal was to continue for another eight days, the brunt of which was to be borne by Cunningham's hard-pressed and over-worked destroyers. While the land battle for Crete hung in the balance they continued to make nightly patrols off the north coast to prevent landings from the sea. On the 23rd, after such a patrol, the *Kelly* and *Kashmir* were set upon early in the morning by 24 dive-bombers and sent to the bottom, their survivors, including Captain Lord Louis Mountbatten, being picked up by the *Kipling* under further heavy attacks.

On the 24th, in reply to a request from the Chiefs of Staff at home for an appreciation, Cunningham gave his opinion that the scale of air attack made it no longer possible for the Navy to operate in the Aegean or near Crete by day. The reaction of the Chiefs of Staff was a message insisting that the fleet and the RAF must accept any losses to prevent reinforcements from reaching the enemy in Crete. In Cunningham's opinion this 'failed most lamentably to appreciate the realities of the situation'.

The facts, indeed, were that reinforcement of the enemy was going on unhindered by means of a stream of Ju.52 transport planes. The Navy could do nothing to stop it. 'It is not the fear of sustaining losses,' replied the Admiral, 'but the need to avoid losses which will cripple the fleet without any commensurate advantage which is the determining factor in operating in the Aegean.' An example of the lack of appreciation of 'the realities of the situation' had occurred during the 23rd. The infantry landing ship *Glenroy* under escort of the *Coventry* and two sloops, had set out from Alexandria with a battalion of infantry reinforcements to be landed on the south coast of Crete. The intensity of air attack south of Crete, as demonstrated by the fate of the *Kelly* and *Kashmir*, convinced Cunningham that 'it appeared to be sheer murder to send her on', and, after consultation with Wavell, he ordered *Glenroy* to turn back during the forenoon. At 1600 the Admiralty sent her a direct order to turn north again which, if Cunningham had not countermanded it, would have meant her arriving to disembark her troops at daylight, and meeting certain destruction at the hands of the unopposed Stukas.

Nevertheless, what could be done was done. Destroyers and cruisers made night runs to Suda Bay to land supplies and ammunition for the Army and to patrol the sea approaches to the island. The *Formidable*, which had managed to build up her fighter strength to 12 Fulmars, sailed out of Alexandria with the *Queen Elizabeth* and *Barham* to launch, early on the 26th, an assault by four Albacores and four Fulmars on the enemy airfield on Scarpanto. Throughout the forenoon the remaining Fulmars fought off the enemy's efforts to take his revenge. It was not until the afternoon that some 20 dive-bombers broke through to hit and seriously damage the carrier as well as the destroyer *Nubian* of the screen. The following day the *Barham* was also damaged. A further effort by the *Glenroy* to get through with reinforcements during the 26th was foiled when she was damaged and set on fire by dive-bombers.

The whole sea area between Crete and the African coast—'Bomb Alley' as it was to be dubbed—was by now dominated by the enemy's overwhelming air strength. Even if Crete could be held, its supply would be virtually impossible. Yet it was at this moment that the Prime Minister cabled to Wavell: 'Victory in Crete essential at this turning point of the war. Keep hurling in all you can.' But the soldiers were at the end of their endurance. They had performed miracles, inflicting such casualties on the German troops that they, too, were at the point of collapse. It was the overwhelming air superiority held by the Germans which decided the issue. A few RAF bombers from Egypt attacked the airfield at Maleme and some Hurricanes fitted with extra fuel tanks were flown to Heraklion; but the effort was too small to affect the ceaseless pounding of the British positions by the German dive-bombers.

On 27 May, therefore, the decision was taken to evacuate the island, the troops in the Suda Bay area being instructed to fall back over the mountains to the little fishing village of Sphakia on the south coast. The force at Heraklion would be evacuated from that port. Once again Cunningham was faced with the daunting prospect of exposing his ever dwindling fleet to certain losses. Already two cruisers and four destroyers had been lost in the battle for Crete; two battleships, the only aircraft carrier, another cruiser and a destroyer had been put out of action, while five cruisers and four destroyers had suffered smaller damage. There was dismay but no hesitation. 'We must not let them [the Army] down'. he signalled to the fleet. When his staff bewailed the heavy cost he told them: 'It takes the Navy three years to build a ship. It would take three hundred to re-build a tradition.'

Evacuation from both points began on the night of 28 May. Four destroyers embarked 700 men at Sphakia and got safely back with them to Alexandria with no more than minor damage to the *Nizam* from a near miss. The force for Heraklion—the cruisers *Orion*, *Ajax* and *Dido* and six destroyers under Rear-Admiral Rawlings—had to pass through the Kaso Straight within 40 miles of the enemy air base on Scarpanto on both the outward and return journey, and met the full fury of the enemy. From 1700 until darkness fell at 2100, the ships raced onwards through a choppy sea with the spray whipping the exposed gun crews as they fought off a succession of attacks which began with the usual contribution of a formation of Italian high-level bombers. The more serious attacks, glide-bombers, dive-bombers and torpedo aircraft, followed.

Sneaking, twisting and turning at high speed, the ships avoided being hit; but near misses there were in plenty. One damaged the *Ajax*, which was sent back to Alexandria; another fell close under the stern of the *Imperial* without apparently doing any damage, but her steering gear had been weakened and it was to cause her loss later. Darkness at last brought relief but no rest to the tired crews. Off Heraklion harbour the cruisers stopped while the darkened destroyers crept in to secure alongside the jetty. Soon the soldiers, indignant at having to retreat from an enemy they had held and defeated, were filing aboard, some 800 to each destroyer which then left harbour and transferred 500 to a cruiser.

By 0320, over an hour later than it had been hoped, all had been embarked and the force turned and raced for the Kaso Straits. Hardly had they settled down when the *Imperial* suddenly veered off course, narrowly missing the *Kimberley* and both the cruisers, and came to a stop. As the remainder of the force disappeared into the darkness, Rawlings sent the *Hotspur* back to find out what was wrong. When the *Hotspur* reported that the *Imperial*'s steering gear had broken down and that she was out of control, the order was given for the crew and troops to be taken off and the *Imperial* to be sunk. It was an hour before this could be completed and two torpedoes had given the *Imperial* her quietus. As the *Hotspur* gathered speed and headed eastwards, the chances of getting through the Kaso Straights in daylight and alone, or of escaping destruction in the Stuka-haunted waters beyond, seemed to her officers so slim, and the thought of what must happen to the 900 men crammed into the little ship was so horrifying, that it was decided to keep close in shore and to turn westwards along the south coast if the Strait was safely passed. Off the beaten track they might escape notice and if the worst occurred the ship could be beached, which would give a chance of life to many of those on board.

To those on the bridge it seemed that the *Hotspur* was doomed as dawn found her streaking through the water for the Kaso Straights alone. The relief which flooded through them as ships loomed up ahead and they realized that Rawlings had waited for them can hardly be exaggerated. They now had six other ships with whom to share the Stukas' attentions, and the gunfire of seven ships would provide a powerful deterrent.

Even so, the ordeal which followed for the next six hours was bad enough, as wave after wave of dive-bombers swooped. Quite early the destroyer *Hereward* was hit and her speed reduced to a crawl. She had to be left to her fate.* Then a near miss on the *Decoy* caused damage which reduced her speed—and therefore that of the squadron—to 25 knots. It was further reduced to 21 by a near miss on the flagship *Orion*. Her bridge was machine-gunned, Captain Back being killed and the Admiral wounded. At 0815 there came a direct hit on the *Dido*'s 'B' turret. At 0900 it was the *Orion*'s 'A' turret that was destroyed.

The most calamitous hit, however, was one on the flagship at 1045 which plunged down into the mess-decks crowded with troops, killing 260

*She was sunk by further air attacks close to the Cretan Coast. The majority of her crew and soldier passengers were picked up by Italian light craft and taken prisoner.

and wounding 280 of the soldiers and ship's company. For a time the *Orion* was out of control and on fire. Subsequently, when emergency steering arrangements had been made and the fire extinguished, sea-water contaminating her oil-fuel intermittently reduced her speed to less than 12 knots. At last the squadron drew out of range of the dive-bombers. Towards sundown the ships reached Alexandria, their crews haggard-eyed with exhaustion and near the end of their endurance, and the *Orion*, with a heavy list and her broken guns tilted awry, under tow.

For the destroyers which had escaped damage, there was more to come. The tired-out crews moved like automatons as they went about the business of refuelling, shifting berth, taking in ammunition and clearing up the cluttered confusion between decks. Then they were off again, this time to Sphakia.

Fortunately the evacuation from Sphakia, which took place on the next three nights, during which some 12,000 troops were embarked, was a much less costly affair, fighter cover being provided by the RAF while the ships were on passage. The cruiser *Perth* had nevertheless to be added to the long list of ships severely damaged, while the anti-aircraft cruiser *Calcutta* was sunk, and the destroyers *Napier* and *Kelvin* damaged.

In all, when the operation ended on 1 June, some 18,000 men had been evacuated. The cost of the battle for Crete to the fleet was three cruisers and six destroyers sunk; two battleships, the aircraft carrier, two cruisers and two destroyers damaged beyond local repair; and three cruisers and six destroyers less seriously damaged.

The credit side of the account was, however, far from negligible. Fliegerkorps XI had virtually ceased to exist. So heavy had been the German casualties in Crete—a total of more than 6,000 in ten days of fighting—that the airborne attack was considered to have been far from an unqualified success. This was to have its influence when proposals for a similar assault on Malta were made later and, in fact, Operation 'Merkur', the assault on Crete, was the last major airborne operation ever undertaken by the Luftwaffe. Furthermore, with the withdrawal of Fliegerkorps VIII for Hitler's Russian campaign, Fliegerkorps X became responsible for the whole of the Central and Eastern Mediterranean area. From a purely air force point of view Greece and Crete now became the most suitable area from which to operate, putting Egypt and the Suez Canal within easy range. The broader strategic view which envisaged the prime necessity of eliminating Malta was lost to sight. The Sicilian airfields were abandoned by the Luftwaffe. For the remainder of 1941 Malta enjoyed a respite during which her defences could be built up and Rommel's supply lines disrupted.

Up to this time Malta's ordeal, though it had been reduced by the redeployment of Fliegerkorps X for the Greece and Crete campaign, had never ceased. Air attacks, concentrated largely on the island's airfields had almost eliminated its usefulness as an offensive air base, though the handful of Swordfish torpedo planes of the Fleet Air Arm continued to make successful attacks on Italian convoys while RAF Wellingtons of No. 148 Squadron harassed the Axis transports with night attacks on their loading and unloading ports. Surface units of the Fleet had been able to operate from the Grand Harbour and the brilliant exploit of Captain Mack's destroyer flotilla has been previously mentioned. Their successors, the cruiser *Gloucester* and Mountbatten's 5th Flotilla, had had no chance to emulate them before being withdrawn to take part in the battle for Crete.

Thus Malta's contribution to the vital task of harrying the Axis sea traffic was mainly confined, for most of 1941, to the work of submarines. The Malta Flotilla was made up of small 'U'-class boats whose size and handiness made them suitable for haunting the narrow waters of the central basin and particularly so for the shallow inshore convoy route from Cape Bon to Tripoli. The first six of these boats had arrived during December 1940 and their first major success had come on 23 February 1941 when the *Upright*, commanded by Lieutenant E. D. Norman, had sunk the Italian cruiser *Armando Diaz*, which was escorting a troop convoy carrying the Afrika Korps to Tripoli.

During March the *Utmost* (Lieutenant-Commander R. D. Cayley), *Unique* (Lieutenant A. F. Collett), as well as the *Upright* had a number of successes. In April came the first major success of the *Upholder*, whose captain, Lieutenant-Commander M. D. Wanklyn, was to make her the most famous of them all. On this patrol he accounted for four transports out of strongly escorted convoys. In May, after sinking an enemy tanker, he took the *Upholder* to lie in ambush for a convoy composed of four large ocean liners, packed with troops for Libya. In spite of asdic and hydrophone out of action as a result of earlier depth-charge attacks, he penetrated the destroyer screen to torpedo and sink the 17,789 ton *Conte Rosso*, subsequently surviving two hours' bombardment by more than 40 depth-charges. The exploit was to be recognized by the award of the Victoria Cross to Wanklyn.

During May, too, Nos 105 and 107 Squadrons of RAF Blenheims replaced the Wellingtons on Malta's airfields and, adding their desperately gallant daylight, low-level bomb attacks to the night torpedo strikes by the naval Swordfish, wrought havoc amongst the Axis convoys. As a result, though General Erwin Rommel's Italo-German armies were able to defeat a British offensive ('Battleaxe') in June, he was too short of ammunition to go over to counter-offensive and was forced to leave the port of Tobruk in British hands behind his lines.

There was, of course, a reverse side to this coin.

As vital to the British as the supply of Rommel's army was to the Axis, was the supply and victualling of Malta. Since January 1941 and the arrival of Fliegerkorps X, no convoys from the west had been attempted.

From February to May, 13 ships had been slipped into Valetta from Alexandria, usually under the cover of fleet movements. The 100,000 tons they brought had kept Malta fed, its few aircraft flying and armed, its submarines fuelled.

Since the end of the battle for Crete, however, and the concentration of Fliegerkorps X in the eastern Mediterranean, the depleted fleet could no longer contemplate trying to fight even single convoys through Bomb Alley between Crete and Cyrenaica. As a desperate stop-gap the larger submarines of the Alexandria flotilla were pressed into service as transports. Between June and December 1941, 16 such trips were run, a typical load being 24 personnel, 147 bags of mail, two tons of medical stores, 62 tons of aviation spirit and 45 tons of kerosene. These trips were to continue until November 1942.

Without them Malta's capabilities of offence and defence would have virtually disappeared. Nevertheless the supplies brought were only a fraction of the requirements. Furthermore, they included no foodstuffs. It was decided, therefore, that a July convoy of six fast store ships must be run from the west. Admiral Somerville's Force 'H', which at this time comprised only his flagship, the battle-cruiser *Renown*, the *Ark Royal*, the cruiser *Hermione* and six destroyers, was reinforced by the battleship *Nelson* and a detachment called Force 'X' under Rear Admiral Syfret, composed of the cruisers *Edinburgh*, *Manchester* and *Arethusa*, the fast minelayer, *Manxman* and 11 destroyers. This latter force was to accompany the convoy through the Sicilian Channel to Malta while the big ships of Force 'H' would await its return to the westward of the Narrows.

Though the Italian battle-fleet at this time included four battleships and three divisions of cruisers, it made no move. It was left to the Italian Air Force to strike at Force 'H' and to a small force of torpedo boats to attack the convoy during its night passage of the Sicilian Channel. During the 23rd a simultaneous attack by high bombers and torpedo aircraft achieved a measure of success. The high-level bombers aimed their bombs with their customary accuracy and lack of concrete result; but they engaged the attention of the defending Fulmars from the *Ark Royal* which climbed up to shoot down two and damage others; and meanwhile six torpedo aircraft, coming in low, sank the destroyer *Fearless* and crippled the *Manchester* which was forced to return to Gibraltar.

It was a skilfully delivered attack, in which the achievement of the torpedo planes compared favourably with any similar daylight efforts by Fleet Air Arm Swordfish. Nevertheless the hot reception they received and the casualties they suffered evidently had a daunting effect. Successive waves of aircraft were driven off by the handful of Fulmars which the Italians complimented by taking for Hurricanes. No further damage was inflicted on convoy or escorts, and that evening they passed into the narrow waters of the Skerki Channel. There during the night two of the MTBs succeeded in attacking and escaping unscathed after torpedoing the *Sydney Star*. The transport was not sunk, however, and, in spite of efforts by German dive-bombers and Italian Savoias to finish her off, she reached Malta on the afternoon of 24 July soon after the remainder of the convoy. The island base was, for the time being, once again viable.

The price could still have been made a painful one had the Italians really been prepared to use their surface fleet offensively. Syfret's Force 'X', after re-fuelling at Malta, had still to make the return passage through the Sicilian Channel. In addition six empty merchant ships and that veteran of the Malta run, the *Breconshire*, were also sent westwards from Malta on the 23rd. An Italian cruiser squadron deployed in the Sicilian Channel might have caused havoc; but the cruisers remained supinely in harbour. Syfret's squadron rejoined Force 'H' early on the 25th without interference, while the empty transports suffered only one damaged as a result of air attacks off the Tunisian coast. As James Somerville commented, 'It was an amazing affair. They had Palermo and Messina packed with cruisers and destroyers and not a move! And so home to bed.' It was indeed a surprising conclusion to an operation which in prospect had seemed so hazardous that Somerville had issued an exhortation to his force preparing them for a hard-fought battle and concluding with the words 'The Convoy Must Go Through!'

Without the massive support of the Luftwaffe, the Italian High Command had little stomach for taking the necessary risks to maintain the siege of Malta. That great courage existed in the fighting units of the Italian Navy was demonstrated by a heroic but unsuccessful attempt to attack the Grand Harbour and the submarine base on the night of 25 July by means of explosive motor-boats and human torpedoes, one of the exploits of the organization known as the Tenth Light Flotilla. It was in Rome that the courage was lacking, the courage to risk much to bring Malta to its knees. Consequently the island's striking forces, now re-supplied, were able to go ahead with ever-increasing success with cutting the Libyan supply line. Rommel, poised on the Egyptian frontier, his eyes on the glittering prize of Cairo and the Suez Canal, remained in frustrated immobility.

During the summer and autumn of 1941 the air strength of Malta was built up, Hurricane fighters being transported in aircraft carriers to within flying range, RAF Wellingtons returned and a squadron of Fleet Air Arm torpedo Albacores sent to reinforce the island's striking force. But by September the need to re-supply Malta had again become urgent. Once again a convoy must run the gauntlet from Gibraltar—nine fast freighters which passed through the Straits during the night of 24 September.

Operation 'Halberd', as it was called, followed the general lines of the July convoy, Force 'H' being composed of the *Nelson* (Admiral Somerville's flagship), the battleships *Prince of Wales* and *Rodney* and

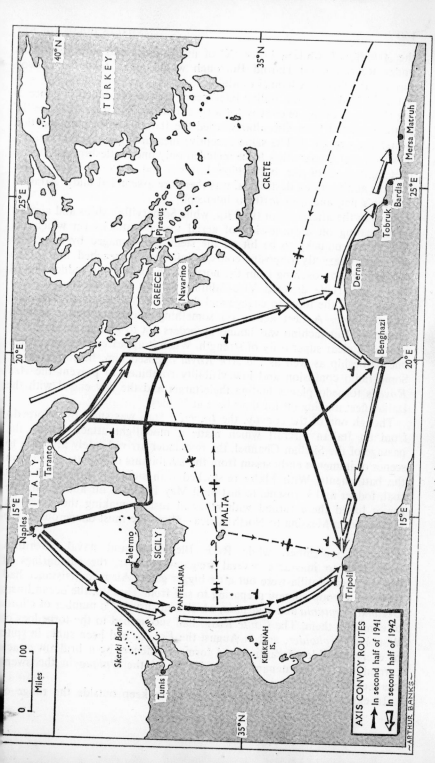

Axis supply routes to North Africa

AXIS CONVOY ROUTES
→ In second half of 1941
⇨ In second half of 1942

~ARTHUR BANKS~

the *Ark Royal*, while a Force 'X' of five cruisers and nine destroyers under Rear-Admiral Harold Burrough would again take the convoy through the Sicilian Channel to Malta.

Efforts to deceive the Italian intelligence service succeeded in concealing the presence of the convoy for a time, but the departure of Force 'H' to the eastward from Gibraltar warned the Italian High Command that something was afoot. The same deceptive measures gave the impression, however, that Somerville's force included only one battleship. An Italian fleet composed of the battleships *Littorio* and *Vittorio Veneto*, five cruisers and fourteen destroyers, was therefore assembled under Admiral Iachino's flag and sent forth to intercept.

Thus in the afternoon of the 27th, while Somerville's ships and aircraft were beating off a succession of aerial torpedo attacks (in which the *Nelson* was unlucky to be hit on the stem and damaged by a torpedo steering an exactly opposite course), information reached him of an enemy fleet approaching from the north. With his flagship reduced to 18 knots, Somerville directed Vice-Admiral Curteis to move out with the remainder of the force to engage and the *Ark Royal* to launch a torpedo striking force. A fleet action on something like equal terms seemed imminent. But Iachino was bound by orders not to join action unless he enjoyed a clear superiority of strength. When it appeared that more than one battleship as well as the *Ark Royal* opposed him, he turned back. Some radio confusion and low visibility combined to prevent the *Ark Royal*'s torpedo planes finding their target and the day ended with the Italian fleet making off for their base at Naples.

Though one of the convoy, the *Imperial Star*, was sunk by a torpedo from an Italian aircraft which made a moonlight attack during the passage of the Sicilian Channel, the remainder arrived safely at Malta to scenes of immense enthusiasm from the inhabitants of Valetta massed on the battlements. With Malta re-stocked with sufficient supplies, except coal, fodder and kerosene, to last until May 1942, the air and submarine forces based there turned with renewed zest to making the short sea passage from Messina to North Africa—about the most dangerous in the world.

During September, while RAF Blenheims and naval Swordfish cooperated to massacre several freighter convoys, the submarines of Malta's 10th Flotilla were out after bigger game. Air reconnaissance had reported a troop convoy preparing to sail from Taranto, the ocean liners *Oceania*, *Neptunia* and *Vulcania*, which had survived a number of efforts to eliminate them. The *Conte Rosso* had succumbed to the torpedoes of Wanklyn's *Upholder*; and in August the *Esperia* had been sunk, in spite of every possible precaution and form of defence, by a brilliant attack carried out by Lieutenant A. R. Hezlet of the *Unique* in the swept channel leading to the port of Tripoli.

In expectation that the troop convoy, to keep outside the range of

37 German Me.110 escorting Italian convoy

38 Troops and supplies for Rommel's Afrika Korps

39 (top) Italian submarine *Axum* 40 (above) Italian 'Chariot' (Maiale) of type which cripple[...]
the *Queen Elizabeth* and *Valiant* at Alexandria

41 Force 'H' under air attack by torpedo planes

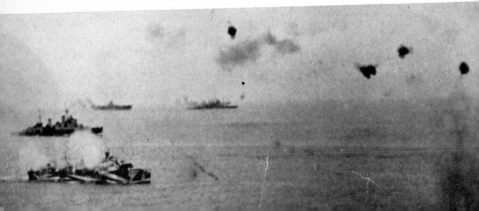

torpedo planes from Malta, would follow the usual easterly route and make landfall 100 miles to the eastward of Tripoli, an ambush by four submarines was set up. At the expected point of landfall was the *Unbeaten*, with *Upholder* and *Upright* along the coast towards Tripoli at 10-mile intervals. At the entrance to the swept channel, 30 miles east of Tripoli was the *Ursula*.

Late on 16 September the three great liners sailed with their five destroyer escorts and headed at high speed across the Mediterranean. Twice during the following day submarine alarms sent the convoy swerving away while the destroyers dropped depth-charges. There were no submarines in fact, but nerves were stretched taut aboard all the ships. There were no further alarms, however, and when at 0330 the following morning Woodward of the *Unbeaten* sighted the convoy against the glow of the rising moon, too far off for him to reach an attacking position, the Italians were unaware of the train of events which was now started by *Unbeaten*'s radio report.

It was taken in by the *Upholder* in time for Wanklyn to steer on the surface to intercept. Half an hour later the bulky shapes of the liners were in sight. Still surfaced, Wanklyn moved in to the attack. He was some way off track and with such fast moving targets he would be forced to fire at long range. The *Upholder*'s gyro-compass had chosen this moment to break down; the little magnetic compass, surrounded as it was by steel, had small directional force. In the choppy sea the helmsman had difficulty in steering and the boat yawed from side to side. Thus when the time came to fire, at a range of 5,000 yards, there was more than the usual need for Wanklyn's personal skill and 'seaman's eye', with the submarine's bow swinging across the firing course. As it swung back he fired again, judging the time lag between barking the order and the moment the torpedo left the tube—until four torpedoes were away on their long run to the target. Satisfied, Wanklyn dropped down through the conning tower hatch as *Upholder*'s bow dipped in a hasty dive.

Luck rewarded his skill. At the angle on which the torpedo tracks met that of the convoy, two of the liners overlapped making virtually one huge target. One torpedo hit the *Oceania* right aft, wrecking her propellers and bringing her to a standstill. Two others travelled on to tear a mortal wound in the side of the *Neptunia*. With a single attendant destroyer, the *Vulcania* put on her best speed and fled towards Tripoli. The *Upright*, which had also received *Unbeaten*'s report, had at once hurried south to get on the convoy's track but, going too far, had the galling experience of seeing the *Vulcania* race by out of range to the north. The *Ursula*, on the other hand, was able to attack but underestimated the liner's speed—she was much the fastest of the trio—so that her torpedoes missed astern.

Meanwhile, the destroyers of the escort were so occupied in taking the passengers and crew off the sinking *Neptunia* and trying to get the *Oceania* in tow that Wanklyn had been able to surface amongst them in

F

the moonlight to survey the situation. Having decided to wait for sunrise before delivering the *coup de grâce* to the wounded *Oceania*, he dived again to make for a position up sun. At the same time, unknown to him, the *Unbeaten*, which had been pounding after the convoy ever since it had passed her, was making for the same position. *Upholder* reached it first and Wanklyn was about to fire when he was forced to go deep by an approaching destroyer. He therefore took *Upholder* under his target and, coming to periscope depth on the far side, put two torpedoes into the *Oceania* which sank her in eight minutes.

While Wanklyn's star was shining out so brilliantly (though soon to be extinguished for ever), Woodward's was in heart-breaking eclipse. Arriving on the scene soon after sunrise, he saw the *Neptunia* slide beneath the surface without any assistance from him. He had just squared up to launch his torpedoes at the *Oceania*, when, through the periscope, he saw the tall columns of water leap up as *Upholder*'s torpedoes robbed him of his victim.

Though the loss of life in this double catastrophe was relatively small, 384 men being lost from the two ships, the destruction of two such valuable and irreplaceable ships almost in sight of Tripoli, in the same month in which supply convoys suffered more severely than ever before, flashed a clear warning to the high commands of the Axis that drastic remedial action was needed if the battle for the Mediterranean was not to be lost.

Cries of alarm came from Admiral Weichold, the German liaison officer with the Italian Naval Staff in Rome, as a result of which the German General Staff informed the German Supreme Command in September:

> The situation as described is untenable. Italian naval and air forces are incapable of providing adequate cover for the convoys. . . . The Naval Staff considers radical changes and immediate measures to remedy the situation imperative, otherwise not only our offensive but the entire Italo-German position in North Africa will be lost.

The 'immediate measures' necessary were primarily a reinforcement of the Luftwaffe in the Mediterranean: if powerful air forces were again stationed in Sicily they could deny the central basin to British ships and neutralize Malta. But, obsessed with the overriding importance of the campaign in Russia, Hitler for the moment refused to divert any further air strength to the Mediterranean. Instead he ordered Fliegerkorps X to be diverted from its offensive task of attacking enemy ships and supply bases in Egypt to that of protecting convoys to North Africa. This might have had a serious effect on air operations from Malta had not Göring contrived to have the order modified, so as to restrict the activities of the Fliegerkorps to protection of convoys running between Greece and Benghazi and along the coastal route between Benghazi and Derna. Hitler also overrode the objections of the German Naval Staff by ordering six U-boats to the Mediterranean.

The inadequacy of these measures was soon dramatically demonstrated. The increased security of the Malta base, and the success which had attended the passage of the two supply convoys in July and September, had satisfied the Admiralty that the time had again come to station there a striking force of surface ships. On 21 October 1941, the cruisers *Aurora* and *Penelope* from the Home Fleet and two destroyers detached from Force 'H', the *Lance* and *Lively*, arrived to form Force 'K' under the command of Captain W. G. Agnew of the *Aurora*.

Their arrival, which was at once known to the Italian Naval Staff, coincided with a temporary stoppage of all convoys for Libya owing to the heavy losses. With Rommel preparing an offensive such an embargo could not be long maintained; but it was nearly three weeks before a suitable target for Force 'K' offered itself. This was a convoy of seven freighters which the Italian Naval Staff, under heavy pressure from the Army command, felt obliged to despatch despite the risk it was bound to run. Powerful protection was arranged for it. Six destroyers under Captain Bisciani of the *Maestrale* formed the close escort, while the heavy cruisers *Trieste* and *Trento* and four destroyers acted in close support, commanded by Vice-Admiral Bruno Brivonesi. To give warning if Force 'K' should come out, several submarines were stationed to seaward of Valetta harbour.

Debouching from the Straits of Messina around midday on 8 November, the convoy was given an air escort of eight Italian and German aircraft until dusk. These were unable to prevent a Maryland on reconnaissance from Malta sighting and reporting the convoy at 1640. An hour later Force 'K' was leaving harbour. No enemy aircraft marked their leaving, nor did the Italian submarines see or hear them. Soon they were racing eastwards, under a clear night sky, through a sea gently ruffled by a light breeze from the north-west.

By midnight the moon had risen and was shining brightly in the east. Forty minutes later, the unsuspecting convoy was sighted at a range of six miles. The British squadron was in line ahead with the *Aurora* leading; and now Captain Agnew signalled for speed to be reduced to 20 knots and led round to the north-east, so that his targets would be silhouetted against the moon, before turning starboard on to a southerly course parallel to that of the convoy.

No inkling of the devastating blow that was about to strike them had as yet alarmed the merchantmen or their guardians. Admiral Brivonesi, unwilling to keep his squadron down to the slow speed of the merchant ships and so expose himself an easy target to any prowling submarine, had been patrolling north and south on the western flank of the convoy—between it and the likely direction of any attack coming from the direction of Malta. Unlike the British squadron he had no radar. Nor were his ships well equipped or his crews well trained for night action. Thus, though Agnew had dimly sighted him to the northeastward during his approach but had ignored him to concentrate on the main object, the convoy, Brivonesi knew nothing of the presence of the British squadron. A little while earlier he had turned north. He had reached a position some three miles astern of the convoy and was now turning back on to the southerly leg of of his patrol when suddenly the horizon ahead was lit up by the bright flashes of gun-fire.

Convoy and escort alike were taken completely by surprise. The destroyer *Grecale* bringing up the rear was immediately hit and brought to a stop, out of action. The *Fulmine*, on the convoy's starboard quarter, survived hardly a minute of the fire from *Aurora*'s 6-inch guns before sinking. The other destroyer on the starboard side, the *Euro*, turned to attack, but, on seeing the dark bulk of the British cruisers, came to the conclusion that they were Italian and that some dreadful mistake was being made. He countermanded the order to fire torpedoes and turned away to seek his senior officer in the *Maestrale*. There Captain Bisciani, under the impression that the convoy was being attacked by aircraft, had given the order for all ships to make smoke. He realized his mistake when the mast with his radio aerial was shot down, thus cutting him off from communication with his squadron. The two destroyers to port of the convoy, the *Libeccio* and the *Oriani*, could not make out what was going on amidst the smoke which blew down over them and were unable to take any useful action.

Similarly the Italian cruisers could make little of the mêlée. They briefly opened fire at their half-seen target but no shell splashes were seen from the British ships. Brivonesi then turned north in which direction he estimated he would be able to intercept the British squadron as it withdrew. Certainly he was too late to prevent the massacre of the convoy, which had been quickly reduced to a number of sinking or burning ships as Agnew led his force in a wide circle, pumping shells into his helpless prey. But a northerly course was a peculiar choice, to say the least of it, as Malta lay to the south-west and it was in that direction that Agnew steered when, a few minutes after 0200 the last merchant ship had been disposed of.

Nothing remained for the Italian escorts but to take the crippled *Grecale* in tow by the *Oriani* and to pick up survivors from the sunken merchant ships. While this was going on, towards dawn a last misfortune befell the ill-starred Italian forces: the submarine *Upholder* put a torpedo into the *Libeccio* which later sank. Not unreasonably, scapegoats were sought amongst the Italian commanders. Admiral Brivonesi and Captain Bisciani were both deprived of their commands, though the former was later exonerated. Responsibility for the disaster could, indeed, not fairly be laid at the door of any individual, arising as it did from the Italian

Navy's neglect of night-action training and equipment, as well as from its lack of radar.

This lightning blow by Force 'K', devastating as it was, was only a highlight of the campaign to destroy Axis supply ships which was being waged by British aircraft, submarines and surface ships. September 1941 had seen the loss of 28 per cent of all cargoes shipped for Libya, October 21 per cent. Now in November it rose to 63 per cent. The situation had become intolerable, not only for the Italians whose merchant marine was being wiped out, but also for Rommel and the Afrika Korps whose planned offensive to capture Tobruk had already had to be postponed from September to October, then to November. Before it could be implemented the British Eighth Army struck, on 18 November. The Afrika Korps, its power of resistance weakened by shortages of every sort of supplies, suffered a resounding defeat.

The Italian Navy made strenuous efforts to bring succour to the hard-pressed Axis armies, but with little success. A convoy of four freighters which set out from Naples on 20 November with the powerful escort of seven destroyers and a supporting force of three heavy cruisers, two light cruisers and seven destroyers, was forced to turn back when RAF Wellington bombers, together with the torpedo-carrying Swordfish and Albacores of 830 and 838 Squadron, attacked. The cruiser *Duca degli Abruzzi* was torpedoed and sent limping back, badly damaged, to Messina. Then the submarine *Utmost* joined the attack to treat the cruiser *Trieste* in the same way. Another small but vital convoy of two German freighters *Procida* and *Maritza*, circling far to the east of Malta to avoid air attack was intercepted by Agnew's Force 'K' during the 24th. Both merchant ships, deep laden with ammunition and bombs as well as petrol and motor transport for the Afrika Korps were sent to the bottom.

Out of all the ships which had set forth in this widespread effort to bring supplies to the armies in Africa which were now fighting desperately to halt the British offensive, only two got through, one to Tripoli and one to Benghazi. On 29 November the Italians tried again, using the same method of despatching a number of small convoys on different routes and adding a battleship to the covering force of four cruisers and nine destroyers. The outcome was no more successful. Blenheims from Malta sank the Italian merchant ship *Capo Faro* and crippled two others. On 1 December Force 'K' caught and sank the auxiliary cruiser *Adriatico*, carrying ammunition, artillery and supplies, and then went on to sink the tanker *Iridio Mantovani*, previously damaged by the Blenheims, and to blow up her escorting destroyer *Da Mosto*. To replenish Rommel's fast dwindling supplies only one ship of all those that sailed reached Benghazi on the 2nd.

For Rommel the situation was almost catastrophic. Though for a time he was able to hold the British offensive launched on 18 November 1941, shortage of supplies and lack of reserves of tanks and fresh troops finally forced him to retreat, declaring it was no longer possible to hold Cyrenaica. On 6 December he abandoned the siege of Tobruk and any hope of relieving the Axis troops encircled and cut off on the Egyptian border, and began a fighting retreat to El Gazala, west of Tobruk. On the 17th that position, too, was abandoned; by 12 January 1942 Rommel was back on the borders of Tripolitania and all Cyrenaica was once again in British hands.

The defeat of the Axis armies and the raising of the long siege of Tobruk painted, to a superficial and landward-looking view, a bright picture of the situation of the British in the campaign for the Mediterranean. In truth, however, the principal factor which had led to this great success had already been removed. This had been the reduction of German air strength in the area, particularly in the Central Mediterranean with the resultant build-up of the offensive and defensive capabilities of Malta, and the virtual strangulation of the Libyan supply line. It was sea power—the ability to use the sea for one's own purposes and to prevent the enemy from doing the same—which, passing into the hands of the British with the withdrawal of Fliegerkorps X from the decisive area, had been the key to the dramatic reversal of fortune in North Africa.

But even while the fruits of British successes, above, beneath and on the surface of the sea, were being gathered in the deserts of Libya, the tree on which they had grown was withering. Within two weeks of Rommel's decision to retreat to El Agheila on the border of Tripolitania, he was once again in a position to mount a successful offensive. This resulted partly from successful German counter-attacks, while Rommel was still holding his Gazala position, which inflicted heavy defeats on the British armoured formations. This offensive could not, however, have been even contemplated by Rommel but for a dramatic change in the situation at sea.

8 The Fight for Malta's Survival

The crippling inroads on supplies to the Axis armies in North Africa—in November 1941 no less than 63 per cent of the cargoes which set out failed to arrive—had led Hitler to respond to the increasingly desperate appeals from the Mediterranean theatre. His first step had been to order four more U-boats to join the six already sent there in September. These quickly achieved two resounding successes. On 13 November the *Ark Royal*, returning to Gibraltar with Force 'H' after yet another sortie into the Central Mediterranean to fly off Hurricane reinforcements for Malta, was torpedoed and sunk in a skilfully delivered attack by *U81*, commanded by Lieutenant Guggenberger. The loss of this famous ship, so often attacked and so often claimed by the Germans to have been sunk, was a severe blow, coming at a time when the *Illustrious* and *Formidable* were still repairing battle damage in the United States, and the *Indomitable* had recently been damaged through running aground off Kingston, Jamaica, while still working up her squadrons and ship's company. Thus no modern carrier was available to take the *Ark Royal*'s place. Without one, the ability of Force 'H' to take further convoys to Malta had gone.

Twelve days later it was the turn of the Mediterranean Fleet to suffer a calamity. It will be recalled that on 24 November Force 'K' from Malta was at sea intercepting a convoy to the north of Benghazi. Simultaneously a detachment from the Mediterranean Fleet, known as Force 'B' and comprising the 7th and 15th Cruiser Squadrons, had been out seeking prey, though without success. In support, Admiral Cunningham had taken his battle-squadron—*Queen Elizabeth*, *Barham* and *Valiant*—to sea with a screen of eight destroyers.

Some 60 miles north of Sollum, *U331*, commanded by Lieutenant-Commander von Tiesenhausen, intercepted the battle-squadron, penetrated its strong screen of destroyers and hit the *Barham* with three torpedoes. She at once took a list to port, which quickly increased until she was lying on her beam ends. A minute later there was a cataclysmic explosion in which the great ship disintegrated. When the smoke and spray cleared, she had disappeared, taking with her 56 officers and 812 ratings.

These two successes by the newly arrived German U-boats were the beginning of a succession of severe blows suffered by the Royal Navy in the Mediterranean.

Meanwhile, ten days after his order for the re-deployment of U-boats, Hitler issued, on 2 December 1941, his Directive No 38, which was to have a vital influence on the battle for the Mediterranean. In it he gave instructions that Fliegerkorps II, under General Lörzer, should be transferred from the Russian front to Sicily and North Africa. Together with Fliegerkorps X, which was responsible for the eastern Mediterranean sector, it would form Luftflotte 2 under the overall command of Field-Marshal Kesselring, who was concurrently C-in-C (Air), South, and in command of all German armed forces in Sicily. The task given to Kesselring was a double one:

(a) to achieve air and sea mastery in the area between southern Italy and North Africa and thus ensure safe lines of communication with Libya and Cyrenaica. The suppression of Malta is particularly important in this connection;

(b) to paralyse enemy traffic through the Mediterranean and to stop British supplies reaching Tobruk and Malta.

Thus was set on foot a re-disposition of German strength which was to reverse the balance of sea power in the Mediterranean and subject Malta to an ordeal by bomb and a siege to which she nearly succumbed and which, if it had been carried through with single-minded vigour to its conclusion, must have made the victory of El Alamein impossible.

While Fliegerkorps II was still moving into Sicily however, and before its effect had begun seriously to be felt, the Italian Navy recorded one of its blackest days as a result of renewed efforts to get supplies through to Africa. At the height of the British offensive a supreme effort to bring aid to Rommel was ordered. On 13 December, five supply ships sailed from Taranto, in three separate convoys. In addition to their close escort of eight destroyers, with each of two of these groups was a *Duilio* class battleship, two or three cruisers and three destroyers in close support, while the *Littorio* and *Vittorio Veneto* were sailed with a screen of four destroyers in general support.

These movements were at once known to Admiral Cunningham, who ordered the 15th Cruiser Squadron—*Naiad*, *Galatea* and *Euryalus* and nine destroyers from Alexandria—to proceed to intercept the enemy. From Malta, Force 'K' sailed to cooperate. Cunningham had insufficient destroyers for screening purposes to allow him to take his battleships to sea. Though these cruiser forces, mounting only 6-inch guns, were prepared to fight at such odds at this critical moment of the land campaign, Cunningham resorted to a ruse which he hoped would make it unnecessary. While strict radio silence was enjoined at Alexandria, the fast minelayer *Abdiel* was sent out to create a radio diversion and give the impression that the battle-squadron was at sea.

The ruse was successful. On the evening of the 13th the Italian convoys were recalled. Even so, they did not escape disaster. Two of the supply ships collided, thus putting each other out of action for some months. Two more were torpedoed and sunk by the submarine *Upright*. Finally the *Vittorio Veneto*, returning to Messina, was torpedoed and severely damaged by the *Urge*. It would be several months before the battleship could operate again.

Meanwhile, on the Palermo–Cape Bon–Tripoli route, Allied destroyers had brought off a brilliant *coup* to complete the Italian discomfiture. Two light cruisers, *Da Barbiano* and *Di Giussano*, loaded with cased petrol had sailed from Palermo on the evening of the 13th in company with the torpedo-boat *Cigno* for a high-speed dash across the Sicilian Straits. Their departure had not escaped the watchful eyes of British reconnaissance planes.

Coming eastwards from Gibraltar at high speed was a force of four destroyers under Commander G. H. Stokes of the *Sikh*, with the *Maori*, *Legion* and the Dutch *Issac Sweers*. A signal went out to him from Admiral Ford, commanding at Malta, that the cruisers of Force 'K' were being despatched to intercept the Italian ships 90 miles south of Cape Bon and that torpedo aircraft would also attack during the night. It was estimated that Stokes could not reach Cape Bon in time to take part but he was told to be prepared for the enemy to break back towards him.

A little later the sailing of Force 'K' was countermanded owing to Malta's shortage of oil-fuel, the last few tons of which had to be reserved against any dire emergency. Thus the Italian cruisers would have had only the torpedo aircraft to contend with had they kept to their planned schedule. For some reason, however, although Vice-Admiral Toscano commanding the squadron had been warned of the approach of the British destroyers, he was more than an hour late in his arrival off Cape Bon. Thus Stokes as he came pounding up from the westward, sighted flashing lights and then the outline of two ships which disappeared behind the steep bulk of the headland.

It seemed as though he was just too late. But luck was running on the British side that night. Toscano had just rounded Cape Bon when he heard overhead the sound of aircraft in formation which he guessed to be torpedo planes. To foil them he reversed his course, so that as the *Sikh* drew clear of the headland Stokes saw his enemy steering towards him and approaching rapidly. He at once led away to get between the Italians and the shore so that he would remain unseen against the backdrop of the headland.

The Italians were thus taken completely by surprise, when at 0223 the destroyers' guns flashed out and torpedoes splashed as they were sent on the short run to the target. A few wildly aimed salvoes from the Italians dropped their shells on the shore beyond their target, but their gunfire soon ceased as three torpedoes hit the *Da Barbiano*, sending her quickly to the bottom, and another hit the *Di Giussano* whose cargo of petrol blazed up. All was over in a few minutes; Stokes's destroyers resumed their passage to Malta, leaving the *Di Giussano* to sink an hour later while the *Cigno* picked up survivors.

Now, however, the scales of fortune were to dip again in favour of the Axis. Lying in wait for Cunningham's force on its return, off the swept channel into Alexandria, was *U557*, which torpedoed and sank the *Galatea*. Her loss, indeed, following that of the *Ark Royal* and *Barham*, was another step towards the eclipse of British sea power in the Mediterranean, being closely followed by a series of disasters as well as the opening of the Luftwaffe's renewed assault on Malta.

It was Force 'K' from Malta that was to suffer the next blow. A further effort by the Italians to pass a supply convoy to Tripoli under cover of their battle fleet during 17 and 18 December had succeeded to the extent that the convoy had arrived unscathed off the port after dark on the 18th. There, however, they had found an air attack in progress. Torpedo planes from Malta had attacked the ships, an Albacore of 828 Squadron obtaining a hit on the steamer *Napoli* which had had to be taken in tow. The convoy therefore anchored off the port for the remainder of the night, but was got safely in during the 19th.

In the hope of catching it still outside, Force 'K', composed of the cruisers, *Neptune*, *Aurora* and *Penelope*, with the destroyers *Lance*, *Lively*, *Havelock* and *Kandahar*, was meanwhile racing through the night from Malta. Soon after midnight disaster struck as they ran into a dense field of mines, long-established but until now unknown to the British. In the next four hours, the *Neptune* was lost with all hands but one leading seaman, and the *Aurora* and *Penelope* were both damaged, the former severely, but reached Malta under their own power. The *Kandahar*, while trying to take the *Neptune* in tow, had her stern blown off and eventually had to be sunk. Force 'K' had virtually ceased to exist.

Even while Force 'K' was suffering this calamity, a heroic exploit off Alexandria was similarly eliminating Cunningham's battle squadron. It was the crowning success of the Italian 10th Light Flotilla, previously mentioned, which specialized in the type of individualistic operation in which the Italian excels—one-man explosive motor-boats (EMB), skin-diving frogmen and two-men 'chariots', called by the Italians 'slow-speed torpedoes', or more familiarly, 'pigs'. These last were submersible craft on which the crew, wearing breathing apparatus, sat astride. On reaching their objective, the explosive head was detached, clamped to the keel, and a time-fuse set.

At 2100 on the evening of 18 December 1941, the Italian submarine *Sciré*, commanded by Lieutenant-Commander Valerio Borghese, was brought gently to the surface 1.3 miles from the lighthouse on the mole at Alexandria. Three chariots, their rubber-suited, helmeted and goggled crews astride them, set off towards the harbour entrance. The submarine sank back into the depths and turned for the open sea.

The pilots of the three chariots, Luigi de la Penne, Antonio Marceglia and Vincenzo Martellotta, were all veterans of the exploits in Gibraltar Bay. Good luck aided their skill, for, as they were contemplating the net defences and preparing to negotiate them, they saw them obligingly drawn open to permit the entry of destroyers of Admiral Vian's force, which were returning from the encounter with the Italian fleet. Narrowly escaping being run down by the destroyers, the chariots passed into the harbour with them.

During these eventful moments the three charioteers lost touch with each other; but each had his assigned target and carried on independently. De la Penne's was the *Valiant*. Negotiating her anti-torpedo net he arrived alongside her safely, but, when submerging, his craft went out of control and plunged to the bottom. Meanwhile his diver, Bianchi, fainting from the long exposure, had lost touch. On coming to, he swam to the mooring buoy and climbed unseen on to it. De la Penne was now faced, single-handed, with the task of hauling his whole craft with its warhead to a position directly beneath the battleship. After superhuman efforts, blinded by the mud stirred up, he succeeded, set the fuse and surfaced, to be taken prisoner with Bianchi.

Refusing to enlighten his captors on the purpose of their mission until shortly before the time set for the fuse to function, they were confined in the hold and were still there when the *Valiant* shuddered under the effect of a terrific explosion. They escaped unharmed, however, to witness the damage they had caused, from which the great ship sank until she was resting on the bottom.

Shortly before this a similar explosion had blown off the stern of the tanker *Sagona*, Martellotta's objective, and badly damaged the destroyer *Jervis* lying alongside her. Martellotta and his companion Marino had reached the shore but were arrested at the dockyard gate. As de la Penne reached the crippled *Valiant*'s deck another violent explosion under the fleet flagship *Queen Elizabeth* told him that Marceglia had been equally successful. With his companion Schergat, he too reached the shore and they were able to make their way into Alexandria and thence to Rosetta off which a submarine was to be lying to pick them up. But the use of English £5 notes with which they had been supplied, currency not in use in Egypt, betrayed them before they could get away and they were taken prisoner.

Thus six brave and resourceful men eliminated at one stroke Cunningham's battle-squadron at a time when replacements were not available. For, eleven days before, the Japanese had delivered their treacherous attack on Pearl Harbor. The battleship *Prince of Wales* and battle-cruiser *Repulse* had gone down before the torpedo aircraft of the Japanese Navy. With what remained of her naval strength Britain turned to defend her eastern Imperial possessions. Sea power in the eastern and Central Mediterranean became seemingly the subject of dispute between Cunningham's exiguous force of three light-cruisers, with two more at Malta and Iachino's four battleships, three heavy and three light cruisers as well as greatly superior destroyer and submarine strength—an unequal contest with only one possible outcome, it might be thought.

In fact, as events were to show, Cunningham's inability to 'field' a battle-squadron was of far less significance than his lack of adequate air support either from a carrier or from shore bases. In the absence of the former, so long as the Cyrenaican airfields were in British hands, Rear-Admiral Vian's 15th Cruiser Squadron was still able to escort supply ships from Egypt to Malta under the nose of the Italian fleet, pre-occupied with the task of protecting its own convoys to Libya. During January 1942 the special supply ships HMS *Glengyle* and *Breconshire* and a convoy of three fast freighters were all successfully infiltrated.

At the same time, however, Axis convoys were enjoying an unwonted period of freedom from attack, re-vitalizing Rommel's armies; so that this brief interlude of uneasy balance of sea power was now to come to an end. As Rommel in North Africa and Fliegerkorps II in Sicily began their offensive the British were thrown back on a desperate defence in which their retention of Egypt and the Suez Canal was largely to depend upon whether Malta could survive an assault far heavier than anything previously experienced.

The counter-attack launched by Rommel on 21 January 1942 was successful far beyond his expectations. The over-extended British Eighth Army was soon in full retreat. By 6 February it was back on the Gazala–Bir Hacheim line to the west of Tobruk—a situation which was to remain stabilized until the end of May while each side refitted and prepared for a renewal of the offensive.

So far as the Axis was concerned, this depended primarily upon achieving permanent security for the lines of communication across the Mediterranean. But whereas the Italian High Command and Field-Marshal Kesselring, the axis air commander, had by this time come round to the necessity of capturing Malta, Hitler and the German Supreme Command were unwilling to commit the necessary forces to the operation. An all-out assault by the Luftwaffe to neutralize the island was ordered instead. It was expected that three weeks should suffice, after which a lower scale of effort would keep her prostrate.

Beginning on 21 December 1941, Fliegerkorps II had launched a steadily mounting air assault. In February they greatly intensified their operations and in March the really massive raids began. The small force of Hurricanes on the island taking off from the cratered, hastily repaired runways, was soon reduced to a handful: Malta's air strike capability was almost eliminated: the 10th Submarine Flotilla continued to haunt the Libyan convoy route successfully for a time, but from early March their base became daily less tenable until at the end of April the Flotilla was forced to abandon it for fear of being penned in port by mines laid in the approaches.

British aims were now simply to supply Malta with the means to survive and to defend herself until the storm blew over. In February an attempt to run a convoy of four fast freighters from Alexandria under cover of Vian's cruiser squadron had been defeated by the incessant air attacks mounted from the Cyrenaican airfields, now once again in German and Italian hands, one of the ships being forced to turn back with bomb damage, the other three being sent to the bottom.

In a belated effort to build up Malta's fighter defences, for which no reinforcements had been flown in since the *Ark Royal's* last trip in November, the Air Ministry at last allocated Spitfires to the island where the Hurricanes had long been outclassed by the Me.109s of Fliegerkorps II. On 7 March, Force 'H', now commanded by Admiral Syfret, came east from Gibraltar with the veteran carriers *Argus* and *Eagle*. From the latter, in a position south-east of Majorca, 15 Spitfires were flown off and arrived safely. It was the first of a succession of such operations, 16 more Spitfires being flown in on 21 and 29 March.

Once again, therefore, Cunningham prepared a convoy. It included— inevitably—that old war-horse, the *Breconshire*, and three fast freighters, *Clan Campbell*, *Pampas* and the Norwegian *Talabot*. On 20 March it sailed with a close escort of the *Carlisle* and seven destroyers while Admiral Vian again provided the covering force with the 15th Cruiser Squadron and four destroyers. His flag flew in the newly joined *Cleopatra* which had replaced the *Naiad*, torpedoed on 11 March off Alexandria. To distract the attention of the Italian and German Air Forces in Cyrenaica, various units of the 8th Army operated to create a diversion. Raids were made by the Long-Range Desert Group on landing grounds far behind the enemy lines while other landing grounds were shelled and sabotaged. No 201 Group RAF made widespread raids on western airfields also. These activites undoubtedly helped to restrict the enemy's air activity against the convoy and for the first two days it enjoyed an unusually quiet passage.

They had not, however, gone unnoticed by the enemy. Italian submbarine on patrol and Ju.52 transport aircraft, flying along the route between Greece and Cyrenaica, reported them. At Taranto Admiral Iachino prepared to intervene with his flagship the splendid *Littorio*, two heavy cruisers *Gorizia* and *Trento*, the light cruiser *Bande Nere* and four destroyers.

Early on 22 March Vian was joined by the *Penelope* and a destroyer from Malta. Vian's force had passed through Bomb Alley between Crete and Cyrenaica without suffering any air attacks; but fighter cover had been overhead during the previous day. Now the convoy was beyond the range of British fighters and during the 22nd must rely only upon the guns of the escort for protection. And, as had been foreseen, soon after midnight the Italian squadron had put to sea, its passing noted and reported by the submarine *P36*. Vian estimated that it would intercept him during the afternoon. He aimed to hold the enemy off until dark by the use of pre-arranged diversionary tactics and the lavish use of smoke which, experience had shown, the Italians were wary of entering.

Meanwhile there were some torpedo attacks by Italian S79s to occupy his attention. The heavy volume of fire developed by the escorts deterred them from pressing their attacks home, and the torpedoes, fired at long range, were avoided. Then, at 1330, an aircraft released signal flares and Vian knew his testing time was at hand. It was confirmed at 1427, when from the *Euryalus*, Captain Bush reported four enemy ships in sight to the north-east. Vian at once set in motion his pre-arranged tactics. While the convoy and its close escort turned away to the south-west, Vian's cruisers and destroyers steered so as to spread a smoke screen between them and the enemy. In the rising south-easterly wind it streamed out effectively.

The Italian cruisers—at first thought to be battleships—opened fire at Vian's ships as they moved out towards them, but soon turned away to the north-west. At this, Vian also turned to overtake the convoy which he could see under a sky filled with black shell-bursts as its escort fought off a heavy attack by Ju.88s. To the C-in-C he signalled that the enemy had been driven off. This was premature. The Italian cruisers had, in fact, only fallen back on the *Littorio* on order from their admiral, and at 1640 their whole force came in sight to the north-east.

Once again Vian moved out in defiance, opposing the 5.25-inch guns of his three cruisers and 4.7-inch guns of his destroyers to the 15-inch, 8-inch and 6-inch guns of the Italian ships. But other factors were in Vian's favour. The south-east wind was steadily increasing to a gale, whipping up a heavy sea. Lacking radar the Italians relied upon optical range-finders which, lashed by spray, were not very efficient. At the same time the smoke from the funnels of the British ships spread in a dense fog between the opposing squadrons. Both sides thus had only fleeting views of their targets as the British cruiser and flotillas emerged briefly from the smoke to fire guns or torpedoes. Nevertheless the *Cleopatra* was hit on the bridge by a 6-inch shell and the *Euryalus* was swept by splinters as a 15-inch shell burst alongside her.

Iachino, anxious to get at the convoy but unwilling to go through the smoke, had the choice of circling the smoke-screen either to leeward by continuing on his south-westerly course or to windward by turning south-east into wind and sea. The rising sea into which his ships would have had to head deterred him from the latter alternative—a decision which the course of the battle was to prove a mistaken one. The smoke, drifting north-westward on the wind, extended so far that it was not until nearly 1800 that he was able to turn south towards the convoy, by which time dusk was approaching, with all its perils for the Italians, lacking, as they did, radar and night fighting capabilities.

Nevertheless, the situation at this time was extremely critical for the British. Vian, suspecting that a portion of the enemy might have made what his seaman's sense told him was the correct move and circled to windward, had taken half his cruiser force to the eastward and thus run temporarily out of the action. His flotilla commanders, Captain Mickle-thwait and Captain Poland, by boldly moving out to attack with torpedoes and closing to within 6,000 yards to do so, saved the situation. The destroyers *Havock* and *Kingston* were hit and damaged by heavy shells and others had narrow escapes, as they raced ahead through a forest of shell splashes to loose their torpedoes. The torpedo threat and the gathering darkness brought the battle to an end as Iachino swung his ships away to the northwards and disengaged.

The Second Battle of Sirte, as it came to be called, thus ended as a tactical and moral triumph for Admiral Vian's force. Though the Italians had suffered but a single hit by a light shell on the *Littorio* which caused only superficial damage, the bold and skilful delaying tactics of the British ships and flotillas had held off their powerful armoured opponents until darkness came to their aid. The convoy, as yet unharmed by the numerous air attacks it had undergone, had been saved. Its four ships were now dispersed and, each with a destroyer escort, ordered to make their best speed for Malta. Meanwhile the Italians were suffering more from the weather than they had from the enemy. On their way back to Taranto, two of their destroyers foundered in the gale, the *Littorio* shipped thousands of tons of water and the *Bande Nere* was damaged. The latter had to be sent to Spezia dockyard for repairs; on passage she was torpedoed and sunk by the submarine *Urge*.

Nevertheless Iachino had partially achieved his aim. The diversion of the convoy to the southward, under the threat posed by his approach, had caused just enough delay to prevent the ships from reaching Malta at first light on the 23rd. They were thus exposed to some hours of air attack before they could reach harbour. Malta's fighter aircraft, their airfields potholed and their numbers reduced by four days of ceaseless, massive attacks, gave what protection they could.

From the moment they came within Hurricane and Spitfire range [Air Marshall Sir Hugh Lloyd, the Air Officer Commanding in Malta at that time, has written], the only occasion when all the available fighters were not over them was when they were flying back to the aerodromes to be re-fuelled and re-armed or to pick up relief pilots. For the last ten miles to the Grand Harbour there was not a moment's respite. Every aeroplane in Sicily seemed to be flying round the island.

The *Talabot* and *Pampas*, in spite of continuous attacks since dawn, reached the Grand Harbour between 0900 and 1000, unharmed except for two bomb hits on the *Pampas* which failed to explode. From the battlements of Valetta the populace, regardless of their own danger from bombs directed at the harbour, watched breathlessly as the ships approached through the leaping bomb splashes and gave them a delirious welcome as they steamed past to their unloading berths.

Meanwhile, however, the gallant *Breconshire*, survivor of so many previous perilous journeys, had been hit and disabled when eight miles from harbour. In the heavy seas running she could not be towed and Captain C. A. G. Hutchinson anchored her. An hour later the *Clan Campbell*, 20 miles out, was sunk by a bomb and the destroyer *Legion*, damaged by a near miss, had to be beached.

Even so, up to this time, losses had not been exorbitant and certainly less than might have been expected. But Malta was now cowering under the intensified air assault which had begun, as planned, on 20 March. The three supply ships gave the Stuka pilots easy targets and an added incentive. No less than 326 bombers and fighters of Fliegerkorps II were expressly directed to their destruction. The outnumbered Hurricanes and Spitfires fought valiantly to protect them and for three days succeeded; but the end was inevitable. On the 26th both *Talabot* and *Pampas* were hit, the former having to be scuttled as fire threatened the ammunition in her hold, while the latter had all but two of her holds flooded. On the following day the *Breconshire*, which in spite of continuous attacks had been towed into a harbour on the south coast of the island, at last succumbed and sank, as did the *Legion* which had been got to the same anchorage. Of the 26,000 tons of cargo which had left Egypt in the convoy, only 5,000 were unloaded.

It was a tragic anti-climax to the gallant deeds performed by ships and aircraft and a bitter disappointment to the almost desperate defenders of Malta. But so long as virtually the whole strength of Luftflotte 2 could be devoted, during the lull in the campaign in Libya, to the reduction of the island, little better could be hoped for.

March 20, as previously mentioned, had marked the opening of the grand assault. A few figures are necessary to show what this meant. During February, when no less than 222 attacks were made on the island's airfields alone, Fliegerkorps II had flown 2,497 sorties. In March this figure rose to 4,927 and in April, when Fliegerkorps X also joined the attack, it was 9,599. During April more than 6,700 tons of bombs were dropped on or around the island.

The schedule for the grand assault as laid down by Field-Marshal Kesselring called firstly for a neutralization of the air defences by forcing the batteries to exhaust their ammunition and their personnel. This was to be followed by mass attacks on airfields and grounded aircraft. Finally the main weight was to be directed against the naval forces, dockyards and installations until they were destroyed. The first of these aims was never achieved. Though ammunition was rationed as a long-term precaution, there was never an actual shortage. As to the second, though the activities of Malta's air striking forces were brought practically to a standstill, more than 350 sorties were flown during April by the fighters which accounted for about half of the Axis planes lost over the island during the month.

The naval dockyard had been a favourite target for the bombers from the start, but, though by February the damage had reached serious proportions, few ships were hit during the early stages of Fliegerkorps II's operations. Only the destroyer *Maori* was sunk at her buoy on 11 February and the *Cleopatra*, arriving *en route* to join the Mediterranean Fleet, was dive-bombed and hit by a 1,000-lb bomb, which fortunately did not explode. Similarly the submarines escaped the enemy's attention until March when the *P39* was sunk and two others damaged. From this time they were kept submerged all day, manned by spare crews.

At the end of March the full fury of the enemy descended on the dockyards. All surface warships that could steam were evacuated directly after the arrival of the March convoy. There remained the *Penelope* and the destroyers *Kingston* and *Gallant*, all damaged in various degrees. Both the latter were destroyed. The story of the *Penelope*'s repair is a fantastic one of courage and dogged endurance under incessant attack, during which fresh damage accumulated while the original was being repaired; during which, too, 6,500 rounds of 4-inch ammunition were fired by her guns, wearing out the new gun-barrels fitted shortly before. It ended with the cruiser, her riddled side plating sprouting hundreds of wooden plugs, slipping away on the night of 8 April for Gibraltar. The foiled enemy sent torpedo planes and bombers after her as she passed along the coast of Tunisia but she arrived without further damage on the 10th.

At the submarine base 1 April saw the beginning of a calamitous period. On that day the *Pandora*, fortunately cleared of the supplies she had brought, was sunk by two direct hits. The *P36* was damaged beyond repair, while the *Unbeaten*, though lying submerged, was so damaged that she had to be sailed for Gibraltar for repairs. Withdrawal of the flotilla was proposed but Captain Simpson, in command, gave his opinion that this 'virtually meant stopping offensive operations against Rommel's supplies; also since the 10th Flotilla was the only remaining means of preventing the enemy from bombarding Malta by heavy surface forces and mindful of the effect of our withdrawal on local morale ... a further effort seems imperative'.

On 4 April the Greek submarine *Glaucos* was sunk and the Polish *Sokol* was so damaged that, after leading a hunted life under camouflage in various corners of the dockyard while temporary repairs were made, she was finally sailed for Gibraltar on the 13th with 200 holes in her upper casing. The rest camps of the submarine crews were daily machine-gunned and bombed. It became almost impossible to service the boats between patrols. (On 14 April it was known that Wanklyn's *Upholder* had been sunk with all hands on her twenty-fifth patrol.)

By 12 April the Admiral Superintendent of Malta Dockyard was reporting that 'practically no workshops were in action other than those underground; all docks were damaged; electric power, light and telephones were largely out of action'. Between the 15th and 30th there were no less than 115 raids, the daily average of bombers attacking being 170. Great hopes were placed in the effect that the big reinforcement of 46 Spitfires, flown in from the US Carrier *Wasp* on the 20th, would have. But Fliegerkorps II watched their arrival on their radar scans and immediately pounced on the airfields. Within three days almost all the Spitfires had been either destroyed or damaged on the ground and the number of serviceable fighters was down to six.

Under these conditions the work of the submarine base was brought almost to a standstill. The decisive factor, however, which made it no longer feasible for the boats to operate from Malta was the inability to give the few remaining minesweepers the fighter protection they needed if they were to keep the harbour approaches clear. The density of the minefields daily increased—between 24 and 27 April no fewer than 123 moored mines with explosive floats and anti-sweeping obstructions were laid by the German 3rd E-boat Flotilla. To avoid being hemmed in, Simpson was at last forced to recommend withdrawal which was agreed to by the C-in-C on 26 April. By 10 May all submarines had gone. They were not to return for three months. The correctness of the decision was painfully confirmed by the loss of the *Urge* on 27 April to one of the newly laid mines; this was a submarine which under the command of Lieutenant E. P. Tomkinson had gained a reputation second only to that of the *Upholder*.

Field-Marshal Kesselring may perhaps be excused for thinking that by this time Malta was totally neutralized and the Libyan convoy route made safe, though his opinion was no doubt influenced both by Rommel's impending offensive to capture Tobruk and demands for air reinforcements, and by the pressure being put on him to release some of Luftflotte 2 for the Russian front. Indeed he had already made it known that he intended to transfer elsewhere two Groups of Ju.88s and two Groups of the Me.109s. Replacement by Italian bombers and fighters would permit, he considered, a sufficient weight of attack to prevent Malta from recovering.

His Italian colleagues were far less confident. Although the results of the grand assault had been good, they said they had not been up to the expectations of Kesselring. Judging by reports from Luftflotte 2 and the Sicilian air force concerning anti-aircraft fire and searchlights, the neutralization was far from complete. Furthermore, the blockade of the island, though very efficient, was not total, Above all, it was proving impossible to stop air reinforcements. In conclusion they gave their opinion that neutralization was only partial and temporary, and that it was necessary to continue and increase blockade operations lest the island should recover and re-assume the offensive.

They were to prove more correct than Kesselring. On 9 May a massive reinforcement of 60 Spitfires reached the island flown off from the *Wasp* and *Eagle*. This time the ground crews were well prepared to receive them. Though they arrived in the middle of a raid, they were so speedily refuelled that some of them were off the ground and going into action within 35 minutes of their arrival. The following day, on which Kesselring reported to Berlin that 'the neutralization of Malta was complete,' for the first time for many months the enemy were met by a superior fighter force. Efforts by the German airmen to hit the fast minelayer *Welshman*, which had arrived with Bofors anti-aircraft ammunition, aircraft spares and ammunition, were foiled and in the process the Germans lost 12 aircraft for the price of three Spitfires.

The transformation in the situation was, indeed, sudden and dramatic. The Malta War Diary records that 'such casualties were inflicted on the enemy that daylight raiding was brought to an abrupt end'. This is something of an exaggeration and presumably refers only to the dockyard area, as there were many more daylight raids recorded elsewhere in the island. Nevertheless, it reflects the wonderful feeling of relief and hope that was suddenly abroad. During May German and Italian losses over Malta increased to 40 against a British loss in combat of 25. Still more significant, British aircraft destroyed on the ground numbered only six as compared to 30 in April.

The crisis of Malta's ordeal by bombs had passed. Nevertheless until it became possible to supply her regularly, her use as a base would remain slight; and, indeed, unless supplies of food and fuel arrived within a reasonable time, the island would fall without need for further effort by the enemy.

In spite of this his intention to mount an assault to capture it still held good. Once again, it must have succeeded if pressed on with: this time it was Rommel who persuaded Kesselring to urge its postponement until he had captured Tobruk, for which purpose he planned to open an offensive on 26 May. As a result Mussolini and Hitler, meeting at the Berghof on

30 April, fixed 10 July as the date for Operation 'Hercules'—the amphibious assault on Malta.

Meanwhile, although convoys to Tripoli and Benghazi were now running largely unmolested, a growing shortage of shipping and of trucks for the long haul along the coast road to the front was restricting Rommel's supplies to little more than the bare minimum required. By the middle of May, however, he had succeeded in accumulating in Cyrenaica four large ammunition dumps, 11,000 tons of fuel and food for 30 days—sufficient for the limited objective of capturing Tobruk which was all that was envisaged. Rommel's strength in tanks was 584, against some 800 British, but the inferior quality and mechanical unreliability of the latter more than squared the odds. In air strength the Axis held the advantage both locally in the Western Desert and in the theatre as a whole. Furthermore many of the British fighters were obsolescent, compared with the German Me.109F.

Such, broadly, was the situation when the Battle of Gazala opened on 26 May, a battle which was to end four weeks later with the fall of Tobruk. It opened with Rommel's favourite gambit—an attempt to encircle the British army. This failed and for a time the Axis forces, pinned between minefields and the British armour and short of fuel and ammunition, were in grave danger of defeat. The attack launched on them failed, however, and the British forces were forced to withdraw with considerable losses. In the south, Free French forces under General König conducted an epic defence of Bir Hacheim against superior forces, from 26 May to 10 June, when the garrison was withdrawn by orders from General Ritchie. In the rest of the battle, fortunes swayed back and forth until the 18th when, with its armoured elements defeated, the Eighth Army was withdrawn to the Egyptian frontier, leaving Tobruk once again surrounded.

Rommel lost no time in attacking, and the assault opened at dawn on the 20th with a massive aerial bombardment in which 85 bombers, 21 Stuka dive-bombers and 40-50 fighter-bombers with 150 fighter escorts, shuttling back and forth from nearby landing grounds, dropped some 365 tons of bombs, stunning and neutralizing the defenders. Early on the 21st Tobruk surrendered. It was a tremendous personal triumph for Rommel who was immediately promoted to Field-Marshal in recognition of it. The objective laid down for his offensive had been achieved. The enemy was back on the Egyptian frontier, much shattered. According to Mussolini's directive of 5 May (Axis forces in North Africa were subject to the Italian *Comando Supremo*), the time had now come for a halt to be made while all efforts were transferred to Operation 'Hercules'. But for Rommel, the opportunist, his confidence and *élan* at full flood after his quick victory, Egypt and the Suez Canal and all that they entailed were beckoning. Amongst the booty captured at Tobruk had been 1,400 tons of petrol, large quantities of ammunition, both British and German, 2,000 serviceable vehicles and 5,000 tons of provisions. It seemed that all his problems of supply had been solved at one blow. Acting on his own initiative and by-passing the *Comando Supremo*, he radioed to the German Supreme Command that:

> The morale and condition of the troops, the quantity of stores captured and the present weakness of the enemy make it possible for us to thrust onwards into the heart of Egypt. Therefore request that the Duce be prevailed upon to remove the present restrictions on movement and that all troops now under my command be placed at my disposal to continue the offensive.

Hitler took little persuading, and on 23 June wrote to Mussolini strongly supporting Rommel's views. The Italian High Command was much less sanguine, but in face of the infectious confidence of the 'Desert Fox', intoxicated by his recent success, Marshal Cavallero agreed to a renewed offensive aimed at an advance into Egypt, while giving warnings of serious supply difficulties which must be expected. Furthermore, powerful units of Luftflotte 2 were to return to Sicily ready for the attack on Malta.

Rommel, forgetting his own warning made to Berlin in February 1941, on taking up his command, that 'Without Malta the Axis will end by losing control of North Africa', had anticipated approval of his plans. By 27 June the Panzer Army, as Rommel's Italo-German Command had become known, using captured vehicles, provisions and fuel, had passed Mersa Matruh and by the end of the month had reached the El Alamein position. Only 60 miles away across the bay was Alexandria and the Mediterranean Fleet, on the edge of the rich Nile Delta which was beckoning the young field-marshal and holding promises of decisive brilliant victory. He at once hurled his forces against the British defensive position. The breakthrough he sought nevertheless eluded him. On 3 July he made a further all-out attempt which again failed—with severe losses. When British counter-attacks were then similarly beaten back, the offensive power of both German and Italian troops had for the time being been exhausted. That night Rommel gave the order for the Panzer Army to go back on the defensive.

Between 15 and 21 July the Eighth Army struck back and, though the attacks in general failed, they were sufficient to make Rommel report that 'if the enemy succeeds in penetrating any farther, our Alamein position will become untenable'. He appealed for reinforcements. Amongst those rushed over to him by air were German and Italian airborne regiments which had been standing by in Sicily for the invasion of Malta. On 20 July, Mussolini, disappointed of his triumph, returned to Italy. The next day Operation 'Hercules' was finally cancelled.

A lull now ensued in the campaign on land, while both armies, exhausted and much shattered, recuperated. It was to last until 30

August. It is time, therefore, to turn back to examine events which had been taking place at sea.

In his directive of 26 June, Cavallero had insisted on 'a quick transfer of air forces from Africa to Sicily in order to increase the attack on Malta again'.

Thus Malta, apparently brought to its knees in May, already again threatened the flank of Rommel's supply line. In the interval its defensive powers had been greatly increased by the many Spitfires which had been flown in from aircraft carriers, with the result that the July 'blitz' on the island was to be a total failure. At the same time the withdrawal of strong units of Luftflotte 2 to Sicily from North Africa had left Rommel's air force inferior to the enemy, a factor which was to play an important part in his failure to break through at El Alamein. Sea power in Italian hands, from January to June 1942, had enabled Rommel to exploit the technical and tactical superiority of the Panzer Army, and inflict a humiliating defeat on the Eighth Army. The Italian Navy had, however, been unable to take full advantage of this sea power delivered to it by the Luftwaffe. Partly owing to a chronic shortage of oil fuel, for which the Italians had to rely upon their ally, but basically owing to the continued policy of a fleet-in-being and a refusal to challenge enemy surface forces even when they could do so in superior strength, they had permitted Malta to be replenished and its air defences to be reinforced. Time and again British and American carriers had been allowed to penetrate to the Central Mediterranean, fly off their deck-loads of Hurricanes or Spitfires and withdraw unmolested. Now, as sea power and control of the central basin became once again in dispute, the Italian surface fleet was at last to exert itself in some measure, but too late and too irresolutely.

Malta, for all its obstinate, fighting spirit, could not survive much longer without a replenishment. Its inhabitants, reduced to a bread ration of ten ounces daily, were being kept from starvation by communal feeding centres. There was no fuel for light and power. The disasters of the supply convoy in March had led to a decision to send no more supply ships until the island's fighter strength had been reinforced. Since then, however, a total of 198 Spitfires had been flown in from aircraft carriers, and it was decided to make a major effort to get supplies through in June.

The plan arrived at was to run convoys through from east and west in a simultaneous operation. From Gibraltar were to come five freighters, the British *Troilus*, *Burdwan* and *Orari*, the American *Chant*, the Dutch *Tanimbar* and a tanker, the American *Kentucky*. Their warship support would be divided, as on previous occasions, into three forces. The covering force, composed of the *Malaya*, the old carriers *Eagle* and *Argus*, the cruisers *Kenya*, *Liverpool* and *Charybdis*, and eight destroyers, would go no farther east than the entrance to the Skerki Channel. The close escort—the anti-aircraft cruiser *Cairo*, five large and four small destroyers—would then take the convoy on to Malta. The operation was given the code-name 'Harpoon' and was commanded by Vice-Admiral A. T. B. Curteis, flying his flag in the *Kenya*.

At the same time from the east, under cover of the Mediterranean Fleet, cruisers and destroyers, reinforced by three cruisers and some destroyers from the Eastern Fleet, was to come a convoy of no less than 11 freighters. The code-name for this part of the operation was 'Vigorous'. Apart from the inevitable air attacks to be expected by both these expeditions—in the Sicilian Channel and in the notorious Bomb Alley respectively—there were Italian surface forces well placed to intervene. At Cagliari in Sardinia was a division of 6-inch cruisers and destroyers. If they were boldly handled and prepared to accept a measure of air attack from Malta, they would comprise a very serious threat to the 'Harpoon' convoy after Curteis's larger ships had parted company with it. The main Italian fleet, grouped round the modern battleships *Vittorio Veneto* and *Littorio*, was at Taranto, only 19 hours' steaming from the route of the 'Vigorous' convoy. Admiral Iachino could intercept it in the early hours of the long calm summer day. This time Admiral Vian would not have the assistance of either darkness or heavy weather to slip the convoy past such an overwhelming threat. On the other hand Malta could now provide a striking force of Beaufort day and Wellington night torpedo planes, while from Egypt could come more Beauforts and some US Army Air Force Liberators equipped with the secret bomb sight of which great things were hoped. Shore-based air power as a substitute for a battle-fleet was thus to be relied upon. In all, 40 torpedo planes and eight Liberators were to be employed—sufficient, perhaps, if thrown in in massed attacks, but not, as experience already indicated, if employed in small units, as their widely separated bases dictated. Nevertheless the attempt had to be made. To control Operation 'Vigorous' Admiral Harwood, the naval C-in-C who had succeeded Andrew Cunningham, and the Air Officer C-in-C, Air Marshal Tedder, set up a 'combined operations room' in the headquarters of No 201 Naval Cooperation Group.

Dawn on 14 June 1942 found the 'Harpoon' force about 120 miles south-west of Sardinia and so within range of attack by the 20 bombers and 50 torpedo planes which, with a numerous fighter escort force, were based there. The Italian 7th Cruiser Division—the *Eugenio di Savoia*, flying the flag of Admiral da Zara, and the *Montecuccoli* with destroyers—had sailed from Cagliari the previous evening. Da Zara had hoped to intercept the speedy minelayer *Welshman*, which was known to have sailed with the convoy, laden with supplies and, as on previous occasions, would be sent ahead to Malta to unload. Finding nothing he had now returned to Palermo to await further orders.

In the other half of the Mediterranean the 'Vigorous' force was well inside Bomb Alley but, thanks to fighter cover detached by the Royal Air Force from the land battle in full swing in Cyrenaica, it was to proceed

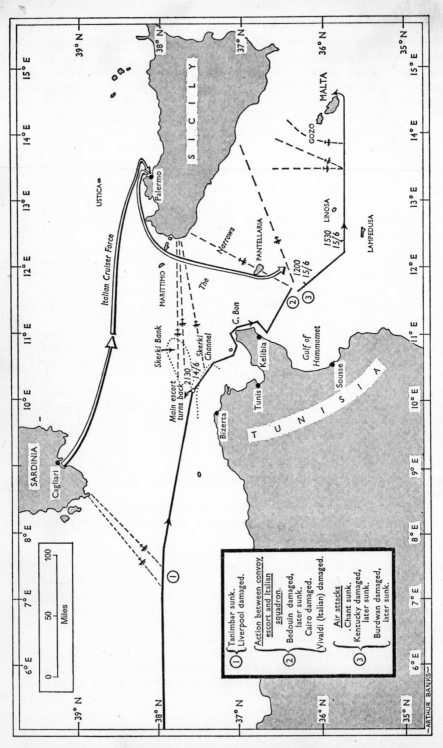

Operation 'Harpoon', 14 – 15 June 1942

MALTA

GOZO

SICILY

SARDINIA

Cagliari

Italian Cruiser Force

USTICA

Palermo

MARITTIMO

The Narrows

PANTELLARIA

LINOSA

1530
15/6

LAMPEDUSA

1200
15/6

Skerki Bank

Main escort
turns back

2130
14/6

Skerki
Channel

C. Bon

Kelibia

Gulf of
Hammamet

Sousse

TUNISIA

Tunis

Bizerta

Miles

0   50   100

① { Tanimbar sunk.
    Liverpool damaged.

② { Action between convoy
    escort and Italian
    squadron.
    Bedouin damaged,
    later sunk.
    Cairo damaged.
    (Vivaldi (Italian) damaged.

③ { Air attacks
    Chant sunk.
    Kentucky damaged,
    later sunk.
    Burdwan damaged,
    later sunk.

—ARTHUR BANKS—

unmolested until the late afternoon when it passed out of range of British-held airfields. Nevertheless, it had suffered losses earlier. One transport had been damaged by dive-bombers and had been detached to Tobruk, and another had been sent back as too slow. Now another ship, the Dutch *Aagtekirk*, had to be sent away to Tobruk for the same reason and before she could reach port was set upon by 40 dive-bombers and sent to the bottom. The convoy was thus down to eight by this time.

At Taranto, Iachino had known during the previous day of the 'Vigorous' convoy. During the forenoon of the 14th his fleet prepared for sea and at 1430 it sailed, in time to intercept Vian's force at 0930 the next morning. Thus the various forces were in motion or poised ready to move towards a clash in the disputed central basin of the Mediterranean; on the result of this clash could depend the survival of Malta and perhaps the whole struggle for the Middle East.

For clarity it is necessary to follow separately the fortunes of the two convoys for Malta, the first of which to see action was 'Harpoon'. The Italians had absorbed the lessons of the past which taught the need for air attacks to be delivered *en masse,* and they had the numbers available to do so. Out of the 16 Sea Hurricanes and four Fulmars embarked in the *Eagle* only a very modest fighter defence could be kept airborne. Though they were to perform valiantly during the day, shooting down 17 enemy aircraft for the loss of seven of their own number, they were too few to deter the swarms of attackers escorted by an almost equal number of fighter aircraft.

An early attack by Italian fighter-bombers did no harm. But when at 1130 a coordinated attack by 28 torpedo planes and 10 high-level bombers developed, escorted by 20 fighters, the defences were swamped. The freighter *Tanimbar* was sunk and the cruiser *Liverpool* damaged, both by torpedoes. The cruiser, taken in tow by the destroyer *Antelope* and steering for Gibraltar, was for some time an irresistible lure for 26 bombers and eight torpedo planes, but escaped without further damage. For the remainder, the afternoon passed uneventfully and it was not until 1820 that the next attack came—this time by Ju.88s of Fliegerkorps II in Sicily. They were set upon by the Fleet Air Arm fighters and their efforts to hit the carriers were foiled.

An hour and a half later came another coordinated, mass attack by Italian torpedo planes and German Ju.88s and Stukas. A wild, thunderous scene of diving planes, bursting bombs and a storm of gunfire was made further chaotic by the boom of depth-charges loosed on what was believed to be a submarine's periscope. From it all the convoy and escort emerged unscathed, though the *Argus* only narrowly avoided several torpedoes.

There was to be one more unsuccessful attack in the dusk by which time the convoy and escort had entered the restricted waters of the Skerki Channel and Curteis and the covering force had parted company. The five remaining ships of the convoy were now kept company by the *Cairo*, nine destroyers—of which four were of the little 'Hunt' class mounting only (like the *Cairo*) 4-inch guns and primarily equipped for anti-aircraft fire—four minesweepers and six minesweeping motor launches In command of the force was Captain C. C. Hardy of the *Cairo*. The night passed quietly and dawn found the force 30 miles south of Pantellaria with Malta less than 12 hours' steaming ahead. Beaufighters from Malta were promised at first light and by noon the convoy should be under cover of Spitfires. The outlook which thus seemed reasonably hopeful was suddenly transformed when, at 0630 on 15 June, Captain Hardy saw that the way ahead was barred by enemy cruisers. A few minutes later they opened fire at a range of over 10 miles, far outside the capability of any of the British guns.

Though the departure of da Zara's squadron from Palermo had been known the previous evening, subsequent shadowing had been impossible owing to a dearth of reconnaissance planes at a time when all attention was being devoted to the Italian battle-fleet coming south from Taranto. Judging from previous form it had been assumed that da Zara was going to join Iachino rather than operate in the Sicilian Channel. Captain Hardy turned a bold face to this unexpected and disconcerting development. His five fleet destroyers, led by Commander Scurfield of the *Bedouin*, raced out to offer battle while the convoy turned back under cover of a smoke screen laid by the *Cairo* and the four 'Hunt'-class destroyers.

Da Zara, steering south across the convoy's route to Malta, divided his fire between the *Cairo*, which was steering a parallel course and screening the convoy with smoke, and the advancing British destroyers. Undistracted at first by fire from the still out-ranged British guns, the Italian cruisers made good shooting. The *Cairo* was twice hit, though she escaped serious damage. The *Bedouin* and the next ship in the British destroyer line, the *Partridge*, were both hit and disabled. On the other hand the two rear ships, *Matchless* and *Marne*, were able to turn their guns with good effect on two of the Italian destroyers, *Vivaldi* and *Malocello*, which had been ordered to break through to get at the convoy. Hit in the boiler-room, the *Vivaldi* came to a stop, on fire, and the *Malocello* stayed to go to her assistance.

Meanwhile Captain Hardy had called for his four 'Hunt'-class destroyers to support him in staving off the surface threat. Thus all the ships with good anti-aircraft capabilities were otherwise engaged when at 0700 eight Stukas screamed down on the convoy. No fighters had opposed them, the original patrol of Beaufighters having returned to Malta and their reliefs having not yet arrived—a common defect of shore-based, as opposed to carrier-borne air defence. With little gunfire to distract them, the Stukas made good practice. The *Chant* was sunk and the *Kentucky* disabled.

As the fight between the two surface forces ran south and the Italian cruisers showed no inclination to penetrate the smoke screen, Hardy turned back towards the convoy. He was followed by da Zara, so that, when he found the convoy steering slowly south-eastward for Malta with the *Kentucky* in tow of the minesweeper, *Hebe*, he ordered it to reverse course again. The position of the convoy nevertheless seemed extremely perilous with the Italian cruisers 6-inch guns about to come into action to make short work of the merchantmen, when at 0840 da Zara suddenly reversed course and made off to the eastward. For some reason he had come to the conclusion that the convoy's course would shortly take it northward to pass clear of a mined area which lay ahead, and he therefore made for the gap between the minefield and Pantellaria to await its arrival. There he waited until noon, being twice attacked—unsuccessfully—by torpedo planes from Malta.

By 0940 Hardy had gathered in his escorts, except for the *Bedouin* and *Partridge* which had repaired her damage sufficiently to take the *Bedouin* in tow, and the convoy was again on course for Malta but at the slow speed dictated by the disabled *Kentucky*. Long-range Spitfires had arrived and at 1040 drove off some German bombers. Once again, however, they had gone back to base and their reliefs had not arrived when the next attack came in, which disabled the transport *Burdwan*.

With Malta still 150 miles away and the air and surface threat undiminished, Hardy now decided that he must cut his losses if he wished to get his last two undamaged ships, *Troilus* and *Orari*, to port. Leaving the *Hebe* to sink the *Kentucky* and the 'Hunt'-class destroyer *Badsworth* to sink the *Burdwan*, he ordered the remainder to increase to their maximum speed. Two hours later, from the *Hebe*, following some 25 miles astern of the convoy after unsuccessfully trying to sink the *Kentucky*, Hardy heard that the Italian cruisers had returned to the scene and had damaged the minesweeper. Taking his three fleet destroyers with him, he steered the *Cairo* to her assistance.

Shortly before 1400 the Italian cruisers came in sight and Hardy prepared to renew the unequal battle. At this moment, however, he saw them turn away to the westward and open fire at some target out of sight beyond the horizon. As he surmised, this was the *Bedouin* and *Partridge* for whom he could do nothing. Forced to leave them to their fate, he turned back to rejoin the convoy.

It was indeed the two destroyers on which da Zara, having given the *coup de grâce* to the *Kentucky* and the *Burdwan*, had turned his guns. Lieutenant-Commander W. A. F. Hawkins of the *Partridge* at once slipped the tow, made smoke to screen the *Bedouin* and stood away to draw the enemy's fire. The *Bedouin* was doomed, however, and her end was only hastened when at 1425 an Italian aircraft put a torpedo into the easy target. The *Partridge* survived to reach Gibraltar. Da Zara, recalled, shaped course for his base.

Though the convoy was attacked by aircraft twice more before dark, no further damage was suffered from that source. But its ordeal was not yet over. Through an error in signalling it steamed into unswept water while approaching Valetta. The *Orari* and several escorts exploded mines, but fortunately only a 'Hunt'-class destroyer was sunk, the remainder suffering no more than minor damage. Thus only two, out of the six transports which had set out, reached Malta with 15,000 tons of desperately needed supplies.

From the strategic point of view, the Italian decision to send surface forces to break up the convoy was one long overdue in the protracted campaign over Malta. Tactically the Italian admiral had failed to act with the boldness necessary to make the destruction of the convoy complete; but by delaying the convoy in waters at the extreme limit of fighter range from Malta and by drawing off the escorts, he had opened the way for Italian and German aircraft to a degree of success that they rarely achieved in the face of determined opposition.

The lesson was taken in by the Italian naval high command, but not by the Luftwaffe or the Regia Aeronautica who took all the credit for such success as had been gained; so that when a similar situation arose two months later the Italian surface ships would be denied the air cover they needed to participate. In consequence what might have been total defeat of an effort to re-supply Malta would be frustrated.

'Harpoon' had proved a costly operation for the British. Two destroyers had been lost, a cruiser, three destroyers and a minesweeper damaged. But Malta was saved at a time when starvation was very near. The island's condition would have been a great deal more satisfactory, however, if the 'Vigorous' convoy had achieved as much as 'Harpoon'. Its failure has, unfortunately, to be recorded. We left it early on 14 June making its way through Bomb Alley. Its escort, commanded by Rear-Admiral Vian in the *Cleopatra*, comprised seven cruisers and 26 destroyers besides anti-submarine corvettes and minesweepers with little fighting value. Admiral Harwood, the C-in-C, had no battleships to oppose the Italian battle squadron should it intervene. As a somewhat desperate bluff the ancient and virtually unarmed battleship *Centurion*, which had served before the war as a wireless-controlled target, was sailed with the convoy.

The real substitutes for battleship strength, some 50 'strike' aircraft of various types, were gathered on Malta and at Egyptian bases. In addition nine submarines would maintain a screen to the north of the convoy's route. This plan accorded with the developments in naval warfare which had come with the improved striking power of aircraft; but the means available to implement it were unsatisfactory in two vital points—the number of aircraft was insufficient and it was impossible to coordinate their attacks owing to the wide dispersal of their bases. Six months earlier *Prince of Wales* and *Repulse* with a screen of four destroyers had been sunk by the massed attack of some 80 Japanese bombers and torpedo planes. The Royal Air Force in the Mediterranean after nearly three years of war could muster only 50 naval strike aircraft and they were intending to throw them in, a few at a time, to attack the Italian battleships accompanied by four cruisers and 12 destroyers. Prewar and subsequent neglect, by a nation dependent for survival on sea power, to build up its maritime air force was once again coming home to roost.

By nightfall on 14 June, the 'Vigorous' convoy had undergone seven air attacks by a total of some 60 or 70 stukas and Ju.88s. The majority had been foiled by the gunfire of Vian's ships and by long-range fighters, but one freighter, the *Bhutan*, had been sunk. Darkness brought little relaxation. Aircraft repeatedly illuminated the force with flares, and German E-boats, sighted at dusk, prowled round the outskirts of the formation awaiting a suitable moment to attack.

By 2300 Vian knew that daylight must bring an encounter with the Italian fleet. That his cruisers and destroyers could not hold it off during the long summer day he also knew. To his inquiry whether he should retire, the C-in-C replied that he should hold on until 0200 and then reverse course. In the interval perhaps Iachino might have been weakened or even halted by air and submarine attack. Vian complied. The inevitable temporary confusion, resulting from such a manoeuvre by 50 ships of widely varied types, gave the E-boats the opportunity for which they had been waiting. The cruiser *Newcastle* and the destroyer *Hasty* were both torpedoed. The former remained capable of steaming at 24 knots, but the destroyer had to be abandoned and sunk.

Meanwhile in the joint operations room at Alexandria the two Cs-in-C waited tensely for news from the four torpedo-carrying Wellingtons of No 38 Squadron which had taken off from Malta at midnight, and from a further force of nine Beauforts of No 217 Squadron which followed three hours later. By 0525 nothing had come in—and, in fact, the Wellingtons, met by the usual Italian defensive measure of a dense smoke screen, had achieved nothing. Harwood nevertheless hoped for good news from the Beauforts, and from the submarines which should be met by the Italian fleet at dawn. He ordered Vian to turn back westwards again.

Dawn did, indeed, break for the Italians in a wild flurry of excitement as the Beauforts streaked in to the attack. It was witnessed through his periscope by Lieutenant Maydon, commanding the submarine *Umbra*, who described it as:

A fantastic circus of wildly careering capital ships, cruisers and destroyers; of tracer shell streaks and A/A bursts. At one period there was not a quadrant of the compass unoccupied by enemy vessels weaving continuously to and fro. It was only possible to count the big ships; destroyers seemed to be everywhere.

It was not surprising that out of such a mêlée Maydon was unable to pick a target for his torpedoes; or that the airmen were uncertain of what they had achieved. They had, in fact, hit and disabled the cruiser *Trento* but thought and reported that both Iachino's battleships had been torpedoed.

Not until well on in the forenoon did this claim reach Harwood and in the meantime a reconnaissance plane had reported the Italian fleet, at 8.28 a.m., still intact, holding on southward and now within 150 miles of the convoy. Once again, therefore, Vian was ordered to turn back on to an easterly course to await results from the attacks being mounted from Egypt. This marching and counter-marching in 'Bomb Alley' exacted its toll. When 20 Stukas pounced during the forenoon, six of them concentrated on the *Birmingham*, narrowly missing her, bomb explosions causing her to whip so fiercely that several of her turrets were displaced and put out of action. In the afternoon, out of 30 dive-bombers, 12 picked the little 'Hunt' class destroyer *Airedale* for their target. When the smoke and spray subsided, she lay dead in the water, completely disabled, and had to be sunk. Fortunately, many of the enemy pilots were lured to attack the *Centurion's* impressive bulk. The sturdy old veteran was not only well able to take their blows but had enough close-range armament to hit back. For the loss of four of their number the Stukas only succeeded in slightly damaging her.

Nevertheless, when at 1.45 p.m. Vian received Harwood's order, given two hours earlier and based on the Beaufort's optimistic report, to turn yet again for Malta, he disregarded it, correctly considering that it had been overtaken by a more recent air report from which it was clear that Iachino was still coming after him in undiminished strength. The air attacks despatched from Egyptian bases had in fact neither slowed nor weakened the Italian fleet. The first to arrive had been the American Liberators. From 14,000 feet they planted their bombs with admirable accuracy all round the battleships—but only one of them hit, on the armourplate of the forward turret of the *Littorio*, doing negligible damage. To the airmen, however, it seemed that both big ships had been heavily hit and they reported accordingly. Before they left the scene they saw—as they thought—further damage inflicted by the Beaufort torpedo planes.

Twelve Beauforts of No. 39 Squadron had taken off from Sidi Barrani to synchronise their attacks with those of the Liberators. Jumped by Me.109s, two had been shot down and five more damaged and forced to return. The remainder carried on and pressed home their attacks in the face of a daunting volume of gunfire. They believed they too had hit a battleship but in fact all their torpedoes were avoided.

Around the British convoy air attack had been following air attack with scarcely an interval between them. Ammunition was being used up fast and the distance to Malta was being steadily increased. Iachino had thus achieved his object by the time the perennial preoccupation of the

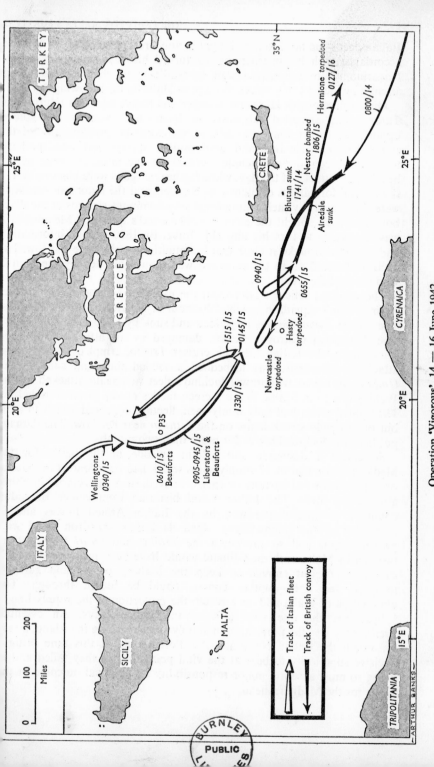

Operation 'Vigorous', 14 — 16 June 1942

Labels within map:
TURKEY
GREECE
CRETE
ITALY
SICILY
MALTA
CYRENAICA
TRIPOLITANIA

35°N
25°E
20°E
15°E

Hermione torpedoed 0127/16
Nestor bombed 1806/15
Bhutan sunk 1741/14
Airedale sunk
0800/14
0940/15
0655/15
Hasty torpedoed
Newcastle torpedoed
1515/15
0145/15
1330/15
0905-0945/15 Liberators & Beauforts
0610/15 Beauforts
○ P35
Wellingtons 0340/15

Track of Italian fleet
Track of British convoy

0   100   200
Miles

ARTHUR BANKS

Italian fleet—the need to avoid night action—reared its head. At 1500, in accordance with his instructions, he turned his fleet away making for Navarino where he was to wait in readiness to challenge any fresh attempt by the British to break through to Malta on the following day.

On learning of this Harwood assumed the Italian fleet was returning to Taranto and signalled jubilantly to Vian that 'Now is the golden opportunity to get convoy to Malta', provided the smaller ships of the escort had enough fuel and ammunition. It was too late—perhaps fortunately, considering Iachino's orders. In the midst of some of the heaviest air attacks of the day, while his heavier guns were blackening the sky around formations of high-level bombers and the automatic weapons were shooting away their ammunition in voluminous streams at the dive-bombers, Vian sought the answer to Harwood's question. Meanwhile it was impossible to turn his unwieldy force. By 1830 enough information had come in to make it clear that ammunition stocks were too low. His decision to hold on to the eastward was soon confirmed by the C-in-C who recalled the whole force to Alexandria.

The effort to relieve Malta from the east had been a dismal failure. Before Vian's squadron reached harbour it suffered further casualties. The cruiser *Hermione* was torpedoed and sunk by *U205* during the night. The Australian destroyer *Nestor*, damaged by air attacks, had to be scuttled. On the Italian side the cruiser *Trento*, crippled by the dawn attack by Beauforts, was torpedoed a second time and sunk by the *Umbra*. During its withdrawal Iachino's fleet was again attacked by the Wellingtons from Malta. Smoke-screen tactics nearly saved it as before. The baffled pilots had only dimly-seen, fleeting targets at which to aim; but one torpedo struck home on the *Littorio* near her bow. The damage put her into dockyard hands for more than two months.

So ended a desperate and gallant episode in the battle for the Mediterranean. Out of 17 supply ships which had been loaded for Malta, only two, with 15,000 tons of cargo, arrived, at a heavy cost in ships, aircraft and lives. The Italian naval historian Commander Bragadin, counts it 'a great battle won by the Italian Armed Forces and in particular by the Italian Navy'. Had da Zara's squadron acted with proper vigour and so prevented the *Troilus* and *Orari* from getting through to Malta such an estimate would have been justified. But their cargoes were just enough to keep the Maltese people and garrison meagrely fed until another convoy could be fought through. The elimination of Malta and, as a result, the protection of the supply line to Libya, was the one vital task of the Italian Navy. An essential preliminary was the prevention of supply ships reaching the island, a task for which the Italian Navy and Air Force could at this time bring a decisive superiority to bear at the vital point. In this they failed and in doing so must accept a major responsibility for the final outcome of the battle for the Mediterranean.

June 1942, it will be remembered, saw not only the failure of the 'Vigorous' operation to relieve Malta but also the withdrawal of the Eighth Army from the Gazala line, a retreat which continued until, on the 28th, Rommel's army was at Mersa Matruh with the Luftwaffe occupying airfields within 160 miles of Alexandria. Faced with the prospect of fighter-escorted bomber raids and even the loss of Alexandria itself, Admiral Harwood took the decision to disperse his fleet to Haifa, Port Said and Beirut, move all ships not required for active operations south of the Canal and transfer his own headquarters to Ismailia.

The evacuation, with its ominous implications and implicit doubts in the Eighth Army's ability to hold the El Alamein position, spread an air of gloom. There was almost a taint of panic amongst the personnel, male and female, of the Alexandria base and administrative staffs as they crowded into Suez and Port Tewfik seeking accommodation. The loss of the submarine depot ship *Medway* to the torpedoes of *U372*, on her way to Haifa on 30 June, probably marked the nadir of British fortunes in the Mediterranean. Sinking in a few minutes she took with her 90 spare torpedoes. The resultant loss of refit and replenishment facilities brought the work of the submarines almost to a halt for some time, and during July the Italian tonnage sunk by them was reduced to a single ship of 792 tons.

That British fortunes had indeed reached their lowest ebb and that the tide was on the turn, though this was far from apparent to the protagonists at the time, can be discerned from a general survey of the situation. On land, Rommel had been brought to a halt and forced on to the defensive. As General Alexander (who relieved General Auchinleck as C-in-C on 15 August) wrote in his despatch on the African Campaigns: 'On 2 July 1942 the Eighth Army defeated the enemy's most desperate efforts to break through ... the old Desert Army gained the vital time necessary for the arrival of the fresh divisions and improved tanks which were to turn the tide of battle.' The new tanks to which he referred were the 'General Sherman', 300 of which, together with 100 105-mm self-propelled guns, had been allocated to the Middle East by President Roosevelt and which were to give the Eighth Army for the first time armoured formations as well equipped as the Panzer Army and in far greater strength.

While the Eighth Army was gathering strength, the Panzer Army, except for the reinforcements hastily flown in from Sicily in the middle of July, was stagnating. Rommel was dissatisfied with the flow of men, vehicles and supplies, all of which were available in Italy but were not reaching him in sufficient quantity or in the right order and proportions. Although, as a result of the German Navy's assumption of responsibility for the coastal supply route, supplies reaching the German Army in July amounted to 26,000 tons, including 12,000 tons of fuel and 1,370 vehicles, Rommel complained that this only met the daily needs and that no reserves were being built up. The position was made worse by the raids of British cruisers and destroyers against the harbour approaches to Mersa Matruh during July, as a result of which three supply ships were sunk. In the same month a Royal Air Force raid on Tobruk hit and destroyed the fuel storage depot there. Rommel's situation was to deteriorate still further as the attacks on the Libyan supply ships were resumed.

The resurgence of Malta, since the middle of May, as an offensive base, had led to the recall at the beginning of July of a number of units of Fliegerkorps II to Sicily and a renewed attempt to neutralize the island. Concentrated bombing attacks on Malta's airfields, during which over 700 tons of bombs were dropped, succeeded in destroying 17 aircraft on the ground and damaging many more; but the bombers were now met by a powerful fighter defence and the brief 'blitz' cost the Axis air forces 65 aircraft against a British loss of 36 Spitfires. By 15 July the attackers had been forced to fall back on tip-and-run raids by fighter-bombers.

Already, on 5 July, Vice-Admiral Leatham, commanding at Malta, had reported that he considered the island could again be used by submarines. By 12 July the swept channel had been cleared of mines and on the 20th the first submarine, *Unbroken*, arrived. Results became apparent during August when submarines sank seven supply ships totalling 40,043 tons.

In the air the Middle East Air Force had at least reached a rough parity with the Axis air strength in the Mediterranean, though the equipment of many of the fighter squadrons with Hurricanes I and II gave the Luftwaffe a qualitative advantage. In addition there were coming into action units of the United States Army Air Force, flying Liberators, Fortresses, Mitchells and Kittyhawks.

Thus everywhere British strength was growing and there were signs that the period of endurance in the face of superior strength was coming to an end. Not least among the omens of approaching victory was the Anglo-American agreement, reached in the middle of July, to launch an expedition through French North Africa in October. Nevertheless much time was needed for the British Eighth Army, situated at the end of its immensely long line of communications round the Cape of Good Hope, to receive the reinforcement and fresh equipment it needed before it could take up the offensive again. The earliest date estimated for this was mid-September, an estimate which was far from acceptable to Mr Churchill and had its influence on his decision to relieve Auchinleck as C-in-C. Under his successor, in the event, the British offensive did not open until 25 October.

On the other hand, time was on the side of the Eighth Army. Its lines of communication, long as they were, were reasonably secure. For Rommel time was running out as losses on the Libyan route mounted in August to 34 per cent. The longer he remained passive the stronger his enemy would become while he himself would not. Retreat was unthinkable in view of his past sanguine utterances. He would therefore be forced to throw his army, in one last desperate gamble 'to win or lose it all', against the vast and powerful defences of the excellent defensive position of El Alamein.

Only in one direction was delay seriously embarrassing to the British. Malta was starving and must be fed. A relief convoy in August was essential. So long as the whole of Cyrenaica was in Axis hands, the experience of the 'Vigorous' operation showed that it was not possible to run a convoy to the island from the east. All efforts must therefore be concentrated on fighting a large one through from Gibraltar. A main escort powerful enough to oppose the Italian battle-fleet was to be assembled, while the Force 'X' which would take the convoy through the Sicilian Channel would this time include modern cruisers and a strong force of destroyers. At the same time the air forces at Malta were to be strongly reinforced for the occasion from Great Britain and from Egypt. The code-name given to the operation was 'Pedestal'.

The Italian Naval Staff had information well in advance, from intercepted radio messages, that an important British operation was impending in the western Mediterranean, and it was not difficult to guess its nature. Consequently, when further information came in during the 9th and 10th of a convoy passing through the Straits of Gibraltar, a huge air fleet of 784 German and Italian bombers, dive-bombers and torpedo-planes, besides scouting aircraft which brought the total to about 1,000, had already been assembled in Sardinia and Sicily. Six Italian and three German submarines had been stationed between the Balearic Islands and Algiers athwart the route to Malta, 11 Italian submarines thronged the approaches to the Narrows and another lurked off Malta. A fresh, temporary, minefield was laid close off Cape Bon in an area that had hitherto always been kept clear for use by Italian convoys for Libya. South of Cape Bon 23 MTBs would be waiting in ambush. Finally a force of three heavy, three light cruisers and 12 destroyers would intercept the convoy south of Pantellaria. This formidable and versatile assembly of air and sea power, which might with some confidence have been expected to bar effectively the passage of any convoy to Malta, was certainly to bring about the most hard-fought convoy battle of the war. Though it proved tactically disastrous for the British, dogged courage and seamanlike skill, particularly on the part of the crews of the merchant ships involved, wrung from it a strategic success which was finally to dispel Axis hopes of victory in North Africa. It is, therefore, worthy of examination in some detail.

In the small hours of 10 August 1942, the convoy of 14 merchant ships for Operation 'Pedestal', with its large fleet escort commanded by Vice-Admiral E. N. Syfret, passed through the Straits of Gibraltar and headed eastwards. It was an impressive armada. The merchantmen were all fast, modern ships, 13 of them freighters carrying mixed cargoes of which, in every case, the main items were flour, petrol stored in five-gallon cans and

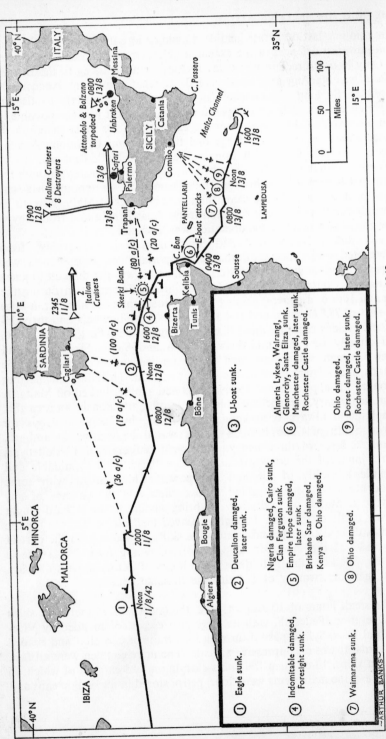

Operation 'Pedestal', 11 — 13 August 1942

① Eagle sunk.

② Deucalion damaged, later sunk.

④ Indomitable damaged, Foresight sunk.

⑦ Waimarama sunk.

③ U-boat sunk.

⑤ Nigeria damaged, Cairo sunk, Clan Ferguson sunk. Empire Hope damaged, later sunk. Brisbane Star damaged. Kenya & Ohio damaged.

⑧ Ohio damaged.

⑥ Almeria Lykes, Wairangi, Glenorchy, Santa Eliza sunk. Manchester damaged, later sunk. Rochester Castle damaged.

⑨ Ohio damaged, Dorset damaged, later sunk. Rochester Castle damaged.

~ARTHUR BANKS~

ammunition—the last two uneasy shipmates on a voyage with such an evil reputation. Two of these ships, the *Santa Elisa* and *Almeria Lykes*, were American-owned and manned. The remainder, the *Port Chalmers*, flying the broad pennant of the convoy commodore, Commander A. G. Venables, RN, the *Rochester Castle*, *Deucalion*, *Glenorchy*, *Empire Hope*, *Wairangi*, *Waimarama*, *Melbourne Star*, *Brisbane Star*, *Dorset* and *Clan Ferguson*, comprised some of the finest ships of Britain's merchant navy. Finally there was one large tanker, the *Ohio*, American-owned but chartered by the British Ministry of War Transport, manned by British seamen and commanded by Captain D. W. Mason of the Eagle Oil & Shipping Company. She carried 11,500 tons of kerosene and oil-fuel, as vital to Malta's survival as the foodstuffs in the freighters.

As on previous occasions, the convoy was to enjoy a powerful protection as far as the Sicilian Narrows. Against submarine attack there were two dozen destroyers. To fend off the bombers and torpedo planes there were 46 Hurricanes, 10 Martlets and 16 Fulmars aboard the carriers *Victorious*, *Indomitable* and *Eagle*, backed by the gunfire of the battleships *Nelson* and *Rodney*, the anti-aircraft cruisers *Sirius*, *Phoebe* and *Charybdis* and the cruisers *Nigeria*, *Kenya* and *Manchester*. Beyond that point, however, there would be only the three cruisers, the anti-aircraft cruiser *Cairo* and half the destroyers.

The passage of this force through the Straits of Gibraltar was known immediately by the Italian high command. Their countermeasures went at once into motion. When the first reconnaissance aircraft gained contact, at 1010 on the 11th, the convoy and escort were already threading their way through the first of the five ambushes awaiting them—the nine submarines spread across the route north of Algiers. It was Lieutenant Rosenbaum of the German *U73* who had the fortune to find himself placed squarely in the way. Skilfully working his way through the destroyer screen and under the convoy columns he put four torpedoes into the *Eagle*. Within eight minutes she had gone down, taking more than 200 of her crew with her.

That evening the convoy came within range of strike aircraft on the Sardinian airfields. Thirty-six Ju.88 dive-bombers and He.111 torpedo planes timed their attack for the half-light, as dusk was settling over the calm sea. Thus they evaded the patrolling fighters; but, met by a storm of gunfire, they achieved nothing and lost four of their number. While they were away, their base airfields at Elmas and Decimomammu were struck by ten Beaufighters from Malta which machine-gunned and destroyed five Italian torpedo planes and damaged 14 more, a loss which the Italian Air Commander, General Santoro, was to hold in some degree responsible for the lack of success on the following day. On the other hand, he was lucky in that American Liberators, which raided the airfields during the night, dropped their loads of delayed-action bombs wide, most of them falling in the open countryside.

Meanwhile Admiral Syfret's force moved on through the night unmolested. Dawn of 12 August broke over the convoy, still at full strength and steaming in admirable order in four columns. Soon after 0600 the fighter patrol of 12 took off from the carriers and it was not long before Martlets from the *Indomitable* had chopped out of the sky the two Italian shadowing aircraft. But, with only about 70 miles to come from their Sardinian bases, the enemy aircraft could have no difficulty in finding their target. Soon after 0900 they arrived, 19 Ju.88s. They had a very rough reception, being intercepted by 16 British fighters. On board the ships men waiting tensed for their ordeal were heartened by the sight of twin-engined aircraft smoking and spiralling down to crash in the sea. Others dropped their bombs wide and fled. Six of the German aircraft were missing when their comrades got back to base.

There was grim satisfaction in the fleet and convoy but no illusion about what was yet in store. And, indeed, at that moment the Regia Aeronautica was preparing to launch its most ambitious coordinated assault by more than 100 aircraft of all types. The first wave, whose primary object was to distract the defences from the torpedo planes following it, was composed of ten Savoia bombers, eight Caproni fighter-bombers and an escort of 14 Macchi fighters. The Savoias were carrying a new weapon, the *motobomba*, a torpedo which, after floating down by parachute, set off on a zig-zag or circling course impossible to predict and difficult to avoid. Ingenious at it was, dropped ahead of the convoy it was no serious threat to one so well drilled and alert as this. At sight of the falling parachutes, the ships turned smartly together 90° to starboard to 'side-step' the danger area, manoeuvring perfectly together in spite of having to fight off simultaneously the Capronis dive-bombing and machine-gunning.

It may be that this unexpected manoeuvre upset the 43 torpedo planes which, while it was in progress, swooped down in two groups, one from each flank. Or they may have been put off by the Sea Hurricanes and Martlets, some of which broke through the escort of 26 Re.2001 fighters to harass them. Certainly the torpedoes were fired at long range and not one found its mark.

The big Italian effort was petering out ineffectually. However, the Italians had other shots in their lockers. The first of these was a Savoia 79, loaded with a heavy bomb, radio-controlled from a Cant float-plane, a sort of pilotless 'Kamikaze'. Unfortunately for them this ingenious device failed to function. The S79 flew off inland and finally crashed and exploded in Algeria. The other consisted of two Re.2001 fighter-bombers, single-engine monoplanes resembling Hurricanes, each carrying a special heavy bomb designed to cause havoc amongst a carrier's deck load of aircraft. The *Victorious*, engaged in landing-on some of her Hurricanes, saw two of them, as it seemed, approaching and took no action till, from their bellies, bombs fell away. One landed squarely on the flight deck and would have had a disastrous effect if it had exploded; but fortunately it broke up on impact and did little harm. The Italian pilots escaped without a shot fired at them.

For all the massive effort made by the Italian Air Force, it was left to a formation of 37 German dive-bombers to achieve the only positive results. Arriving just as the torpedo planes were retiring, only 11 managed to evade the defending fighters and attack. Picking the Blue Funnel ship *Deucalion*, a veteran of the Malta run, which was leading the port wing column of the convoy, they concentrated their bombs on her. Only one hit her and this passed right through the ship; but others fell and exploded so close around her, smashing a lifeboat in the process, that the whole ship was lifted and shaken as by a giant hand. Captain Ramsay Brown rang down for the engines to be stopped and lifeboats cleared away while the mate and carpenter sounded the wells and inspected the damage.

It was not Ramsay Brown's first experience of being damaged while in convoy and he had no intention of being left behind if he could help it. Unfortunately, many of his seasoned crew had recently been replaced; and now, without orders, some greasers and assistant stewards in panic lowered two of the lifeboats and pulled away in them. When it was found that the damage was by no means fatal and the ship could get under way again, these two boats and their crews had to be recovered, which caused an hour's delay. Left far behind, the *Deucalion*, escorted by the destroyer *Bramham*, turned towards the Tunisian shore, hoping to avoid the attention of the enemy by following the coastal route. Ramsay Brown's plan came near to success. Though towards evening the ship was again attacked by two dive-bombers and the resultant near misses again lifted and shook her, her sturdy construction saved her and as dusk came down she was still plodding along at 12 knots. But, with the last of the light, two torpedo planes found her. A torpedo burst against her side. Aviation petrol and kerosene caught fire, sending flames up to twice the height of her masts. The ship was an inferno and it was only a matter of minutes before the explosives in her hold would blow up. Abandon ship was ordered and the crew rescued by the *Bramham*.

In the meantime much had been happening around the convoy. Having beaten off, for the loss of the *Deucalion*, the enemy's major effort of the day, Syfret's force had reached the approaches to the Sicilian Narrows thronged with Italian submarines. The glassy calm summer sea provided the worst possible conditions for asdic detections, as temperature layers in the water deflected the sound beams to give faulty indications and a multitude of false alarms. Throughout the afternoon destroyers were engaged sniffing suspiciously at contacts and from time to time dropping depth-charges to scare off the hidden attackers. At 1640 suspicions were confirmed when from the *Tartar* a torpedo track was seen. Then the Lookout astern of her sighted a periscope. In the hunt which followed, the submarine *Emo* was shaken and damaged by the depth-charges; but the destroyers could not linger for long and she escaped with nothing worse.

At almost the same time, away on the other side of the widespread concourse of ships, the *Ithuriel* also spotted a periscope and the top of a conning tower as a submarine broke surface momentarily. Racing to the spot her depth-charges caused such damage that the submarine *Cobalto* was forced to come to the surface where she was rammed and sunk. While the survivors were being picked up a fresh air attack by a small force of Caproni fighter-bombers was developing. Intercepted by the fleet's Hurricanes and daunted by the volume of fire reaching up towards them they preferred to take on the solitary destroyer. *Ithuriel*'s gunners were ready for them and the Capronis retired with nothing achieved.

So far the losses suffered by the British, grievous as they were, represented a failure on the enemy's part to take advantage of the tactical situation presented by his successful concentration of aerial and underwater forces. Brushing aside the repeated efforts of submarines and bombers to get at the all-important merchantmen, the British force had swept steadily onwards, the convoy maintaining its compact rectangle in good order. This state of affairs was shortly to be dramatically transformed.

By 1830 the convoy had come within reach of the Sicilian airfields and therefore of the deadly Stuka dive-bombers. Twenty-nine of these now arrived simultaneously with 14 Italian torpedo planes, the whole escorted by a swarm of fighters. In a perfectly synchronized attack, the torpedo planes came in from either flank while the Stukas screamed down from ahead and astern. One group of dive-bombers concentrated on the *Indomitable*, diving down to 1,000 feet to make sure of a hit. Three bombs burst on her flight deck making it unusable, her fighters subsequently having to land on the *Victorious*. The remaining Stukas achieved nothing, while the torpedo planes' only victim was the destroyer *Foresight* which with her stern blown off, had to be sunk.

The convoy steamed on undiminished. But now had come the critical time as, towards the end of the day, Syfret's battleship and carrier force had to turn back from the restricted waters of the Skerki Channel ahead. At the same time Commodore Venables' well-drilled, compact convoy had to become a long double line in order to thread its way through the narrow channel, a manoeuvre which inevitably led to some loss of unity in the convoy and of cohesion with the escort.

With all this to distract the escorts, the slender periscopes of two Italian submarines, turning their baleful eyes on the busy scene, went unobserved. They were the *Axum*, commanded by Lieutenant Renato Ferrini, and the *Dessie*, Lieutenant Renato Scandola. Ferrini had had his first sight of the British force, dimly in the distance, at 1820 and had steered, submerged, to close it. Twenty minutes later two columns of

42 HMS *Ark Royal* under air attack

43 Malta-bound merchantman ablaze

44 HMS *Indomitable*, *Victorious* and *Eagle* in Operation 'Pedestal'

45 Malta under air attack

smoke and anti-aircraft bursts in the sky confirmed the nature of his sighting. Let his log-book take up the story here.

1841   Alter course North to close.

1850   Observe bearing of smoke now 300°. Dive to 20 metres and steer course 030 at full speed.

1927   Periscope depth. Enemy formation spread between bearings 290-010°, distance 8,000 metres, course 110°. Alter course parallel to study situation.

1933   Fresh observation. Enemy's course 140, i.e. enemy, has altered course in the interval 30° to starboard. Alter course to starboard to 180°. Am able meanwhile to establish that the formation comprises about 15 steamers, two cruisers and numerous destroyers. They are in three columns with the steamers divided amongst the three lines, the two cruisers in centre and the destroyers spread on an outer line. Note further, but imprecisely because masked by other units, a ship with three lattice masts, similar to those of American battleships. Able to take a quick general view only as in the flat calm the feather of the periscope is conspicuous even at minimum speed.

1937   Fresh estimate of distance 4,000 metres. Course of enemy 140. Speed 13. Alter course starboard to 220 to reach firing position.

1942   After a quick look at periscope depth, dive to 15 metres and go half speed ahead on both engines to close.

1948   Periscope depth. Angle of sight of cruiser in the second line 28°. In the nearer line, ahead and astern of the cruiser, are respectively a destroyer and a large merchant ship.

1955   Fire bow tubes in order 1, 4, 3, 2 of which 1 and 2 straight, 3 and 4 angled respectively 5° to starboard and 5° to port.
Directly after firing, disengage. Distance at firing from first line 1,300 metres, from cruiser 1,800 metres.
63 seconds after firing hear first explosion. 90 seconds after firing, two explosions close together. This leads me to assume a hit on a unit in the first line and successively on one in the second line. Calculating from speed of torpedoes, distance on firing was less than estimated, being actually about 1,000 metres from the first line and 1,400 from the second.
4m. 30 sec. after firing, while at 65 metres depth, the hunt begins with a pattern of depth-charges; dive to 100 metres and stop all machinery. The hunt continues with deliberate attacks for two hours, patterns of depth-charges being fired. It is noticed that each time the boat rises to between 80 and 90 metres the transmissions of the asdics are clearly heard, followed immediately by depth-charges. Decide to remain between 100 and 120

metres, particularly as at 2135 a destroyer passes overhead from
bow to stern and besides the noise of the propellers is clearly
heard another like a vibrating wire leading me to think it comes
from an explosive sweep.
After 2215 the hunt draws away.

2250   Surface. 3,000 metres ahead is a big ship in flames. On
starboard bow another burning with much smoke. 70° on port
bow a third ship already burnt out from which still comes,
however, the characteristic dense grey-black smoke. The flames
of the first ship clearly illuminate me and immediately afterwards I see two destroyers in motion and signalling; since it is
essential for me to replenish air bottles and recharge batteries, I
submerge to avoid being further hunted and leave the area.

Although the *Dessie* fired torpedoes at almost the same moment, the
Axum's torpedoes probably hit three ships, the *Nigeria*, flagship of Rear
Admiral Burrough commanding the 'through escort', the *Cairo* and the
tanker *Ohio*. This simultaneous triple catastrophe in the gathering dusk
not unnaturally threw the whole force into considerable confusion.
Destroyers of the escort scurried this way and that, going to the assistance
of the stricken cruisers and seeking the hidden assailant. In the convoy
the *Ohio*'s sudden halt forced the *Empire Hope*, astern of her, to reverse
engines in order to avoid collision. Other ships swung aside independently
to 'comb' the torpedo tracks. All order was lost for the time being. And,
in the middle of it, out of the dark eastern sky roared a mixed force of
German Ju.88s and Italian torpedo-carrying Savoias. Guns blazed wildly
in every direction but with little effect—perhaps fortunately as one of the
targets selected was a formation of long-range Beaufighters from Malta,
come to take the place of the carrier fighters.

Confusion mounted to chaos as the *Empire Hope*, hit by bombs, burst
into flames and had to be abandoned; *Clan Ferguson* and *Brisbane Star*
shuddered to a stop, hit by torpedoes either from the submarine *Alagi* or
from the torpedo planes.* Certainly it was a torpedo from the *Alagi*
which at this time hit the *Kenya* and damaged her, but not so badly as to
put the cruiser out of action.

This is how the savage scene had appeared to Lieutenant Sergio
Puccini, captain of the Italian submarine:

0900   Begin to hear explosions which during the course of the day
become louder and more frequent. Steer for the south-eastern
part of the patrol area where it is estimated the convoy will be at
sunset.

2000   Through periscope can see on a bearing 300° a tall column of

---

*The *Clan Ferguson* sank; *Empire Hope* remained afloat until nearly midnight when she
was sunk by a torpedo from the submarine *Bronzo*. The *Brisbane Star* was got under
way again.

smoke and, a little later the masts of ships distant about 20,000 metres. Alter course towards.

2020   Convoy attacked by aircraft. Violent anti-aircraft reaction. All ships alter course together to starboard, steering south. A destroyer is hit by a bomb. I can count 15 ships comprising cruisers, destroyers and freighters.

2040   Ships alter course again and reform; almost at their head is a cruiser of the *Southampton* class. Range 8–10,000 metres. Manoeuvre to attack this ship.

2100   Third air attack begins, more violent than the others and two (about)   merchantmen are hit and set on fire. A destroyer stops near them, perhaps to render help. A storm of bombs near the other ships raises tall columns of water, some of them are not more than 3–4,000 metres from the submarine. The cruiser which has a merchantman very close ahead of her seems to have reduced speed to keep with the convoy, scattered by the violent bombardment.

2105   Course 214°, range 1,500–2,000 metres, launch four bow torpedoes at the cruiser.... While disengaging hear three explosions quite different from those heard during the bombing. Since, owing to the spread, the cruiser could not have been hit by three torpedoes, I think I must have hit the merchantman immediately ahead of her.... Disengage and settle on bottom at 90 metres.

2126   Hear a violent explosion. Meanwhile on the hydrophones are heard other units passing through the area. It must be a second group of ships steering towards Cape Bon.

2313   Surface. The horizon between bearing 180° and 240° is a continuous line of flame from the burning, sinking ships.

2350   A burning ship blows up.

Meanwhile, amongst the survivors of the harried British force, after the confused sound and fury of the simultaneous air and underwater attack, a sudden quiet had settled down with the darkness. Astern of them the night was lit by the lurid glare of blazing ships.

Destroyers sped hither and thither rounding up the uninjured ships and shepherding them into some sort of order. After transferring to the destroyer *Ashanti*, the Admiral had ordered the crippled *Nigeria* to return to Gibraltar. The *Ohio*, with a hole 24 feet by 23 in her side, had come to a stop, on fire. Officers and men had set to, however, extinguished the fire and shored up bulkheads in the first of a succession of damage repairs which were to make the story of the *Ohio* an epic of the sea. By now she was under way again, limping after the convoy as best she could, steering by emergency means and without a serviceable compass. The *Cairo* was so damaged that she had to be sunk.

The largest organized group at this time consisted of the cruisers *Kenya* and *Manchester* followed by the American ship *Almeria Lykes* and the *Glenorchy*, the whole led by two destroyers with mine sweeps streamed. The remainder were coming on alone or in company with shepherding destroyers of the escort. Coming up from astern carrying the Admiral, the *Ashanti* overtook the *Ohio* and, at the request of the master, Burrough sent the destroyer *Ledbury* back to guide the compass-less ship through the narrow channel. By daylight the sturdy tanker, the twisted, buckled plates of her damaged hull groaning at the strain on them, would have worked up to 16 knots and rejoined what was left of the convoy. Besides the *Ohio*, another crippled ship had been able to get under way again. This was the *Brisbane Star* whose resourceful master, Captain Riley, finding himself left far behind, had decided to hug the Tunisian shore and try to make his own way to Malta as opportunity offered. In this he was to be successful. By fine seamanship and resource he overcame all difficulties to reach Valetta with the majority of his desperately needed cargo unharmed.

About midnight the various groups and single ships rounded Cape Bon. Lying in wait, their engines stopped, invisible in the darkness against the loom of the land to the southward, were the German and Italian E-boats. The calm sea was ideal for them. Their youthful captains proceeded to make the most of it. From 0100 the next four hours saw a succession of confused melées marked by the sudden glare of search-lights, the bright coloured streams of tracer bullets, the deep-throated roar of E-boat motors and from time to time the boom of exploding torpedoes. It is impossible to extract a clear detailed picture of events from the accounts of the many attackers and their victims.

Certainly it was two Italian boats, *Ms16* and *Ms22*, commanded by Lieutenant-Commander Manuti and Sub-Lieutenant Mezzadra, which had the first success, each of them putting a torpedo into the *Manchester* which wrecked her propellers and left her immobilized, to be abandoned and scuttled the following day. The *Almeria Lykes* was the next to go, torpedoed by an invisible assailant, and soon on her way to the bottom. Her crew were rescued by the destroyer *Somali*, which also saved the survivors of the *Wairangi*, another E-boat victim. Soon after 0200 the *Glenorchy* was suddenly illuminated by a searchlight, turned at once towards it, but was hit almost immediately by two torpedoes which tore open her hull and flooded the engine-room. The ship was abandoned at the order of the master, Captain G. Leslie, who himself stoutly refused to leave in spite of repeated appeals by his officers and men. The boats were finally towed to the nearby Tunisian coast and the majority of the crew interned by the Vichy French. The mate, Mr Hanney, with a volunteer boat's crew went back at daylight to the *Glenorchy* to try once again to persuade the captain to leave; but as they approached the ship they saw her turn over and sink. At this moment the *Ms31* (Lieutenant Calvani), which had torpedoed the *Glenorchy*, returning to the scene of his success, came upon the boat and took its occupants prisoner. Captain Leslie was not seen again.

Two other ships were torpedoed before the coming of dawn brought the attacks to an end—the American *Santa Eliza* and the *Rochester Castle*. The former, trailing astern owing to engine defects caused by near bomb misses on the previous day, beat off one E-boat with her machine guns, but a second came in unseen on the other side. The torpedo exploded amongst the canned petrol and set off an uncontrollable blaze. The crew abandoned her barely in time before the flames reached the explosives and she blew up. Her survivors were taken aboard the destroyer *Penn*.

Captain Richard Wren of the *Rochester Castle* had already managed to elude a number of attacks, weaving in and out of torpedo tracks, when at last a torpedo reached his ship, tearing a huge hole in her side abreast the forward holds. But the ship was a credit to her builders. The bulkheads held, her engines continued to function and at daybreak Captain Wren found himself leading the undamaged survivors of the convoy—the *Waimarama* and *Melbourne Star*, followed at a little distance by the *Ohio* and further astern the *Port Chalmers* and *Dorset*.

It was to the sky that the haggard eyes of all in the British force were now lifted, knowing full well what they must expect. Beaufighters and long-range Spitfires were coming from Malta; but with both the fighter-direction ships *Nigeria* and *Cairo* gone, their capabilities would be much reduced. There was time for all hands to eat their breakfast before the first alarm at 0800, though not many can have had much stomach for it.

For Rear-Admiral Harold Burrough, in the *Ashanti*, there was another preoccupation as 13 August dawned, besides the certainty of a massive air attack. On the previous evening a reconnaissance aircraft from Malta had reported an enemy force of six cruisers and 11 destroyers in the Tyrrhenian Sea steering south. A simple calculation showed that they should reach the convoy south of Pantellaria by dawn, just as da Zara's squadron had done in June—but in much greater force than on that occasion. And though Syfret had sent the light cruiser *Charybdis* and two destroyers to Burrough's aid, the arrival of such an enemy squadron could mean nothing less than the annihilation of the convoy.

The fate of the British force, of Malta and, it may well be, of British fortunes in the Middle East hung, indeed, by a thread. The intervention of their cruiser-squadron had been an integral part of the plan of the Italian Naval Staff, who had absorbed the lesson of the June convoy. But past experience also gave them a healthy respect for British torpedo planes. They had, therefore, secured promises from both Kesselring and the *Comando Supremo* of fighter cover for their ships in the Sicilian Channel.

When the chiefs of the two Air Services—Luftflotte 2 and the Regia Aeronautica—realized that by the end of the second day their huge and costly efforts had contributed comparatively little to the destruction so far achieved, they were determined that a maximum effort should be made on the 13th. To mount it, every available fighter would be required to escort the strike aircraft. None could be spared for the Italian Navy—for which, in truth, the airmen had developed considerable contempt since da Zara's failure in June.

To inter-service rancour, which had dogged the Italian Navy and Air Force throughout the war, were added the demands of political expedience when Mussolini was appealed to by the Naval Staff. Unwilling to offend Kesselring and through him Hitler, he decided in favour of the Air Forces. The decision robbed the Italian Navy, already almost immobilized through lack of oil-fuel, of its last chance to win a decisive victory. It also saved Malta. At 0130 the Italian cruiser squadron was recalled. The following morning it was intercepted by the submarine *Unbroken*, commanded by Lieutenant Alastair Mars. Firing four torpedoes, Mars achieved a remarkable success. The heavy cruiser *Bolzano*, hit amidships and set ablaze, had to be beached. The light-cruiser *Attendolo*, with her bows blown off, managed to reach Messina. Neither ship was able to play any further part in the war. As for the *Unbroken*, in spite of a counter-attack lasting eight hours during which Mars counted 105 depth-charge explosions, she emerged unscathed to return in triumph to Malta.

At the very moment that Mars was thus engaged, the ordeal of the convoy, now south-east of Pantellaria and 200 miles from Malta, had begun at 0800, when 12 Ju.88s dived on the merchant ships. The *Waimarama* was hit, the aviation petrol in her cargo blazed up and in a moment the ship had disintegrated in a monstrous explosion. Captain MacFarlane of the *Melbourne Star*, following close astern, was just able to steer clear of the flames though he was driven to take cover from the searing heat and the hail of debris falling aboard. Thirty-six of his crew, imagining it was their own ship which had blown up, had leaped overboard. Together with the tragically few survivors of the *Waimarama*, they were rescued by the *Ledbury* from the flame-covered sea. In the *Ohio*, next in line, burning debris started a fire in her cargo of kerosene which was with difficulty extinguished.

An hour later another formation of enemy aircraft was sighted, eight of them with the characteristic gull-wing of the deadly Stuka. These were Italian-manned planes, however, and the pilots were no doubt unfamiliar with the technique. Their bombs missed; one was shot down by a Sptifire; another, hit by gunfire, crashed into the *Ohio*'s starboard side, parts of it falling on board; its bomb failed to explode. The solitary tanker was inevitably the favourite target. Near misses shook up her machinery and defects were accumulating. When the next attack by a mixed force of

Ju.88s and 87s came in at 1050 a salvo of six bombs, all near misses, brought her long-suffering machinery to a shuddering stop.

The same attack had started a fire in the *Rochester Castle* but had not stopped her. The *Dorset*, however, had been crippled and lay immobilized. Admiral Burrough sent the destroyer *Bramham* to stand by her and the *Penn* to the *Ohio*. There now began a heartbreaking struggle to take the huge, unwieldy, deeply laden tanker in tow, a struggle in which only the desperate need to get at least some of her cargo of oil to Malta led her rescuers to persist long after all hope seemed to have vanished. For a time the *Penn* alone tried to get her moving, but it was impossible. While the efforts were being made, bombers swooped again and again and further near misses increased the damage and flooding. At 1400 the *Ohio* was temporarily abandoned, the crew going aboard the *Penn* to await darkness and further help.

One last attack had meanwhile descended on the main body—by Italian torpedo planes, some carrying *motobomba*. Their weapons were prudently launched at long range. Nevertheless the Commodore's flagship, *Port Chalmers*, which had throughout borne a charmed life amidst countless bombs and torpedoes, had yet another miraculous escape.

One torpedo passed directly beneath her; another was seen passing close up her starboard side. Soon afterwards her starboard paravane wire began to vibrate violently, indicating some object caught up by it. The ship was stopped and the paravane hoisted out of the water to reveal a torpedo firmly entangled with it, its deadly warhead swaying to and fro a few feet from the ship's hull. Delicately it was lowered into the water and the paravane wire was slipped while the ship hastily backed away. After an interval which gave the ship time to get clear, there was an explosion which seemed to lift her out of the water as the torpedo hit the sea bottom; but she escaped damage.

By now this main body, three merchantmen and escort, was nearing Malta and the minesweeping squadron under Commander Jerome came out to take charge, one of them, the *Rye*, being sent to join the *Penn* and *Ohio*. Admiral Burrough could now take his depleted Force 'X' to rejoin Syfret to the westward, running the gauntlet of the Narrows again in the reverse direction. E-boats, submarines and aircraft all tried to bar his way, but without any further success.

During the afternoon the *Rye* and two motor launches joined the *Penn*. The combined efforts of the warships at last got the *Ohio* moving at some five or six knots and under a precarious control. Hardly had this been achieved when once again there came attack from the air, one bomb falling close under the tanker's stern, another plunging down into the engine-room where it exploded. Other bombs fell close alongside the *Penn* and *Rye*. The tanker's crew were again taken off.

At this time, 70 miles away, to the frenzied cheers of the people and garrison of Malta, the *Port Chalmers*, *Rochester Castle* and *Melbourne Star*, their scarred and blistered sides providing evidence of the ordeal they had survived, were sliding slowly between the arms of the breakwater of Valetta Harbour. Yet Malta's survival could still hang on the outcome of the valiant fight being made for the life of the *Ohio*.

During the night, while the crew of the *Ohio* lay in the deep sleep of the utterly exhausted, Lieutenant-Commander Swain of the *Penn* and Lieutenant J. A. Pearson, RNR, of the *Rye* concocted some ingenious and unorthodox methods of getting the huge tanker moving, and at one time had succeeded in achieving four knots with her; but then the towing wires parted and all was to do again. Further help now joined in the shape of the destroyers *Bramham* and *Ledbury*. The *Bramham* had been standing by the *Dorset*, but the crippled merchantman had made an easy target when Stukas had swooped on her and three bombs had sent her to the bottom. Lieutenant-Commander R. P. Hill had brought the *Ledbury* back after an unsuccessful search for the scuttled *Manchester*. By 1045 in the morning of 14 August, the *Ohio* was moving again with the *Rye* towing, the *Penn* lashed alongside and the *Ledbury* secured to her stern to keep her heading in the right direction. Gathered round protectively were the *Bramham* and the minesweepers *Speedy*, *Hebe*, and *Hythe*.

Then came again the growl of aircraft engines—Ju.88s coming in for a final effort to deny Malta the oil without which she could not survive. Spitfires streaked down to engage them. The German formations broke up. Some came flaming down. Others loosed their bombs wide, but one bored doggedly on, its 1,000-lb bomb bursting close under the tanker's stern, tearing another hole in her hull. The *Rye*'s towing wire parted.

This was the last attack to get through the fighter defences. From then on the problems were confined to salvaging the slowly sinking tanker. Not the least was the exhaustion of the men of the little warships, the *Rye* still towing and the *Penn* and *Bramham* lashed on either side of the *Ohio*. Time and again the wires parted, only to be renewed by the sleep-starved sailors. Other difficulties, too many to be recounted, were dealt with by splendid seamanship. It was, indeed, by little short of a miracle of skill and endurance that the *Ohio* was finally got into the Grand Harbour of Valetta. The 10,000 tons of fuel oil and kerosene salved from her torn hull set the final seal on Operation 'Pedestal'. Malta was saved.

In his report, Admiral Syfret said that he and all officers of the Royal Navy who saw 'the steadfast manner in which [the merchantmen] pressed on their way to Malta through all attacks . . . will desire to give first place to the conduct, courage and determination of their masters, officers and men'— a judgment with which the passage of time has brought no reasons for disagreement.

9 *Disaster in the Barents Sea*

Operation 'Pedestal' was the last major encounter between the opposing naval forces in the Mediterranean. Before the re-supply of Malta became critical again the situation on land had been transformed by the defeat of the Panzer Army at the Battles of Alam el Halfa and El Alamein, followed by its eviction from Libya, leaving the key to sea power in the eastern Mediterranean—the Cyrenaican airfields—in Allied hands. From that time onwards the maritime part of the campaign was no longer a struggle to establish sea power in the area, but the application of it by the dominant Allied navies. The classic way of doing this was, of course, by amphibious assault behind the enemy's front on land. We shall see in later chapters how this was done.

Elsewhere, however, Allied sea power was still being vigorously challenged, not least in the Arctic, storm-swept and dark in winter, or shrouded in icy fog; in summer mostly calm under the midnight sun with extreme visibility alternating with dense fog.

On 22 June 1941, three weeks after the evacuation of Crete was completed, the uneasy, false friendship between the two dictators, Hitler and Stalin, had dissolved as the legions of Nazi Germany rolled across the Russo-German frontier. The relief that the launching of Operation 'Barbarossa' had brought to the hard-pressed British in the Mediterranean had been immense.

But while 'Barbarossa' had thus brought some easement of the situation in the Mediterranean, elsewhere it had imposed a new commitment on the Royal Navy. For Russia, caught unprepared, if left to her own resources would go down in defeat before the splendidly equipped, veteran armies of Germany as she had done 23 years before.

Alternatively, if Russia could be kept in the ring, Hitler's defeat was now certain. Military aid by Britain, the only country still in the fight and striving desperately to renew her strength after the disasters of 1940, was out of the question. But, by taking advantage of her one great asset, command of the sea, Britain could, in spite of her own desperate needs, send material help, particularly in the two weapons of which Russia was most urgently in need—tanks and aircraft. Sympathy for a country treacherously attacked by the common enemy, combined with self-interest, led to an offer of such help, which was readily, though hardly gratefully, accepted.

Thus to the Royal Navy, its resources already stretched almost to the limit by world-wide, unaided responsibilities, an additional burden was assigned—that of opening and protecting a new shipping route which, unlike the trans-Atlantic, was exposed for a great part of its length to enemy-held territory on its flank.

The original understanding was that Russian merchant ships would carry the cargoes but, in the event, these proved quite inadequate in numbers. Britain's merchant navy, already being decimated by the U-boat attacks in the Atlantic, was called on to make up the deficiency.

The offer made and accepted, no time was lost in getting to work. Less than two months after the German attack on Russia, the first convoy of seven ships sailed for Archangel. This early demonstration of goodwill set the pattern for what was to follow. At tremendous sacrifice in weapons and munitions critically needed by our own forces, at a terrible risk of naval disaster at the hands of the superior air and surface forces deployed in Norway and at a grievous cost in ships and men, convoys were fought through to Murmansk and Archangel for the rest of the war, only pausing for the mid-summer months when continuous daylight made their defence impossible in the face of shore-based air attacks.

With the entry of the USA into the war six months later, the Americans joined wholeheartedly in the enterprise, American ships in the convoys often outnumbering the British. American material made up the bulk of the cargoes. But the responsibility for the safe and timely arrival of the convoys was solely that of the Home Fleet of the Royal Navy. It entailed their defence against the battleships, cruisers, destroyers and submarines of the German Navy, all of which were brought into play, and against the high bombers, dive-bombers and torpedo planes of the Luftwaffe.

A glance at the map will give an idea of what this involved. Leaving Iceland, a convoy for North Russia would head north-east for the vicinity of Bear Island. The decision whether to pass north or south of that desolate Arctic upthrust of rock depended on how far south was the barrier of solid ice. By the time that nearer, lonely Arctic island, Jan Mayen, had been passed, the convoy route, still some 1,400 miles long, was continuously in range of airfields in Norway; its ability to evade the U-boats waiting in ambush was limited by the ice barrier in the north and the proximity of airfields to the east and south-east.

As the convoy approached the North Cape, its dangers were multiplied by the possibility of the enemy's heavy warships, the gigantic *Tirpitz*, the powerful battle-cruisers *Scharnhorst* and *Gneisenau*, the pocket-battle-ship *Lützow* and the heavy cruisers *Hipper* and *Prinz Eugen*, slipping out at their own chosen moment from their safe bases in Norway and falling on the convoy and its escort of lightly armed anti-submarine and anti-aircraft ships. These dangers persisted right to the mouth of the Kola Inlet, a bare 30 miles from enemy territory.

Thus the problem for the C-in-C Home Fleet, with his ships based far away at Scapa Flow, was, having given the convoy a sufficient escort of light forces to drive off U-boat and air attacks, to provide cover against any sortie by the German heavy ships without unnecessarily exposing his own battleships and cruisers to the overwhelming air attack that the enemy could concentrate against them from his shore bases. It was a problem of the utmost nicety. In the story of the Arctic convoys, we shall see with what success it was met.

It began less than two months after the German attack when a convoy of seven ships sailed from Iceland for Archangel on 22 August 1941. It was followed, before the end of the year by seven others, all lightly escorted, usually by a cruiser and two destroyers from the Home Fleet. The Germans were slow to react, perhaps because they were confident that Russia would go down to their *Blitzkrieg* before the Allied aid could affect the issue. The first six reached Archangel or the ice-free port of Murmansk unscathed; the seventh lost one ship from U-boat attack.

The first convoy of 1942 also suffered U-boat attack, the destroyer *Matabele* of the escort being sunk, all but two of her crew succumbing to the killing cold of the Arctic seas before her consorts could rescue them. It was not until the spring of that year, however, that a serious threat to the convoys developed; not so much from any German appreciation of the importance of the traffic to North Russia as from the workings of Hitler's 'intuition' that Norway was about to be invaded.

Not only was the exasperated Dönitz ordered to send eight U-boats to the north at the very moment that the new field of operations on the American coast was opening rich prospects of destruction to him, but the splendid battleship *Tirpitz* was transferred to Trondheim. The battle cruisers *Scharnhorst* and *Gneisenau* and the heavy cruiser *Prinz Eugen* were extricated from Brest by their daring dash up Channel only to have the first two mined; the *Prinz Eugen* was similarly put out of action by the submarine *Trident* as she was sailing north with the pocket-battleship *Admiral Scheer* in February. Nevertheless the *Tirpitz* and *Scheer* with their accompanying destroyers constituted a new and serious threat to the Arctic convoys, one which called for the cover of the entire Home Fleet. At the same time the Home Fleet was restricted in its movements by the increased Luftwaffe strength on the northern Norway airfields where, for the first time, torpedo planes had joined the bombers. Thus a major problem for Admiral Sir John Tovey, C-in-C Home Fleet, was to deploy his force so as to bring his solitary carrier *Victorious* within Albacore torpedo plane range of the *Tirpitz* if she should sortie, yet not so close to the massive air threat by German shore-based bombers and torpedo planes that the *Victorious*' few fighter planes would be overwhelmed.

These arrangements were tested when the *Tirpitz* with three destroyers sailed to seek out and attack the outward-bound convoy PQ12 and the homeward-bound QP8, while the Home Fleet hovered in a position to cover both as best it could.

The widespread game of blind-man's-buff which ensued between these ships and the German squadron is no part of our story. It is sufficient to say that in the mist and smother of those smoky seas, they advanced and retreated and passed on opposite courses without ever meeting each other, as though in some vast maritime minuet. Meanwhile the two convoys moved on towards each other.

The outward-bound PQ12, meeting pack-ice, was forced further south than had been planned and, at noon on 7 March, passed QP8 on an opposite course. Barely 80 miles to the southward, the *Tirpitz* and her three destroyers were casting north-westward on the trail of the defenceless prey they sensed was somewhere near at hand. Not far to the westward, Tovey, unable to operate his aircraft owing to thick weather and severe icing, was also blindly groping for his opponent.

A clash between the *Tirpitz* and QP8 seemed inevitable—a clash which must have led to a fleet action as soon as the alarm was flashed to Tovey. But in those days of early, primitive radar sets, the weather was still the master at sea.

Lieutenant-Commander Seymour of the *Hazard*, senior officer of the escort of QP8, which consisted of but two minesweepers and two little corvettes, never knew that at one moment, ten miles ahead of his convoy in the murk, the great battleship was sweeping past; while astern of the convoy, the German destroyers, similarly screened by the northern mists, were passing so close that they encountered a straggler, a Russian ship, which they quickly sank. Any one of these enemy units could have wiped out the weak escort. But they drove on unsuspecting and the homeward convoy was saved.

Foiled in his search, the German Admiral Ciliax pressed on north-wards where sound reasoning told him he might still fall in with the outward convoy. By the narrowest of margins he failed. PQ12, hoping to pass north of Bear Island, had again recoiled from the ice barrier and been forced to make a long diversion to the south which took it once again within 80 miles of the questing *Tirpitz*. Contact there would have spelt catastrophe for the convoy, for Tovey was hundreds of miles away to the southwest, bent on intercepting the enemy as he returned to Narvik. But luck and the weather were on the convoy's side. It ploughed on, unalarmed and unaware of the danger so closely threatening.

The German Admiral Ciliax now decided to abandon the search; he recalled his destroyers and steered south to return to Trondheim. But when, early on the following morning a carrier-type plane was sighted

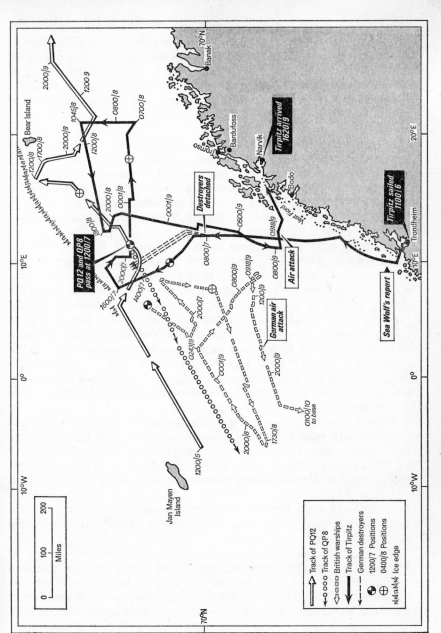

Operations round Arctic Convoys PQ12 and QP8, March 1942

shadowing, it was the *Tirpitz*'s turn to become the hunted. Ciliax turned east for the coast at once to take shelter in the Vestfiord. But a striking force of 12 Albacores had taken off from the *Victorious* at the same time as the search planes; and at 0917 they attacked. In spite of great determination and dash to which the enemy paid respect, no hits were made, two Albacores were shot down and the *Tirpitz* reached Narvik unscathed.

Nevertheless, this narrow escape by the *Tirpitz* so soon after the loss of her sister-ship *Bismarck* in the Atlantic so alarmed Hitler, to whom his surface ships were primarily a defence against the forecast invasion, that he forbade her future employment against convoys without his express permission, which would only be given if the Home Fleet carrier had been located and put out of action. During the passage of the next four convoys, therefore, she remained idle.

Attack by other means began steadily to increase, however. Convoy PQ13 lost two of the 19 ships with which it started out, from aerial bomb attack, two from U-boat torpedoes; three German destroyers came across a straggler and sent her to the bottom; when they closed in to attack the rear of the convoy, a confused fight ensued amidst the Arctic mists and snow during which the German *Z26* was sunk and the British *Eclipse* damaged, while the escorting cruiser *Trinidad* suffered the calamity of being hit by one of her own torpedoes which malfunctioned in the bitter cold and circled back. Heavily damaged, the cruiser managed with difficulty to limp to Murmansk only to be sunk by air attack two months later as, temporarily repaired, she set out on the homeward voyage with a destroyer escort.

PQ14 was reduced to only eight ships out of 24, the remainder being forced to turn back to Iceland after encountering pack ice. PQ15 lost three of its number to the first German torpedo-bomber attack of the war by He.111 planes. The escorting cruiser, *Edinburgh*, was first torpedoed and crippled by *U456* and then given the death blow by a torpedo from one of three German destroyers which attacked as she was being towed to Murmansk. In reply the *Edinburgh* and her destroyer escort sank the destroyer *Hermann Schoemann* at the cost of damage to the British destroyers *Foresight* and *Forester*.

PQ16 had five ships sunk by bombs, one by aerial torpedo and one by U-boat. The returning empty convoys did not attract the same attention as the outward-bound with their cargoes of tanks and fighter planes for the Russians. Nevertheless, by this time the mounting toll of losses from the latter had led the senior British officers directly concerned, Admiral Tovey and his cruiser commander, Rear-Admiral S. S. Bonham-Carter, to express themselves as strongly against continuation of the convoys during the summer period of continuous daylight, and they had warned of heavy losses to be expected. The arrival of PQ16 with only seven ships lost was rated by the C-in-C as a 'success beyond all expectations'. The

First Sea Lord, Admiral Sir Dudley Pound, writing to his American equivalent, Admiral Ernest King, confessed that the 'whole thing is a most unsound operation with the dice loaded against us in every direction'.

But the desire of Winston Churchill and Franklin Roosevelt to satisfy the understandable yet unreasonable demands of the hard-pressed Russian ally, was the deciding factor: during June a large convoy PQ17 was assembled in Iceland. The story of its passage to Archangel was to comprise one of the most calamitous episodes of the naval war.

It is not surprising that the story of hazardous voyages of the Arctic convoys, growing ever more so with each one, should have begun by now to play on the nerves of the staff officers responsible. At the Admiralty and in the operations room of the Home Fleet flagship the progress of every one was watched with deep anxiety as the symbol representing it crawled so slowly across the wall maps. Intelligence of U-boat concentrations and of impending air attack would come in. Tidings of how the convoy was coping with them would be awaited, if not with fear, certainly with misgivings.

Beyond all reasonable expectations, these two forms of menace had, up to now, failed to achieve any great measure of success. The dogged determination of the masters of the merchantmen not to be intimidated into breaking formation had contributed largely to the defeat of both of them. So long as the convoy remained a compact body, the enemy airmen and U-boat captains had to face a formidable, concentrated defence in order to press home their attacks. This, more often than not, they jibbed at doing.

If these had been the only threats confronting the convoys, the future could perhaps have been regarded with reasonable confidence. The escorts available were increasing in number. New types designed for anti-aircraft defence were coming into service at last. But always a gnawing anxiety to the naval staffs were the German heavy ships in Norwegian harbours. It was inexplicable that, except for the *Tirpitz*'s abortive sortie against PQ12 in February and the two unimpressive attempts by the German destroyers, the enemy had not tried to cut up a convoy in the Barents Sea. To the Admiralty there seemed to be no defence against such an attack except by our submarines who were maintained on patrol off the Norwegian coast. But the chances of one of these being lucky enough to bring off an attack against a German force sweeping by at high speed were too remote to be counted upon.

The heavy ships of the Home Fleet, which alone could meet the available force of German heavy ships, had the primary task of preventing a break-out into the Atlantic. If, to cover a convoy, they passed into the Barents Sea without sure knowledge that they would find the enemy there, they would be leaving the door wide open behind them.

They could only wait in the background until it was known that the *Tirpitz* and her lesser consorts were committed and then hope to intercept them as they retired to their bases.

The Home Fleet cruisers, on the other hand, could not stand up to the greatly superior power of the *Tirpitz* and the pocket-battleships. West of Bear Island, they could, if they accepted the risk from U-boats' torpedoes, give anti-aircraft support to the convoys and cover them against attack by cruisers or destroyers. In the Barents Sea they seemed, on paper, to be a hostage to fortune and to run an unreasonable risk.

Such was the strategic position as it appeared to the anxious naval staffs. It was, said Admiral Tovey, 'wholly favourable to the enemy'. Knowing, as we do now, that the German surface fleet was labouring under such restrictive instructions from Hitler that it was virtually impossible to take it into action, it is tempting to criticize this appreciation. But the Admiralty had no such knowledge. Certainly they had seen the lack of stomach for a fight displayed by the German destroyers on two occasions. They had also previous examples of German unwillingness to risk their ships in battle during the Atlantic excursions of the *Hipper*, *Scharnhorst* and *Gneisenau*. All these were typical of the tactics of a weaker naval power following the strategy of maintenance of a 'fleet in being'.

But the Admiralty could not bring themselves to base their strategy on such an assumption. A Nelson, with the nerve to follow his 'hunch' as he did when he followed the French fleet to Egypt or across the Atlantic, might have done so. But Nelsons come few and far between. The naval staff's caution, wise or excessive as the reader may judge for himself, is the key to events that were shortly to unfold.

While the ships that were to form PQ17 were assembling in Hvalfiord, a new German C-in-C, Admiral Schniewind, had hoisted his flag in the *Tirpitz*, lying with *Hipper* and four destroyers at Trondheim. At Narvik, further north, were the *Scheer* and *Lützow* with six more destroyers. The 'new broom' was full of ideas for taking his force out to intercept the next Arctic convoy. But even as he laid his plans, reiterated orders came down from the Fuehrer further restricting the freedom of movement of the fleet. Not unless and until the Home Fleet's aircraft carriers had been located and attacked by the Luftwaffe might he leave harbour. By then it would certainly be too late, if he remained at Trondheim, to get at a convoy. He planned therefore, as soon as the next convoy was known to have sailed, to move *Tirpitz* and *Hipper* to Vestfiord and the *Scheer* and *Lützow* to Altenfiord in the far north. Operation 'Rosselspring' (Knight's Move), he called it.

In order that he should get the necessary intelligence as early as possible, Admiral Schniewind sent three of his ten available U-boats to patrol the north-sea sector of the Denmark Strait as early as 5 June. In view of this German zeal in reconnaissance, it was disappointing for the British that a dummy convoy of four colliers and five large minelayers,

46 Admiral Sir John Tovey greets Commodore J. C. K. Dowding of PQ17

47 Rear-Admiral Louis Hamilton

48 Arctic convoy skirts the pack ice

49–50 Escorts with Arctic convoys—HMS *Lotus* (top); HMS *Ashanti* and *Onslow* (above)

51 Battleship *Tirpitz* fires one of the few broadsides of her career

which sailed from Scapa on 29 June to induce the Germans to commit their forces prematurely, was never sighted by the enemy in spite of trailing its shirt for a few days.

However, the position, from the Admiralty's point of view, was no worse than it had been. A careful watch was kept by aircraft of RAF Coastal Command on the enemy's ships and any movement should be detected at an early stage. Preparations for the sailing of PQ17 and its opposite number, QP13, went ahead. The outward convoy was to comprise 35 ships, 22 of them American, led by Commodore J. C. K. Dowding, RNR, no newcomer to the Kola Run, though he had not so far experienced a summer convoy.

As for previous convoys, a very large naval force was to be deployed, consisting of a 'Covering Force' of battleships, an aircraft carrier and destroyers led by the C-in-C in the *Duke of York*, a 'Support Force' of cruisers, two British and two American, under the command of Rear-Admiral Louis Hamilton, besides the close escort. The covering force, however, was to cruise well to the west of Bear Island whence they would only move on receipt of definite intelligence which would enable them to intercept the *Tirpitz*. Hamilton's cruisers would cruise in support to the northward of the convoy route, their task being to engage any surface forces, other than the *Tirpitz*, which threatened.

The close escort, under Commander J. E. Broome in the destroyer *Keppel*, was numerically impressive, comprising six destroyers, four corvettes, three minesweepers, four anti-submarine trawlers, two submarines and two converted AA ships, *Palomares* and *Pozarica*. The destroyers, however, consisted of the *Keppel*, *Fury* and *Offa* and the ex-US 'over-age' *Leamington*, primarily equipped to hunt U-boats, though they retained their torpedo tubes, and two little 'Hunt'-class armed with 4-inch high-angle, anti-aircraft guns only. The submarines were included with the idea that they might be able to get into position to attack any surface forces which succeeded in intercepting the convoy.

With the convoy sailed also three rescue ships, *Rathlin*, *Zaafaran* and *Zamalek*. These craft, the need for which experience in the Atlantic had shown, were small passenger steamers in which a medical staff was carried, sick bays and extra accommodation fitted. Their low freeboard and the 'scrambling nets' which could be lowered over the side and up which men from boats and rafts or swimming could clamber, enabled them to embark survivors with the least possible delay. They thus relieved the escorts of this responsibilty, leaving them free to concentrate on their duties of defence. They also saved them from the heartbreaking and all too common experience of having to leave men struggling in the water while they dealt with an enemy U-boat or aircraft.

The rescue ships played a heroic and largely unsung part in the convoy battles in the Atlantic as well as the Arctic. It took iron nerve and cool courage to lie immobilized in the middle of an attack, an easy target for torpedo or bomb, while survivors were helped on board, often a long and difficult business in rough weather and icy seas.

'Jackie' Broome was an experienced escort force commander and he looked forward to the voyage with quiet confidence. The route was a great deal longer than on previous occasions as the withdrawal of the edge of the ice-barrier allowed the convoy to reach far up into the Arctic before turning eastwards to pass north of Bear Island. The destroyers would consequently need to refuel at least once, so two tankers sailed with the convoy, the *Grey Ranger* and *Aldersdale*, the former to transfer to the homeward QP13 when it passed.

Except for the reduction of the convoy to 34 through a freighter running aground off Iceland soon after sailing on 27 June, all went smoothly and well for the first few days. In fine, calm weather, the convoy settled down under Commodore Dowding's leadership and made good progress. Lonely Jan Mayen Island had been passed, far out of sight over the horizon, on 1 July, when the enemy first discovered that PQ17 was at sea, U-boats on patrol reporting it that day. Some of these were sighted on the surface and destroyer escorts drove them off. But the damage was done and at noon the inevitable reconnaissance aircraft arrived.

At German naval headquarters in the north, great excitement prevailed. Ten U-boats were sent instructions to concentrate to shadow and attack, while the *Tirpitz* and the pocket-battleships were brought to short notice for steam, ready for the first moves of 'Rosselspring'. At the same time the Luftwaffe prepared to launch their first attacks.

The German Air Force available comprised 103 Ju.88 and 30 Ju.87 dive-bombers, 15 He.115 torpedo seaplanes, 42 He.111 torpedo (land) planes and 74 reconnaissance aircraft.

July 1 passed quietly in PQ17. Taking advantage of the fair weather, all destroyers filled their fuel tanks before the *Grey Ranger* should leave early on the 2nd to join the approaching QP13. The homeward convoy, favoured by thick weather throughout their voyage, had not been molested at all. At noon on the 2nd, it passed by on opposite course, leaving PQ17 the sole object of the enemy's attentions.

Fog over the airfields kept the majority of the German strike squadrons grounded that day and only the He.115 torpedo seaplanes stationed at Kirkenes were able to operate. Nine of them, homed on to the target by the signals of the shadowing plane, came in skimming low over the water at about 2100. Met by a storm of gunfire from the escorts and the ships of the convoy, several were seen to be hit, the majority swerved away after dropping their torpedoes ineffectively at long range. The squadron commander, however, flying through the convoy columns to press home his attack, was forced down in a crash-landing right ahead of the convoy. With superb skill and gallantry, his wingman alighted alongside and, ignoring the shell splashes leaping all around, picked up the crew and took off again.

'Jackie' Broome had reason to be pleased with this first showing of the escort under his command. The situation was further improved that night when the convoy slipped into a sheltering mantle of thick fog. He was not to enjoy the resultant immunity for long, however. For, during the following forenoon, the weather cleared and, though 'Snooper Joe', the shadowing aircraft, had apparently been thrown off the scent, it was not long before it was evident that U-boats had clung to his trail. The afternoon was spent driving off any that came too close. But another day had gone by and the convoy still drove on, its numbers complete.

That evening, Admiral Hamilton's cruisers, hovering over the horizon to the north, were also sighted by the enemy and reported. At this time, too, Hamilton received the first news that the German heavy ships were on the move. These movements had begun on the previous afternoon when, in anticipation of the Fuehrer's permission for a sortie, Schniewind had given orders for the *Tirpitz* and *Hipper* to leave Trondheim for the Vestfiord with their escort of four destroyers. At the same time the *Scheer* and the *Lützow*, with their six destroyers weighed anchor to move from Narvik to Altenfiord.

Misfortunes befell the Germans almost at once. The *Lützow*, negotiating a narrow fiord, ran aground, receiving such damage that she would have to return to Germany for repairs. Then, when the *Tirpitz*'s force reached Vestfiord, three of its destroyers making up the Ofotfiord to Narvik also grounded and were put out of action. The German force was still, however, a formidable one. Operation 'Rosselspring' could go ahead. As soon as Admiral Tovey's fleet was located and his carrier successfully attacked by the Luftwaffe, the way would be clear for the *Tirpitz* and her consorts to sail. Perhaps then some action experience would re-vitalize the drooping morale of the German crews chafing and discontented at the soul-destroying monotony of life aboard their harbour-bound ships.

All that was known to the Admiralty, however, was that the *Tirpitz* and *Hipper* had left Trondheim. Bad weather in the north had prevented air reconnaissance of the Narvik area. Anxiety began to mount in London. The four heavy German ships might be anywhere at sea. In fact, during the night of the 3rd, the *Tirpitz* had moved on from Narvik to join the *Scheer* at Altenfiord. So that, when at last the weather cleared sufficiently on the 4th for a clear view of Narvik from the air, that harbour, too, was seen to be empty.

The situation had arisen which the British naval staff had long foreseen and feared. With a valuable convoy just entering the Barents Sea accompanied by an Anglo-American cruiser squadron which would be outclassed in an encounter with the German fleet, Schniewind's ships had vanished into the blue. Even if the Admiralty and the C-in-C had been prepared to take the only British battleship and the only available aircraft carrier into the U-boat-infested and Luftwaffe-dominated waters of the Barents Sea, where a lucky torpedo hit might leave one of these valuable ships crippled with no destroyer screen owing to lack of fuel, they could not do so until location of the *Tirpitz* made it clear that it was against the convoy that she was steering.

In this moment of crisis the First Sea Lord, Admiral Sir Dudley Pound, called a staff meeting at the Admiralty on the evening of 4 July to consider what should be done.

At sea, 3 July had passed quietly. Dönitz's U-boat commanders were writing in their logs, 'Unable to close to the attack owing to powerful escort.' The Luftwaffe was hanging back, unwilling to risk another dose such as had been administered to their torpedo squadron on the previous day. At midnight American Independence Day began. In the light of the midnight sun, seen through breaks in the fog, large Stars and Stripes unfolded at the mastheads of this predominantly American convoy. Sixty miles due south lay Bear Island. Soon, according to his orders, Admiral Hamilton's squadron would be leaving, after which PQ17 and its close escort would be on their own.

But all hands were in good heart, confident that, though not without some loss, they could fight their way through to Archangel in the face of anything the Luftwaffe or Dönitz could do. Even when, through a hole in the fog, a single torpedo-bomber suddenly dropped down to put a torpedo skilfully into the *Christopher Newton,* just before 0500, confidence remained firm. When the crew had been taken aboard a rescue ship, an escort sent the immobilized freighter to the bottom. The convoy plugged doggedly on.

By midday, however, the growing anxiety felt in London was making itself evident in an increasing number of signals to Admiral Hamilton from the Admiralty. The cruisers had instructions not to go further in company with the convoy than the meridian of 25°E. But at noon, Hamilton was given leave to stay longer, subject to any contrary orders from the C-in-C. Admiral Tovey, fretting, not for the first time in his tenure of command, at such interference by the Admiralty with the operational control of his forces, intervened at once with a signal to Hamilton instructing him to leave on reaching 25°E unless the Admiralty could assure him that he could not meet the *Tirpitz*.

At this, Hamilton replied that he would withdraw to the westward at 2200 when the refuelling of his destroyers would be completed. Barely had this decision been communicated when from the Admiralty came the order to remain with the convoy pending instructions as further information might be available shortly.

Taken in conjunction with the earlier news that the German heavy ships had been stirring from their long inactivity, this seemed to indicate to both Hamilton and Broome that the time had come to consider what their tactics would have to be if enemy surface forces were met. Neither of them lacked confidence that, by skilful use of smoke screen and torpedo threat, they could hold off an enemy who had before now shown himself unwilling to 'mix it' in a sea fight.

While his destroyers went, one by one, to the *Aldersdale* for oil, Hamilton's squadron zigzagged to and fro across the line of advance of the convoy some ten to 20 miles ahead of it. July 4 wore on without incident until 1930 that evening when an ill-coordinated attack by bombers and torpedo-planes achieved nothing. The US destroyer *Wainwright*, arriving to fuel, gave an impressive demonstration of long-range controlled anti-aircraft fire which did much to lower the enemy's zest. Bombs and torpedoes all went wide.

So far the vaunted Luftwaffe had been singularly unsuccessful. It may be that scathing criticism from on high had served to put some backbone into the next squadron that attacked, or it may simply be that it was the 'First Eleven' which was now being brought into play. It is possible, too, that the success they now achieved was due entirely to the resolute courage of their leader. For when 23 torpedo-bombers came streaking in, fast and low, from the starboard quarter, the leading aircraft, ignoring the tempest of fire from all around, held on till he was well into the convoy before dropping two torpedoes aimed at point-blank range at the freighter *Navarino*. A moment later it crashed in flames just ahead of the escort leader *Keppel*.

His followers were not so bold. Jackie Broome, giving credit to a gallant foe, said later, 'Had they kept with him, dividing and generally embarrassing the AA fire, many ships would have been sunk.' But meeting the wall of shell bursts and the deadly streams of tracer shells, they split up, jinking like a wisp of snipe, unable to aim their torpedoes with any accuracy. Only two more ships were hit, the *William Hooper* and the Russian tanker *Azerbaidjan*. The *Navarino* and the *William Hooper* had to be sunk by the escorts, but the Russian was found by Broome, when he closed to see how she was getting on, to be 'holed but happy and capable of nine knots'. She regained her station in the convoy and was eventually to reach harbour safely. Three aircraft destroyed and at least one damaged was the price the enemy paid for this success.

After this heavy and unusually well-led attack, Broome was supremely confident that he had the measure of the enemy. As he was to write later, 'My impression on seeing the resolution displayed by the convoy and its escort was that provided ammunition held out, PQ17 could get anywhere.'

But even as the gunfire died away, as the convoy got into its stride again and every gunlayer in the force was gleefully claiming the destruction of one of the crashed planes, a decision was being taken at Admiral Pound's staff conference that was to lead to repercussions whose echoes would take many a year to die away and to recriminations which are still repeated to this day.

As we have seen, on the afternoon of the 4th, the Admiralty was bereft of all information as to the whereabouts of the *Tirpitz* and *Hipper*. The air reconnaissance which might have discovered them where they lay at anchor at Altenfiord, awaiting Hitler's permission to sail, had again failed to materialize, though from photographic reconnaissance our intelligence was able to say that it was 'tolerably certain' that *Scheer* and *Lützow* were in Altenfiord. But by the evening the *Tirpitz* had at last been located. Confronting the First Sea Lord's staff meeting was the knowledge that she could be amongst the convoy by 0200 on 5 July.

Such a situation with a convoy in the wide waters of the Atlantic was catered for and had been successfully met in the past. When an attack by superior forces was known to be imminent and unavoidable, the technique was for the escort to engage the enemy, if possible screening with smoke the convoy, which thereupon scattered. This was a pre-arranged manoeuvre in which each ship had a course to steer differing from that of its neighbours. Thus, on the order to scatter, the convoy would open like the petals of a symmetrical flower. By the time the raider had dealt with the escort, the ships of the convoy would be steering away to every point of the compass, making it a lengthy business for the raider to round them up one by one and sink them.

This, in fact, was how it had fallen out when, in November 1940, the *Scheer's* topmasts hove over the horizon in sight of Captain Fegen of the armed merchant cruiser *Jervis Bay*, the sole escort of an Atlantic convoy of 37 ships. Giving the Commodore the order to scatter the convoy, Fegen steamed gallantly into action against hopeless odds, to his death and a posthumous Victoria Cross. When the *Jervis Bay's* last gun had been silenced and the *Scheer* could turn her attention to the convoy, most of the ships were disappearing over the horizon in every direction. Six of them only could the *Scheer* dispose of before fear of being trapped by avenging British forces forced her to scurry away to another part of the ocean.

Such were the tactics which Sir Dudley Pound was considering ordering PQ17 to carry out now. But in what different circumstances from the *Jervis Bay* incident! There, the decision was taken by the man on the spot, the enemy plainly in sight and bearing down on the convoy. Now it was to be taken by an authority remote from the scene who could not have the latest information of weather or of air or U-boat threat, nor, indeed, of the surface threat either.

Jervis Bay's convoy had the whole wide Atlantic in which to scatter and in which a sparsely distributed U-boat force was the only other danger to face. PQ17 was restricted to the north by the ice barrier and to the south by an enemy-held shore. Ahead and astern U-boats were concentrated and enemy aircraft roamed at will in large numbers.

Yet when the First Sea Lord put his proposal to the staff meeting, there seems to have been no voice raised in disagreement; only a comment by the Vice-Chief of the Naval Staff, Vice-Admiral H. R. Moore, that if the convoy was to scatter it must do so soon or it would have no sea room.

So the die was cast. The convoy would be ordered to scatter. Whether the decision was right or wrong—and here it must be said that Admiral Tovey, Rear-Admiral Hamilton and Commander Broome all deemed it disastrously wrong—is a question of high technicality and hedged with imponderables. Schniewind did eventually sail to attack the convoy and might have, as planned, wiped out the escort with one half of his force while the other half massacred the convoy. But some of the many British and Russian submarines on patrol in the area might have got home an attack on the German ships first—the Russian *K21* did, in fact make an unsuccessful attack. Rear-Admiral Hamilton's cruisers, boldly handled under cover of smoke screens, as he planned to use them, might have outmanoeuvred Admiral Schniewind in whose ears rang Admiral Raeder's damping warning words that a naval reverse at that time would be particularly unfortunate.

Let us leave the question of right or wrong at that, remembering how Nelson once wrote, 'Nothing is certain, in a sea fight above all others.' What is sure, however, is that the decision once taken, lack of imagination on the part of the naval staff in drafting the necessary signals gave those at sea an entirely false impression of the situation.

Meanwhile, on the bridge of the *Keppel*, Broome was in an exuberant mood, for he had just seen his force deal very adequately with as weighty an air attack as had so far been mounted against the Arctic convoys. He and Commodore Dowding 'were sharing', as he wrote, 'the wave of confidence which swept the convoy and escort after the air attack. The tails of PQ17 were well up!'

Broome and Rear-Admiral Hamilton had been expecting a signal from the Admiralty giving the 'further information' which they had said might be available shortly. Instead, came the first message drafted by the Admiralty staff following on the First Sea Lord's conference: 'Most Immediate. Cruiser force withdraw to westward at high speed.' Only on occasions of the utmost urgency could the priority indication 'Most Immediate' be used.

The message therefore seemed to indicate that some force in overwhelming strength was moving to entrap Hamilton's cruisers. The next signal heightened this impression. 'Immediate. Owing to threat of surface ships, convoy is to disperse and proceed to Russian ports.' It seemed quite clear now that surface attack was imminent. The orders were categorical no matter how much Hamilton and Broome disliked receiving

The massacre of Convoy PQ17, July 1942

52 Ammunition ship blows up

ARCTIC CONVOY PQ18

53 HMS *Avenger* and a near bomb miss

54 Escorts narrowly missed by bombs

ARCTIC CONVOY

55 Swordfish from the escort carrier on patrol

them. The Admiralty must have information denied to the two sea commanders.

When, a few minutes later, a further signal came in drafted by someone in the Admiralty who realized that the wrong terminology had been used in telling the convoy to 'disperse', which is quite different from 'scattering', it sounded like a despairing, warning shriek. 'Most Immediate. Convoy is to scatter.'

This last signal more than either of the others gave the impression that the enemy's mastheads might appear over the horizon at any moment. A fleet action was imminent! Broome naturally felt that in that case there was little that his destroyers could do amongst the scattering convoy, but that his torpedoes would be a considerable access of strength to Admiral Hamilton's force in the coming action. Sore at heart therefore, but confident that he was doing right, having passed the order at 1015 to an astonished Dowding that his convoy was to scatter, he ordered the remainder of the escorts to proceed independently to Archangel. With that, he called in his destroyers and steered to join Hamilton's cruisers which had just turned to the westward and would shortly sweep past the convoy at twenty-five knots. 'In the eyes of all who did not know the full story,' as Hamilton said, 'running away, and at high speed.'

At this stage none of the escorts thought that they were running away. On the contrary, they thought that a desperate fight lay ahead of them as an exchange of signals between the *Keppel* and one of the submarines shows. Ordered to proceed independently, the submarine sent the informatory signal to the *Keppel*, 'Intend to remain on the surface as long as possible'. With grim wit, Jackie Broome replied, 'So do I'.

Alas, though owing to the Admiralty's deceptive signals Hamilton did not realize it, running away is exactly what he was unwittingly doing. 'Had I been aware', the Admiral went on, 'that the Admiralty had no further information of the enemy heavy units than I myself possessed, I would have remained in a covering position until the convoy was widely dispersed, when I could have parted company in a less ostentatious manner.'

But once the convoy had scattered, the presence of the cruisers would have made little difference. By simply shifting her anchorage the *Tirpitz* had done what massed U-boats and aircraft had failed to do. She had broken the cohesion of the convoy, the principal defence against both those methods of attack. Even had Broome's destroyers been sent back when it became clear that there was, in fact, no danger of an immediate surface attack, there was little they could have done. Perhaps a few ships might have been saved, but losses would still have been calamitous. The following day the wolves descended on the scattered flock which they had hardly dared to attack while the shepherd was there to guard and the sheepdogs snarled round the outside of the fold.

To Commodore Dowding, even less 'in the know' than the escorts as to what was going on, the order to scatter came as a fearful shock. Disbelieving it at first, he asked for the signal to be repeated. When Broome's last signal came to him, 'Sorry to leave you like this. Good luck. Looks like a bloody business', he knew it was only too true. The necessary signal was hoisted in the Commodore's flagship, *River Afton*, left flying for a short time until its import had been taken in by the masters and then hauled down. PQ17 had ceased to exist.

In its place was a disorganized body of ships steering so as to put the greatest possible distance between themselves and their neighbours in the shortest possible time, and a handful of escort corvettes with orders to proceed independently to Archangel. That the convoy scattered exactly as laid down in the signal book speaks much for the fine discipline of the masters, for it meant that some had initially to steer to the west or south-west, away from their hoped-for destination and in the direction whence an enemy might be expected to arrive.

Once the manoeuvre of scattering had been completed, however, each merchant ship master had to decide on his future course. A few re-gathered in small groups for mutual protection; others steamed on their own over a glassy sea under a blue sky with visibility extreme in every direction; all were conspicuous targets for the bombers and torpedo planes which streamed out from the airfields of Banak and Bardufoss and for the trailing U-boats which now came to the surface and set off in exultant pursuit.

The corvette *Dianella*, the rescue ship *Rathlin*, and two freighters steered boldly on a direct course for Archangel and arrived safely on 9 July. The remainder, however, decided that their best chance of safety lay in making for the Matoschkin Strait, Novaya Zemlya and waiting there for escort. Many were pounced upon on 5 July and either sunk in short order or so damaged that their crews took to the boats, sometimes prematurely. The temptation to get away, without haste, while all boats were in sound condition must have been strong to crews demoralized by the desertion of their escort, the blank loneliness of the Arctic scene, the freezing breath coming off the ice, the endless daylight, exposing their defencelessness to U-boats and aircraft alike. It was a weird, terrifying world to most of the crews, made worse by the effect of the mirage by means of which they could sometimes see their late convoy companions mirrored in the sky from over the horizon, being bombed.

One or two crews thus decided they would rather submit to the hazards of a boat trip of several hundred miles than stay aboard, trying to keep their slightly damaged ships afloat, to await their apparently certain end at the hands of aircraft or U-boat. Strangely enough those who took this line, favoured by fair weather, either succeeded in reaching Novaya Zemlya, where they were taken aboard ships which had already got there, or were picked up in good shape by escorts searching for survivors. One crew which had taken to the boats actually refused to be picked up by another merchant ship which found them. They reckoned they were safer where they were, and perhaps they were right for their would-be rescuer was later torpedoed.

The majority of the crews, however, stuck to their ships with great gallantry and were often left with only rafts on which to get away. One of these was the Commodore's *River Afton*. For more than three hours Dowding, a steward and a deck boy shared four barrels lashed together, in water not far above freezing level. He has related how he saw other survivors drifting around in boats and on rafts and most of them amazingly cheerful though chances of rescue seemed very faint. Even in such a pitiable situation, Dowding's sense of humour did not desert him and he derived grim amusement from the sailor in charge of one of the rafts whom he could hear abjuring a particularly sodden, shivering and complaining shipmate not to be 'so bloody wet'!

In hope of rescue, smoke floats were lighted but in the flat calm the smoke drifted away low along the surface and it seemed unlikely that it would do much good. But 20 miles away, in the corvette *Lotus*, searching for survivors, it appeared, owing to mirage, as a dense column in the sky. Thus, an hour later, Dowding and the master and crew of the *River Afton* joined the many other survivors aboard the *Lotus*. The corvette continued with her rescue work as she steered towards Novaya Zemlya and was repeatedly aided by this mirage. The inverted image of a ship, hanging in the sky on the horizon, would suddenly be surrounded by bomb splashes but, of course, stretching downwards to the horizon instead of upwards into the air!

Some of the most splendid examples of devotion to duty were given by the guns' crews of the merchant ships. In British ships—and in some of the American freighters also at this time—these were gunners belonging to the DEMS (Defensively Equipped Merchant Ship) service. In other American ships they were naval reservists under the command of young Ensigns and were known as the Armed Guard.

More than one of the masters paid glowing tribute to their guns' crews for rallying the demoralized ships' companies when they wanted to abandon ship prematurely. In one American ship, when the crew panicked and made to abandon ship, the matter was referred to the leader of the British DEMS gunners who answered roundly, 'It is our duty to stand fast and take defensive action until the ship sinks.' This stout-hearted rejoinder put an end to the panic and restored morale.

By the end of 5 July, six ships had been sunk by bombs, another six by U-boats' torpedoes. On the next day one more ship was sunk by air attack. Between the 6th and 8th, U-boats accounted for four more. There is no space here to recount the adventures of the survivors from all these ships, which is a pity, as the resource and dogged endurance which they displayed constitute a bright gleam against the sombre background of the story. We must follow instead the fortunes of those which escaped the first onslaught of the enemy as he found, to his incredulous delight, that the impenetrable phalanx from which he had recoiled in attack after attack had broken up into defenceless units.

The shelter for which most of these ships made was the deep inlet on the west coast of Novaya Zemlya known as Matoschkin Strait. Here, by 7 July five had arrived, as had many of the escorts, including the *Lotus* with Commodore Dowding aboard, and the anti-aircraft ship *Palomares*. After a conference in the last-named, a convoy was formed and sailed that evening. Fog and drift ice off a harsh, inhospitable coast made a nightmare voyage at first. One of the ships, *Benjamin Harrison*, lost touch and returned to the shelter of Matoschkin Strait. From time to time boatloads of survivors were sighted and the occupants taken on board the escorts. When the weather cleared on the 9th, the little convoy found itself off the southern point of Novaya Zemlya faced with pack ice which forced an alteration of course to the westward along its edge. By the evening they had rounded it and were heading south for the White Sea. A bare 60 miles from the Russian coast, 40 high-level bombers arrived and for four hours made repeated leisurely attacks undisturbed by sight or sound of a Russian fighter. Though four of them were believed to have been shot down, when the attackers finally drew off at 0230 on the morning of the 10th, two more ships had been sunk by near misses.

Even the imperturbable Dowding was in low spirits as he penned his first report. His bitter understatement, '*Not* a successful convoy! Three ships brought into port out of thirty-seven!' contained a note of heartbreak. But then he heard of the arrival of the *Rathlin* and two others on the 9th and, when news began to come in of others sheltering in Novaya Zemlyan waters, he roused himself. Dowding was not the man to rest while there were any more of his convoy to be brought in. He demanded transport to go out and join them, and escorts to bring them in.

On the 16th, therefore, he left Archangel in the corvette *Poppy* in company with the *Lotus* and the Free French *La Malouine*.* The calm weather had broken, and it was after three stormy days that the first sheltered bay on the coast of Novaya Zemlya was reached, Byelushya Bay, where 12 survivors from the torpedoed *Olapana* were found ashore and taken aboard. Searching northwards along the coast, they first came upon the American *Winston Salem* aground on a sandbank. Without tugs there was little they could do for her for the time being. Reporting her position they passed on up the cruel, ice-bound coast.

The next inlet was Moller Bay where they found the CAM ship *Empire Tide* at anchor and swarming with survivors from other ships. Promising

* Manned by a British crew.

to pick her up on their way south, the little force pressed on to Matoschkin Strait and were cheered by the glad sight of five more merchantmen from the convoy, a Russian ice-breaker *Murman* and a trawler the *Kerov*. Proudly ruling this flotilla was the trawler *Ayrshire* commanded by Lieutenant L. J. A. Gradwell, RNVR.

While the Commodore is arranging to embark in the *Murman*, from which he intends to lead this new convoy southward, we should listen to the tale of Gradwell, a barrister turned sailor 'for the duration', for it is not without interest and charm.

While the convoy scattered on the evening of 4 July and the various escorts picked on ships or groups of ships to shepherd, Gradwell took under his mantle the three American ships *Silver Sword, Ironclad* and *Troubadour*. They were already heading northwards in accordance with the orders for scattering. Gradwell persuaded them that the further they could go in that direction the better until the first fury of the enemy attack had spent itself. So, northwards they continued until they came to the ice-packs when, for a time, they turned eastwards.

But the *Ayrshire*'s radio was full of SOS messages from ships being attacked not far to the south of them. Gradwell therefore led his little convoy boldly up the lanes in the pack-ice until he had put some twenty miles between it and the open sea. This made them safe against U-boat attack. But against the gleaming white of the ice, the black and grey ships stood out like sore thumbs and must soon be seen by roaming aircraft. Very well! All hands paint ship! As the *Ayrshire* slowly converted herself to a yacht-like appearance, the merchant captains caught on to the idea and soon all were a stark white.

The ruse was entirely successful. For the next two days the four ships lay undisturbed in the ice. As the hubbub on the radio died away and Gradwell judged that the enemy were satisfied that there were no more targets for them—in the northern part of the Barents Sea, at any rate—the convoy got under way again and headed for the Matoschkin Strait. There they safely arrived on 11 July. After a brief stay there, Gradwell decided that it was time to move on to Archangel. But, with no charts of that dangerous coast, the *Ironclad* ran twice aground and was refloated with the help of the *Ayrshire*. When the *Troubadour* then did the same, and was with difficulty extricated, Gradwell judged it would be better to await assistance.

Feeling his way carefully up the strait, he led the merchantmen 20 miles up it and there the party anchored, well camouflaged in their white paint and overlooked by several reconaissance enemy aircraft.

The praises of Britain's amateur sailors who manned the vast majority of her little warships have been sung by many authorities on many occasions. But the conduct of the pair of legal lights who formed the captain and executive officer of the *Ayrshire* stands high as what Admiral Tovey described as 'a splendid example of imagination and initiative', an opinion which was warmly endorsed by the masters of the ships the trawler led so skilfully to safety.

But now Commodore Dowding has transferred to the *Murman.*

After a conference on 20 July, all the ships in Matoschkin Strait followed the *Murman* out to sea and down the coast. The *Empire Tide* with her load of survivors joined as the convoy passed Moller Bay. The voyage to Archangel was unmolested, which was just as well judging from Dowding's experience with the Russian staff in the *Murman.* When well into the White Sea, two Russian aircraft appeared right ahead and dropped a single smoke flare, obviously some form of recognition signal, and then flew back whence they had come.

At once there was tremendous excitement amongst the Russians. 'Turn the convoy, Commodore,' they shouted. 'The aircraft has attacked a submarine.' The alarm bells clanged, at which every man on board donned a steel helmet. Nothing would disabuse the Russians of their idea nor would they agree that the strong force of British escorts could well deal with the U-boat, if U-boat there were. On the other hand, nothing was going to persuade Dowding to make a fool of himself by turning the convoy. As the Russians' excitement reached fever pitch, they suddenly rang down for full speed and swung away to port until they had put several miles between themselves and the convoy.

Dowding signalled to the senior officer of the escort to disregard the Russians' antics and, as the convoy sailed serenely on without further alarm, the *Murman* was brought back finally to rejoin it. It was not surprising, if this was typical of the Russian naval mentality and efficiency, that the approaches to Kola and the White Sea were a happy hunting ground for German U-boats at times.

The long agony of PQ17 was nearly over. With the salvaging of the *Winston Salem* under the superintendence of the American Naval Attaché, who flew to Novaya Zemlya in a Catalina flying boat, the last survivor reached port, making a total of 11 out of the 37 which had originally sailed. Besides the 24 freighters lost, the faithful *Aldersdale* had gone and the rescue ship *Zaafaran.*

As for the *Tirpitz* which had caused all the trouble, she did eventually sail on the afternoon of 5 July. With *Scheer, Hipper* and seven destroyers she steered north-eastwards into the Barents Sea for a few hours; but, on the sighting reports of the Russian submarine *K21* and the British *P54* being intercepted, the German naval staff at once began to get cold feet. Calculations showed that Admiral Tovey could get close enough to launch an air attack from his carrier on the German force before it could get back to harbour if it continued with the operation. In any case the scattering of the convoy had delivered it into the hands of the Luftwaffe and the U-boats. Soon after 2130 on the evening of 5 July, the *Tirpitz* turned back to harbour.

10 *Intervention of the Escort Carrier*

The traditions of the Royal Navy, which called for its units to fight against any odds and, if necessary, to sacrifice themselves in protection of merchant ships under their escort, had been broken in the débâcle of PQ17; and though the participants could not have acted otherwise than they did, the reputation of the Navy had suffered a lasting blow; justifiably, it must be held, as the decision to scatter and abandon the convoy had been taken personally by the professional head of the Service.

Nevertheless, although in the light of all the facts which were eventually to be known it seems likely that Hitler's obsessive anxiety not to risk his surface units would have prevented any effective attack by the *Tirpitz*, the First Sea Lord's opinion, previously quoted, was undoubtedly right; that to run convoys to Russia during the period of perpetual daylight when a combination of submarine, surface and air attack could be brought against them was 'a thoroughly unsound operation, with the dice loaded against us in every direction'.

Political forces pressed inexorably, however. Plans were laid for PQ18 in September 1942. This time, however, its defence was to be in far greater strength and organized on different lines. Two principal innovations were involved.

The first was the inclusion of the auxiliary carrier *Avenger*, carrying 12 Hurricane fighters and three anti-submarine Swordfish. The second was the provision of a strong 'Fighting Destroyer Escort'. Realization of the German unwillingness to face a powerful torpedo threat on their few, and therefore highly valued, surface ships, led to the decision to rely upon such a defence in place of the misnamed 'battleship covering force', which had been shown to be incapable of providing cover east of Bear Island. It was to be made up of destroyers of the Home Fleet.

The sailing date for PQ18 was fixed for 2 September from Loch Ewe on the west coast of Scotland where its assembly would not be so exposed to premature discovery as in Iceland. An opposite convoy, QP14 would sail, composed largely of survivors from PQ17, on the 13th. In fact, the Germans, who at this time were able to read many of the British naval cyphered messages, knew that the operation was in the offing and were making preparations. Indeed, one of the features of the actions which were to develop round PQ18 was the complete knowledge held by the enemy of all British plans with regard to it.

By the end of August the opposing sides had completed their preparations. For both the coming operation was to be a real trial of strength. The German air squadrons were burning to repeat their easy triumph and had little need of the stringent orders being passed down from Hitler's headquarters for a great effort to be made. Their torpedo-bomber force had now reached a new total strength of 92 aircraft while their bombers numbered more than 130. The knowledge that an aircraft carrier would be with the convoy added zest and provided a valuable target which could be singled out for attention.

A large force of U-boats was at sea also and the German Naval Command was avid to use some, at least, of their big ships to attack the homeward QP14.

On the British side, a force prepared to accept the challenge had been assembled. Besides the through escort, under Commander A. B. Russell, of two Western Approaches destroyers *Malcolm* and *Achates*, two anti-aircraft ships, *Ulster Queen* and *Alynbank*, four corvettes, three minesweepers, four trawlers and two submarines, there was to be the fighting escort of 16 destroyers under the command of Rear-Admiral Bob Burnett, flying his flag in the new anti-aircraft cruiser *Scylla*, and the auxiliary aircraft carrier *Avenger* with her personal escort of two destroyers. In the background would be the covering force of cruisers, while off the Norwegian coast would be our submarines lying in ambush for the enemy surface ships.

The *Scylla*, commanded by Captain Ian Macintyre, was a splendid addition to the force. Originally designed as a 6-inch gun cruiser, she had been armed instead with eight 4.5-inch guns as an anti-aircraft ship. These smaller guns, mounted in the turrets intended for 6-inch guns, gave her an odd appearance and earned her the nickname amongst the sailors of 'The Toothless Terror'. She was to gain a very different reputation amongst the pilots of the Luftwaffe and was to become a familiar figure on the Kola Run.

It will be seen from the size of the escort, none of the destroyers of which could complete the voyage without re-fuelling at least once, that even with tankers waiting in Spitzbergen, careful organization was needed if the convoy was not to find itself bereft of part of its escort at the moment when the enemy chose to launch an attack. The through escort of anti-submarine vessels which must accompany the merchant ships to their destination had first call on the tankers with the convoy. To reduce their requirements, it was arranged that a local escort would bring the convoy as far as the Denmark Strait where Archie Russell's escort group would take over on 7 September.

Then, on the 9th, the *Scylla* and half the destroyer force, known as Force 'B', would join, while the other half, 'Force 'A', would have gone ahead to Spitzbergen so as to join, with tanks full, on the 13th. Half of Force 'B' would also refuel at Lowe Sound on 12 September. Thus, when the most hazardous part of the convoy's journey began on the 13th, the escort would be at full strength. On the other hand there would be a period between the 11th and the 13th when, in spite of this somewhat intricate arrangement, the escort would be at its weakest. It was felt, however, that this was acceptable as, during that time, only U-boat attack was likely. The whole scheme relied, of course, on reasonable weather permitting the convoy to keep up to schedule, never a very safe bet in the Arctic.

So it was all arranged. Force 'A under Captain H. T. Armstrong of the *Onslow*, included the *Onslaught*, *Opportune* and *Offa* of the 17th Flotilla and *Ashanti*, *Eskimo*, *Somali* and *Tartar* of the 6th. Force 'B' came under Captain Ian Campbell, Captain (D) of the 3rd Flotilla in the *Milne* with the *Marne*, *Martin* and *Meteor* and *Faulknor*, *Intrepid*, *Impulse* and *Fury* of the 8th. The convoy sailed on time and was duly met, north of Iceland by the through escort on the 9th.

With the arrival of the Admiral to assume control, there was a bustling of escorts to their screening positions and signal lamps winked excitedly. Gradually the flurry died away as the last ship reached her station. The *Scylla* had taken up a position in the convoy leading the column next to the Commodore's, while the *Avenger* tagged on astern of a column whence she could readily turn into wind to fly her aircraft on and off.

So quiet settled down as the convoy drove on at a steady nine knots through blue summer seas. But it was an ominous quiet to those who saw the wireless signals warning that the enemy had located the convoy as early as the 8th when still north of Iceland. It could easily be surmised, as was indeed the fact, that a dozen or more U-boats were even then speeding on the surface across the empty Arctic Ocean to take up patrol positions where they could lie in wait.

But the *Avenger*'s Swordfish planes were aloft, patrolling round the horizon and any approaching U-boat would be forced to submerge and would not find it easy to get within range of the convoy.

On the 10th, more evidence arrived of the enemy's intention. The *Scheer*, *Hipper* and *Köln* had been sighted by all four of the British submarines patrolling the Norwegian coast, as they sped northward from Narvik to Altenfiord. It began to look as though the fighting destroyer escort was to be given a try-out. The torpedo tubes' crews went about their work of maintenance and preparation of torpedoes with an increased air of purpose as the news filtered down to them.

But there had been no further sign of enemy activity when, on the 11th, Bob Burnett signalled the 3rd Flotilla to join him as he swung away in the *Scylla* bound for Spitzbergen, to top up fuel tanks, leaving the other half of Force 'B' to fuel from the tankers in the convoy.

So far, the Kola Run had provided little excitement, which was as well, as it gave the large escort force time to settle down. In the fine, clear weather, the perpetual daylight and the crisp cold were showing their more attractive side. There had been no cause yet to curse the absence of any darkness during which there would be some respite from the threat of air attack; nor had it been weather to bring the freezing spray laying a skin of ice on to everything, the whirling snowstorms and the icy breath coming out of the north. The Arctic was proving thoroughly invigorating, in fact.

On the afternoon of the 13th, Force 'B' rejoined the convoy. Force 'A' had joined earlier, so now the escort would be at full strength. And an impressive armada it made—20 destroyers and 11 smaller warships ringing the central mass of the convoy in which three anti-aircraft ships and a carrier were waiting to show their teeth if any aircraft penetrated the screen.

But that other insidious enemy, the U-boat, had already clashed with the convoy in the absence of Force 'A'. During the 12th, the patrolling Swordfish had sighted the wolves closing in but had managed to keep most of them at bay. Some, however, had reached a position directly ahead of the convoy where they could wait, submerged, for their target to come to them. The first of these, *U88*, had lain patiently waiting, each observation through the periscope showing the ships looming larger, the roar of their propellers in the hydrophones getting louder. A little before 2100 the U-boat captain took his last look before going deep to let the escort screen pass over him. It was to be his last sight of the world above for, at that moment, the questing sound beam of the asdic in the *Faulknor* pinged against his hull and sent back the echo which told of a submarine in its path. Soon the depth-charges were sinking remorselessly down to erupt around the U-boat and send it to its lonely grave on the bottom of the Arctic Ocean.

It was first blood to the British. But *U88* was only one wolf of a pack which had gathered and which was snarling round the outskirts seeking a way in. Time and again during the 13th the *Avenger*'s Swordfish detected others on the surface, trying to gain bearing so as to come in to the attack from ahead. Each time they were forced to dive their speed became limited to a crawl and the convoy drew ahead. But persistence on the part of the U-boats brought its reward eventually when one at last got through the screen and torpedoed the *Stalingrad* and the *Oliver Elsworth* in the starboard wing column.

The ominous gap in the line of ships was there to see and to whet the escorts' vigilance as the destroyers dispersed to their screening stations.

But they had barely reached them when the air battle for PQ18 opened. Above the almost continuous layer of cloud, its base at about 4,000 feet, could be heard the throbbing roar of a formation Ju.88s seeking gaps in the cloud through which they could dive to drop their bombs. On the *Avenger's* flight deck, there was bustle and activity as Hurricanes were manned and their engines started with a cough and a roar. The carrier turned into wind and five fighters took the air and climbed away to seek the enemy above the clouds.

A confused mêlée ensued as the Hurricanes chased fleeting targets in and out of the clouds while the guns of the escorts banged away at briefly sighted bombers emerging momentarily to drop their bombs. Neither side achieved any results. Bombs burst harmlessly between the ships; no bombers were hit.

But, whether it was the enemy's intention or not, he had for the time being drawn the sting of the carrier. This was the first time that a carrier had been used to provide fighter defence for a convoy. The technique was yet to be developed. Commander Colthurst of the *Avenger*, galled by the immunity enjoyed by the shadowing aircraft droning impertinently round the horizon, had sent away sections of two Hurricanes each to deal with them, only to find that his obsolescent Mark 1 fighters, armed with light machine-guns, could make no impression on the armoured Blohm and Voss 138 reconnaissance aircraft or the Ju.88s which worked in groups of as many as nine planes at times.

While some of his Hurricanes were thus employed, the bombing attack had developed and his remaining fighters were sent up. Thus, when the really dangerous attack developed 30 minutes later, as more than 40 He.111s and Ju.88s each carrying two torpedoes, swept in low from the starboard side of the convoy, not one fighter was available to meet it. Those which were still airborne had used up all their ammunition on the armoured Ju.88 bombers. Now they did what they could by making feint attacks on the oncoming Heinkels, but to little effect.

Watchers in the ships gazed with undisguised awe on the approaching swarm, spread clear across the southern horizon in line abreast, 30 to 40 feet above the water, looking, as Commodore Bodham-Whetham so vividly described them, 'like a huge flight of nightmare locusts'.

With a roar the guns of the escorts opened up, a barrage to be followed, as the enemy came closer, by the mad clatter of Oerlikons and the staccato bark of pom-poms. The *Scylla*, at full speed, had drawn away ahead of the merchantmen to get a free arc of fire for her guns, her quick-firing 4.5-inch guns spitting viciously.

But it was all of little avail against the serried array of planes, their pilots, urged on by the memory of exhortations for a 'special effort' against this convoy, keeping perfect station, grimly determined to get through the screen and into the mass of merchant ships. A few, smashing headlong into a destroyer's shell or a stream of machine-gun fire, staggered, burst into flame and plunged into the sea. But the majority survived the barrage, zoomed over the escorts and pressed on for the convoy.

In the Commodore's flagship, a flag signal ran up the halliards and a plume of white steam appeared as her siren bellowed to draw attention to it. It was the signal for an emergency turn of 45° by each ship of the convoy simultaneously to starboard, that is to say in the direction from which the attack was coming. Such a turn would make it easier for any ship seeing a torpedo approaching from the starboard side to swing parallel to its track and so greatly reduce its chance of hitting.

But by now, bedlam reigned in and around the convoy as the guns in every ship came into action. The masters of the ships of the two starboard columns, attention riveted on the on-coming aircraft even now dipping down to loose their torpedoes, saw nothing of the Commodore's signal, or, if they did, were too stupefied to take action. Like oxen to the slaughter, they ploughed straight ahead as the great swarm of torpedoes sped straight for their vitals.

Of the seven ships remaining in the two starboard columns, six were hit, one vanishing in a terrifying detonation. In the middle of the convoy, also, torpedoes found their mark in two more ships. The convoy steamed on, eight ships fewer. The smaller escorts and the rescue ships were already picking up survivors while the enemy were still attacking. Gradually the firing died away. The 'nightmare locusts' could be seen growing smaller and smaller as they retreated towards the southern horizon.

The torpedo attack had been a startling and woeful experience. Though there had been little chance from the escorts on the screen to see much of what was going on in the convoy while the wild mêlée continued and the ships lurched and trembled at the shock and recoil of the guns coughing out their barrage and the pom-poms and Oerlikons blazed away as targets came fleetingly within range, the eight new gaps in the ranks were now plain to see. Even the thought-deadening hammer of the guns had been unable to conceal from anyone the awful fate of the exploding merchantman.

But there was no time to ponder on it just yet for more torpedo-bombers had come in sight, three approaching from ahead and six from astern. However, this was not in the same calibre at all as the earlier attack and, as the guns roared into action, the pilots made haste to drop their torpedoes at long range and get away, though not before two of them had been shot down. The torpedoes were of no danger to the convoy, but for a time the water round the ships screening ahead was alive with tracks, which were only narrowly avoided by the *Scylla* and some of the destroyers.

At last quiet settled down again and stock could be taken. There was no doubt that the enemy had scored a notable success with his mass attack. At a cost of five aircraft, he had eliminated nearly a quarter of the convoy. It was a rate of exchange which simply could not go on. The convoy had six more days to go before it could reach harbour. Furthermore, ammunition had been used up at a tremendous rate during the attack. In the 'M'-class destroyers, for instance, from each of the three twin turrets, 4.7-inch shells could be fired at the rate of between 12–15 rounds per minute. Thus, in barrage fire, when the rate of fire was not slowed down through the need to lay the guns accurately on to a target, ammunition was being used up at about a ton a minute. It would not last long at that rate and Captain Campbell gave orders to his ships to limit the duration of barrages.

But, in fact, that first attack on 13 September marked the high water of enemy air effort against the Arctic convoys. Never again would they get together such a number of torpedo planes for a massed assault. At the same time, some lessons learnt by the defence were being studied. In the *Avenger*, the disadvantage at which she had been caught owing to the premature launching of her very limited force of fighters was bemoaned and vows made not to be caught that way again. Instead of launching the Hurricanes piecemeal against small and unimportant attacks, they would be held on deck until the enemy was committed to his mass torpedo-bomber assault and then they would be operated in a continuous cycle so that some sections were always airborne while others were being re-armed and re-fuelled.

In the anti-aircraft ship, *Ulster Queen*, too, Captain Adam had fretted at the orders which kept his handy little ship tied to a station in the convoy where his guns could not be brought into action against approaching low-flying aircraft. Admiral Burnett's orders had been framed with the prospect of high-level bombing in view when, no doubt, the *Ulster Queen* would perform better as a steady gun platform in the middle of the convoy. But after the experience of the 13th Adam decided that he would take advantage of his ship's good manoeuvring powers and move out of the convoy to bring his guns to bear if a further torpedo attack impended.

So, in the various escorts the situation was examined and plans laid to beat off the enemy's next effort. But thoughts turned from time to time to the crews of the merchantmen. Everyone wondered how they were taking the ceaseless suspense and foreboding. Knowing little of the tactical or strategical situation or the relative strength of the opposing forces, unable to do anything to defend themselves, but forced to stand and wait for whatever fate might be in store for them—an instant launch into eternity as had happened to the crew of the ship which had blown up, or a hasty leap from their sinking ship into icy Arctic seas—it must have been an experience of long-drawn terror for them. Many, indeed, collapsed and lay helpless in extremities of fear; but others displayed qualities of cool courage and heroism that have rarely been equalled.

All of them must have felt what Rear-Admiral Bodham-Whetham described later to Bob Burnett as 'a funny feeling to realize one is sitting on top of 2,000 tons of TNT, but we nearly all carry between that and 4,000 tons. I don't think the bigger amount would make more than some tiny fraction of a second's difference to the time one entered the next world.' As far back as May, Admiral Bonham-Carter had said, 'It is beginning to be too much to ask of the merchant seamen.' PQ17 and PQ18 showed how right he had been.

Survivors from the sunken ships swarmed in embarrassing numbers in the minesweepers which had joined in the rescue work. In the lull which lasted through the dog watches, they were taken one by one alongside the *Scylla* which had more space to accommodate the unfortunates.

Even in the escorts it was with no light-hearted insouciance that the prospect of the next few days was faced; but at least they were free to manoeuvre clear from the path of torpedoes if they could see them in time; they could hit back hard, too, and while doing so there was no time for anyone to be frightened. It was sheer fatigue that weighed most heavily on the warships' crews, with no moment throughout the 24 hours when vigilance could be relaxed against the double menace of the U-boat and the bomber.

At 2030 that evening, the 13th, came another effort by some dozen torpedo-carrying Heinkels. Attacking in small numbers, they failed to penetrate to the convoy, however, and dropped their torpedoes ineffectively at long range. For the rest of the night, U-boat alarms were incessant. Bearings obtained by ships fitted with radio direction finders betrayed the fact that at least five of the sinister craft were hovering around. Asdic operators were keyed up to the highest pitch of alertness.

But in spite of this, at 0330 in the morning of the 14th, a torpedo struck home in the *Atheltemplar*, one of the tankers on which the escorts were relying for fuel. The blow was not a mortal one, but with other U-boats in the vicinity, there was nothing for it but for an escort to take off her crew and sink her. Another fine ship gone! With so large an escort, it was galling that U-boats should be able to get through the screen; but it was known that the water conditions in the Arctic, especially in the summer, reduced the efficiency of the asdic and gave the submarine a big advantage.

As the sun reappeared from just below the horizon that morning, Bob Burnett could not look back with much satisfaction on the results of the first day of the battle for PQ18. If the Germans could keep up the same weight of attack, prospects for the future did not seem bright. But the various elements of his force, many of them new to this form of warfare, had absorbed the lessons of the previous day and were ready for the second round. A dogged defence on the one side and a failure on the other to follow up the first assault with the same vigour as before were now to turn the tide of fortune.

The first to fall a victim to the increasing efficiency of PQ18's combined air and surface escort was one of Dönitz's U-boats—*U589*. Surfacing safely out of sight of the convoy, as her captain thought, she was sighted by one of the *Avenger*'s Swordfish soon after 0930 on 14 September and forced to dive.

Reporting the position to the flagship, the pilot marked it with a smoke float and waited near it for the destroyer he felt sure would be sent out to cooperate. And, indeed, the Admiral had at once despatched the *Onslow*, whose captain, 'Beaky' Armstrong, was an old hand at submarine hunting, with an experienced anti-submarine team under him.

But even at 30 knots it would be nearly an hour before she could be on the scene. While the 'Stringbag' waited impatiently, German eyes from the cockpit of a reconnaissance plane fell on the slowly circling biplane. The much faster Ju.88 came swooping down. Almost defenceless against its much more powerful opponent, the Swordfish turned to run for the shelter of the convoy's protection, using its ability to turn in tight circles and to fly at a slow speed—impossible to the high-performance mono-plane—to evade its attacks.

It escaped unharmed, but the U-boat captain, searching the sky with his·periscope, saw that he was again free to surface to continue the charging of his batteries and to keep touch with the convoy. Thus, when the *Onslow* came dashing out, Armstrong saw the low silhouette against the horizon and could mark the U-boat's position on his plot. So when the submarine dived again at a range of six miles, it was a fairly limited sea area that had to be searched by the destroyer's asdic.

Even so, asdic search was a slow process. A cast in the wrong direction could give the submarine time to get well away, every minute undetected greatly improving its chances of escape. But luck and skill were now combining on PQ18's behalf. From the long ping-g-g . . . of the *Onslow*'s asdic suddenly came back the sharp pip of an echo and the hunt was on. For three hours, as the U-boat twisted and turned, accelerated and stopped, plunged deeper and deeper to evade the deadly patterns of depth-charges, the asdic team held contact. At length, after many accurate attacks, the answering echo faded and died.

Not daring to hope that this spelt success at last, 'Beaky' cast this way and that to pick it up again should the U-boat have, in fact, managed to sneak away. But then, returning to the scene of his last attack, Armstrong came upon the evidence he needed. In the midst of a widening pool of oil on the surface, great bubbles were bursting and wooden debris was floating. *U589* would haunt the convoy routes no more!

But, while the hunt was still in progress, PQ18 had been demonstrating the new ability to defend itself which it had gained from the experience of the previous day. At the warning of a strong formation of more than 20 torpedo-bombers approaching, besides the familiar sight of the *Scylla* streaking out ahead to gain a free arc of fire for her guns, the convoy saw the *Avenger* disengaging and manoeuvring inside the screen, with the *Ulster Queen* in support. Six Hurricanes were all ready ranged on deck, their propellers turning.

As the enemy aircraft in two groups neared the outer screen, the destroyer barrage opened up. One group chose the screen and *Scylla* as targets, but they soon regretted it. As the leaders met the barrage they smashed headlong into the sea. The remainder hastily dropped their torpedoes at long range and swerved away.

The larger group evidently had orders to concentrate on the carrier, but the *Avenger*, attended by her two destroyers and the *Ulster Queen*, sent her brood of fighters streaming into the air while her escorts blazed away with every gun they had. The Heinkels made a desperate effort to get her, chasing persistently after her as she circled the convoy. No less than 17 torpedoes were launched at the *Avenger*; but, with Hurricanes tearing into them from behind and a seemingly impenetrable barrier of shell bursts and tracers ahead, the pilots' aim was understandably poor and *Avenger* avoided them all. When the enemy at last drew off, they left 11 of their number destroyed and not a single ship hit.

A feeling of immense exhilaration spread through the escorts at this success. Bob Burnett called it 'a most gratifying action'. Commander Colthurst signalled light-heartedly to claim the 'honour of being the sole object of the attack'.

But there was little time for self-congratulations. There had been barely time to clear away the litter of cartridge cases around the guns and to pass a hurried action meal of soup and sandwiches to the men at their quarters when the next alarm came crackling over the radio telephone. Bombers, coming in high above the overcast, had appeared on the radar screens and soon the throbbing drone of them could be heard.

Avenger was not going to be lured into sending her fighters after them—indeed they were still being hastily re-fuelled and re-armed. So it was left to the guns to engage the Ju.88s which came momentarily out of the clouds, one by one, over the next hour to drop their bombs and climb back into safety. It was nerve-racking to have to wait passively under the continuous rumble of aircraft, listening for the rising change of note that heralded one of them going into a dive, while the gunners tried to forecast where it would appear and everyone wondered if his ship was to be the selected target.

Fortunately, it was not a very effective form of attack and, though many ships, including the *Avenger*, had narrow escapes, none was hit and one aircraft was shot down. But as the Ju.88s expended their last bomb, Colhurst's wisdom in holding on to his fighters was seen. Another swarm of more than 25 torpedo-bombers came swooping in.

Once again they made the carrier their principal target as she manoeuvred on the starboard quarter of the convoy. Ten Hurricanes had been launched and soon the air was full of a mad whirl of aircraft, shell bursts and tracers as the Heinkels came boldly in to close the range to drop their torpedoes and the *Avenger*'s fighters followed them, disregarding the storm of shell through which they were flying. Aircraft were plunging into the sea in every direction, including three Hurricanes, whose pilots were picked up safely, however. Miraculously the carrier avoided every torpedo aimed at her.

But in the midst of this fantastic circus of whirling wings, roaring engines and the thought-deadening bedlam of gunfire, there came a cataclysmic thunderclap as the *Mary Luckenbach* in the starboard column blew up. As the last shattered morsels of debris from her fell back into the sea, nothing remained but a tremendous cloud of smoke reaching up and flattening itself against the overcast.

For a moment the gunfire died away as guns' crews contemplated in awe the frightening happening. Then it burst out again. But the fight was nearly over and the survivors of the enemy formation, leaving nine crashed behind them, were streaming for home.

The convoy's new-found confidence was temporarily shaken by the manner of the *Mary Luckenbach*'s passing and the thought of the appalling loss of life. But there was still cause for grim satisfaction at the outcome of this latest effort by the enemy. They were losing aircraft and highly-trained crews fast. At a cost of 21 aircraft they had succeeded in depleting the convoy by only one more ship.

However, to temper any false confidence there now came a reminder of that other threat to the safe passage of the convoy, the huge *Tirpitz* and her smaller but still powerful consorts lying in wait on the flank of the route to Russia. Reconnaissance of the Narvik area on this day, the 14th, had disclosed that the *Tirpitz* had left harbour and had not since been located.

She might be out, therefore, making for a rendezvous with *Scheer*, *Hipper* and *Köln* off the advanced base in Altenfiord to bring against the convoy that overwhelming force which was the constant pre-occupation of the Admiralty and the C-in-C. The bad luck which seemed to dog the Royal Air Force reconnaissance in the North at crucial moments now caused a hiatus in their scouting operations. As a stop-gap the squadron of Hampden torpedo-bombers was itself sent out to search and to attack if the enemy were found at sea.

As it turned out, the enemy surface ships had not left harbour and the Hampdens found nothing. But until they were re-located there were too many threats looming for any easy confidence amongst the escorts. Indeed, as the naval staff had pointed out before, if the German resources were boldly and skilfully handled they ought to be able to prevent any ships getting through to North Russia.

For the rest of the afternoon of 14 September, some Ju.88s harried the convoy, dropping their bombs through holes in the cloud layer or occasionally making surprise shallow-dive attacks. But few would face the volume of fire which the strong escort could put up and none of their bombs did any damage. How quietly reassuring it sounds, writing of it thus so long afterwards. But at the time nerves were kept at full stretch for hour after hour in escort and merchant ship alike.

Any one of the attacks might be the exception to the rule and be boldly and skilfully carried through, sending a bomb crashing into a ship's hull in spite of all that the guns could throw at the aircraft. Eyes grew tired and sore from ceaseless search of the sky. Unable to relax, bodies became deadly weary. Food, hastily snatched at odd intervals, lay heavy in stomachs gripped by a sensation reluctantly acknowledged as fear. Running through it all, in the escorts, was the leitmotiv of the never-ceasing, 24 hours a day 'ping ... ping ...' of the asdic. The subconscious mind listened unceasingly for an echo to it. The slightest variation in it brought an immediate, anxious attention.

The closing down of night, or more accurately twilight, brought some relief as the enemy airmen seemed unwilling to venture on the long sea passage to the convoy then. But it was now that the U-boats liked to close to the attack, their periscopes less visible in the gloom. So, for the escort captain night brought little real rest. The little box-like sea cabin under the bridge was there with a bunk for him to rest in, but he was never out of hearing of the ping—nor did he want to be—and in the difficult water conditions common in the Arctic, repeated false alarms kept him continually dashing up and down, which in heavy cold-weather clothing was very wearying.

So captains rarely left the bridge except to eat, wash or perform the natural functions. In most destroyers, there was fitted a stout wooden chair beside the binnacle, with an alternative position in the sheltered fore end of the bridge. In it they spent most of their time when attack threatened, dozing when things were quiet, instantly awake at the slightest change in the even tempo of the bridge routine.

No doubt, as they steadily ran more into debt to sleep, efficiency seeped gradually out of them, but at the time it was not apparent. It is, however, noticeable that in reports on Arctic convoy operations, comment was sometimes made that calamities had occurred towards the end of a long period of tension when the escorts were perhaps no longer at their best. But, short of neglecting their responsibilities in command, responsibilities which can never be shared, there was no remedy for the captains of ships.

The night of the 14th passed quietly. During the forenoon of the next day, too, some relaxation was possible for, with the convoy now well into the Barents Sea, 400 miles lay between it and the German Air Force base at Banak. Taking off at dawn, the enemy aircraft were not to be expected before midday.

Sure enough at 1245, after radar warnings, there came the growl of aircraft engines above the clouds. With the overcast at 4,000 feet, the enemy obviously feared to face the gunfire to press home their attacks with accuracy. In groups of three, they came briefly out of the cloud base to attack. Greeted by a great volume of fire, they lingered only long enough to take a browning shot at the convoy before retiring to safety again. Such methods relied largely upon luck to achieve anything and the luck had now turned against the Germans.

From the *Avenger*, sections of Hurricanes were sent off to harry the bombers and, for nearly three hours the enemy airmen were chivvied above the clouds by the fighters and shot at whenever they appeared below, doing which they lost three of their number.

Thoroughly disgruntled at this churlish reception, the enemy took to circling hopefully inside the clouds, waiting for the convoy to pass into a clear area to give them a chance. Appreciating this, Admiral Burnett was just considering diverting the convoy for a time to keep it under cloud when the German leader was heard ordering his flock to return to base and jettison bombs, being at the end of their fuel endurance.

It had not been a very high-spirited effort and one wonders what the German high command thought of it after their frenzied appeals for a 'special effort' against PQ18!

Meanwhile the U-boats were doing no better. Never less than three were always in contact during all this time but none could bring itself to face the very powerful screen.

The bombers were still playing hide-and-seek in the clouds above, when that other hazard, the enemy surface ships was brought to mind. From one of the wing escorts came a report of two columns of smoke on the southern horizon.

It could not be known at the time—the *Tirpitz* was still unlocated, *Scheer*, *Hipper* and *Köln* were still poised for a sortie from Altenfiord—but there was, in fact, no question of the German forces coming out at that period. Hitler's infatuation with the idea that an invasion of Norway was planned by the Allies effectively tied the hands of the German naval command in the matter. On no account were any risks to be run which might imperil their availability to counter such a move by the Allies. With such instructions, it is not surprising that Admiral Raeder vetoed the plan of the German Command, North, to sail the three ships at Altenfiord. The temporary disappearance of *Tirpitz* was later found to be owing simply to her being engaged in exercises in the Vestfiord.

In any case, there now came the reassuring report from the *Opportune*, sent out to investigate, that the smoke was simply the exhaust, much magnified by mirage, from two U-boats on the surface, away beyond the horizon. They dived on sighting *Opportune*. There were no dividends to

be had from hunting U-boats so far from the convoy, so they were left to
their own devices—to stay where they were, harmless, or to engage the
escort on its own terms in the vicinity of the convoy.

It may have been one of them which did the latter in the early hours of
the next day. At 0300, the asdic operators in the *Impulsive*, in her
screening position ahead of the convoy, gained a contact. There was an
experienced and well-drilled team in the *Impulsive*. Her captain,
Lieutenant-Commander E. G. Roper, had just time to make one quick
attack before the advancing convoy ran over his target. He was then
forced to wait, chafing impotently, until the lines of merchant ships had
made their stately way past before he could return to the attack. But
when the time came, there was no need for further depth-charges. A
growing circle of wreckage and oil told their tale. Later it was established
that it was *U457* which had ventured once too often within range of a
convoy escort.

The score was levelling up in the record of PQ18. It was nearly further
evened later that forenoon when *Opportune* and *Offa*, sighting another
submarine on the surface, gained contact with it after it had dived and
attacked it heavily. But they could not claim a kill. ◊

That morning came the first sign that the most dangerous part of the
convoy's voyage was nearing its end, when the first Catalina arrived from
the squadron based in North Russia to take over the duties of anti-
submarine patrol from the devoted, tireless Swordfish of the *Avenger*.
The homeward QP14 would be passing soon and Bob Burnett's force
would have to transfer it, to give it the same cover that PQ18 had
enjoyed. In theory, cover from Russian fighters would be available for
PQ18 from now on and, though experience had not bred any confidence
that any such thing would be provided, priority of task for Burnett's
squadron obviously lay with QP14 from this point.

So, during the 16th, in three separate groups so as not to make it too
obvious to the enemy, *Scylla*, the destroyers, *Avenger*, the two fleet oilers,
the *Alynbank* and the two submarines parted company. We will join them
later, but for the moment let us follow the fortunes of PQ18 to the end.

Early on the 17th came further signs which, like the dove from Noah's
ark or the signs of land which restored Columbus' confidence, told of
friendly territory not far ahead. For two Russian destroyers now joined,
and it was known that they never ventured far from their own coasts!
However, these, with their fine armament of four dual-purpose 5-inch
guns each, and two more, smaller Russian destroyers which arrived early
on the 18th were a very welcome addition to an escort which looked
alarmingly sparse to Archie Russell when the last of Burnett's force
left.

The Russians were to have plenty of opportunity to show their
skill—and indeed they did put up a splendid performance when put to
it—for the German Air Force was being urged on by Reichsmarschall

Göring, furious at the impending escape of so much of the convoy, to persist in their attacks right to the very entrance to Archangel harbour.

As the convoy passed Cape Kanin at the entrance to the White Sea early on the 18th, radar warnings came from the *Ulster Queen*, which had fortunately been retained as part of the escort, that aircraft were again gathering for the attack. With full daylight they arrived—12 torpedo-bombers spread in line abreast and coming in low over the water from astern.

In the absence of the strong outer screen from which they had shrunk before, the airmen were able to get their torpedoes well into the convoy. But, running almost parallel to the ships' tracks, they were all avoided by individual alterations of course—all but one, which hit and damaged the *Kentucky*, which dropped astern immobilized. At the same time there arrived the Ju.88 bombers. But they lacked the nerve of the torpedo-bomber pilots. Attacking intermittently through gaps in the clouds, they failed to score any hits until they decided to take the easy target of the stationary *Kentucky*, whose destruction they completed.

At this stage Archie Russell decided that the moment had come to release the Hurricane which throughout the voyage had sat on its catapult in the *Empire Morn*. Available for just one flight only, it was always most difficult to know when to throw the solitary trump card on the table. But now Flying Officer A. H. Barr, the Hurricane's pilot, made the most of his opportunity. Tearing into the enemy formation, he shot down one torpedo-bomber and then, by the bare threat of his empty guns, repeatedly drove off others. Finally, with just enough petrol remaining, he left to seek an airfield near Archangel, 240 miles away, which he succeeded in doing with just four gallons splashing in the bottom of his tank when he landed.

A second torpedo attack an hour later than the first failed to score any success whatsoever and three of the enemy fell to the guns of the escort—two to those of the *Ulster Queen*. It is impossible not to speculate on the astonishing lack of success of the German airmen against the Arctic convoys with the exception of rare occasions such as the first torpedo attack on PQ18. At much the same period, in the Mediterranean, Italian and German airmen were playing havoc with the convoys being fought through to the relief of Malta under very heavy escort.

It is tempting to ascribe the difference to the employment of lower grade, less well-trained pilots in the Arctic theatre, but this does not, from German records appear to be so. In September there were no great climatic difficulties of maintenance or operation either. Yet even after the withdrawal of the carrier and its fighters and a huge reduction in the fire power of the escort force, egged on by a frantic Göring, the German airmen could account for but one merchantman in their repeated attacks.

One is forced to the conclusion that the long sea passage between target and base, with the prospect of a 'ditching' resulting from even minor damage during the attack, took the guts out of airmen of a land-trained air force. In the Mediterranean, a flight of 50–100 miles brought them to their objective; a warm sea waited for them if they were forced down. In the Arctic there were hundreds of miles of icy water and a poor chance of survival. It may be that here is the one crucial reason why the Arctic convoys got through against all that the enemy air force could bring against them.

We have seen how Hitler's famous 'intuition' was inhibiting any surface attack. As for the U-boats, it was in the Arctic that the solution to the problem of their defeat was first demonstrated in the employment of a combined sea and air escort throughout the convoy's voyage.

But to follow PQ18 to the end, the attacks on 18 September might have been expected to have been the end of their ordeal, for on the next morning the convoy arrived off the Dvina Bar. But the long, weary voyage, already 17 days in length, with six of them under incessant enemy attack, was to be cruelly prolonged. A gale descended to hold the ships at sea; and while they tried to find shelter from the elements, Ju.88s made yet another effort to retrieve their lost reputation. But even with the convoy so handicapped, the enemy utterly failed to achieve any success.

The gale, indeed, was more to be feared than the foe, for three merchant-men of the convoy were stranded for a time. Even then, with targets stationary, though guarded by the faithful Ulster Queen, two bombers which attacked during the afternoon of the 21st failed to achieve a hit.

So ends the story of PQ18. At a heavy cost, techniques had been learnt which would have their application elsewhere in the war. QP14, to which we must now return, was to point another lesson, again, unfortunately, at a grievous cost.

The company which formed the convoy QP14 was one composed mostly of the much-tried survivors of PQ17. For two weary months they had suffered the monotony of life at Archangel where amenities were almost non-existent, the flat, barren countryside making a backdrop of unutter-able dreariness to the scene. Now at last, under the leadership of Commodore Dowding, his flag in the Ocean Voice, they were heading thankfully for home. Admiral Burnett's force joined it on 17 September.

The names of the ships of the close escort as well as those of the convoy will be familiar to those who have read the misadventures of PQ17. In command of it was Captain Crombie in the minesweeper Bramble. Under him were the two anti-aircraft ships Palomares and Pozarica, the destroyers Blankney and Middleton, corvettes Lotus, Poppy, Dianella and La Malouine, the minesweepers Leda and Seagull and those veterans of the Kola Run, the trawlers Lord Middleton, Lord Austin, Ayrshire and Northern Gem.

With the convoy of 15 ships were the rescue ships *Zamalek* and *Rathlin*. Sailing, rather ominously to the superstitious, on 13 September, they had made good progress for the first four days and, though the enemy undoutedly knew their position, they had been left alone, partly owing to welcome thick weather and partly because the Luftwaffe was concentrating all its effort on PQ18.

We have seen how the German Naval Command's intention to send *Scheer*, *Hipper* and *Köln* to attack QP14 had been hamstrung through Hitler's misunderstanding of the strategical situation. It is profitless but nevertheless fascinating to speculate what might have happened if the German Navy had been given a free hand. It is difficult to see how disaster to the convoy could have been avoided, though perhaps the RAF squadron of Hampden torpedo-bombers might have made the enemy pay heavily for any successes.

However, the fact remained that when Burnett's force joined the convoy far up in the Barents Sea, its passage had been entirely peaceful. Now, in intermittent fog and snow it was heading westwards to pass close south of Spitzbergen. Though the enemy shadowing aircraft had lost touch in these conditions, they had seen enough to direct U-boats to the scene, and by the 18th reports by escorting Catalinas and Swordfish revealed that some were in touch and prowling round.

It was bitterly cold far up into the Arctic. The convoy was not far from the ice barrier as the appearance of that curious phenomenon 'ice-blink' told, a dazzling, eye-hurting light caused by the reflection off the ice. In sight passed what must be one of the loneliest, dreariest islands in the world, named for some unexplained reason Hope Island. From time to time the motionless, dead, yet menacing bulk of great icebergs loomed by, seeming but to stress the lifeless desolation of the Arctic.

While the sea remained calm, the destroyers went in turn alongside the two tankers to replenish their fuel tanks; but long before their thirst was satisfied the available stocks in the oilers were exhausted. So the Admiral sent away two destroyers to fetch one of the tankers lying in Lowe Sound to join him, which she did on the following evening.

By the morning of the 19th, the South Cape of Spitzbergen was abeam and now the Admiral put into execution a plan designed partly to keep as great a distance as possible between the convoy and the German air bases and partly to try to shake off the trailing U-boats. Sending two Swordfish up to ensure that no U-boats were on the surface to watch and a screen of destroyers and minesweepers out to the southward to keep the submarines down, he altered the convoy's course north-west up the coast of Spitzbergen, intending to keep on that course for the rest of the day before turning again south-westward for home.

Though U-boats were sighted by the Swordfish and duly forced to dive, Bob Burnett's plan came to naught so far as deceiving the enemy went, for at the very moment of altering course a shadowing aircraft arrived to note and report it. However, whether the Admiral's stratagem was the reason or not, it was a fact that PQ14 was not attacked from the air at all during its passage. Only U-boats were to harry it.

A considerable pack of these had gathered round by the evening of the 19th, and for the next three days they were handled with skill and unusual boldness which brought them a rich reward. It began with the sinking of the minesweeper *Leda*, torpedoed in her screening position astern of the convoy in the last hour before dawn of the next day. Eighty-six of her crew were rescued but the submarine responsible, *U435*, escaped.

In spite of repeated sightings and persistent hunting and attacks by aircraft and destroyers, none of the wolf pack was accounted for, though one had a narrow escape when one of the two British submarines sent to patrol astern of the convoy sighted *U408*. In and out of snow squalls, *P614* stalked its surfaced and unsuspecting quarry. But the fleeting glimpses of it through the periscope were too infrequent to allow an accurate attack. The torpedoes went wide, the startled enemy hurriedly diving when he saw their tracks in the calm sea.

On the evening of that day QP14's very strong screen suffered the humiliation of seeing one of the convoy torpedoed. A U-boat had got through in spite of all their vigilance. But at that time it was not altogether appreciated to what an extent water conditions in the Arctic often stultified the use of the asdic, the only means available of detecting a submerged submarine.

Particularly in the summer, varying layers of temperature played queer tricks with a sound beam and might deflect it above or below its target so that a submarine could pass closely by, undetected. It was fortunate that the enemy did not understand this either, so that it was only the occasional U-boat, more boldly handled than usual, which reaped the benefit without realizing why.

The best defence for a convoy under these conditions was provided by continuous air patrols preventing U-boats from surfacing to run at high speed to positions ahead of the convoy whence they could make their approach submerged. This the *Avenger*'s three Swordfish had been doing with considerable success on behalf of PQ18 as well as QP14. But now these aircraft and their crews were showing signs of strain after so many days of almost continuous operation. Commander Colthurst decided they must be given overhaul and rest.

Learning of this, the Admiral, appreciating that air attack was by now most unlikely, decided to detach both the *Scylla* and the *Avenger* to return to base. He himself would shift his flag to the *Milne*. Accordingly shortly before dusk on the 20th, the *Milne* was taken alongside the *Scylla* and as the two ships steamed along together at 14 knots Bob Burnett, enthroned on a modern, steel version of a bosun's chair, was hoisted by the cruiser's boat-crane and delivered to the deck of the *Milne*.

He was received, in spite of this novel form of embarkation, with due formality and twittering of bosuns' pipes. At the masthead his rear-admiral's flag was broken out.

The *Scylla* was undoubtedly best away out of it. To keep her tied to the slow-moving convoy, a constant encouragement to any U-boat commander anxious to earn his Knight's Cross, would certainly have been wrong now that the danger of air attack was past. But the absence of *Avenger*'s splendid old 'Stringbags' circling on the horizon to keep the U-boats down was a different matter. The Admiral had asked for and confidently expected air escort to be provided by Coastal Command of the Royal Air Force; so that when Commander Colthurst reported that his three hard-worked Swordfish and their patrols had reached the end of their endurance and must be given refit and rest, the valuable carrier was but a hostage to fortune if she remained in the convoy. It seemed as well to send her off also.

But Coastal Command was still far from being able to meet all the requirements of the war at sea. A convoy battle in the North Atlantic now absorbed all its resources, leaving nothing for QP14. Though one Catalina did arrive on the 21st, it was early damaged in an attack on a submarine and forced to alight near the convoy which was left from then on with no air escort. It was to cost it dearly.

Already at the time of the *Avenger*'s departure the absence of air patrols during the day had allowed a U-boat to reach ahead of the convoy and lie in wait. Hardly had the carrier gone than calamity struck. The large 'Tribal'-class destroyer *Somali*, port wing ship of the convoy screen, was torpedoed. Brought to a standstill, she showed no signs of sinking and was taken in tow by Richard Onslow's ship *Ashanti*.

Bob Burnett decided that *Somali* was worth a big effort to get home and sent *Eskimo*, *Intrepid* and *Opportune* as well as the trawler *Lord Middleton* to escort her and the *Ashanti*. It was a big bite out of the convoy's available escort but it still left 12 destroyers and nine smaller craft which should have been ample to guard 15 ships. When the Catalina arrived the next day it seemed to make the convoy doubly safe; but alas this was the aircraft which crashed after a few hours and was the only one to arrive.

The absence of the *Avenger*'s Swordfish was now to be sorely felt. With asdics almost useless in a sea which had been calm for a period unusual in those latitudes and cooled on the surface by freezing polar air and the melting of innumerable icebergs there was every chance of a U-boat which had got ahead of the convoy penetrating the screen submerged and undetected. With no aircraft there was no way of preventing them from running at high speed on the surface beyond the horizon to gain such a position.

When the *Milne*, returning from taking the Admiral to see how *Somali* and *Ashanti* were getting on, sighted a U-boat which dived when only four miles away, her asdic team failed to get even a breath of contact. *Bramble* and *Worcester* had a similar experience with another one.

Had the U-boat commanders appreciated the fact, they could have done what they liked. But for a day and a night the convoy steamed on unmolested and at daylight on the 22nd Burnett decided that there was no further need for so senior an officer with the convoy. Turning over command of the escort to Captain Scott-Moncrieff in the *Faulknor*, he left in the *Milne* for Seidisfiord in Iceland to transfer back to the *Scylla*.

One less destroyer in the still large escort can have been of little significance. But an hour after *Milne* had left, a submarine, slipping submerged between escorts, got amongst the convoy. Within five minutes of each other, *Ocean Voice*, *Bellingham*, and the fleet tanker *Grey Ranger* had been sunk. Poor Commodore Dowding was once again adrift in the Arctic Ocean. Fortunately it was not for long as the rescue ships were quickly on the scene, scooping up the crews of the torpedoed ships. Fortunately too this U-boat was the only one to try breaking through the screen and by the next day, with Iceland and its guardian minefields drawing near, the submarines abandoned their efforts and withdrew.

Now came a northerly gale with blinding snowstorms to harry the convoy as it shaped course to pass down between Iceland's rock-bound east coast and the minefield to seaward of it. It was tough on the acting-commodore, Captain Walker of the *Ocean Freedom*, who was responsible for the navigation of the gathering of unwieldy merchantmen in ballast, riding high out of the water and often barely manageable in such conditions.

It was hard on the escorts too. They had been by now fifteen days at sea under attack or threat of imminent attack and the commanding officers were near the end of their tether when at last, two days later, the local escort arrived to relieve them off Cape Wrath. The convoy gladly headed for the shelter of the Minches and Loch Ewe. The destroyers turned for the meagre comforts of Scapa Flow. The *Somali* had meanwhile foundered while in tow of the *Ashanti*.

11 Entry of America: Decision Postponed

Though 13 ships lost out of the 40 which sailed in PQ18 was no light price to pay to bring aid to the Russian ally, the inclusion of an auxiliary aircraft-carrier in the escort had indicated how convoys might be fought through even during the long daylight of the summer months. The risks had been weighty, nevertheless: bad weather or the precious tankers falling victims to the torpedo planes, might have prevented the escorts re-fuelling at sea, forcing the convoy either to turn back or go on with a much depleted escort and suffer heavier losses. If the enemy had mounted a simultaneous air and surface attack, losses in the convoy must again have been heavy.

It is only of academic interest, however, to speculate on what might have been the outcome if a further trial of strength had been staged in the following month. For after three years of trial and tribulation when the Allies, standing on the defensive, had had to make do everywhere with inadequate forces, it was now Germany which was forced to transfer forces from one place to another as she tried to stop the leaks in her widespread frontiers. One such move was that of the majority of the Luftwaffe units from northern Norway to the Mediterranean where the tide of fortune was turning strongly against the Axis.

Events in that theatre were in any case to bring the Arctic convoys to a temporary halt: for every ship which could be spared from the Home Fleet was wanted to take part in Operation 'Torch', the great Anglo-American landing in North Africa. Not until winter clamped down on the Arctic would the 'Kola Run', as it was called amongst its disgusted initiates, be re-opened.

We shall turn, therefore, to follow the course of the Battle of the Atlantic which we left at the moment the United States' armed neutrality in that ocean was converted to full belligerent participation in December 1941.

The declaration of war by Germany on the United States of America on

11 December 1941, from the German point of view, only regularized a situation which had for some time existed in the North Atlantic. Step by step the American Government had been steadily increasing its aid to Britain and her Allies. As long ago as July 1940 President Roosevelt had announced that his Government's policy was 'all aid [to Britain] short of war'. In the same month had come the agreement in principle to the exchange of leases of British bases in the Western Hemisphere for 50 old US destroyers. March 1941 saw the passage of the Lend-Lease Bill under which ten US coastguard cutters were transferred to the Royal Navy. The next month the American Defence Zone was extended to 25°W—more than half-way across the Atlantic.

These developments were, plainly enough, in direct aid to Britain and hostile in intent to Germany. It was not, however, until July 1941, when American troops relieved the British garrison on Iceland and the US Navy was ordered to escort convoys to and from Iceland—convoys which merchant ships of any flag might join—that a real danger of warlike incidents between German U-boats and US naval forces came into existence. That the American Government accepted this possibility became clear, when, on 1 September 1941, the US Navy began also to take a share in escorting trans-Atlantic convoys in the western half of the ocean on the disingenuous grounds that they included ships for Iceland. The situation could not yet be described as undeclared war. It was more of the nature of an uneasy armed truce in which any trigger-happy person on either side could start active hostilities. Such an incident occurred on 4 September 1941.

The US destroyer *Greer*, proceeding independently to Iceland, received a signal from a patrolling British aircraft that a U-boat had been seen to submerge ten miles ahead of her. The American captain at once increased speed and on a zig-zag course made for the position given him. Reaching it, he slowed down, put his asdic into operation and very soon was in contact with the submarine. This he held, without attacking, for some three hours. When the aircraft again signalled to the *Greer*, asking if she was intending to attack, the reply was 'No'. The aircraft then dropped its load of depth-charges more or less at random and set course for base. The captain of the U-boat understandably attributed these depth-charges to the destroyer. When the opportunity came he fired a torpedo at the *Greer* in retaliation. This the destroyer was able to avoid, after which she in turn counter-attacked with depth-charges. A second torpedo from the U-boat failed to find its mark and, when the *Greer* lost contact soon afterwards, her captain continued his passage to Iceland.

President Roosevelt pronounced the U-boat's act to be piracy. A few days later he announced that 'From now on if German or Italian vessels of war enter these waters they do so at their own peril'. This gave American ships of war the right to strike first in any encounter with U-boats. An undeclared state of war between the USA and Germany thus existed in the North Atlantic as from that date. The first clashes were not long in coming. The first trans-Atlantic convoy to be escorted by United States warships was HX150, which sailed from Halifax on 16 September 1941. Had the concentration of U-boats off Greenland not been discovered through the devastating attack on SC42 described in an earlier chapter, and HX150 diverted clear of it, this first wholly American escort must have found itself involved thus early in a full-scale convoy battle. In the event it passed on unmolested and it was not until October that the American and German Navies had their next encounter. This occurred when SC48 was beset on 15 October 1941. To its aid were sent five US destroyers from Iceland. During a heavy night attack one of them, the *Kearney*, was torpedoed and badly damaged, suffering a number of casualties.

Fourteen days later the USS *Reuben James*, one of an American escort to HX156, was torpedoed and sunk, her casualties amounting to 115 including all her officers.

Thus it might have seemed as though Germany's declaration of war would not greatly alter the situation already existing in the Atlantic. But in fact, as President Roosevelt had shrewdly understood, American intervention on the trans-Atlantic convoy routes had not been sufficient to force Hitler into a general war with the USA. The shipping thronging the routes along the coast of North America from the Caribbean to New York had been left unmolested. Now the whole vast sea area became a war zone, the ships in it open to attack. In view of the hard-won experience of the British in anti-submarine warfare, the fruits of which had been freely and unstintingly made available to the United States Navy, the events which were to follow during the first few months of 1942 were calamitous and, to a great extent, unnecessary. Though war with Germany had for some time been inevitable and foreseen, no steps whatever had been taken to prepare for the institution of a convoy system on the American east coast, along which ran the densest and most valuable stream of shipping in the world at that date, carrying cargoes of cotton, sugar, oil, iron, steel and bauxite.

When Admiral Dönitz learnt, on 9 December 1941, of the lifting of the frustrating handicaps under which his U-boats had been working, which forbade operations against American ships or operations in the Pan-American security zone, he at once proposed to the Naval High Command that 12 boats should be sent to American east coast waters. He saw the brilliant opportunity being offered; but his clear vision, which never allowed him to waver in his appreciation that their Atlantic shipping was the Allies' most vulnerable point, was denied to the High Command. His proposal was rejected. The Mediterranean was to remain the primary area. It was therefore with only five boats that the attack on

American east coast shipping was initiated. The blow fell nevertheless with devastating effect.

Between the 12th and the end of January 1942, 46 ships had been sunk in the North Atlantic. Of these, 40, all sailing independently, had been west of 40°W, mostly off the American seaboard. In February the number rose to 65 ships sunk in American waters, out of a total for the North Atlantic of 71. March saw 86 ships lost in the same area. A slight drop in April to 69 rose again in May to 111, in June to 121. Then, in July, came the introduction of a widespread convoy system from the Gulf of Mexico to Canada. The result was a dramatic change to almost total immunity in the areas where previously the sea had been littered with burning and sinking ships. These figures are vividly reminiscent of those in 1917 when a similar holocaust, which had brought Britain to the brink of total defeat, was stopped at once by the introduction of convoy. It is sad to relate that, in spite of this example before them and of further lessons passed on to them from experience in the Second World War, the American naval authorities still held to doctrines and methods whose falsity had been starkly exposed.

The ultimate responsibility for the defence of shipping in American waters belonged to the C-in-C of the US Atlantic Fleet, Admiral Ernest J. King. Soon after the outbreak of war, King was elevated to the post of C-in-C, US Fleet, while that of C-in-C, Atlantic Fleet, fell to Admiral R. E. Ingersoll. King remained the guiding genius of American naval strategy, however, and it was his views which decided the broad lines on which naval forces were employed.

In addition to the ships and aircraft of the Atlantic Fleet, there were other forces under the operational control of the local naval commands known as Sea Frontiers. These were certainly inadequate in numbers and quality for the task which faced them. So far as surface craft were concerned they consisted of coastguard cutters, converted yachts and a few armed trawlers lent by the British. Specialized anti-submarine craft were being built, but, owing to a mistaken conception of the type of ship required, they were fast, light craft to hunt U-boats instead of more sea-worthy, if less glamorous, craft for escort duties. The submarine-chasers, as they were called, proved unsuitable for anti-submarine work in anything but the calmest weather.

With regard to aircraft the situation was even worse. An Army Appropriation Act passed by Congress in 1920 had decreed that the US Army should control all land-based planes and the Navy sea-based aircraft. In consequence the US Army absorbed almost the entire supply of US military, land-based planes. It had not even a component equivalent to Coastal Command of the RAF which, however inadequate, was trained to fly over the sea and cooperate with the Royal Navy. US Army pilots were neither trained in shipping protection duties nor to bomb small moving targets such as submarines. Nevertheless, at the

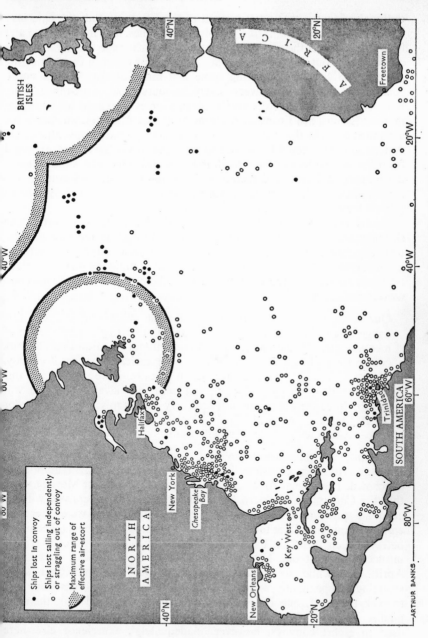

The U-Boat's second 'Happy Time', 1 January – 31 May 1942

- Ships lost in convoy
- Ships lost sailing independently or straggling out of convoy
- Maximum range of effective air-escort

NORTH AMERICA

SOUTH AMERICA

AFRICA

BRITISH ISLES

Halifax
New York
Chesapeake Bay
New Orleans
Key West
Trinidad
Freetown

40°N
20°N
20°W

40°W
60°W
80°W

—ARTHUR BANKS

outbreak of war it was upon aircraft of the US Army that the US Navy had to rely for anti-submarine patrols and searches. The inexperience and lack of training of the pilots no doubt made the shortage of aircraft of less consequence; but, in fact, in January 1942 the air effort in the area of the Eastern Sea Frontier, covering some 600 miles of the Atlantic coast consisted of two daylight sweeps every 24 hours by six short-range Army bombers. This paucity of anti-submarine forces available to the Commander Eastern Sea Frontier, Admiral Adolphus Andrews, was made the argument to show that the institution of a convoy system was impossible. American naval thought had gained less than might have been expected from the experiences of the British in two world wars. The same belief in the purely defensive—and therefore discreditable—nature of convoy, the same pursuit of the offensive against an infinitely elusive enemy, had to be paid for in millions of tons of shipping and vital cargoes.

It was not any mistrust of convoy as the basic means of protecting shipping which befogged US naval thought. Indeed, in the face of their own experience in the protection of trans-Atlantic shipping this could hardly be so. Furthermore they must have had in mind the dictum of their own great seaman of the First World War, Admiral W. S. Sims, who had written at that time:

Our tactics should be such as to force the submarine to incur this danger [that of encountering the escorts] in order to get within range of merchantmen. It, therefore, seems to go without question that the only course for us to pursue is to revert to the ancient practice of convoy. This will be purely an offensive action because, if we concentrate our shipping into convoy and protect it with our naval forces, we will thereby force the enemy, in order to carry out his mission, to encounter naval forces ... we will have adopted the essential principle of concentration while the enemy will lose it.

In spite of this admirable and irrefutable argument, two fatal objections to its acceptance were raised by the US naval authorities concerned. The official American naval historian, Professor Morison, says that the Commander Eastern Sea Frontier 'knew that a convoy without adequate protection is worse than none'. His forces were therefore employed on 'patrolling the sea lanes' and hunting for U-boats when they betrayed their positions by sinking merchantmen. They were invariably unsuccessful. Not one U-boat was sunk off the American coast until April. Meanwhile so totally unprotected were the merchant ships steaming independently within sight of the shore that U-boats were able to pick them off, one by one, and even to surface and sink them by gunfire. Had only the meagre forces available to Admiral Andrews been used to escort convoys, however 'inadequately', experience elsewhere shows that a U-boat would have been unlikely to sink more than one or two ships, probably at the expense of most of her torpedoes. The

Admiral's contention that a 'convoy without adequate protection is worse than none' cannot therefore be accepted.

The other objection to the institution of convoy stemmed from a misreading of the situation. Having studied, and experienced, the pack tactics used against Atlantic convoys in mid-ocean, the Americans evidently assumed that the same methods of protection and similar escort forces would be necessary for coastal convoys; whereas, in fact, pack tactics could never be brought into play close to an enemy coast where reinforcements, air and surface, for a convoy beset could quickly be summoned to the scene. Thus a Committee, appointed by Admiral King in February 1942 to study the subject, reported:

> It should be borne in mind that effective convoying depends upon the escorts being in sufficient strength to permit their taking the offensive against attacking submarines without their withdrawal for this purpose resulting in unduly exposing the convoy to other submarines while they are on this mission. Any protection less than this simply results in the convoy's becoming a convenient target for submarines.
>
> As a result of experience in the North Atlantic it now appears that the minimum strength that will afford reasonable protection is five escorts per convoy of 40 to 50 ships.

An admirable summary of the situation in mid-Atlantic, but, remembering that the U-boat campaign on the American coast was being conducted by only five U-boats, all operating separately, it was quite out of touch with the situation there. Nevertheless, Admiral King wrote on 2 April that 'the principles enunciated and the general procedure suggested in this excellent report are concurred in'. On the basis of it he decided that until more escorts became available a convoy system would have to wait. It is necessary, therefore, to examine the numbers of anti-submarine ships and aircraft which were actually available. Professor Morison in discussing this question quotes only the figure of those available for the exclusive use of the Sea Frontier Commander—'pitifully inadequate' he calls them, with which we will not disagree. But, in fact, there was also available in the area a considerable force of destroyers of the US Atlantic Fleet. In the face of a violent newspaper agitation for something to be done, Admiral Andrews asked for 15 of them in February. He got seven. These were sent out on patrol which proved uniformly futile. Racing from one spot to another in which U-boats had been located, they never succeeded in gaining contact with any of them. Professor Morison comments:

> No scientific method of search to regain sound contact with a submarine had been worked out. US destroyers were then so ill-fitted for search and so imperfectly trained for attack that to use them as a roving patrol was worse than useless. It resulted only in the loss of the *Jacob Jones* [torpedoed on 28 February].

1

While Morison is no doubt justified in his criticism of the efficiency o
US destroyers—a shortcoming not unusual in the armed forces of
country freshly involved in war—he is not justified in ascribing th
uselessness of roving patrols to this cause. Statistics and the experienc
of the most skilled anti-submarine forces show that hunting and patro
unrelated to the movement of a convoy—the lure which must dra\
U-boats to it if they are to fulfil their mission—are rarely effective. Th
point is, however, that, had there been an appreciation of the prim
necessity to get merchant ships into convoy at all costs, escorts could hav
been found. It will be recalled that convoy was instituted by the Britis]
on the outbreak of war with an available escort strength of 112 surfac
vessels and 45 aircraft. Opposed to them were 18 U-boats—a numbe
which rarely dropped below 14 for the remainder of 1939. According t
the US Fleet Anti-Submarine Summary produced in July 1945, the anti
submarine forces available to the Americans in the North Atlanti
in January 1942 comprised 173 surface craft and 268 aircraft. In Apr
the number of surface craft was the same but aircraft had risen to 58S
In the middle of May, when shipping losses were reaching intolerabl
proportions, convoy was at last instituted on the United States east coast
the average size of convoy being about 21 ships and of escorts never les
than five. The publication quoted above gives the figures of anti
submarine forces available as 197 surface vessels and 643 aircraft.

Thus, if Admiral King's contention that convoy could not be institute
in January 1942 on account of shortage of escorts is to be accepted,
appears that the addition of 24 escort vessels was sufficient completely t
reverse the situation and put ships into convoy with a comparativel
lavish escort. The improbability of this makes it seem more likely that
change of heart took place in American naval circles as a result of th
complete failure to their 'offensive' methods. This is borne out by a
exchange of messages between Admiral King and General Marshal
Chief of Staff of the United States Army. The latter was deeply concerne
at the heavy losses of army transports:

> We are well aware of the limited number of escort craft available, b
> has every conceivable means been brought to bear on this situation?
> am fearful that another month or two will so cripple our means c
> transport that we will be unable to bring sufficient men and planes 1
> bear against the enemy in critical theatres to exercise a determinin
> influence on the war.

In his reply, King announced his views with all the fervour of
convert. 'Escort is not just one way of handling the submarine menace;
is the *only* way that gives any promise of success. The so-called patr
and hunting operations have time and again proved futile.' How differe
from the reply given to Admiral Pound, British First Sea Lor
when he told King on 19 March 1942, that he 'regarded the introductio

of convoy as a matter of urgency'. Like Admiral Andrews, King at that time pronounced that 'inadequately escorted convoys were worse than none'.

Enough has been said, however, to establish the fact that it was primarily the complete organizational unpreparedness of the Americans, coupled with a failure to benefit from the lessons so hardly learnt by their Allies, that provided the U-boat commanders with the second of their 'Happy Times' and exposed American and Allied shipping to an unprecedented massacre. It remains to record the magnitude of the disaster and the means whereby it was encompassed.

Dönitz's first five boats—long-endurance, 1,000-ton boats—set out from their Biscay base at the end of December 1941, 'taking with them', the Admiral writes, 'high hopes such as we at U-boat Command had not had for many a day'. These hopes were to be richly fulfilled. Though America had had five weeks grace in which to prepare for the assault, the U-boats found conditions little different from those of peace. Ships steamed independently along the normal routes, their navigation lights burning. Lighthouses, beacons and buoys flashed their signals though with reduced brilliancy. As for defensive measures, Dönitz records:

There were, admittedly, anti-submarine patrols, but they were wholly lacking in experience. Single destroyers, for example, sailed up and down the traffic lanes with such regularity that the U-boats were quickly able to work out the time-table being followed. They knew exactly when the destroyers would return, and the knowledge only added to their sense of security during the intervening period.

In such conditions the U-boats could attack at leisure and in complete safety. By day they lay on the bottom in security, surfacing at dusk to pick their targets from the defenceless stream of shipping. This was made all the easier by the brilliant illuminations of the coast resorts against which the ships stood out in clear silhouette.

These first five boats, working between the St Lawrence and Cape Hatteras, not unnaturally had a great and easy success. Three more large boats joined them off Chesapeake Bay before the end of January and added to the havoc being caused. Between them they sank no less than 40 ships between 13 January and the end of the month. Their achievements led Dönitz to decide to deploy his whole available strength in the western Atlantic. New boats completing their training in the Baltic were ordered as soon as ready to make for the Biscay bases at high speed, there to be prepared to cross to America. But at this moment Hitler's 'intuition' came to the Allies' aid.

Believing that an Allied invasion of Norway was planned, he gave orders for eight boats to be stationed in the north for its protection. Once again Dönitz found himself frustrated at the moment that a resounding triumph seemed imminent. He decided, therefore, that his smaller, 750-

ton boats, which up to now had been operating off Nova Scotia and Newfoundland, must be used to reinforce the attack on the American shipping. In the north these smaller boats had found little but driving snow, ice and winter gales. The first group, having arrived on their station after some of their fuel had already been expended on patrol off the Azores, could not be diverted to the new happy hunting ground. The next group of 750-tonners, however, were sent to operate south of Halifax. Owing to their limited endurance, it had not been expected that they would be able to remain long on station. But enthusiasm to take full advantage of the conditions off the American coast led their engineers to try a number of ingenious methods of saving fuel on passage. In addition, water tanks were used for fuel, while the crews' living quarters were cluttered with stores, spare parts and food so that they might remain longer in so fruitful an area. Thus they were able to press on southwards to New York and beyond, and remain there for two or three weeks.

In the meantime a second wave of five 1,000-ton boats had already crossed the Atlantic bound for the Caribbean. By 16 February they were on station, and Dönitz gave the order for a simultaneous attack. Now the whole length of the American coast from Trinidad to New York became the graveyard of Allied shipping. Wolfgang Frank, author of *The Sea Wolves*, describes the happy conditions that the U-boat commanders found.

There was still no evidence that the Americans were switching over to war-time conditions. After two months of war their ships were still sailing independently. Their captains stopped close to torpedoed ships and asked for information over the loud hailer: should a ship be hit but remain capable of steaming, the captain never bothered to zig-zag or vary his speed so as to impede the U-boat in dealing the *coup-de-grâce*. And they had no idea of security; they chatted about everything under the sun over the 600-metre wave band—and as if that were not enough, the coastal defence stations sent out over the air a regular programme of information, giving details of rescue work in progress, of where and when aircraft would be patrolling and the schedules of anti-submarine vessels.

Gradually, however, these aids to the U-boats were reduced. In the four months following the opening of the U-boat offensive, the Americans tried everything—except convoy—to master the situation. Ships were routed close in shore, which only served to increase the density of the traffic stream and worried the U-boats not at all. Then shipping was restricted to moving only in daylight, anchoring for the night in Chesapeake or Delaware Bays or in protected anchorages prepared for them. By this system, known as the 'Bucket Brigade', Jacksonville to New York could be made in four daylight runs. In spite of all, the shipping losses mounted steeply. The U-boat commanders brought a light-hearted verve to their work of destruction in conditions so much less rigorous than the pursuit of escorted convoys in the gales and fogs of the north. Wolfgang Frank records how one of them, Jochen Mohr of *U124*, reporting a score of nine ships sunk during his patrol did so in verse,

> *The new-moon is black as ink*
> *Off Hatteras the tankers sink*
> *While sadly Roosevelt counts the score*
> *Some fifty thousand tons—by Mohr.*

But at last, in May, the Americans were ready to institute a convoy system along their coast. The result is best given in Dönitz's own words:

> At the end of April the heavy sinkings off the east coast of America suddenly ceased. As this was a full moon period, I hoped that the dark nights to follow would restore the situation and that the sinkings would regain their previous high level. Instead, there was a steady increase in signals from the U-boats reporting no shipping sighted. . . .
> In the light of unfavourable conditions off the coast of America and favourable conditions in the Caribbean, U-boat Command at once transferred six boats from the former area to the latter and four further U-boats on the way to American waters from the Biscay ports were sent to the Caribbean.

Thus the simple act of gathering the merchant ships together in groups, and removing the stream of independently sailing ships, achieved what had been previously considered impossible unless escorts in sufficient numbers to take the offensive could be provided. It was a remarkable vindication of the convoy system. So long, however, as the system was not extended to the Gulf of Mexico and the Caribbean, Dönitz's assault on Allied shipping could be maintained at the same high level as before. Forty-one ships of nearly 250,000 tons, more than half of which were tankers, were sunk in the Gulf of Mexico alone. Another 38, more than 200,000 tons, were sent to the bottom in the Caribbean area.

Up to now sinkings had been limited by the short time the submarines could remain on station after the long passage from France, before they had again to leave with enough fuel and stores remaining for the return journey. On 21 April there sailed the first of the U-tankers or Milch-cows, *U459*. A large clumsy boat of nearly 1,700 tons, she had no offensive capabilities; but besides a quantity of stores and spare parts she carried 700 tons of diesel fuel of which some 600 tons were available to refuel other boats. In this way she replenished 12 of the smaller and two large U-boats. As a result the number of boats on station in May was greatly increased, about 12 being spread along the American East Coast, nearly 20 in the Gulf of Mexico and Caribbean area. The latter group, roving happily amongst the streams of shipping sailing independently along the established routes from the oil ports and the West Indies, accounted for 148 ships with a total tonnage of 752,009 tons during May and June. In his *Memoirs*, Admiral Dönitz recounts how, in 1957,

> Admiral Hoover, who in 1942 had been in command of the Caribbean and had done everything possible with the naval and air forces at his disposal to stem the onslaught of our boats, wrote me a friendly letter in which he said, 'The years 1945-6 must have been a great strain on your nerves, but 1942, when you conducted your astonishing U-boat war against me in the Caribbean was, for me, an equally nerve-shattering period.'

The strange thing about this extract is that the American Admiral should still, long afterwards, call the operations of Dönitz's U-boats in the area of his Command 'astonishing'; whereas it was in reality his failure to use his forces as convoy escorts, however meagre, that was astonishing. 'From the end of June, however', Dönitz goes on,

> Results in these areas, too, began to deteriorate. Here, too, as had happened off the east coast of the United States at the beginning of May, the convoy system was gradually introduced; and it became obvious that in the near future the main effort of the U-boat war would have to be switched back to wolf-pack attacks on convoys.

So the second 'Happy Time' came to an end. The decisive clash between the wolf-packs and convoy escorts could not much longer be postponed. As in one area after another the Allies closed their ranks and put shipping into escorted convoys, it was to mid-Atlantic, the last region not yet within range of shore-based aircraft, that the U-boats gravitated. There, in the ten months from July 1942 to May 1943, the battle was to be fought out to a decisive conclusion.

Although by July 1942 the period of easy success for his U-boats had been brought to an end by the widespread introduction of convoy in American waters, Admiral Dönitz was by no means discouraged. However, in a radio speech to the German people he did warn them that they must expect greater casualties. The convoys and their escorts would now have to be faced. The decisive struggle was impending. It would be undertaken, he believed, under greatly improved conditions for the Germans. The number of boats available had increased and they should now be better able to intercept the convoys and concentrate against them in the 'black gap' in mid-Atlantic where no air escort could reach.

On the other hand, though Dönitz could not know it, the opposition his boats would be meeting was by now much improved in quality. Most of the escorts had received the new 10-centimetre radar equipment which gave detections of surfaced submarines at ranges of four miles or more. Many of them also had the high frequency direction finder by means of which the bearing and, to some extent, the range of a unit transmitting on short-wave radio could be determined. The combination of these two devices made the U-boat tactics of the wolf-pack and the night surface attack far more hazardous than previously. The wireless messages, necessary to keep the U-boat Command informed of the situation and to enable the pack concentration to be effected, gave the escort commander warning of an impending attack. Under favourable circumstances they could betray, with considerable accuracy, the position of the boat which had transmitted, bringing down on it a hunting group detached from the escort. By night, or in thick weather, an approaching submarine could be detected by radar far outside visibility range. Thus, the escorts now had the advantage of the first 'sighting', which the U-boats had enjoyed in those earlier times, when they could approach on the surface, confident that they could see before being seen. The use of radar by night or in fog also meant that the escort commanders were no longer preoccupied with maintaining proper station and avoiding collisions. They could now concentrate exclusively on detection of their lurking enemy.

Once detected, the U-boats also faced a more formidable attack. No longer could they gain immunity by diving to great depths. Depth-charges were now available which could be set to explode at a depth of 500 feet. Furthermore, escorts were fitted to fire patterns of ten charges, giving a greater probability of one of the charges exploding at a lethal distance from the target. Should the enemy remain at lesser depths and hope to evade attack by agility of manoeuvre, another weapon was now beginning to be fitted in the escorts. Known as the 'Hedgehog', this was a multi-barrelled mortar which fired bombs, filled with a new, higher-powered explosive, Torpex, to a fixed range of 250 yards ahead of the ship. This form of attack, unlike a depth-charge attack, gave the submarine no warning to enable it to take evasive action.

The problem of maintaining escorts at full strength for the whole of the long trans-Atlantic voyage had been eased by the introduction of a system of re-fuelling at sea from tankers sailed with the convoys for this purpose. The operation required reasonably good weather, however Another innovation at this time, though actually a lesson from the First World War re-learnt, was the inclusion in convoys of specially fitted rescue ships. Their duty was to pick up survivors from sunken ships. They thus relieved the escort commander of the necessity to divert one or more of his few ships at the expense of hunting down the attackers. By now, also, many of the escort group commanders and the captains of the individual escort ships, after many months engaged in the specialized business of convoy escort, had achieved an 'expertise' which only time could give them. They had developed an instinct which enabled them to weed out false alarms and to know when it was possible and politic to thin out the defensive screen so as to go over to the attack. They were able to see into their opponents' minds and foresee their probable tactics. Thus it was not only the improved methods of detection which led to U-boat commanders suffering the frustration of being discovered and driven off, time after time.

For all these improvements, however, the escorts were still weak numerically. The US Navy's heavy commitments elsewhere, in the Pacific as well as along their Atlantic coast and in escorting troop and transport convoys to the Mediterranean, had led to its virtual withdrawal from the North Atlantic. This left the Royal Navy to shoulder 50 per cent of the burden in that vital area and the Royal Canadian Navy 46 per cent. America's four per cent was represented by one or two coastguard cutters which led a mixed escort of American, British and Canadian ships, and a few destroyers based in Iceland. Early in 1943 the latter were also withdrawn, but their departure was more than compensated for by the formation of the US escort carrier *Bogue* and her destroyer screen into a Support Group in March of that year. Though British and Canadian forces had grown considerably since the early days of the struggle, at this time they still averaged only five or six escorts to each convoy, a figure much below the minimum required. Not all of them had yet received the new equipment. Nor had they all achieved the same standard of training, either individually or as flotillas. Thus much would still depend upon the relative efficiency of the opponents when they met in combat around the convoys.

Such was the general situation in the summer of 1942 when the contest in mid-Atlantic was resumed in August. It followed the course predictable from a full knowledge of the factors which prevailed on both sides. A majority of the convoys ran without loss; either because, through skilful diversion by order of the shore command, based on the information collected by the U-boat tracking organization, the submarine patrol lines were avoided; or because air or surface escorts were able to detect and hold down, drive off or perhaps destroy the first U-boat making contact, thereby preventing the position and route of the convoy being reported.

But where the escort was weak, ill-assorted or lacking in group training, the wolves were able to gather round. Such was the case with the slow, homeward-bound convoy of 36 ships, SC94, which was beset in the first week of August 1942. The ocean escort was not unduly weak numerically, comprising as it did six small warships. But of these only one was a destroyer, HMCS *Assiniboine*, commanded by Lieutenant-Commander J. H. Stubbs, RCN. The remainder, including the ship of the senior officer of the escort, HMS *Primrose*, were corvettes. Such ships, besides being too slow to chase away any U-boats working round the convoy to their attacking positions ahead, were unable to mount the H/F D/F equipment; nor had they, for the most part, the new 10-centimetre radar. When the *Assiniboine* was damaged and forced to return to base, the odds turned heavily in favour of the U-boats. Individually, the escorts were well-trained and experienced. On the other hand, they had not been trained to work together; nor was a Flower-class corvette a suitable ship, on account of space or equipment, from which to exercise command. It was by the accident of seniority of rank, that Lieutenant-Commander A. Ayre, RNR, of the *Primrose*, found himself called upon to do so.

In the five days' running fight which began on the afternoon of 5 August, these disadvantages were to prove calamitous. During the 3rd, SC94 had been enveloped in the dense fog which hangs over the Grand Banks at this time of the year. When an alteration of course was ordered by the Commodore by signal on the siren, six ships on the port side failed to hear and, with the two escorts on that side, *Nasturtium* and *Orillia*, became detached from the main body. It was not until the afternoon of 5 August, by which time the weather had cleared somewhat, that the senior officer of the escort learnt their whereabouts and sent *Assiniboine* out to contact and shepherd them back into the fold. Before this could be effected the first blow fell as one of the stragglers, the ss *Spar*, was torpedoed and sunk.

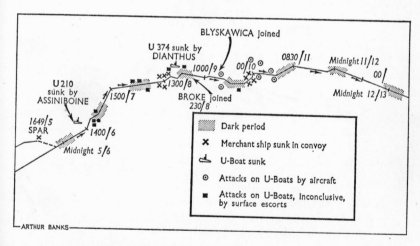

The passage of Convoy SC94, August 1942

No contact with the attacker was made. The first round had gone to the enemy. What was worse, the U-boat was left free to follow to see the junction with the main body and report the convoy's position and course. Soon the other boats of the patrol line were running hard on the surface to intercept. Towards midday on the 6th the first arrived. Fog patches, lingering over the calm sea, hid the convoy until, as the U-boat ran out of one, it was suddenly in sight at six miles. At the same moment the U-boat was seen from the bridge of the *Assiniboine*. Followed by the corvette *Dianthus*, the destroyer swung away in chase, forcing the submarine to seek safety by diving. *Assiniboine*'s asdic went into operation and as contact was gained the depth-charges were sent plunging down. Three attacks were made before contact was lost. With *Dianthus* in company, *Assiniboine* searched, probing with the asdic, weaving in and out of the fog patches. It seemed as though her quarry had given her the slip.

But the depth-charges had done their work. Heavy damage had accumulated in the U-boat. She was forced to come up and try to escape on the surface. Sighted by the *Assiniboine* at five miles' range, a wild chase through fog patches developed. As the destroyer overhauled the submarine, gun crews on both sides went into action. A shell hit the submarine's conning-tower. In reply a shot went home on the starboard side of the destroyer, starting a dangerous fire, killing one man and wounding 13 others. Meanwhile the U-boat was frantically twisting and turning to avoid Stubbs' efforts to ram her. Three or four times *Assiniboine*'s sharp bow just failed to hit. The destroyer was so close that her guns could not be depressed sufficiently to be aimed at the submarine almost alongside. Suddenly the U-boat slowed down. It started to dive. But before it could do so the *Assiniboine* had clawed round under full helm and rammed. It was not a fatal blow and, as the submarine came fully to the surface, *Assiniboine* again thrust her bow against it in a glancing blow. As she slid on beyond the now stationary boat, the destroyer's depth-charges, set to burst shallow, took up the fight. Then a 4.7-inch shell hit the submarine in the bow and all was over. *U210* went to the bottom as the *Dianthus* slid out of the fog just in time to see her go. Pounding along behind at her best speed trying to get into the fight, the little corvette had only succeeded in being in at the death. But now she had the satisfaction of taking 22 of the enemy prisoners, the remainder being picked up by the *Assiniboine*.

This was a heartening success for the convoy defence. Had it only occurred a day earlier and so disposed of the first submarine to gain contact, that which had torpedoed the *Spar*, the convoy might well have passed through the U-boat patrol line without further trouble. Instead, opportunity had been given for the pack to gather. Even while *U210* and *Assiniboine* were playing their deadly game of hide-and-seek amongst the mists, the conning-tower of another submarine had been sighted from the corvettes *Primrose* and *Chilliwack*, ahead of the convoy. Three hours later the corvette *Orillia* was hunting another which she had seen on the surface and forced to dive. Finally, as darkness was settling down, a signal came in to the escort commander from *Dianthus* telling him that she, too, on her way back to rejoin, had discovered and was hunting a third. For the time being the situation was in hand. Surprised on the surface through the lifting or parting of the fog, the would-be attackers were being driven off. Three of them were damaged. They were not put out of action, however, and there were several long days ahead in which to renew their efforts. Meanwhile the escort had been reduced to four slow corvettes until the *Dianthus* could rejoin, as the only destroyer, *Assiniboine*, was limping back to base licking the wounds she had received in her action with *U210*.

Nevertheless when, after a quiet day on the 7th, the U-boats renewed their attempts to get at the convoy under cover of darkness they were detected by radar and again held off. With their slow speed, the corvettes could not, however, go over to the offensive with prolonged hunts which would have at least forced their opponents out of action. Nor could they afford to extend their search beyond the horizon when daylight came. Thus, they could not prevent others of the wolf-pack from using their high surface speed to circle wide round the convoy, attain a position ahead and there wait, submerged, for the convoy to approach. August 8 was a calm, summer day with only a slight haze to reduce visibility. Through the forenoon and past midday the 32 slow merchantmen plodded eastward at $7\frac{1}{2}$ knots, while the escorts weaved to and fro in their stations, trying to cover the broad sea miles between them and the neighbouring corvette.

In merchantman and escort alike, watchkeepers who had spent much of the night peering into the darkness, and gun and depth-charge crews who had been in action were taking advantage of the unwonted peace of the hot afternoon to get some sleep against the probability of another night of activity. This placid scene was shattered by a succession of explosions coming across the still air and thudding through the ships' hulls. Within three minutes five merchantmen had been torpedoed. Three of them, including the Commodore's flagship, *Trehata*, went quickly to the bottom. The other two remained afloat for a time. The sudden onset and the extent of the catastrophe sent a wave of panic through the convoy. Three ships stopped engines and their crews took to the boats, while the British gun crew of a Dutch ship leapt overboard. For a time complete confusion reigned. The escorts, instead of being free to hunt the attackers, were forced to devote themselves to picking up survivors from the sunken ships and cajoling the crews of others to return aboard and get their ships under way. The coloured crew of one of the latter, the *Radchurch*, refused to do so and the ship had to be abandoned. Not until shortly before nightfall did the convoy reform itself.

In the meanwhile events had been taking place which were to some extent to even the score temporarily. From the *Dianthus* a conning-tower had been sighted on the horizon. At the order of the senior officer of the escort, her captain, Lieutenant-Commander C. E. Bridgeman, RNR, took her away in chase. It seemed a forlorn hope as a U-boat on the surface could outpace the corvette. Furthermore, the distant enemy was soon lost in a rain squall. Nevertheless Bridgeman plugged doggedly on and was rewarded after a time by the sight of not one but two submarines. At a range of six miles, *Dianthus* opened fire with her solitary 4-inch gun. The chances of hitting the tiny targets at that range were remote, but as Bridgeman had hoped, the U-boat commanders, rather than accept the risk, submerged. Half an hour later the corvette had reached the diving position on one of them and had begun a systematic search around it. For an hour and a half this was continued without result. Meanwhile darkness had fallen. Bridgeman had almost decided that he must abandon the hunt and return to the convoy when there came a shout from his signalman. He had a dark object held in his binoculars. It was almost certainly a U-boat. Star shells from *Dianthus*'s gun blossoming above it confirmed it. The U-boat dived and almost at once was caught in the asdic beam. Two accurate depth-charge attacks, and *U379* came spouting to the surface heavily damaged. Bridgeman spun his ship round. As *Dianthus* rammed and slid on beyond, further depth-charges were exploded round the crippled submarine. Four more times the corvette crashed into it before, soon after midnight, *U379* sank leaving survivors of its crew in the water. By now the *Dianthus* was in a bad way herself with her fore compartments flooded and much down by the bow. Little attention could be given to rescuing the submarine crew; but some of them were taken aboard and a Carley Raft launched for the remainder before Bridgeman set course to rejoin the convoy while his crew turned to repair the damage to their ship.

While *Dianthus* was away, occupied with her private battle, the convoy had received a welcome reinforcement from Iceland in the shape of the destroyer *Broke*, whose captain, Lieutenant-Commander A. F. C. Layard, became the senior officer of the escort. The situation he found as night fell was not a happy one. The *Primrose* was the only other warship in company, while several U-boats were known to be about and no doubt planning further attacks. The night, however, passed uneventfully. By dawn the convoy had reformed and more corvettes were back in their stations. The Polish destroyer *Blyskawica* was also about to join up. At midday there came the heartening sight of the first Liberator aircraft which were thereafter intermittently to accompany and escort the convoy. In conjunction with the H/F D/F now available in the *Broke*, there seemed a good prospect of interrupting the free movement of the enemy and preventing him from reaching an attacking position. Towards evening one of his craft was reported by the aircraft nine miles on the port beam of the convoy. The *Blyskawica* streaked away to hunt it, and keep it down. Shortly before dawn another boat was heard signalling close astern. *Primrose* sent to search along the bearing sighted it, opened fire and forced it to dive. A two-hour asdic search was unproductive, but, as the corvette steered to rejoin the now distant convoy, yet another submarine was sighted, chased and forced to dive.

The U-boats were certainly being harassed. But, as was to be found on other occasions, once the pack had gathered it required continuous air support, backed by fast escorts, to hold all of them. During the forenoon of 10 August the convoy was bereft of air escort, the first aircraft arriving at noon, and meanwhile one or more submarines had evidently achieved a position along the convoy's route. Lying submerged and undetected, their opportunity to attack came at 1022, when in quick succession four more merchantmen were torpedoed. In spite of all efforts by the escorts, the attacker escaped scot-free to bring the total casualties up to 11 merchantmen at the price of two U-boats. The ordeal of SC94 was at last at an end. Destroyer reinforcements and a more continuous air escort frustrated all further attempts by the enemy. The much depleted convoy sailed on to its destination without further loss.

The lessons to be learnt from SC94 had already been pointed time and again, and were to be repeated in the future. The capacity of the individual units making up the escort to hunt U-boats efficiently was not enough. They must also be trained to work together as a team. The force escorting SC94 was a mixed force of British and Canadian ships thrown together for the occasion. Its senior officer had neither the equipment to hold them together and direct their activities, nor had he had the opportunity to train them to work together with a minimum of direction from their leader. Admiral Dönitz, when he received details of this action, concluded that 'the fact that the boats succeeded in pressing home their attacks in spite of the strength of the escort is the deciding factor which justifies the continuation of our war on convoys'. But in fact the total number of escorts with a convoy was less important than the proportion of escorts with a high turn of speed. Destroyers could be sent out to a submarine detected near a convoy, could hunt it for an effective period and return to the convoy before other U-boats could take advantage of the gap left in the screen. The 'Flower'-class corvettes, with a maximum speed of 15 knots, could not be used offensively, or, if they were sent out to hunt a submarine, they left the escort weakened for long periods. What was likely to happen then was demonstrated, not for the first time, in October 1942. Convoy SL125, homeward-bound from Freetown, 37 ships carrying, besides full holds of cargo, a large number of servicemen, was sailed with an ocean escort of only four corvettes. When it ran into a concentration of ten U-boats north-east of Madeira, the escort under Lieutenant-Commander J. M. Rayner, RNR, of the *Petunia*, was helpless to prevent the loss of 12 ships with a tragically heavy toll of life; nor was it able in return to inflict any loss on the enemy.

Another factor which befogged Dönitz's appreciation of the facts of the situation in the Atlantic was that the escort groups varied in the quality of the equipment they carried. At this time the rapidly expanding Royal Canadian Navy, eager to stand on its own feet, had formed its own escort groups which took their turn with the British groups to shepherd convoys on the trans-Atlantic run. In retrospect this must be judged premature, as their ships lagged behind their British sisters in modern equipment, lacking in particular the 10-centimetre radar which was so crucial a device. When a westbound convoy, ON 127, with a strong Canadian escort, was brought to action in September 1942, the destroyer *Ottawa* and seven merchant ships were torpedoed and sunk, and four more of the convoy torpedoed and damaged. The U-boats responsible escaped unscathed. Fortunately by the late summer of 1942 regular escort groups had been formed and assigned to the trans-Atlantic run, each of which usually included two destroyers. A convoy escorted by a well-trained and well-led escort group of this kind had little to fear or, if for some reason the escort was unable to prevent the concentration of a wolf pack on it, the U-boats were likely to be made to pay heavily for any successes they achieved.

Thus in the same month of that year, the slow, homeward-bound convoy SC104 was intercepted by a submarine pack of 13 in the 'black gap' where no air escort could be given it. The enemy's arrival on the scene was at once detected by the H/F D/F operators as they crouched in their cramped cabinets, listening hour after hour to the German radio traffic. The senior officer of the escort, Commander S. Heathcote, in the destroyer *Fame*, had under him another British destroyer, *Viscount*, and four corvettes, *Pontentilla*, *Eglantine*, *Montbretia* and *Acanthus* of the Royal Norwegian Navy.

As evidence came in to him of the wolf-pack gathering, his ships were sent out at their best speed into the darkness, along the bearings indicated by the direction finders. The weather, a gale from the south-west raising a steep sea with intermittent snow showers, handicapped them, the wild motion of the ships and the tall waves making both radar and asdic inefficient, while the spray sweeping across their bridges blinded look-outs. No submarines were therefore sighted or detected, but these sorties had the desired effect, forcing the U-boats to dive and preventing them getting at the convoy. Nevertheless, it was not possible to drive off every one of such a strong concentration. While the screen was depleted one submarine was able to infiltrate through it and soon after midnight torpedoed and sank three ships of the convoy. Dawn the next day, 13 October, spread over a still wild and stormy sea, but visibility had improved. Escorts sent out towards enemy radio transmissions caught sight of the submarines responsible, but the heavy weather kept speeds low and enabled the U-boats to dive when still many miles away, making very slim the chances of a successful hunt.

At dusk three of the escorts were still away leaving only *Fame*, *Montbretia* and *Acanthus* to cover the convoy of 44 ships. During the night four more ships of the convoy were sunk. Meanwhile, however, the escorts were not idle, and only the heavy weather saved the wolf-pack from loss. Lieutenant-Commander John Waterhouse of the *Viscount*, for instance, had been coming up from astern to rejoin the screen after a sortie, and was still seven miles behind, when the first attack occurred. Soon afterwards he sighted two stragglers, one of which was the huge whaling depot ship, *Southern Empress*, which had been torpedoed but was still able to proceed at slow speed. As Waterhouse watched, two more torpedoes exploded against the *Southern Empress'* side, finally sinking her. Calculating the probable position from which the submarine had fired, Waterhouse steered for it and was rewarded by the sight of her coming to the surface, unaware, no doubt, that a warship was near by. A wild scrambling encounter followed during which Waterhouse's attempt to ram the submarine and *Viscount*'s gunlayers' efforts to get a shell home in her before she dived again were all foiled by the blinding spray and the black darkness. Once the submarine had submerged she was safe, the wild conditions on the surface making operation of *Viscount*'s asdic almost impossible. The convoy being again under attack, Waterhouse set course to rejoin. The other destroyer of the escort, *Fame*, had a similar encounter a few hours later when, following an attack on an asdic contact, a submarine came to the surface. In the chase which developed down wind and swell, from the destroyer's lurching bridge the submarine was hard to distinguish among the white-crested waves. When the range had come down to 500 yards, the U-boat dived again; but this was not at once realized. The *Fame* careered on for a while before turning and trying, unsuccessfully, to regain asdic contact.

Inconclusive as these encounters were, the narrow escapes must certainly have shaken the U-boat commanders concerned and made them chary of approaching the convoy again. The gale began to take off during the next day, 14 October, and the escorts were able to range farther afield keeping the pack at a distance. With nightfall the U-boats probed inwards trying to get at the convoy. But each time they approached the escorts' radar detected them. Out of the darkness came the white flurry of a bow wave forcing them to crash dive and give up the attempt. The *Acanthus* was the first to have such an encounter. In her station on the port beam of the convoy her radar detected something at a range of five miles. Lieutenant-Commander E. Brunn, Royal Norwegian Navy, set off in chase and narrowly missed ramming the submarine which came in sight at 400 yards. The *Montbretia*, Lieutenant-Commander Halvos Soiland, on the other side of the convoy, was the next. In a brief encounter at short range in the darkness, her 4-inch gun put a shell into the U-boat before she was lost to view. It may well have been this same submarine which *Viscount*'s radar picked up an hour later. Running down the radar contact, when the range came down to 2,000 yards Waterhouse ordered 26 knots and steered for a ram. As the U-boat came in sight her commander simultaneously saw the destroyer's sharp bow bearing down on him. Too late he began to weave back and forth to avoid it. The *Viscount*'s stem crunched into her hull, lifted on a wave and crashed down, pinning the submarine down for some 15 seconds before she dragged clear. Her back broken, *U619* plunged to her end. *Viscount* herself was heavily damaged. Until bulkheads forward had been shored up and the fore end of the ship lightened to bring her bows out of water, she dare not go ahead at more than 7 knots. This was increased to 13 when repairs had been completed but her need for the shelter and facilities of a base were urgent. Waterhouse was instructed to carry on alone. The escort was reduced to five, but by now, with the improvement in the weather, the fight had fairly turned in favour of the defence. Before dawn *Fame* and *Potentilla* each encountered and attacked other U-boats trying to penetrate the screen. They did not manage to destroy them, though *Fame* hammered one with three depth-charge attacks and *Potentilla* damaged another with gunfire and depth-charges. With daylight the escorts resumed their repeated outward sweeps to drive off others whose signals had been picked up on the H/F D/F.

In his account of the long five days of unceasing action, Commander Heathcote paid tribute to his gallant Norwegians who 'pounced like terriers' whenever an opportunity arose, in spite of the tempestuous weather in which their little corvettes rolled and lurched in wild exhausting motion, swept by spray and their decks awash. Nevertheless, the wolf-pack continued to cling to the outskirts. When the convoy at last came inside the range of Liberator aircraft from Iceland, the first to arrive with sunrise on 16 October soon reported that it had sighted a submarine and forced it to dive five miles astern. That at least one U-boat had succeeded in pressing on ahead to lie submerged in ambush was to be discovered when, soon after midday the *Fame*, two miles ahead, gained asdic contact with it, After his many frustrating and disheartening encounters during the preceding days of heavy weather, Commander Heathcote was now able to employ his anti-submarine team in good conditions. His first attack forced *U353* to the surface. His ram, which followed, delivered only a glancing blow, the submarine scraping down *Fame*'s starboard side. By now the convoy had come up. The gunners of the merchantmen passing by to either side went gaily into action at this first sight of the enemy who had been tormenting them. It was too much for the U-boat's crew who abandoned ship. A party from *Fame* got aboard her and were able to spend five minutes in the control room gathering papers before hurriedly escaping as *U353* took her last plunge.

It was fortunate that the dogged defence and the arrival of air escort had by this time discouraged the wolf-pack, for the last remaining destroyer of the escort was now put out of action. *Fame* had suffered an ugly tear in her hull along the water-line from the U-boat's sharp hydroplanes. Her after magazine was flooded and her stem badly buckled. As she limped away, Lieutenant-Commander C. A. Monsen, RNN, of the *Potentilla*, became senior officer of the four corvettes left to defend the convoy. Had a further concentrated attack been attempted it might have gone hard with the convoy. As it was there was only one more encounter in which the *Potentilla*, following up a radar contact, met a U-boat head-on steering for the convoy. As the two ships raced by on opposite courses, the corvette's 4-inch gun scored several hits and her depth-charges were bursting round the submarine as she dived. The strong smell of oil which lingered behind raised hopes that another of the enemy could be counted destroyed to offset the losses in the convoy. Though it was not so, the long fight was over. Against the grievous loss of seven merchantmen and their valuable cargoes, two U-boats had been sunk and a number damaged.

12 *Amphibious Assault: Sea Power on the Offensive*

How fiercely contested was the struggle for control of the Atlantic between the growing swarm of German U-boats and the Allied escort forces during the autumn and winter of 1942 has been told elsewhere in this volume. Critical as it was at times, to get the whole picture in perspective it is necessary to appreciate that in October and November of that year, the greatest convoy operation in history up to that time was launched and completed without loss along routes in that ocean extending over many thousands of miles across which as many as 75 U-boats could have been concentrated. This was Operation 'Torch', the Allied invasion of French North Africa.

The decision on this had been taken by the Combined Chiefs of Staff on 25 July 1942 and in the following month Admiral Sir Andrew Cunningham had been appointed Allied Naval Commander Expeditionary Force (ANCXF) under the supreme command of General Eisenhower. Simultaneous landings were to be made on 8 November at Casablanca on the Atlantic coast and at Oran and Algiers inside the Mediterranean. For the first of these an assault convoy of 38 ships designated UGF1, escorted and covered by a US naval force of 56 ships, designated the Western Task Force under the command of Rear Admiral H. K. Hewitt, USN, was to be sailed directly from the United States, to be followed five days later by UGF2, consisting of 24 ships, and other follow-up convoys at regular intervals.

For the other landings, two convoys, a slow and a fast, KMS1 and KMF1 of 47 and 39 ships respectively, were to sail from Scotland, dividing off Gibraltar into KMS(0)1 and KMF(0)1 for Oran and KMS(A) and KMF(A), for Algiers. These were to be followed by KMS2 of 52 ships and KMF2 of 18. The troops for Oran were to be American; for Algiers a mixed British and American force followed up by the British First Army. The escort and covering force would be British, a Central Task Force of 57 warships for Oran under Rear-Admiral H. M. Burrough and an Eastern Task Force of 56 ships for Algiers under Commodore T. H.

Troubridge. Also covering the landings at Oran and Algiers against any possible interference by the Italian Fleet was the British Force 'H' comprising two capital ships, two fleet carriers, three cruisers and 17 destroyers. The initial move in Operation 'Torch' had begun on 2 October when KXI, the first of several advance convoys, including a variety of supporting vessels such as colliers, tankers, ammunition ships, tugs, trawlers, etc, sailed from the Clyde for Gibraltar. Elaborate precautions were made to keep the assembly and destination of the various convoys secret. In the event the Germans were unable to decide which of numerous possible invasion points reported by their agents, ranging from the Mediterranean to Norway, was the true one; and, although KMF1 convoy was sighted on 2 and 3 November by U-boats and the British carrier force by a German reconnaissance plane on 31 October and a heavy southward flow of shipping was apparent, almost complete surprise was achieved.

A vital necessity for the success of any opposed assault landing must be the accuracy of the movements of the various units, the punctual rendezvous of fast and slow convoys, the punctual and navigationally accurate dispersal of the Landing Ships, Infantry, to their individual lowering positions whence the first wave of assault troops set off in their Landing Craft, Assault, for the beaches which must be reached exactly at zero hour.

Much larger landing operations and against much fiercer opposition were to be executed in the Pacific and against Normandy. But Operation 'Torch' was the first large-scale assault to be mounted by the Allies. The technique was new and largely untried. For the central and eastern assaults the exactness of the organization was all the more important on account of the approach through the eight-mile wide narrows of the Straits of Gibraltar. These were smoothly traversed by the 86 transports and their escorts and their covering forces between 1930 on 5 November and 0400 on the 7th.

During the 7th the complicated schedule for the rendezvous of the fast and slow portions of the assault convoys and their division into groups allocated each to their various beaches was achieved without a hitch. During that night they steamed for their respective 'release positions' to which they were 'homed' by submarines and where the landing craft were hoisted out and led by motor launches to the beaches where pilots in folding boats from the submarines were stationed to guide them. H-hour was scheduled for 0100 on the 8th.

At neither Algiers nor Oran did the final phase of this procedure go according to plan at all the landing points, owing largely to an undiscovered coastwise current. Some confusion and delay resulted, but in the absence of any immediate opposition the consequences were not serious. At Algiers the important Maison Blanche airfield was captured by 0640 and was in use by RAF fighters from Gibraltar soon after 0900.

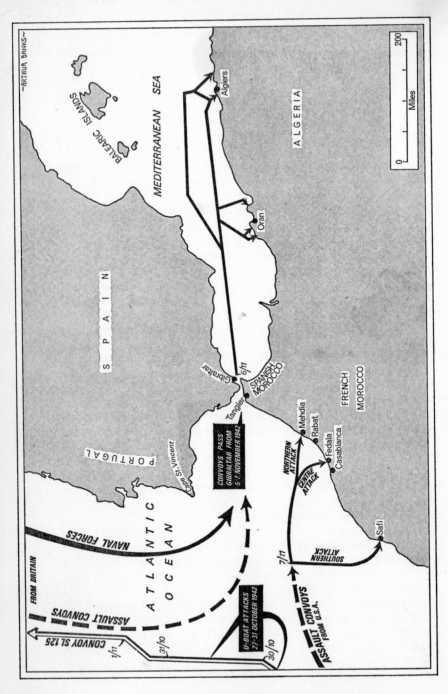

Operation 'Torch', November 1942

At the other airfield, Blida, history was made when Lieutenant B. H. C. Nation of the *Victorious*, leading a patrol of Martlet fighters, seeing white handkerchiefs being waved, landed his plane and accepted the surrender.

At Oran naval aircraft succeeded in neutralizing the La Senia airfield and though a parachute assault to capture the main airfield at Tafaroui mounted by an American unit from England got scattered and driven off by flak, ground troops had captured the field by noon.

The capture of both Algiers and Oran was assured by the successful landing of the large bodies of troops; but it was important that the harbour and facilities should fall into Allied hands as little damaged as possible. A separate assault inside each of the harbours was also planned, therefore. At Algiers the destroyers HMS *Broke* and *Malcolm*, carrying three companies of US infantry, were detailed to force the booms protecting the two entrances and place themselves alongside the quays. Their efforts were at first unsuccessful, being unable, in the dark, to locate the southern entrance which was their first objective. The *Malcolm* was hit by gunfire from the French forts, and forced by damaged boilers to withdraw. It was not until dawn, two hours after her initial approach, that the *Broke* succeeded in charging and breaking through the boom. She went alongside a quay where the troops were landed and took over the power station and oil installation; but with damage from gunfire and casualties accumulating, the destroyer was forced to withdraw leaving some 250 men ashore; she herself sank the next day when rough weather blew up.

The approach of this same heavy weather had begun during the 8th to cause a number of casualties among the landing craft. It was fortunate, therefore, the French resistance at the port ceased that evening under the bombardment by guns of the covering force and by aircraft from the carriers, enabling the sheltered harbour to be used from then on. That day, too, enemy aircraft arrived to attack Allied shipping with bombs and torpedoes, but succeeded only in damaging the destroyer *Cowdray*. At dawn on 9 November Rear-Admiral Burrough's flagship, the headquarters ship *Bulolo*, entered the harbour and berthed alongside, enthusiastically greeted by large crowds of the inhabitants.

The plan of operations for forcing the harbour of Oran was one fraught with desperate hazard. The ex-American coastguard cutters, HMS *Walney* and *Hartland*, lightly armed and very vulnerable, were selected to force the naval port where a cruiser and a number of destroyers and other warships were lying, preceded by loud-hailer appeals not to resist. The leading ship, *Walney*, would then have to traverse the long, narrow basin between the jetty, running parallel to the shore and the various moles of the dockyard. Though two motor launches were to lay a smoke-screen under cover of which the cutters were to break the boom, the enterprise must be suicidal if seriously opposed: and so it proved.

When the loud-hailer appeals resulted only in a searchlight being trained on the *Walney* and heavy machine-gun fire, she charged the boom and, under withering fire which killed nearly all her crew, drifted helplessly up the harbour finally to capsize and sink. The *Hartland*, following five minutes behind, as planned, was crippled even sooner by point-blank fire from French destroyers. With the majority of her crew killed and the remainder fighting uncontrollable fires, she anchored in the harbour where the French then humanely ceased fire. Finally abandoned by survivors, the cutter disintegrated in a tremendous explosion which damaged buildings in a large area around.

Captain F. T. Peters, who led this 'forlorn hope', and Lieutenant-Commander Billot, RNR, of the *Hartland*, were amongst the very few survivors. The former, pursued by a cruel fate, however, was killed a few days later when the aircraft in which he was returning to England crashed on landing. The American Distinguished Service Cross and the Victoria Cross he had earned were awarded posthumously.

The loss of the *Walney* and *Hartland* was avenged when some of the destroyers from Oran emerged, with a gallantry which must be admired, to be engaged by the cruiser *Aurora* and British destroyers. One was sunk, another forced to beach herself and a third escaped back into the harbour. Two more Vichy destroyers were engaged the next day, one being driven ashore in flames, another put to flight. French naval losses amounted in all to one flotilla leader, *Epervier*, three destroyers, *Tramontane*, *Tornade* and *Typhon*, the corvette *Surprise*, six submarines, three armed trawlers and five minesweepers sunk by gunfire or scuttled by their crews.

After some stiff resistance on shore had been overcome, Oran finally capitulated at 1230 on 10 November.

The assignment of Rear-Admiral Hewitt's Western Task Force was to prove more hazardous and difficult than the assaults on Oran and Algiers. The powerful French coastal defences had been fully alerted half an hour before the scheduled H-hour—0400 on the 8th. A French naval squadron including the battleship *Jean Bart*, the heavy cruiser *Primauguet* and a number of destroyers and submarines was at Casablanca, ready to intervene; and the landing beaches were exposed to the swell rolling in from the Atlantic, raising a heavy surf. This, indeed, came near to causing a last-minute abandonment and substitution of landings inside the Mediterranean which would have defeated the important objective of winning Morocco and Algeria simultaneously. Fortunately, however, Hewitt's meteorologist was able to forecast moderating weather and the decision was taken to adhere to the original plan. The amphibious assault was, however, to meet difficult conditions.

The Casablanca landing was in three separate operations. The main (Centre) Attack Group was to land 18,700 men over beaches at Fédala, 15 miles north of Casablanca; from the Northern Attack Group, with the object of capturing the principal Moroccan airfield of Port Lyautey, 9,000 men were to land on beaches either side of the town of Mehdia at the mouth of a winding river up which a destroyer was to carry a raider detachment to capture the airfield some six miles upstream; the Southern Attack Group had the task of landing the Force's Sherman tanks for which the port of Safi, 110 miles down the coast from Casablanca, was to be captured.

The various sections of the Western Task Force had concentrated in mid-Atlantic on 28 October and at dawn on 7 November the Force was some 150 miles from the Moroccan coast, having crossed the ocean without loss and without detection by the enemy. There the Southern Attack Group—five transports and a cargo ship carrying 6,423 troops and 54 light and 54 medium tanks, escorted by a battleship, a cruiser, an escort carrier and ten destroyers—parted company and steered for Safi. Beach landings to the north and south of the harbour were successfully accomplished, meeting no resistance. The key to the operation, however, lay with two assault destroyers, *Bernadou* and *Cole*, which were to rush the harbour and throw some 400 soldiers ashore to seize the port facilities, while the shore defences were kept neutralized by the guns of the heavy ships of the escort. Though the *Cole* went astray during the approach and was delayed some 40 minutes, this part of the operation was also entirely successful; few casualties were suffered and by 1430 Safi was in American hands and the transport *Lakehurst* carrying the Sherman tanks was entering the harbour.

It was fortunate that at Mehdia no opposition was met on the beaches, although the French were alerted around midnight through a chance encounter between a coastal convoy and the American transports, for the landings were a confused and muddled affair, assault craft getting lost and scattered and arriving often at the wrong beaches where surf with six-foot high breakers caused them to be stranded and damaged. Confusion occurred also between troops attempting to capture the battery of 138-mm guns at the river mouth, the main French defence, and the cruiser *Savannah* trying to destroy it by bombardment. As a result operations were held up throughout the first 48 hours, the troops ashore in action with the French who were advancing from Port Lyautey being left short of water, medical supplies and ammunition; the destroyer *Dallas* with the raider detachment was driven off and not until the morning of the 10th was she able to get up river and seize the airfield. Fighting was still, indeed, occurring when, at midnight 10–11 November, an order from Admiral Darlan for all French forces in North Africa to cease resistance was received and obeyed.

Around Casablanca itself the same difficulties beset the troops of the Centre Attack Group, the featureless coastline hampering pilotage and the surf wrecking nearly half the assault craft. As elsewhere, only the absence of opposition on the beaches prevented disaster, and during the first hour 3,500 men managed to scramble ashore. Capture of the little port of Fédala at 1430 on the 8th eased the situation, though it was not until the following afternoon, by which time some 140 stranded landing craft were littering the beaches, that the first transport docked in the harbour.

Meanwhile during the morning of the 8th as soon as it was daylight the four 138-mm guns of the Port Blondin coastal battery opened fire on the transports and warships and were at once engaged by the cruisers *Augusta* and *Brooklyn* and three destroyers until 0730 when the battery fell silent. The same destroyers were replying to batteries near Fédala and beating off attacks by French aircraft when shells from Vichy warships from Casablanca began to fall closely round them, forcing them to retire seawards, the destroyer *Ludlow* being heavily engaged.

Two sharp engagements followed with French warships, led by the cruiser *Primauguet*, which, with sacrificial gallantry for a cause they must have known to be unworthy, sallied forth against overwhelming odds. As a result the *Primauguet* and the destroyer leaders *Milan* and *Albatros* were driven ashore heavily damaged and on fire, the destroyers *Fougeux*, *Boulonnais*, *Brestois* and *Frondeur* were sunk. Eight French submarines also put to sea to attack the Task Force. Some made unsuccessful torpedo attacks; three were sunk by the bombs of American naval planes as they left harbour; depth-charges destroyed two more off Casablanca and a third was caught and sunk a few days later on her way to Dakar; one reached Cadiz where she was scuttled by her crew; the eighth was lost from unknown causes. When the battleship *Jean Bart* brought her 15-inch guns into action from inside the harbour on the 10th, air attacks and bombardment by the battleship *Massachusetts* heavily damaged her as well as two destroyer leaders, three destroyers, three sloops and a minesweeper—a bitter price to pay for hopeless defiance of those who were soon to be Allies.

By the evening of the 10th the invading army had surrounded Casablanca and a general assault for the following morning had been ordered. Happily, however, before that moment arrived Admiral Darlan's order to cease resistance had been obeyed. Only then did German U-boats reach the scene, the *U173* sinking a transport and damaging the destroyer *Hambleton* and a tanker. On the following day *U130* sank three transports. This intervention was too late to affect the issue, however. The Allied lodgement in North Africa was assured. The potentiality of sea power had been resoundingly demonstrated. It was soon to be so again.

While the British 8th Army from the east and now General Eisenhower's Anglo-American armies from Morocco and Algeria fought their way into Tunisia to drive the Axis armies out of North Africa, the question of where next to assault the enemy had been under debate. At the Casablanca Conference in January 1943 the Americans had been persuaded that the resources necessary for the hoped-for assault across the English Channel could not be assembled that year and they had accepted the British proposal for an amphibious operation across the Mediterranean.

After discarding a British suggestion for a landing in Sardinia, the Combined Chiefs of Staff decided to make Sicily the objective; occupation would ensure the safety of Allied shipping in the Mediterranean as well as opening the 'Second Front' to divert enemy strength from hard-pressed Russia. By the middle of March a plan had been devised by which British and Empire troops were to assault on either side of Cape Passero, between Catania and Gela, the south-east corner of Sicily, while an American army would invade the far western coast of the island aiming at an early capture of Palermo.

General Montgomery, however, whose Eighth Army was to form the main part of the eastern invasion force, objected to this dispersal of the Allied force as a whole and of his own force which he also insisted should be strengthened. After much argument and several changes of plan, it was finally agreed that the British and Empire troops should assault between Syracuse and Pozzalo with the aim of a quick capture of Syracuse and the airfield at Pachino, with the Americans being thrown ashore immediately on their left between Scoglitti and Licata, charged with an early capture of the south coast airfields of Ponte Olivo, Biscari and Comiso and the port of Licata. Strategically sound as this was, the lack of adequate harbours on the south coast of Sicily would call for supply of the American army over beaches on a scale never before attempted. Nevertheless the risk was taken.

The orders for Operation 'Husky' as it was named, were finally completed on 11 June 1943. The forces engaged were divided into an Eastern Task Force (British and Canadian) and a Western Task Force (American). At 'H'-hour (0245 on 10 July) the former would launch some 115,000 Empire troops over beaches in four sectors—the XIIIth Corps in 'Acid' on both sides of Avola with the object of capturing Syracuse; the XXXth Corps in 'Bark East', 'Bark South' and 'Bark West' which enclosed the promontory of Cape Passero, to capture Pachino airfield. The assault troops for Acid and Bark East, the 5th and 50th Infantry Divisions and three Commandos were to come from Egypt in convoy MWF36 (fast) embarked in Landing Ships, Infantry, from which the Landing Craft Assault that would take them to the beaches would be hoisted out. A slow convoy of MT (Mechanical Transport) ships, MWS36, would follow with their heavy equipment.

The landings at Bark South were to be a 'shore to shore' assault with the troops, except for those in four LSIs, making the whole journey from North Africa (Sfax) and Malta in Landing Craft, Infantry (LCI), in which they would assault the beaches, Landing Craft, Tank, and Landing Ships, Tank, all of which could run their bows up on the beaches to disgorge their men and vehicles. The convoys in which these ships and craft were organized were designated SBS1, SBM1 (medium speed) and SBF1, all starting from Sfax, with follow-up convoys of LCIs, SBF2 and 3, from Malta.

Meanwhile, coming from the UK, where they had assembled in the Clyde, were convoys KMF18—three LSTs and eight LSIs with the assault troops of the 1st Canadian Division for Bark West—and KMS18 with their vehicles in LSTs and MT ships.

All these convoys sailed from their various ports and proceeded so as to converge on a rendezvous some 50 miles south of Malta at noon, 9 July, whence they turned north to steer during the night for their several release positions off their allotted beaches. Tanks for all the Eastern Task Force sectors sailed in a special convoy of 15 LSTs and 48 LCTs from Tripoli and was designated MWS36X.

Following the KM convoys along the route running close to the African shore came the American convoys of the Western Task Force. For the assault areas 'Cent'—each side of Scoglitti—and 'Dime' for Gela, 22 Combat Loaders (LSI) and seven MT ships for the initial assaults were to transport the 1st and 45th US Infantry Divisions in convoy NCF1 from Oran and Algiers, and the follow-up convoys NCS1 and 2 and NCF2. For the most westerly area, 'Joss' in which was the port of Licata, a 'shore to shore' assault by the US 3rd Division, was to be transported in convoys TJF1 of 106 LCIs, and TJS1 of 100 American and 16 British LCTs from Bizerta and Tunis, with 76 American and two British LSTs carrying further vehicles in the medium speed TJM1. Air power for the operation was represented by more than 4,000 Allied aircraft of which the heavy types were to pound Naples, Messina and Palermo to hinder the despatch of reinforcements; fighter cover for the assaulting forces was to be provided from Tunisia, Pantellaria and Malta. For a week prior to the assault, Sicilian airfields were kept under heavy air attack.

A powerful covering and support force for the whole operation had been assembled. Force 'H'—the battleships *Nelson, Rodney, Warspite* and *Valiant*, the carriers *Indomitable* and *Formidable*, six light cruisers and 18 destroyers—was to hover to the east of Sicily to guard against any interference by the Italian Fleet. Two further battleships *Howe* and *King George V*, two light cruisers and six destroyers held in the Western Basin of the Mediterranean to deceive the enemy into believing Sardinia was the objective, were to bombard Trapani and Marsala as a diversion. Each Task Force included a force of cruisers and destroyers to work close in shore assisting the Landing Craft, Flak, and Landing Craft, Support, in providing close gun support for the troops and to guard against raids by enemy light forces. Submarines would act as navigation beacons and provide beach marking parties as in Operation 'Torch' and would land raiding parties.

Finally, a large-scale airborne landing was included in the plans for each of the two main assault sectors. In the east, 1,600 men of the British 1st Airborne Division in 137 gliders towed by powered planes, mostly Dakotas, were to seize a strategic position south of Syracuse. In the American sector 2,600 parachute troops were to be dropped from 266 Dakotas, to capture Ponte Olivo airfield and act as a diversion for the 'Dime' assault troops.

To mislead the enemy as to the objective of the Allies' impending move, various ruses were employed of which the most bizarre and, in the event, the most successful, was the jettisoning on the Spanish coast of a corpse carrying spurious documents which duly reached the German High Command. The more immediate cause of the surprise that was, in fact, largely achieved, has been ascribed to the rough seas raised during the 9th by a stiff north-westerly wind which, while it slowed down the convoys of landing ships and craft, delaying the assaults and making a misery of the voyage for the embarked troops, also lulled the Italians into a false sense of security.

Except for delays caused by this minor storm, none of which proved significant, the deployment of this vast array of shipping in the operational area proceeded with hardly a hitch. Losses prior to the assault were confined to three ships from convoy KMS18B attacked by U-boats off Cape Tenez and one from MWS36 off Derna. The safe passage of the remainder from as far apart as the USA, Great Britain and Egypt and the achievement of effective surprise at the end of it, was an impressive demonstration of sea power.

Details of the various landings, few of which went off exactly as planned in the inky darkness before dawn and after the waxing moon had set, make a story of difficulties encountered through unexpected off-shore reefs, navigational errors overcome by skilful improvisation, and a dashing spirit amongst the assault troops which quickly silenced the light resistance encountered.

Taking the Eastern sectors first, at 'Acid', events opened with tragic disaster to the airborne operation. The effect of the strong north-westerly wind was not correctly taken into account. Half the gliders were released too soon and came down in the sea and losses amongst the troops were heavy. The seaborne assault craft, however, touched down on time, though many did so at the wrong place; the troops scrambled ashore through the surf. When coast defence batteries opened up at first light, inflicting a number of casualties, the destroyer *Eskimo* quickly silenced them. Dawn was at 0545, and by 0600 all the assault troops were ashore and in control of the beaches where the beach parties' bulldozers were soon clearing exit routes for the tanks which came rumbling ashore an hour later. At about the same time the transports of the slow convoy MWS36 came to their anchors and were soon unloading stores and vehicles. By the time the first enemy raid took place at 1300, the LSIs which had brought the assault troops were already cleared and on their

The Invasion of Italy

way back to Malta or North Africa. Though the air attacks, often heavy, continued at intervals for the rest of the day, not until after dark was any ship sunk. This was the hospital ship *Talamba*, lying fully illuminated some five miles to seaward and so clear of the smoke screens which shrouded the anchorage. Deliberately bombed, she went down with a heavy loss of life. Ashore, progress had been so good that British troops had entered Syracuse by nightfall.

At Bark East the story was much the same. A coast defence battery which attempted to interfere with the landing was silenced by the Netherlands gunboats *Flores* and *Soemba*. The troops for Bark South who, except for those in the four LSIs of convoy SBF1, were all in landing craft or ships, had a miserable passage as their bluff-bowed vessels punched into the rough sea, the LCTs making barely 3½ knots and arriving two hours late. The landings were slowed up by the awkward swell but very little by the enemy's opposition which was quickly silenced by the destroyers, LCS and LCF of the gun support force. Particularly impressive were the six LCT (R), launching simultaneous showers of rocket projectiles which were in action for the first time here. Another innovation first deployed in this operation, was the DUKW, a vehicle which could proceed afloat or on shore. Here they proved their worth, when some LSTs grounded on a false beach some distance off shore, by enabling stores to be got quickly ashore from them. During the afternoon of D-day a further 4,000 men streamed ashore over the lowered ramps of their beached LCTs. By dark the 51st Division was ashore and moving forward towards their objectives.

At Bark West the beaches to the west of the Cape Passero peninsula were the disembarkation point for the men of the 1st Canadian Division and two Royal Marine Commandos who had been at sea since leaving the Clyde 12 days earlier. Tank support for the assault came in LCTs of MWS36X from Tripoli, which were also used to transport some of the assault troops ashore from the LSIs. On that side of the peninsula, the swell and surf were unpleasantly high, making transfer of the troops difficult, particularly for the LCTs; but in spite of off-lying false beaches the delay was not serious. Opposition was mainly from coastal defence batteries which were engaged by the destroyers *Blankney* and *Puckeridge*, with LCGs adding their gunfire from close inshore with considerable effect. One battery of five guns proved hard to silence, surviving even a cannonade by the 15-inch guns of the monitor *Roberts*. By 0530, however, the beaches were secured. In the subsequent landings many landing craft stranded on the shifting sandbanks and once again the DUKWs came effectively to the rescue. Though vehicles and stores were safely landed throughout the 10th and 11th, the Bark South beaches were proving so much better that it was decided to close down Bark West. Meanwhile, during the 11th, bombardments by the *Roberts* and the destroyers *Blankney* and *Brissenden* brought about the surrender of the town of Pozzalo to landing parties from the destroyers which were gaily greeted by the inhabitants. On the same day the port of Syracuse was brought into use for unloading supplies and on the 13th the follow-up convoy MFW37 was able to enter and unload in a few hours. Soon afterwards Augusta, too, was in Allied hands. Nevertheless stores and vehicles continued to be put ashore over the Bark beaches for another ten days and over the Acid beaches where the 78th Division was disembarked, until 5th August.

In the American sectors success had been equally complete. As with the Eastern Task Force, the assault forces were made up of 26,000 fresh troops from home for one sector ('Cent'), though in their case their two convoys had had two weeks at Oran for reorganization and training before sailing from Oran and Algiers on 5 and 6 July in Convoy NCF1 composed of 22 Combat Loaders (the American equivalent of LSIs) in which 19,250 troops for the 'Dime' sector were also embarked. Troops for 'Joss' to the number of 27,650 set out from Sousse in 54 LCIs and 85 LCTs from Tunis to make a 'shore to shore' assault.

In spite of the weather and the head seas encountered after turning north from the African coast, all these convoys arrived with great precision at their initial positions. In the Gela landings the landing craft of the Dime force were hoisted out with admirable skill and promptness; after a wet and alarming passage of the seven miles to the shore, the assault troops were greatly relieved when they poured happily out on to *terra firma* to find no enemy opposition. It was not until DUKWs and vehicles from the LSTs reached shore that trouble was met from minefields, with bulldozers and trucks being blown up. Resultant delay in landing tanks and anti-tank guns made the enemy's counter-attacks when they finally developed, and their harassing gunfire from positions inland, the most effective resistance encountered anywhere. This was met by fire from the cruiser *Boise* and the destroyers *Shubrick* and *Jeffers* and from the monitor, HMS *Abercrombie* whose 15-inch guns pounded the observation post and strong point of Niscemi, eight miles inland. Nevertheless there was bitter fighting all D-day in and around Gela and it was not until the next day the beach-head could be said to have been secured and it was 0845 on the 12th before the Ponte Olivo airstrip was captured.

The difficulties encountered by the Dime force were increased by the partial failure of the parachute assault scheduled for first light on D-day, when the 2,800 paratroops were dropped over a wide area and unable to concentrate. A second airdrop of a complete division on the night of 11–12 July met disaster when the transport planes came first under fire from American Army guns and then, as they swerved away out to sea just as an air raid was taking place, from the guns of the ships. Twenty-three of the 144 aircraft were destroyed.

In the Cent sector, landing troubles occurred from the awkward swell, on account of which an hour's delay had to be imposed, and from the surf and false beaches at the landing places. Many of the crews of the landing craft were very inexperienced and 'broaching-to' on the beaches and other mishaps caused nearly 200 wrecks. Luckily, however, the enemy was in much smaller force here than in the Dime sector and bombardment by supporting warships made the resistance they could offer slight. In spite of much confusion and congestion on the wreck-littered beaches, troops were able to advance and capture Scoglitti by the afternoon of D-day and Comiso airfield on the 11th.

Professor Morison, official historian of the US Naval Operations, says that the 'key to the success of the Joss landings' was the smooth working of the plan whereby, as at each of the three American and four British sectors, a British submarine—in this case the *Safari* (Lieutenant R. B. Lakin)—acted as an off-shore beacon. Another factor contributing to the smoothness with which this complicated assault operation went off was undoubtedly the thoroughness with which Rear-Admiral Connolly and Major-General Truscott had trained and rehearsed the landing craft and troops for this 'shore to shore' assault. Combined with very light resistance in the area, the Joss force made such rapid progress that Licata was in its hands by noon on D-day.

With the defeat of the enemy's counter-attack in the 'Dime' sector, the way was now clear for General Patton's 7th Army to advance to the occupation of Western Sicily which progressed so rapidly that Palermo was captured on 22 July. The 7th Army, supported by an American naval Task Force, then turned east along the north coast of Sicily, the northern jaw of the Allied pincer movement to seize Messina.

The British 'jaw', moving north from Syracuse and Augusta, met a determined resistance from German troops defending Catania and were repulsed with severe losses. Rather than pay a further heavy price for its capture, General Montgomery altered his line of advance to circle to the westward of Mount Etna. Admiral Cunningham, in his subsequent despatch, regretted that Allied sea power was not used to by-pass and isolate Catania which might have saved much time. As it was, when the American 7th Army reached Messina on 17 August followed two hours later by advanced units of the British Eighth Army, the Axis armies had had time to evacuate the city and escape across the straits to the 'toe' of Italy.

So ended 'Husky', a classic example of the successful use of sea power to attack a land power at a weak point of one's own choosing in its vast coastal perimeter. The exposing of such a huge armada of vulnerable shipping to attack by powerful land-based air forces and numerous submarines was a risk; but in the event it proved to have been a well calculated one. The 'exchange rate' with enemy submarines was decidedly in favour of the Allies, three German and nine Italian submarines being sunk between D-day and the end of July during which time four merchant ships and two LSTs were sunk, three merchantmen and the cruisers

Cleopatra and *Newfoundland* were damaged by submarine attack. In the same period seven transports, two LSTs, a destroyer, a minesweeper and three minor craft were sunk by air attack which also damaged the carrier *Indomitable*, the monitor *Erebus*, two destroyers and several transports and landing craft.

Such a price was a small one to pay to penetrate the enemy's defences on so massive a scale.

The invasion of Sicily had been a textbook example of the use of sea power to gain a local success against a numerically superior enemy by a surprise descent on a sector of the long perimeter which could not be everywhere defended in strength. As in Operation 'Torch', surprise had been a vital feature; disaster could have overwhelmed the unfledged assault troops as they scrambled ashore from the landing craft stranded or wrecked by inexperienced crews if opposition had been assembled at the threatened points.

For the next move, following the eviction of the Axis armies from Sicily, surprise was likely to be much more difficult to achieve. It would call for an assault point well away from the toe of Italy where the enemy would be gathered in force ready for the Allies' advance across the Straits of Messina. The alternatives for a seaborne expedition which the Combined Chiefs of Staff had been considering since June, were Sardinia, where a measure of surprise and less opposition could be hoped for, or a landing in the Gulf of Gioja where the assault could expect support from the Allied troops advancing from Messina and would be under effective air cover from Sicilian airfields. It could also be within the compass of the greatly reduced supply of landing ships and craft that General Eisenhower would have available owing to the decision to send a great many to the Indian Ocean where a large-scale amphibious operation on the coast of Burma was being prepared.

In mid-July, however, the Combined Chiefs of Staff became seized with the idea of landing far behind the enemy's front in the vicinity of Naples. The problem of providing air cover would be partially met by naval fighters operating from a squadron of British escort carriers. Asked for his views, General Eisenhower was less than enthusiastic, considering that such an operation would need more landing craft than were available and that as the proposed area was at the extreme range of single-seater fighters from Sicily, reliance upon escort carriers for air support was too hazardous.

The Americans continued to insist on the withdrawal from the Mediterranean of large numbers of their landing craft in favour of the Pacific theatre as well as the Indian Ocean. Admiral Sir Andrew Cunningham, the naval C-in-C in the Mediterranean, appealed forcefully to the Admiralty against orders for a similar reduction of British landing craft and finally succeeded in retaining what was to prove a bare minimum for the operation. Amongst other arrangments, ten large troopships were returned to the Mediterranean from British ports.

The decision to make the assault in the Naples area (Operation 'Avalanche') was finally taken on 16 August at the 'Quadrant' summit meeting being held at Quebec. A suitable phase of the moon to meet Army preference for landing in darkness dictated 9 September as D-day.

The Admiralty had ordered the fleet carrier *Illustrious* to join the *Formidable*, already in Force 'H', which was to provide cover for the expedition against any sortie by the Italian Navy. The escort carriers *Attacker*, *Battler*, *Hunter* and *Stalker* and the *Unicorn* (an aircraft repair ship adaptable as a carrier) were formed into a squadron under Rear-Admiral Sir Philip Vian and embarked a total of 110 Seafire fighter planes. To replace the cruisers *Cleopatra* and *Newfoundland*, damaged during 'Husky', the cruisers *Scylla* and *Charybdis* were added to this squadron as part of its escort.

As early as 31 July, before the objective had been decided, Vice-Admiral H. K. Hewitt, USN, who had commanded the Western Naval Task Force in 'Husky', had been appointed, with the same title, to command the naval forces for 'Avalanche'. These were divided into two naval assault forces, the northern commanded by Commodore G. N. Oliver, the southern by Rear-Admiral J. H. Hall, USN. When Eisenhower's choice of the Gulf of Salerno for the assault—the nearest point to Naples which could be given any cover by fighters from Sicily—was approved at the end of August, little time was left for a finalized plan to emerge from the various responsible authorities scattered between Sicily, Malta and North African ports and for orders to be completed and issued. Nevertheless a very complicated programme for convoys starting from Tripoli, Bizerta, Oran and Algiers, in which British and American ships and craft mingled and British and American troops were embarked in ships and craft manned by their allies, was prepared and carried out with very few misunderstandings and mistakes. Details will therefore be omitted. It will be sufficient to give some idea of the magnitude of the operation to register that some 700 ships and craft made up the assault and early follow-up convoys.

The 5th Army under General Mark Clark, which was to make the assault, was divided between the two Assault Forces. The Northern, composed of the British X Corps (46th and 56th Divisions) two Commandos and three US Ranger Battalions, were transported mainly in landing ship and craft from Tripoli to make a 'shore to shore' assault. The Rangers and Commandos were to land near the townships of Maiori and Vietri on the northern shore of the gulf to cut road and rail communication with Naples and to seize the small port of Salerno. The remainder were to be landed on beaches close to Montecorvino airfield, the capture of which was their first objective before pressing on inland to seize the road and rail junction at Battipaglia and a bridge across the River Sele, which formed the dividing line between the two assault areas.

Troops of the Southern Assault Force, the US VI Corps, were embarked mainly in Attack Transports to make a 'ship to shore' assault on beaches abreast of Paestum; their main objective was the occupation of the high ground from which their beaches could be commanded by the enemy's artillery. H-hour for the assaults was 0330 on the 9th, one hour before sunrise. The plan included no preliminary softening-up bombardment as the Army hoped to achieve surprise. Naval forces were to stage diversionary operations in the vicinity of Naples, and Allied bombers were to neutralize airfields from which the enemy might launch attacks on the beaches. Fighter cover over the beaches would be provided as far as possible from Sicilian airfields backed up until the capture of Montecorvino (expected on D-day) by the Seafires from Admiral Vian's squadron which, in turn, would be given cover by fighters from the *Illustrious* and *Formidable* of Force 'H', operating further to seaward.

The first of the many convoys for Salerno to get under way, a slow convoy of 29 LCTs and ten Support Landing Craft from Tripoli, sailed early on 3 September. At about the same hour the first wave of landing craft carrying Montgomery's Eighth Army set out from Messina and headed across the straits while the monitors *Abercrombie*, *Roberts* and *Erebus* with their 15-inch guns, the cruisers *Mauritius* and *Orion*, six destroyers, two gunboats and the Eighth Army's own artillery laid down a devastating barrage on the far shore. The troops met no opposition and were soon in possession of the port of Reggio and, their supplies assured, were advancing northwards.

Further developments of great importance were also taking place while the convoys for Salerno were on their way. Mussolini had been arrested on 25 July and a new Italian Government under General Badoglio formed. It had at first announced its intention of continuing the war, but by mid-August secret emissaries to negotiate peace had arrived in Madrid. A treaty was finally signed on 3 September by the terms of which the Italian fleet, gathered mostly at Spezia, was to sail for Malta to surrender. News of this was kept secret until the evening of the 8th when news of an armistice was broadcast from London.

At 0300 on the 9th, the battleships *Roma*, *Vittorio Veneto* and *Italia* (ex *Littorio*) with six cruisers and eight destroyers sailed and steered to the westward of Corsica before turning south. That evening they were attacked by a new German weapon, the FX1400 guided armour-piercing bomb. A squadron of fast Dornier 217 bombers armed with these had taken off from the south of France and, unopposed by the Italians who thought they were Allied planes, they scored a direct hit on the *Roma* which blew up and sank, taking with her Admiral Bergamini and most of her crew. The *Italia* was slightly damaged but with the remainder reached

Malta safely, being joined there by the rest of the Italian fleet from Taranto. On 11 September Admiral Sir Andrew Cunningham was able to signal to the Admiralty: 'Be pleased to inform their Lordships that the Italian battle-fleet now lies at anchor under the guns of the fortress of Malta.'

This spectacular demonstration of the final passage of sea power in the Mediterranean to the Allies was a timely encouragement. For in the Gulf of Salerno, where the assaults had met stiff opposition from high-grade German troops, things were in a critical state.

In both Northern and Southern Assault Forces, the assault convoys had fulfilled their intricate programmes admirably, arriving on time in their correct initial positions shortly after midnight 8–9 September. They had not achieved surprise, however. They, as well as Force 'H' covering them, had been attacked by German aircraft while on passage. One LST had been hit and forced to beach herself. One LCT had been sunk. Now the assault ships and craft came under fire during their approach and suffered damage and casualties. It was not enough to dislocate the assault at this stage but it presaged tough fighting ashore with a fully alerted enemy.

In the northern sector, minesweepers having cleared and buoyed a channel through the defensive minefield, the Commandos and Rangers touched down on time. They met little opposition on the beaches, but had to fight hard to hold their objectives. On the main beaches, in spite of an error at one of them which led to confusion, congestion and severe casualties, and with the support of gunfire from the destroyers which engaged enemy tanks and batteries continuously with great effect, the beach-head had been quickly secured and LSTs were beaching themselves and unloading by 1030.

In the American sector further south, the assault waves correctly identified their beaches and in spite of heavy fire on their run-in and on the beaches, the troops were quickly ashore and moving inland. But the enemy artillery kept up such a heavy fire that LCTs bringing the tanks were at first driven off; then the big LSTs were delayed, forced to abandon some of the allotted beaches, causing congestion and confusion on those which could be used. Disaster loomed but was staved off by the gunfire support given by the monitor *Abercrombie*, the US cruisers *Savannah* and *Philadelphia* and several destroyers; in spite of all, by the evening of the 9th, Paestum was in American hands and the VI Corps were astride the railway and main road. They were still short of most of their objectives, however.

During the 10th the advance inland continued against mounting opposition and at a dangerously slow pace. For until the enemy was driven back out of artillery range of the beaches there was a great danger of the troops being cut off from their supplies. In the northern sector, though Salerno and Montecorvino airfields were both captured, enemy artillery fire made both useless, while at Battipaglia, which British troops had also taken, counter-attacks drove them out again. Progress came to a halt and by the 13th, having suffered more than 3,000 casualties the weary X Corps was nowhere more than five miles from the beach. In the southern sector the Americans had made slightly better progress, but even they were no farther than six miles from the shore.

And now the Germans, having concentrated their reinforcements near Eboli prepared to launch a powerful counter-offensive on the evening of the 13th. The crisis of the battle had arrived. Before we tell how it developed, however, we should turn our eyes seaward to find out how the naval forces had been faring.

We have mentioned the support given to the northern assault by destroyers. These were mainly the *Laforey, Loyal* and *Lookout, Mendip, Brecon* and *Blankney*, to whose contribution in knocking out the enemy gun batteries the 56th Division HQ were to pay tribute. The *Laforey* also had the satisfaction of blowing up the ammunition dump of one battery shortly before she herself was forced temporarily to retire to make repairs, as a result of five shell hits. In the anchorage area the 12th and 13th MS Flotillas after clearing the approaches to the beaches and to Salerno had set about sweeping the whole area and before the operation was over accounted for 171 mines. Farther out the cruisers *Mauritius* and *Orion* and the monitor *Roberts* were deployed for longer range bombardment but calls for their support were few until the 10th after which their bombardments of gun positions, tank and troop concentrations, ammunition dumps, etc., played an increasingly important part in the critical situation. Meanwhile, during D-day, the escort carrier force, from 0615 when they flew off the first sortie of Seafires, until 1930 when the last aircraft landed on, maintained patrols of about 20 fighters over the area being controlled from the AA ship *Palomares*. The 265 sorties flown that day should have been their full contribution; but with Montecorvino still unusable, and with the number of planes available progressively reduced by deck accidents to the fragile Seafires, flying at the same intensity continued throughout the 10th and 11th and during the forenoon of the 12th.

By that time the Seafires, operating from the 18-knot escort carriers in very light winds, had been reduced to only 26 serviceable out of more than 100 with which they had started. The Americans having by then prepared a landing strip at Paestum, these were flown there and continued to operate until the 15th. The unsuitable aircraft with which the Fleet Air Arm was equipped at that time had made the operation less effective than had been hoped for. Apart from the heavy accident rate, the Seafire IIC was too slow at low level to catch the enemy's fighter bombers. Nevertheless, though they achieved few combat successes and lost ten of their number in action, they drove off a great many attackers and played an important part in the air defence of the beach-head over which the shore-based Allied fighters could spend only a few minutes during each sortie.

During the night 10–11 September, the enemy's naval forces appeared on the scene in the shape of MTBs which attacked an American transport convoy as it was leaving the area. The convoy was successfully defended but one of the escort, the US destroyer *Rowan*, was torpedoed and sunk. It was the air squadron of Do.217s, however, which gave the most trouble. These aircraft were too fast to be caught by any Allied aircraft in the area except the American long-range Lightnings. Against the FX bombs the Dorniers launched, there was no other defence. Arriving over the 'Avalanche' area early on the 11th, they landed one of them 15 feet from the USS *Philadelphia*, fortunately without causing serious damage. Their next bomb scored a direct hit on the *Savannah*, however, causing damage which forced her to limp away to Malta for repairs. The next to suffer was HMS *Uganda* that afternoon and she, too, was put out of action. To replace these two casualties, the USS *Boise* and HMS *Aurora* and *Penelope* were brought forward to join the bombardment forces.

Now we must return ashore to the critical situation about to develop there. During the night 13–14 September a German spearhead of infantry supported by a powerful armoured column including the respected Tiger tanks, thrust down the Sele Valley at the junction between the two Allied Corps. This weak point, held by troops exhausted by four days and nights of fierce fighting, was pierced. By dawn a salient two miles wide yawned between the British and Americans. Withdrawals all along the Allied line enabled a concentration of enemy artillery to play upon the ever more densely-packed beach-head.

Disaster seemed imminent. General Mark Clark asked for plans to be concerted for the troops of one sector to be evacuated and transferred to the other. Admiral Hewitt ordered unloading on the southern beaches to cease. At a conference in his HQ ship, Commodore Oliver protested that General Clark's proposal was suicidal; he appealed to Admiral Cunningham for support. The C-in-C at once ordered the cruisers *Euryalus*, *Scylla* and *Charybdis* to embark reinforcement troops at Tripoli for Salerno; the battleships *Valiant* and *Warspite* with six destroyers were ordered forward. Meanwhile the ships already present brought a heavy cannonade to bear on the enemy, while the Allied Air Forces made the most concentrated attack ever made. By late afternoon pressure on the beach-head had sufficiently reduced for unloading to be resumed. Early on the 15th, General Alexander, the Army C-in-C in the Mediterranean, arrived at Salerno. At 5th Army headquarters he expressed his disapproval of the withdrawal plan, of which no more was heard. And, indeed, the crisis had been overcome, thanks largely, as the Germans acknowledged, to the sea and air bombardments they suffered. These were almost continuous throughout the day, some 2,000 bombing sorties being made while the British and American warships, joined that evening by the *Valiant* and *Warspite*, pounded enemy targets with great effect. By the evening the enemy's advance had been finally halted.

The bombardment was resumed in full fury on the 16th, once again with notable results; encouraged by these, the troops of the 5th Army forced the enemy to abandon his salient. Once again, too, the only serious opposition to the bombardment ships was the FX guided bomb. The *Warspite* had just completed a successful shoot culminating in the blowing up of an enemy ammunition dump, when three of these missiles plunged vertically on her. Two missed her narrowly but the third pierced through to a boiler room before exploding, causing heavy damage, flooding and a loss of all steam power. She was towed off to Malta for repairs.

By the 17th the situation ashore had been restored. The 5th Army was in touch with the Eighth advancing north from Messina and now was able itself to resume the offensive. The assault phase of Operation 'Avalanche' was over, giving way to the build-up and advance inland. Salerno itself was finally secured and opened on 25 September; Castellamare and Torre Annunziata, up the coast towards Naples, on the 28th and 29th; Naples was entered on 1 October. The German counter-attack at Salerno had gained them time for a thorough destruction of the port facilities, much ingenuity to prevent clearance being employed. But the Allied salvage parties with the experience of other similar situations behind them achieved miracles. Berths for five Liberty ships were cleared in two days; a month later the port was working to full capacity to support the Allied armies.

Operation 'Avalanche' had been a classic example of the use of sea power to turn a hostile enemy's flank and penetrate in its rear. The risks of major disaster if surprise is not achieved or if the assault troops are unable quickly to advance inland and secure their beach-head were also demonstrated. So, too, was the price the naval forces may be called on to pay to support the expeditionary force under such circumstances.

At Salerno this price did not approach an unacceptable level. The next amphibious operation of the kind undertaken in the Mediterranean was to be more costly. This was the landing of the VI Corps, composed of the US 3rd Division and the British 1st on either side of the port of Anzio on 22 January 1944. Space will not permit any detailed account. It must be sufficient to say that the assault phase achieved perfect surprise; and, indeed, it was later to be known that there was nothing to stop the troops advancing to the Alban Hills, 20 miles away, had they seized the opportunity, though it is not sure that they could have secured a position there.

By the end of D-day over 36,000 men with 3,069 vehicles and a large quantity of stores had been safely landed with trifling casualties. This brilliant feat was to be largely wasted, however, by the slowness of the VI

Corps to advance so as to put the beach-head out of range of enemy artillery and the speed with which the Germans moved in opposition. As a result not only was the Allied expeditionary force pinned down for nearly three months during which they came near to being driven back into the sea, but the naval supporting forces and the transports bringing in supplies were exposed for the whole of that time to intensive air attack, including glider bombs and aerial torpedoes, attack by E-boat and U-boat and to the gunfire of enemy batteries on shore.

Glider bombs sank the light cruiser *Spartan* and the destroyer *Inglefield* with heavy loss of life; they also sank two Liberty ships, and damaged the destroyer *Jervis*. A torpedo plane sank the destroyer *Janus*. Bombs sank the Hospital Ship *St David* and damaged an American destroyer. The USS *Mayo* was mined. The cruiser *Penelope* and two LSTs were sunk by U-boats. To add to the naval problems, repeated gales hampered operations and unloading.

Nevertheless by 29 January no less than 68,886 troops, 508 guns, 237 tanks and 27,250 tons of stores had been landed, bringing the Allied strength up to approximately four divisions; but the Germans were deploying in equal strength and when the VI Corps attacked they were unable to make any headway. On 3 February the Germans were able to counter-attack in superior numbers and for the next two weeks the issue was in the balance. Allied bombers of the Tactical Air Force gave continuous massive support, while the cruisers *Orion, Mauritius, Phoebe, Penelope*, the USS *Brooklyn*, the Dutch gunboats, *Soemba* and *Flores* and every available Allied destroyer brought their guns into action to harass the enemy's concentrations with an effectiveness that brought rueful acknowledgements in the German War Diary. By the 20th the enemy's effort was spent. The stalemate ashore that followed and continued for more than three months, while Allied strength was built up to seven divisions, left the port of Anzio, the beaches and the anchorage under artillery fire and subjected to ceaseless fighter-bomber and other types of air attack.

Not until 23 May were the Allied troops able to go over to the offensive and by the end of the month the fighting had advanced beyond supporting gun-range and the Navies' part in the operation was virtually over.

The great opportunities that sea power can provide had been again demonstrated at Anzio. So, too, had the risks which attend any amphibious descents. Though the landings had achieved surprise and been carried out with great skill and expertise, the strategic situation had, perhaps, been misjudged and for a while there had been a real danger of disaster to the land forces.

We must return now to a theatre where the application of Allied sea power was still being challenged.

13 *The German Surface Fleet's Failure*

While the fortunes in the Battle of the Atlantic swayed back and forth through the winter months 1942-43, working up to the climax of the following spring, in the Arctic, resumption of the convoys to Russia in December 1942 led to that confrontation between the escorts and the German heavy units stationed in northern Norway which the Admiralty had always feared and to which no feasible counter appeared possible. Indeed, looked at as a strategic problem in a staff college 'war game', the Arctic convoys had always been an unsound operation, passing, as they did, within 200 miles of enemy sea and air bases. When their viability was finally put to the test, however, other factors than a simple comparison of the forces each side could bring to bear were to intervene.

The new series of convoys to Russia were planned on different lines from those during the summer. The almost total absence of real daylight as well as the transfer of the Luftwaffe squadrons from northern Norway made provision of strong anti-aircraft defence unnecessary. U-boats, however, were coming to sea in ever-greater numbers as Germany's submarine effort was reaching its peak. Air escort could do little to help until daylight returned in which the carriers could operate. It was not until a later stage of the war that operation of aircraft from the decks of auxiliary aircraft-carriers by night became possible.

Defence therefore lay with the destroyers and corvettes of the close escort with a force of cruisers in the offing ready to intervene should a surface attack be launched by the enemy. The Admiralty's plan for the first convoy was for one of 30 ships with a destroyer escort comparable to that of PQ18. But experience with a winter convoy of that size which had been run in November to bring back empty ships from Archangel caused the C-in-C Home Fleet to propose instead that two east-bound convoys of 15 ships each should be sailed a week apart. Plans were therefore made for 15 ships to sail from Loch Ewe on 15 December and a further convoy of 14 on the 22nd.

The nomenclature of this new series of convoys was changed, the eastbound being known as JW convoys, the homeward as RA. The first JW having been thus split, the two halves were numbered JW51A and JW51B, while the first homeward convoy would be RA51.

JW51A duly sailed from Loch Ewe on 15 December and made a quiet and uneventful passage, arriving safely in the Kola Inlet on Christmas Day. The covering force of cruisers under Rear Admiral Burnett with his flag in the *Sheffield* and accompanied by the *Jamaica* carried on to Kola Inlet to wait there until it was time to sail to provide cover for RA51 and JW51B.

The senior officer of the close escort for JW51B was Captain R. St. V. Sherbrooke, commanding the destroyer *Onslow* and the 17th Flotilla (*Oribi*, *Obedient*, *Orwell* and *Obdurate*); construction of these ships had outstripped the manufacture of the six 4.7-inch guns in twin turrets each were designed to mount; instead they had only four 4-inch dual purpose (H/A L/A) guns. The remainder of the escort was composed of the old destroyer *Achates*, the corvettes *Rhododendron* and *Hyderabad*, the minesweeper *Bramble* and the trawlers *Vizalma* and *Ocean Gem*.

At the convoy conference before sailing, Sherbrooke outlined to the assembled merchant ship masters and the convoy commodore, Captain R. A. Melhuish, Royal Indian Navy (Retired), his intended tactics in the event of attack by German surface warships. At the first alarm, the destroyers of the escort would concentrate on the threatened flank and would then steer to meet the enemy. While the remaining escorts gathered in a close screen and laid smoke, the convoy itself would be turned away from the enemy, each ship dropping smoke floats at intervals. Meanwhile, he assured them, the cruisers of the covering force would be hurrying to the scene to take over the defence.

They were simple and indeed the obvious tactics. What Sherbrooke could not enlarge upon, though it was no doubt clear to the audience of experienced master mariners, was the element of doubt as to how soon the cruiser force, hovering out of sight and perhaps uncertain of the position of the convoy, could come into action through the dim Arctic twilight and the fog or snow of the northern seas. All that Sherbrooke could assure his listeners, by implication rather than in words, was that the enemy would have to destroy every one of the British destroyers before he could with impunity proceed to attack the convoy.

Unseasonable calm weather favoured the convoy at first; but on 28 December, when it was half-way between Jan Mayen and Bear Island, this gave way to the more usual furious gale with driving snow squalls. During the black winter night two escorts, *Oribi* and *Vizalma*, and five merchant ships lost touch. *Oribi* and one of the merchantmen never succeeded in regaining contact in the brief daylight hours and they eventually arrived at Kola independently. Three of the freighters rejoined during the 29th. The *Vizalma* and one merchant ship followed a route

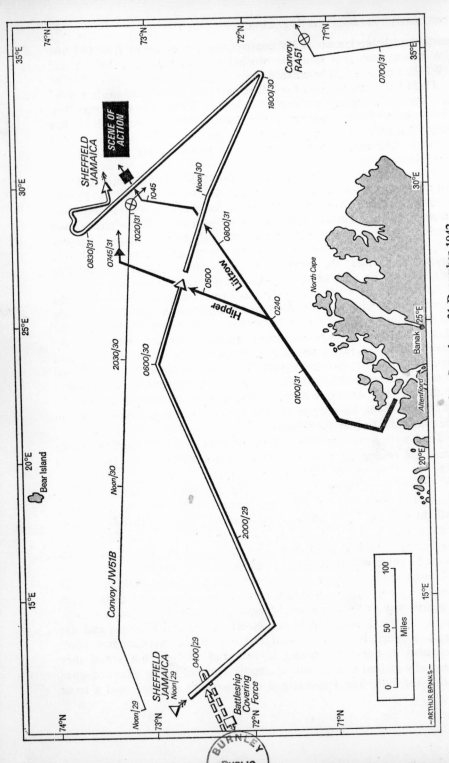

Repulse of German Surface Squadron, 31 December 1942

—ARTHUR BANKS—

well to the northward of the convoy and would be on their own until New Year's Day.

By the 30th the gale had died away. The fresh breeze from the north-west which took its place brought an icy breath from the polar ice cap. Sixteen degrees of frost in the air laid a hard skin of ice over everything on the upper decks, constantly thickened as spray which fell on deck instantly froze.

So far there had been 'no enemy but winter and rough weather'. No knowledge of the progress of the convoy had reached German naval headquarters. But now, on the forenoon of the 30th, came a U-boat alarm. From the *Obdurate* a conning-tower was sighted some distance away. Streaking after it, the destroyer forced the U-boat to dive, preventing it from getting in to attacking distance. But the convoy's position was now known to the enemy. Surfacing as soon as he could, the U-boat captain sent his message, 'Convoy bound for North Russia, south of Bear Island. Lightly escorted.'

This was the news for which Admiral Schniewind, the German commander in the north, had been impatiently waiting since it became known that the convoy had sailed. The heavy cruiser *Admiral Hipper* (eight 8-inch, 12 4.1-inch guns), flagship of Vice-Admiral Kummetz, the pocket-battleship *Lützow* (six 11-inch, eight 5.9-inch, six 4.1-inch guns) and six destroyers (five 5-inch guns each), already at short notice for sea in Altenfiord, were at once ordered out to the attack.* Heading north, they steered to intercept the convoy on the early morning of the next day so that they would have the whole of the few hours of twilight in which to hammer it before night again came down.

Unknown to Kummetz, Admiral Burnett's two cruisers had sailed from Kola on the 27th and were ranging to and fro in the area between Altenfiord and the convoy's route. However, in ignorance of the convoy's true position and thinking it to be further north and east than it was, Burnett swung north-westward on the evening of the 30th, intending to be only a few miles north and some 40 miles astern of it on the next morning. Then, should an attack develop, he would be able to come into action with the advantages of the feeble daylight on his side. Due to the position error, he was in fact to find himself about 30 miles due north of the convoy at that time, but the advantage of light would still be with him.

So through the night of 30 December the convoy plugged steadily on through the clear frosty darkness, fading from time to time into the grey obscurity of snow squalls. Escorting the 12 ships still in company were now five destroyers, two corvettes and a trawler. Some 45 miles to the north were the *Vizalma* and one merchantman. Somewhere in the vicinity was another straggler and the minesweeper *Bramble* searching for her.

Steering across the convoy's route ahead of it were *Sheffield* and

Tirpitz and *Scheer* were both away refitting at this time.

Jamaica, hoping to pick up radar contact with it but actually passing too far ahead to do so. None of these scattered British forces knew even approximately where the others were, for strict wireless silence had been enforced for many days to avoid detection through the enemy's radio direction finders.

Finally, coming up from the south, all unknown to the British, was the German squadron. Vice-Admiral Kummetz had evolved a plan whereby *Hipper* and *Lützow*, each accompanied by three destroyers, would fall separately on the convoy from two directions. Ruling out any idea of night action which he felt would give the destroyer escorts a dangerous ability to bring off unseen torpedo attacks, Kummetz planned to bring *Hipper* in from the port quarter of the convoy at first light. This, he rightly judged would draw off the escorts in his direction while the convoy would veer away from him to the south-east—into the arms of the *Lützow* and her destroyers.

The plan was a good one; but the best-laid plan of battle must go awry if the will to carry it out with courage and determination is lacking. Kummetz was labouring under the same disadvantage that had hamstrung previous sorties of German surface warships—Hitler's hysterical insistence that no risks must be taken and that he must avoid action with equal or superior enemy forces. Furthermore, even against the destroyers of the convoy escort one of his heavy ships, the *Lützow*, was expected to avoid taking any injury. For on completion of the operation she was under orders to make for the Atlantic on a commerce-raiding expedition. It was vital that she should be fully fighting-fit for such a task.

However, serious opposition was not expected, for Kummetz was unaware of the presence of Burnett's ships, and at 0240 on the morning of the 31st the German force divided in accordance with Kummetz's plan. With *Hipper* went the destroyers *Friedrich Eckhold, Richard Beitzen* and *Z29*, while the *Z30, Z31* and the *Theodore Reidel* accompanied *Lützow*.

As the dim, grey Arctic day was coming unwillingly to life, the stage was thus set for the sort of disastrous encounter which the Admiralty had always feared must one day befall the convoys to North Russia and against which it was so difficult to provide an adequate defence.

The curtain rose at 0820 on the morning of New Year's Eve, the scene disclosed being the bridge of the corvette *Hyderabad* on the starboard quarter of the convoy. Her captain, searching the murky horizon as feeble daylight grew, sighted two dim shapes identifiable as destroyers, steering north across the convoy's wake. Knowing that two Russian destroyers were due to join the escort, he gave a grunt of satisfaction at this unusually punctual arrival, which he took it to be, and took no further action.

But ten minutes later, from the *Obdurate*, the same ships were sighted. Her captain, Lieutenant-Commander Sclater, was not so easily satisfied

A signal was at once on its way to the *Onslow*—'Two unidentified destroyers bearing west, course north.' Already *Obdurate* had swung round and was nosing after the strangers when Sherbrooke's reply came back—'Investigate'.

Sherbrooke had little doubt as to what the *Obdurate*'s report signified. He piped his ship's company to breakfast and to shift into clean underclothes, a traditional though rather alarming prelude to naval battle, a precaution against infected splinter wounds, an order rarely given since the passing of the era of predictable pitched battles at sea.

It was some time before confirmation of his belief came, however. Chasing after the German destroyers, which were soon seen to be three in number, Sclater could get no clear view of them against a background of black snow clouds. By 0930 the range had closed to a mere four miles but there was still not enough light by which to identify them. But then all doubt was set at rest as a ripple of flashes from the German guns was seen and the tall water-spouts of shell splashes rose from the sea nearby. Sending off an immediate enemy report, Sclater swung his ship round to fall back on the support of his flotilla-mates.

The Germans, too, turned away. They had been detached by Admiral Kummetz to search eastwards along the convoy's track and had been about to comply when this sighting of the *Obdurate* made further search unnecessary. Now, with singular lack of enterprise, they veered north-eastward to rejoin the *Hipper* where first contact with the convoy escort was also about to be made.

Before *Obdurate*'s alarm signal had reached the bridge of the *Onslow*, Sherbrooke was already steering his ship for the gunflashes and calling for *Orwell, Obedient* and *Obdurate* to join him. Thus his plan which he had outlined at the convoy conference was at once put into operation and the remainder of the escort force knew just what they had to do. *Achates*, which was on the convoy's port quarter and so between the enemy and the convoy, began to belch out a cloud of black, oily smoke from her funnels and white smoke from smoke floats on her quarter deck and to steam up and down laying a dense screen which drifted slowly on the wind after the merchant ships.

But now Sherbrooke obtained some idea of what he was up against as, at 0939, out of the hazy gloom to the north-west the massive top hamper of a large ship loomed, heading straight for him. As he peered at the dim outline, trying to identify it, he saw it swing away to port, disclosing its silhouette, unmistakably the *Hipper*. A definite enemy report could now be radioed to the cruiser force. Here was an opponent which would need more than a flotilla of destroyers to combat. Five minutes later Bob Burnett, who had been decoyed away to the north by the need to investigate a radar contact of the *Vizalma* and her straggler, was reading the message which at once resolved his doubts as to what he should do. He had already seen the gunflashes far to the south at 0930 but until more definite news had come in he had not been able to neglect the contact to the northward which might have been that of the enemy's main force. Piling on speed until the two cruisers were racing along at 31 knots, he turned to the support of the convoy and its escort.

Meanwhile, the *Hipper's* turn to port had been made with the object of bringing all her guns to bear on the little *Achates*, standing out stark against the black background of smoke. *Achates* was hit but not seriously damaged before the *Hipper* shifted her fire to the *Onslow*, now accompanied by the *Orwell*, as they came into view. At a range of five-and-a-half miles, *Hipper* and the two British destroyers exchanged desultory fire as both sides ran in and out of smoke patches and snow squalls, the British firing by radar.

It was at once clear to Sherbrooke that his opponent was far from willing to mix it, probably fearing to run into torpedoes fired, unseen, from the British ships. With their camouflaged hulls merging with the grey background of sea and sky, *Onslow* and *Orwell* were difficult targets and hard to see. Rather than close and smash them with his much heavier armament, Kummetz kept the *Hipper* away, hiding in smoke whenever possible and edging his way to the north-east.

He could, indeed, well afford to; for now the convoy was behaving as he had forecast, turning away behind the smoke screen to the south-east where Kummetz knew the *Lützow* must be waiting to spring on it. Sherbrooke had no knowledge of this second threat but instinctively he refused to be lured away by his slippery opponent. He was concerned as to what the three destroyers originally sighted might be up to—they had, in fact, been ordered to rejoin *Hipper*. As the *Obedient* and *Obdurate* came streaking up to join him, he ordered them to turn back to guard the convoy against them. Meanwhile he decided that he himself with the *Orwell* would keep *Hipper* in sight and withhold his torpedo fire, keeping it as a constant threat. He rightly judged that so long as the enemy remained unwilling to face this threat, the *Hipper* would be unable to break through to the convoy.

Nevertheless the situation was one of the utmost peril for the British force. Five destroyers could not indefinitely hold off a heavy cruiser and three larger destroyers boldly handled. Sherbrooke believed Burnett to be a long way off and that it might be many hours before he could come to his aid. But now came a signal from the *Sheffield* which altered the whole situation. It told Sherbrooke that she and *Jamaica* were approaching on a southerly course at 31 knots. As the glad tidings filtered down to the guns' crews and on to the supply parties in the magazines, the stokers in the boiler-rooms and the engine-room crews, cheering broke out in all the ships.

At this moment the *Hipper* was seen to haul away to the north and break off the action. She had up to now made a very poor showing. Unable to get a clear view of the camouflaged British destroyers as they slipped in and out of smoke clouds and snow squalls, her gunlayers seemed to shoot in a most aimless and erratic fashion. The gunnery of the British destroyers was similarly handicapped, as well as by the constant icing-up of gun barrels and of the ammunition at their unsheltered gun mountings. No hits on the enemy had been obtained.

Kummetz's turn to the north had been made with the object of drawing the British destroyers after him. But when they failed to follow him Kummetz suddenly turned back again and for the first time the *Hipper* brought accurate fire to bear. What had always been inevitable in the long run but had been so fortunately long delayed, now occurred. At 1020 a salvo of heavy shells fell square around the *Onslow*. Four hits in rapid succession wreaked fearful destruction. Both the destroyer's forward guns were knocked out, fierce fires raged in her fore superstructure and on her mess decks. A hole was torn in her side abreast the engine-room.

Across the bridge, splinters had flown from a shell which had burst against the funnel. One had hit Sherbrooke, inflicting a dangerous and horribly painful wound in the face, partly blinding him. In spite of pain and shock, Sherbrooke held to his post on his shattered bridge, giving orders to *Onslow* and *Orwell* to turn away under cover of smoke before *Hipper*'s new-found aggressiveness could do further damage.

Meanwhile a signal had gone to Lieutenant-Commander Kinloch of the *Obedient*, the next senior officer present, ordering him to take over control of operations. But not until confirmation came that the signal had been received in the *Obedient* would Sherbrooke allow himself to be led away to have his wounds treated, wounds which the doctor thought at first must be fatal.

Fortunately at this perilous moment a heavy snowstorm swept across the scene bringing a lull in the action. As the damaged *Onslow*, unable further to play an active role, limped away to join the convoy, *Obedient*, *Obdurate* and *Orwell* also turned south, refusing to be lured too far from their charges. And now Kummetz, all unaware that 12 miles to the north-west, in radar contact and tearing along towards him, were the *Sheffield* and *Jamaica*, had his attention distracted by a fresh target. Out of a snow squall to the eastward of him emerged the little *Bramble*, which since the previous day had been wandering solitarily in search of the two missing stragglers from the convoy.

It is doubtful if her two 4-inch guns even came into action before she was overwhelmed by a blast of fire from her huge opponent and was reduced to a smoking wreck. Leaving the destroyer *Eckholdt* to give the *Bramble* her quietus, Kummetz swung southwards again at 1047 to find the British destroyers as soon as the snowstorm in that direction should have passed on.

Behind him, still out of sight, were coming the two British cruisers, curling bow-waves mounting white up their forecastle sides, their hulls trembling as the high-pressure steam from the boilers forced the

screaming turbines round at maximum revolutions. Their ensigns stood
out stiff and crackling in the wind of their wild progress. Halliards slatted
impatiently against the masts as though to whip the ships on to greater
speed. On their bridges, huddled figures peered through the murk and
snowfall ahead for the first sight of the enemy being fast overhauled.

Meanwhile the denouement for which Kummetz had planned was
taking place to the southward. While the *Achates* still prowled back and
forth across the rear of the convoy laying smoke to shield it from the
Hipper, and Obedient and her companions were still to the north of the
convoy for the same reason, from the corvette *Rhododendron* came a
report of smoke to the south-west, amplified ten minutes later into news
of a large warship steering across ahead of the convoy. The *Lützow* had
arrived punctually on the scene, an almost defenceless prey presented to
her and her three destroyers.

At this moment Fortune cast in her lot with the British. For the same
thick screen of snowfall which had saved *Onslow* and *Orwell* overtook
and blanketed the convoy. Captain Stange of the *Lützow*, mindful of his
instructions to risk nothing, decided to stand off to the eastward until the
weather should clear. With him he retained his three destroyers which
could, with a brief cannonade, have sent most of the 12 merchant ships to
the bottom before any aid could have reached them.

Kinloch, his hands already uncomfortably full with the difficult
situation to the control of which he had succeeded, was unwilling to
believe that a second enemy heavy ship could be on the scene. When no
signal came from the *Hyderabad*, which must have been even closer to the
reported ship, he decided that *Rhododendron* must have been mistaken.

There was, indeed, little that he could do about it in any case, with the
Hipper hovering menacingly to the north. He therefore kept his force
where it was, between *Hipper* and the convoy which, as things turned
out, left him well placed to fend off the *Lützow* also when the time came.
In the meanwhile he contented himself with ordering the *Achates* to
reinforce the crippled *Onslow* at the head of the convoy.

So for a few minutes silence settled down over the scene with all ships
shrouded in the softly falling snow. On a score of ships' bridges, warships
and merchantmen alike, captains and masters waited and wondered what
would be the situation to meet their eyes when the weather cleared.

At 1100 it suddenly did so. From the *Obedient*'s bridge Kinloch sighted
an enemy capital ship and two destroyers to the north-east and realized
that *Rhododendron*'s report had been all too true. It was the *Lützow*,
steering south-east to head off the convoy. Kinloch at once led off towards
her and then turned parallel to her course, laying smoke between the
enemy and the convoy. As both forces ran to the south-eastwards thus,
gunflashes from beyond the *Lützow* suddenly appeared. The *Hipper*
coming south at full speed after the convoy had sighted the *Achates* as

she cleared her own smoke screen, obeying the order to make for the head of the convoy.

Almost at once the *Achates* received a devastating hit which crippled her, reducing her speed to a painful 12 knots with a heavy list. Amidst a shambles in which more than 40 men had been killed, her captain, Lieutenant-Commander A. H. T. Johns, lay dead. Her second-in-command, Lieutenant Peyton-Jones, assuming command at this critical moment, realized that in her broken state the ship could do little good by trying to overtake the convoy. With superb disregard of danger he decided therefore to continue for as long as possible to interpose his smoke screen between his assailant and the convoy.

Turning to meet this more urgent threat, Kinloch had led his three ships round on to a north-westerly course and now, mercifully, the *Hipper*'s fire was shifted from *Achates* to *Obedient* which, with her companions, had opened fire on the *Hipper* at 1120. In a brief, fierce exchange of shots, *Obedient* was closely straddled, the near misses putting her wireless equipment out of action. But once again fear of the British destroyers' still unexpended torpedoes induced Kummetz to turn away to the northward. Well satisfied, Kinloch swung back towards the convoy to await the next attack.

Now came the crowning moment of this long-drawn, confused drama, played out amidst the drifting banks of smoke, the sweeping snowstorms, against a back-drop of grey sea and grey sky pricked with the intermittent flicker of gunflashes. As the *Hipper* turned north-west at 1125 to bring her guns to bear on the *Obedient*, her dim shape, which could at last be made out from the bridge of the approaching *Sheffield*, was seen in silhouette and identified. At a range of six-and-a-half miles, the British cruiser's guns opened on the unsuspecting German. Four times salvoes fell closely round her, scoring one damaging hit, before the *Hipper*'s crew recovered from their surprise and brought their own guns into action.

Making smoke to screen herself, the *Hipper* swung round in a full circle before steadying on an escape course to the south-westward, but not before two more hits from *Sheffield*'s 6-inch guns had smashed home. Kummetz lost not a moment in calling off his whole force. Already he had done what he had been so strictly enjoined not to do—allowed one of Hitler's precious ships to be damaged in action. A signal went out ordering all German forces to break off action and retire to the westward.

Now from the *Sheffield*, with *Jamaica* in line astern of her, were sighted two German destroyers emerging from the gloom some 4,000 yards ahead and well placed to deliver a dangerous torpedo attack. They were the *Eckholdt*, returning from sinking the *Bramble*, and the *Beitzen*. The former had mistaken the British cruisers for *Hipper* and *Lützow* whom she was trying to rejoin. Before the error was realized, the range was down to point blank. Every gun in the *Sheffield* from 6-inch down to pom-poms opened up on her a devastating hurricane of fire reducing her almost at once to a sinking, shattered wreck, dire vengeance for the little *Bramble*'s traceless doom.

The *Beitzen*, turning away at once under fire from the *Jamaica*, escaped unharmed. The brief action had, however, taken the British cruisers round on to a northerly course, causing them to lose touch for the time being with the *Hipper*, retiring at her best speed to the westward.

Meanwhile the convoy, shying away from the more immediate threat of the *Lützow*, had altered course to south and later to south-west. Captain Stange, maintaining his incredibly timid behaviour, thereupon turned back to the north-west to keep in touch with the *Hipper*. As he did so, however, some ships of the convoy came into sight clear of the smoke and at 1141 the *Lützow* opened fire on them. At once Kinloch's destroyers, where a feeling of great elation had swept through everyone at the welcome sight of the flashes of Bob Burnett's guns, turned to renew the covering of smoke and to engage as best they could the barely visible pocket-battleship.

For about five minutes the *Lützow*'s cannonade continued, during which one merchant ship was damaged. But then the destroyers' smoke once again drew a protective veil and firing ceased. But now once again to the north, *Hipper* and her two remaining destroyers came in sight steering to the south-west and therefore offering again an apparent threat to the convoy. The indomitable British destroyers turned with undiminished vigour to oppose them, their very appearance out of the murk causing the enemy to veer hastily away to the west.

But the *Lützow*, now intent only on rejoining the *Hipper* (an order which the irresolute Captain Stange had gladly accepted), had not yet been shaken off. Opening fire on the *Obdurate*, which was then leading the line of destroyers, she soon found the range and a near miss caused some damage. However, with all the enemy ships steering away again, the escorts' task was for the moment fulfilled and they could turn back to the convoy and out of range.

Their task was indeed fulfilled, for Kummetz had already repeated his order for all German forces to withdraw to the west. The convoy was saved. One further short and inconclusive encounter there was between *Sheffield* and *Jamaica* and the German heavy ships but by 1236 the enemy had fled far to the west and Bob Burnett, unwilling to get too far from the convoy, gave up the unnatural chase of two heavy ships and five destroyers by two light cruisers.

The short hours of daylight were already drawing to a close. As darkness fell, the escorts gathered once again round the convoy and course was resumed for Kola.

But one more heroic tragedy of that day was still being played out. Throughout all this time the *Achates*, though mortally wounded, had continued to steam slowly up and down screening the convoy with smoke.

Gradually her bows had sunk deeper in the water, her list had steadily increased. Peyton-Jones had scorned to call for assistance while every ship was fully occupied driving off the enemy. He had, however, asked the trawler *Ocean Gem* to stand by. When, at 1300, the list had increased to 60° and it was no longer possible to keep steam, the end was obviously near and Peyton-Jones called the trawler alongside to take off the 81 surviving members of the crew. This had hardly been done when at 1315 the gallant little *Achates* suddenly capsized, lingered thus for a while and then sank.

It was the end of a story worthy of the honoured name she bore. Twenty-six years before, the previous *Achates* had distinguished herself at the battle of Jutland where another and better-fought *Lützow* had been an opponent and, flying his flag in her had been the Kaiser's brave battle-cruiser admiral, Hipper.

Captain Sherbrooke was awarded the Victoria Cross for his leadership and gallantry in this action. It was a well-deserved honour, but no one will wish to dispute that there were others on that memorable day who shared in that supreme award which Sherbrooke received as leader of them all. It was fitting, too, that Kinloch's name, at the very time he was leading his destroyers so skilfully and bravely into action, appeared in the naval half-yearly list of promotions to Commander.

The convoy sailed on, arriving at its destination without further adventures, while the west-bound convoy RA51, benefiting by the enemy's preoccupation, reached Loch Ewe in safety, undetected and unassailed. The battle had been an insignificant action in its scope and in the record of damage inflicted on either side. But its effect on morale was supremely heartening from the British point of view, while in the field of grand strategy and the higher direction of the war, its results were to be crucial.

'That an enemy force of one pocket-battleship, one heavy cruiser and six destroyers, with all the advantages of surprise and concentration, should be held off for five hours by five destroyers and driven from the area by two 6-inch gun cruisers is most creditable and satisfactory,' said Admiral Tovey, with customary economy of praise. A wave of increased confidence went through the Royal Navy, at last emerging from the bitter years of defensive warfare with inadequate and insufficient weapons in its hands, a confidence which was to play its part in the decisive battle with the U-boats which was nearing its climax in the Atlantic.

The Germans had relearnt the old lesson that the personnel of a fleet kept mewed in harbour can never meet on equal terms a fleet used to keeping the seas constantly in all weathers; that a service with a tradition of attack regardless of loss, in defence of merchant convoys, will not be defeated by even a greatly superior force which is timorously handled. From Admiral Kummetz himself down to the destroyer commanders, irresolution, ineptitude and an astonishing lack of confidence were shown.

That the big ships should have held back was perhaps understandable in the light of Hitler's prohibition against taking any risks. But that the fast, well-armed destroyers should have rejected their opportunities to pounce on the convoy and its remaining close escort of two badly damaged destroyers and two corvettes is incomprehensible in spite of Kummetz's lame explanation, 'To make a destroyer attack was out of the question owing to possible confusion with the enemy. As the action developed I should no longer have been able to assemble our destroyers round *Hipper* before darkness and would thus have left her without destroyer protection at a difficult period.'

Only an admiral commanding a squadron seriously lacking in tactical experience at sea could speak in such terms. Only a fleet devoid of morale and self-confidence could behave in so poor-spirited a fashion. From the Germans themselves comes a lament at the sorry outcome of the action. In the War Diary of the *Lützow*, written as she made for Altenfiord, her foray into the Atlantic abandoned, is found the sad comment, 'As we withdrew from the scene of action the unsatisfactory feeling reigned that, in spite of the general position which was apparently favourable at first, we had not succeeded in getting at the convoy or scoring any successes at all.'

The German Navy and, through it, the German people as a whole, were to pay heavily for this shameful display. Hearing the news first from the BBC, Hitler gave way to paroxysms of rage at his navy's craven behaviour, ignoring the fact that his own restrictions on their acceptance of risks were largely to blame. Summoning Grand Admiral Raeder to his headquarters, for an hour and a half he stormed and raged at his unfortunate C-in-C, expressing his belief that the big ships of the German Navy were nothing but a waste of men and material. Raeder was to produce a detailed plan for the paying-off and laying-up of all of them. Palace politics took a hand as Göring gleefully seized the opportunity to point out how many Luftwaffe squadrons were tied up guarding the capital ships as they swung uselessly and endlessly round their anchors in harbour.

Raeder's pleas for a reprieve for the navy in the creation of which he had played the leading part could not shake Hitler's 'firm and unalterable resolve' to pay off the big ships. Rather than stay to supervise such an emasculation of the fleet, Raeder handed in his resignation and passed into retirement. In his place reigned the ambitious Dönitz, with his faith in the ability of his U-boats to win the naval war on their own.

Following the battle of 31 December 1942 round JW51B two more convoys each way were run, suffering almost negligible losses. This, and the evident paucity of enemy air strength in Norway led once again to proposals to continue the Arctic convoys through the summer. From

Moscow the pressure for more and more supplies to be sent never ceased. Had Hitler's 'irrevocable decision' to lay up the German surface fleet not been abandoned, convoys might well have been run in March. But Dönitz, once he had settled in Raeder's chair, had seen the wisdom of his predecessor's insistence on the maintenance of a balanced fleet. Being high in the Fuehrer's favour, he had been able to make such views prevail.

On 11 March 1943, the *Tirpitz* was sighted leaving Trondheim and it was not long before air reconnaissance revealed that not only she, but the battle-cruiser *Scharnhorst* and the *Lützow* were all in Altenfiord. Admiral Tovey at once told the Admiralty that under these circumstances he did not consider the continuance of Arctic convoys justifiable. Only by taking his battle fleet into the Barents Sea, which he had never considered a worth-while risk for the comparatively minor object of covering a convoy, could he give protection against such a formidable force.

The C-in-C's objections gained support from an unexpected direction. The Russians chose this moment when they were pressing with unabated vigour for a continuation of the convoys, to make it more difficult for us by obstructive tactics. Two British wireless stations in the Murmansk area were ordered to close down and the entry of the Royal Air Force ground staff for the squadrons to be based there was forbidden.

It was not difficult therefore for the Admiralty to persuade the Government, when the Battle of the Atlantic reached a critical stage in March, that all possible escort craft and destroyers would be better thrown into that decisive struggle than dissipated on operations of doubtful wisdom to fight Arctic convoys through.

Not all Home Fleet destroyers could be spared to reinforce the Western Approaches Command, of course. The Home Fleet still had to bar the way to the Atlantic against any sortie by the German surface fleet and a certain number of flotillas had to be retained. But none could be spared for Arctic convoys of which none was to be run for the next seven months.

14 *The U-Boats Mastered*

In the Atlantic the autumn of 1942 found the battle still in the balance. From the German point of view U-boat losses were by no means insupportable. Merchant ships were being sunk at a rate greater than they could be replaced. On the other hand, by far the greater number of these were still ships out of convoy, and the convoy system was constantly being extended. These convoys were receiving improved protection, not only by stronger, better equipped and trained escort groups but, at least as important, by the very long-range Liberator aircraft which were at last being supplied, in increasing numbers, to squadrons of Coastal Command.

That a climax in the Atlantic was approaching, was clear; Karl Dönitz was not optimistic as to its outcome. He quotes from his War Diary for 21 August 1942, that 'these ever-increasing difficulties which confront us in the conduct of the war can only lead, in the normal course of events, to high, and indeed intolerable losses'. To counter this situation, urgent measures to improve the U-boats' equipment and weapons were put in hand. A search receiver, which picked up radar signals and warned the submarine commander that he had been detected, was produced and fitted. The development of a submarine with a high submerged speed was pressed ahead urgently. A torpedo which could 'home' acoustically on to the sound waves emanating from a ship's propellers was being experimented with as a weapon with which to hit back at escorts. The search receiver was not greatly to affect the issue as it was designed to pick up the transmissions of the early, $1\frac{1}{2}$-metre radar and was useless against the 10-centimetre radar which, unknown to the Germans, was being increasingly fitted in warships and aircraft. The new-type submarine and the acoustic torpedo were eventually to be very effective, but the issue was in fact to be decided before they were ready to enter the battle.

Dönitz's chief preoccupation at this time was the increasing amount of air escort being given to the convoys and the shrinking gap in mid-

Atlantic, where alone his U-boat commanders could operate without the constant fear of being surprised on the surface by aircraft which now carried highly lethal depth-charges. How right he was in his foreboding will be seen later. Even at this time, the closing months of 1942, when the Allied very long-range aircraft, still numbering only 10, had not yet perfected their technique and skill, it was being demonstrated how the provision of air escort, even only for a few hours, at the crisis of a convoy battle could turn the scales. The onset of a concentrated submarine attack inevitably disorganized the defence as individual escorts became detached chasing or hunting an enemy or rescuing survivors. Air escort, by harassing other attackers working their way in through the depleted surface escort, disorganized and delayed the attack while the defensive screen was reforming.

Meanwhile, as the wild Atlantic winter set in with the steady succession of cyclones sweeping across the convoy routes, whipping up monstrous seas, the intensity of the conflict flagged. Although two U-boat groups were always on station in the North Atlantic and achieved some success, much of Dönitz's force was widely dispersed. At first, seeking soft spots in the Allied defence, submarines were sent to the Trinidad area, where the convoy system had been slow in establishing itself, and to the waters off South Africa, where anti-submarine forces were weak and ill-organized. In both areas the submarines had considerable success without serious losses.

Then came the Allied landings in North Africa early in November 1942. Taken completely by surprise, the German High Command had failed to order U-boat dispositions to intercept the huge troop and supply convoys which thronged the Atlantic in the last half of October. The submarine group which might have done so was fully occupied in decimating the weakly escorted convoy from Freetown mentioned earlier. Thus the far more important convoys for North Africa arrived unscathed. Too late, Dönitz directed his boats to the Moroccan coast, the Straits of Gibraltar and the western Mediterranean. They found no shortage of targets, but the convoys were strongly defended. In achieving a few successes the U-boats lost seven of their number in the space of a single week. The lesson was quickly absorbed by Admiral Dönitz. He correctly divined that to provide such strong escorts the Allies must have had to denude the regular trans-Atlantic convoys, the theatre in which Dönitz never ceased to insist that his boats could deliver a decisive blow. Ordered to send more boats into the Mediterranean to make good losses and to maintain 20 boats west of Gibraltar and Morocco, he protested that it 'would have disastrous effects on the war against shipping in the Atlantic, which U-boat Command has always regarded, and still regards, as the primary task of the U-boat arm.... This is a question of decisive importance.'

Dönitz's plea was disregarded. The year 1943 thus opened on a comparatively quiet note. During January only 15 ships were lost out of convoys in all areas. Yet indications emerged even from the few engagements, fought out amidst tempestuous weather, that the crisis of the battle was approaching. The Monthly Anti-Submarine Report for January, compiled in the Admiralty, contained the prophetic comment that 'a bolder and more reckless strategy is now characteristic of the enemy. The tempo is quickening and the critical phase of the U-boat war in the Atlantic cannot long be postponed.' In February, 34 ships in convoy were sunk, representing 14 per cent of the ships in convoys attacked. Against this, 12 submarines were sunk in the Atlantic, a rate of exchange which must have given Dönitz unpalatable food for thought.

Many convoys were crossing the Atlantic both ways in close succession without loss. Admiral Dönitz was disturbed and puzzled by the failure of his widespread patrol lines to find them. That it was partly owing to the Admiralty's uncannily accurate knowledge of his dispositions he knew. Able at this time to decipher British signals, he received the Admiralty's daily signalled 'U-boat Situation Report'. Thus he realized that to some extent the convoys were being diverted from danger areas by long-range control. What was not clear to him was that, in addition to this, the better-trained and equipped escort groups, in conjunction with air escort, by efficient use of H/F D/F and radar were often preventing the U-boats nearest to their route from closing to sight and report the convoy for which the wolf-pack was searching. A submarine forced to dive by a patrolling aircraft might be held down for the crucial period during which the convoy was passing through the patrol line. At other times accurate knowledge of the position of the shadowing submarine would enable an escort commander to detach a pair of ships to hunt it, keeping it down and perhaps destroying or damaging it. Meanwhile the convoy would make a drastic alteration of course, leaving the converging wolf-pack to cast vainly in the wrong direction. What, in fact, Dönitz could not know was that the escort forces were reaching a state of efficiency such as his wolf-packs had never previously experienced.

In November 1942, Admiral Sir Percy Noble had come to the end of his term of office as C-in-C, Western Approaches. In the period since 17 February 1941, when he had taken up the appointment, tremendous advances had been made, not simply in the strength of the forces he had been able to gather to throw into the battle but also in their organization, equipment and training. Under constant pressure to release his personnel, officers and men, experienced in the specialized form of warfare around the convoys, for the superficially more important tasks of manning the new ships going to swell the fleets in other theatres, he had yet succeeded in largely keeping together the trained escort groups which experience had shown to be essential. Bases for them had been built up from nothing at Liverpool, Greenock and Londonderry, where the storm-battered ships were taken in hand for maintenance and repairs between voyages, and their crews underwent the intensive training so necessary to keep them at a peak efficiency, with a knowledge of the latest weapons and tactics.

Thus when his successor, Admiral Sir Max Horton, took over, he found in his hand the weapon with which he was to win one of the most clear-cut and decisive victories of the war. Though Max Horton will be remembered as the victor in the Battle of the Atlantic, Percy Noble can justly claim to have been the architect of that victory. A school, known as the Western Approaches Tactical Unit, had been set up in Liverpool in February 1942 to give synthetic training to escort captains and group commanders in the tactics of convoy battles. It had done much to instil a common doctrine of convoy defence, together with the team spirit and initiative which were the mark of a well-trained escort group. In January 1943, to this theoretical type of training was added practical application at sea of the lessons learnt, by the institution of a school housed in Mr Tom Sopwith's steam yacht, serving the Royal Navy as HMS *Philante*, to which were attached a number of training submarines. Before setting out with their convoys, escort groups would be given intensive practice under the guidance, firstly of Captain A. J. Baker-Cresswell and later of Captain L. F. Durnford-Slater, both experienced escort commanders, and a staff of specialist officers.

In these ways the quality of the escort groups was raised and kept at a high level. Their numbers were at the same time being increased. Whereas up to this time there had been a permanent shortage of escorts, resulting in convoys being weakly defended, it now became possible not only to increase the size of escort groups from an average of five-and-a-half to seven-and-a-half for each convoy, and to allow time between voyages for their essential training, but also to begin the formation of Support Groups —reserve groups which could be sent to reinforce the regular escorts when a convoy was threatened or was passing through a concentration of U-boats. This had been for a long time an agreed requirement, but shortage of suitable ships and experienced captains had prevented its adoption.

The emergence of the necessary surplus came about largely as a result of the labours of scientists engaged on operational research under Professor P. M. S. Blackett, who had gone to the Admiralty in January 1942 after nine months' work for Coastal Command. In the autumn of that year, by statistical examination of the battle figures up to that time, Operational Research deduced a number of facts of which perhaps the most important, because it could not otherwise become apparent, was that, whereas the number of ships lost in a convoy battle depended, as might be expected, upon the number of U-boats attacking and the size of the escort, it was quite independent of the size of convoy. Thus by increasing the size of convoys from an average of 32 ships to 54, which reduced the *numbers* of convoys open to attack at any one time, losses could be lessened by 56 per cent.

The results of taking such a step would be cumulative. They would

firstly enable more escorts, air as well as surface, to be allocated to each
convoy. Statistics showed that by increasing the number of escorts from
six to nine, losses would be reduced by 25 per cent, whereas, if air escort
could be supplied for eight hours each day, the reduction would be no less
than 64 per cent. The apparent objection that the value of larger escort
would be offset by the larger area to be defended was met by the
elementary mathematical fact that, whereas the area of a convoy is
proportional to the square of its dimensions, the length of perimeter to be
occupied by the escorts is proportionate only to the length of the radius.
Secondly, an increase in the number of escorts might enable an escort
commander to station them in a double ring round the convoy thus
achieving a defence in depth. Furthermore, he would be able to go over to
the offensive more readily as he could afford to detach hunting sections
more frequently and allow them to stay away longer, without too
seriously reducing the screen round the convoy. Then, as has been said,
the economy of force, achieved by reducing the number of convoys to be
defended, provided a surplus of warships which could be formed into
Support Groups. These in themselves resulted in a further economy. For
provided that the convoy escort could be reinforced during the passage of
the most dangerous areas, a smaller escort could safely be given for the
remainder of the convoy's voyage. Thus Operational Research, too often
neglected or ignored, was responsible for a revolution in organization
which came about in March 1943 with an adjustment of the North
Atlantic convoy cycle, whereby fewer and larger convoys were sailed each
way.

The startling forecast of a 64 per cent reduction of losses in convoy
which would be achieved by a regular provision of air escort was not,
however, given its due weight. The limited number of Liberator aircraft
which were adaptable for the very long range work necessary for the
purpose, were coveted by Bomber Command of RAF, who had the
backing of the Air Staff in their belief that priority had to be given to
maximum bombing effort on Germany. Furthermore, a number of those
available to Coastal Command were employed on unproductive patrolling
of the U-boats' transit areas—between Iceland and the Hebrides and in
the Bay of Biscay. Consequently at the turn of the year there were still no
more than ten VLR Liberator aircraft able to operate in mid-Atlantic.
Yet this handful of aircraft was time and again to intervene decisively in
convoy battles, while the number of U-boats sunk by aircraft on the
'defensive' work of convoy escort was far in excess of those which were
destroyed by 'offensive' patrols. In the nine months from June 1942 to
March 1943, while aircraft operating as air escorts or in direct support of
convoys in the North Atlantic destroyed 22 enemy submarines, the 'Bay
Offensive', which involved 3,500 patrol hours each month and the loss of
some 100 aircraft, accounted for only seven.

After the withdrawal of the U-boat packs from the North Atlantic

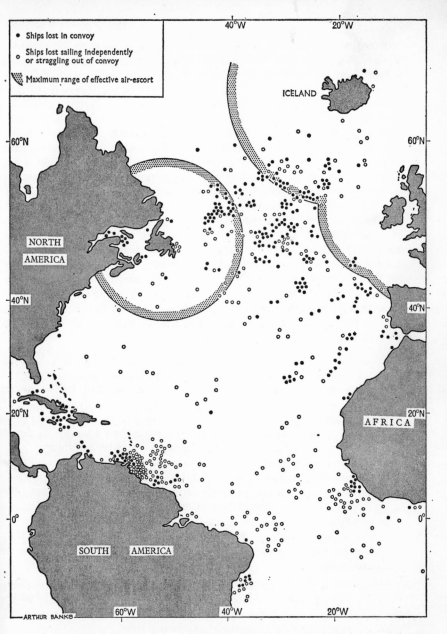

Merchant ship losses before closing of the 'Black Gap', 1 August 1942 – 31 May 1943

convoy routes at the end of May 1943 which, together with the presence
of aircraft-carriers with the convoys, released many of the shore-based
aircraft from escort duty, it was possible to saturate the Bay of Biscay
with aircraft. Even so it was only a tactical error by the enemy that led to
a temporary achievement of worthwhile results. The inability of the U-
boats to detect transmissions from 10-centimetre radar had led to a few of
them being caught on the surface at night by aircraft and sunk or badly
damaged. Dönitz therefore decided to increase the anti-aircraft armament
of his boats, which were then sailed in groups and ordered to fight it out
with the aircraft. These tactics were only momentarily successful. As
soon as they were appreciated, a technique to defeat them was adopted.
The first aircraft to come on the scene called up reinforcements. A
synchronized attack was then delivered—with devastating results. Thus
in June and July 1943 the Bay Offensive at last paid a worthwhile
dividend, 17 U-boats being sunk by aircraft in that area. When on 2
August 1943, the enemy reverted to independent sailings, surfacing only
for the minimum time to recharge batteries, submarine losses on passage
at once returned to the previous low rate, only four being destroyed in the
three months following. So far as the rival claims of Bomber Command
were concerned, Professor Blackett was able to show, as he recorded in
an article in *Brassey's Annual* for 1953:

> From the figures on the effectiveness of air cover, it could be calculated
> that a long-range Liberator operating from Iceland and escorting the
> convoys in the middle of the Atlantic *saved* at least half a dozen
> merchant ships in its service lifetime of some thirty flying sorties. If
> used for bombing Berlin, the same aircraft in its service life would drop
> less than 100 tons of bombs and kill not more than a couple of dozen
> enemy men, women and children and destroy a number of houses.
>
> No one would dispute that the saving of six merchant ships and their
> crews and cargoes was of incomparably more value to the Allied war
> effort than the killing of some two dozen enemy civilians, the
> destruction of a number of houses and a certain very small effect on
> production.
>
> The difficulty was to get the figures believed. But believed they
> eventually were and more long-range aircraft were made available to
> Coastal Command.

Nevertheless the Prime Minister's Anti-U-Boat Committee, examining
the claims of the various contestants, achieved only a compromise which
by March 1943 raised the number of VLR aircraft from ten to 40,
allowing about 13 to be operational at any one time.

It was in March 1943 that an escort aircraft carrier, the USS *Bogue*,
made its first appearance with a trans-Atlantic convoy. British ships of
this type had been operating for some time; but, though they were
intended to give convoys the continuous anti-submarine air escort which

experience was soon to prove would give them almost complete immunity from submarine attack, they had at first been diverted to take part in the North African landings. There they had performed valuable service in providing fighter cover for the fleet until fighters of the Royal Air Force were able to establish themselves on airfields ashore. It was not to be until April 1943, therefore, that these ships were able to take up their predestined role and supply one of the most important ingredients of the victory about to be won. Similarly it was not until April that the advantages accruing from the changes in the convoy cycle were to be fully enjoyed, particularly in the shape of Support Groups. One of these was to be made up of an escort carrier and three destroyers and was to prove its great worth immediately.

Nevertheless, March 1943 opened with brighter prospects in Allied view than ever before in the long-drawn Battle of the Atlantic. The majority of escort groups were imbued with a well-founded confidence that they were a match for the wolf-packs. Yet this month was in fact to prove to be one of the most disastrous of the war in terms of merchant shipping lost. It was the dark hour before the dawn. In the first ten days of March, 41 ships were lost, world-wide; 56 more were to be lost in the next ten days. These figures alone were not enough to indicate catastrophe. Nor was the fact that nearly two-thirds of this number were sunk in convoy; for, in fact, during March the submarines, swarming in unprecedented numbers, only sank 11 per cent of the ships in the convoys they attacked, a not insufferable loss rate.

It was two other factors which caused alarm to rise to the level of crisis. Three homeward-bound convoys, set upon by large concentrations of U-boats, lost no less than 34 of their number, at a cost to the enemy of only one submarine. Also only six of the enemy were destroyed by air or surface escorts round the convoys during the whole month. Thus, while the U-boats were accounting for 12 merchant ships for every one of their number destroyed, there seemed to be evidence that convoy defence was helpless against really massive concentrations of attackers. The first of these convoys to suffer was the slow, homeward-bound SC121. It was beset by every form of foul weather. A gale of wind, raising towering seas and driving a swirling blanket of snow before it in which the convoy became scattered, was followed by fog which made its reassembly slow and difficult. Seventeen U-boats had doggedly pursued it through the storm. Some fell upon the stragglers and picked them off one by one. Others were able to get through the disorganized defence and sink more from the main body.

Some indications of how the U-boats were able to range freely amongst the ships of the convoy is given by the account of the master of the freighter *Kingswood*, Captain R. Coates, who describes how, in the darkness and the gale, as he peered anxiously out from his bridge, his eye was caught by what seemed to be a particularly heavy breaking sea on his port bow. Then he saw that the white flurry was travelling with some speed towards him. 'It's a torpedo', he shouted to the mate standing beside him. But almost at once he realized that he was in fact looking at the wash of a submarine travelling at high speed on the surface. He ran to the telegraph and gave a double ring, calling for utmost emergency speed and steered to ram. 'I really felt we could not miss,' he recorded.

Collision seemed inevitable. About this time I heard the U-boat's engine and a voice in the distance. I was sort of hanging on waiting for the crash when I saw the submarine's wake curling round—the voice I had heard must have been the U-boat's commander shouting, 'Hard a port' in German. The submarine's wake curled right under my stem— how its tail missed us I still do not know.

The ship's 4-inch gun and machine guns let fly at the conning-tower but the submarine vanished quickly into the night to seek other victims.

Thirteen ships were sent to the bottom from SC121 without loss to the attackers. Yet, at about the same time, another group of U-boats, falling in with the east-bound convoy from Halifax, HX228, meeting a better organized and more resolute defence, lost two of their number while sinking only four of the convoy and a destroyer. The destroyer *Harvester* was commanded by Commander A. A. Tait, senior officer of a group of British, Polish and Free French escorts, one of the groups which had reached a high state of efficiency under their experienced leader. Running down a radar contact, Tait sighted *U444* on the surface and rammed her. This usually most effective and certain way of destroying a submarine had its dangers, however. As the *Harvester* drove through and over, the submarine scraped and bumped its way along the destroyer's keel and became wedged under her propellers. The two vessels lay locked in this way for a time, and, by the time the U-boat finally broke free, *Harvester*'s propellers and shafts had suffered so much damage that she was reduced to a slow crawl on one engine.

The French corvette *Aconit*, coming to her leader's help, found *U444* still miraculously afloat and delivered the *coup de grâce* by ramming her again. Meanwhile, Tait, in spite of *Harvester*'s heavy damage, had rescued 50 survivors from one of the sunken merchant ships before limping slowly on. *Aconit* was ordered away to rejoin the convoy; but soon after daylight *Harvester*'s propeller shaft cracked, bringing her to a standstill. Called back again to *Harvester*'s aid, *Aconit* was still some distance away when a column of smoke on the horizon and a last signal told Lieutenant Levasseur, her captain, that the helpless and immobilized destroyer had been torpedoed. Hurrying to the rescue, *Aconit* was rewarded with an asdic contact. Depth-charges brought a U-boat to the surface and once again Levasseur had the satisfaction of ramming and sinking one of the enemy—a satisfaction deepened by the discovery that his victim, *U432*, had been responsible for torpedoing the *Harvester*. Loss of life from *Harvester* was tragically heavy, and included her captain. But this drawn battle had again showed that a first-class escort group could hold the wolf-packs at bay and make them pay heavily for any successes.

Besides the two submarines destroyed, at least one other very nearly suffered the same fate. *U121* was responsible for two of the merchant ships sunk. One of them, carrying explosives, blew up. Debris crashed against the U-boat's periscope, damaging it. While thus blinded, Korvetten-Kapitän Trojer, the submarine's captain, heard the thrash of a destroyer's propeller. As he took his boat down in a crash dive, depth-charges exploded around, causing the conning-tower hatch to leak, letting in a mass of water. *U121* escaped destruction by going deep but it was a very narrow escape.

The other side of the coin was to be seen when the next two homeward convoys, HX229 and SC122, met the U-boat swarm in mid-Atlantic. The former, with a weak and ill-assorted escort gathered together at random, was set upon by 38 U-boats where no air escort could be given. No rescue ship having been included in the convoy, the escort was at once faced, when the attack developed, with the bitter choice between leaving the survivors from torpedoed ships to their fate or disorganizing and weakening the already quite inadequate defence. The dilemma was an insoluble one and, in the course of two days, 13 ships of the convoy were sent to the bottom.

HX229 had meanwhile been overhauling the slow SC122. As the two convoys drew close to each other the attack was extended to them both. SC122 had a regular group of reasonable strength but it was swamped by the weight of the attack and lost eight ships. Liberator aircraft from Iceland joined the defence on the second day, and the resultant harassment of the U-boats, culminating in the destruction of one of them, finally brought the battle to a close. Although Admiral Dönitz records that 'nearly all the other boats suffered from depth-charges or bombs and two were severely damaged', it was a clear victory for the attackers.

As the mounting tale of convoy losses reached the Admiralty something approaching dismay or even despair developed. Voices were raised questioning whether the virtue had gone out of the convoy system. To quote from Captain Roskill's official history, *The War at Sea*, the Naval Staff were later to record that 'the Germans never came so near to disrupting communications between the New World and the Old as in the first 20 days of March 1943', and 'it appeared possible that we should not be able to continue [to regard] convoy as an effective form of defence'. This was tantamount to an admission of defeat. For there was no possible alternative, as a glance at the record of ships sailed independently made abundantly clear. Disastrous as were the stories of a few of the trans-Atlantic convoys at this time, many others were being brought or fought through relatively unscathed, so that the total losses represented no more than 2.5 per cent of the ships sailed in convoy. Even considering the convoys which were attacked, the losses were only 11 per cent. Independently sailing ships, on the other hand, suffered a loss rate of more than double that of convoys, while independents which came under actual attack lost no less than 80 per cent of their number.

In fact a set-back on one part of the battlefield was being unreasonably looked upon as a herald of general defeat. The crisis passed. As March gave way to April the escort forces were gathering their strength to deliver the knock-out blow.

March 1943, with its grim tale of convoy losses, shook the Admiralty's confidence in the future prospects of the Battle of the Atlantic. And indeed from the comparatively detached viewpoint of Whitehall this was perhaps natural. Those closer to the fighting, however, such as the C-in-C, Western Approaches, and his staff at Liverpool, the captains commanding the escort bases and the escort commanders themselves were by no means so dismayed. They were better able to appreciate the results to be expected from the imminent arrival on the scene of the special Support Groups, of the escort carriers which provided continuous, direct air escort and of increased numbers of shore-based, long-range aircraft. Even without these reinforcements, some of the escort groups, particularly those with a high proportion of destroyers in their composition, were demonstrating on trip after trip, that, by efficient use of the equipment and weapons now available, even powerful concentrations of U-boats could be held off while the convoys passed on their way unscathed or with very minor losses.

Already, before the month of March was out, the tide of battle had begun to turn. Following their success in mauling HX229 and SC122, as related previously, fresh U-boat packs were concentrated to intercept the next two homeward-bound convoys. Though submarine patrol lines were correctly stationed and both convoys were intercepted, they were shepherded safely through without loss. First of all, the U-boat making initial contact was detected by H/F D/F, pounced upon, put down and held down so that the wolf-packs, deprived of a shadower to guide them to their prey, were prevented or delayed from concentrating round them; then, a Support Group was brought in to reinforce the convoy escorts through the danger area; and finally, as the convoys came within range of air escort from Iceland, the long-range Liberators so harassed the pursuing U-boats that they were forced to withdraw, empty-handed. This combination of efficient use of the improved weapons available to the convoy escorts—H/F D/F, 10-centimetre radar and the latest asdic sets—of reinforcement in the danger area and of close cooperation with shore-based aircraft, now also fitted with 10-centimetre radar, was the classic form of defence at last perfected and was the basis on which victory was to be won. It was to be made more certain by the imminent

60 A cruiser punches into heavy seas

ARCTIC WEATHER

61 An insidious threat—ice accumulation on upper works

62 RAF Hudson of Coastal Command   63 RAF Liberator of Coastal Command

AIRCRAFT V. U-BOAT

64 U-boat under depth-charge attack from   65 U-boat surrenders to RAF Hudson
the air   aircraft

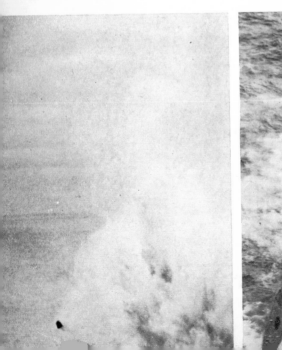

addition of the escort aircraft carrier which would abolish the mid-Atlantic gap in air cover.

The turn of the tide of battle was somewhat obscured at this time, however, by conflicting cross-currents. During the last 11 days of March only 15 ships were lost in the North Atlantic compared with the dreadful total of 107 during the previous three weeks; but this period was one of tempestuous weather in which the storms normal in that time of year rose to the intensity of hurricanes. Merchantmen, escorts and submarines were alike too absorbed in a struggle for survival to give much thought for the enemy. Whether eastward-bound, deeply laden and with deck cargoes of landing-craft, lorries or tanks, which often made them dangerously crank, or west-bound in ballast, riding high, with their screws thrashing on the surface, the merchant ships were forced to heave-to and concentrate on their own safety. Convoys became widely scattered. The Commodore's ship of one of them capsized and was lost with all hands. The little ships of the escort force climbed the steep sides of the monstrous waves and hung momentarily poised on their crests with bow and stern out of water before plunging dizzily down the farther slopes. For hour after hour this process repeated itself. Damage mounted, hull plates splitting, rivets shaking loose, boats being smashed, men swept overboard and the delicate electric and electronic anti-submarine devices put out of order. The German submarines, though they had proved their staunchness and sea-keeping qualities in three North Atlantic winters, found themselves similarly reduced to a single-minded struggle with the elements. Admiral Dönitz quotes from the log of *U260* which in these conditions came across a merchant ship running before the gale and attempted to attack her:

2200. Pursuit broken off. While trying to run before the storm at full speed, the boat dived twice. By blowing tanks, putting my helm hard over and reducing speed I managed to hold her reasonably well on the surface. To remain on the bridge was impossible. Within half an hour the captain and the watch were half-drowned. Five tons of water poured into the boat in no time through the conning-tower hatch, the voicepipe and the diesel ventilating shaft.... With a heavy heart I abandoned the chase.

Thus, for a time both sides turned to face a common enemy. The new trend in the battle was also obscured during the last days of March and the first half of April 1943 by a temporary reduction in the number of U-boats at sea. Those which had taken part in the big battles of mid-March had returned to base to re-arm and re-fuel. Only one group was stationed at the beginning of April on the trans-Atlantic routes. This intercepted HX231 which was escorted by one of the 'First Division' teams, led by Commander Peter Gretton. The reception awaiting any wolf-pack which accepted combat with a well-escorted convoy was demonstrated. Though

L

handicapped by having only one destroyer, only one ship fitted with H/F D/F and by the absence of a rescue ship, Gretton's team, helped by good cooperation by Liberator aircraft from Iceland, beat off a concentrated attack, losing only three ships at a cost to the enemy of two of his submarines and others severely damaged, a rate of exchange the Germans could by no means afford. Unfortunately this satisfactory result was obscured by the loss of three more ships which had belonged to the convoy. One had dropped behind with engine trouble, while two foreign ships, a Dutchman and a Swede, broke convoy at the first attack and paid the inevitable penalty.

Yet even such a repulse of the wolf-packs, satisfactory as it seemed in a cold, statistical light, had to be paid for in harsh, human tragedy of the kind which runs through the whole story of the Battle of the Atlantic. Lack of space in a book of this kind and a necessary avoidance of repetitive narrative prevents much reference to it; but it should not be forgotten. The absence of a rescue ship placed the escort commander in an agonizing dilemma. It was familiar to all engaged in convoy defence. Commander Gretton has described it on this occasion:

> The unfortunate ship which had been hit was loaded with iron ore and sank within two minutes. Searching for the U-boat, we passed survivors who were scattered in the icy water, each with his red light burning. Some were on rafts, some were alone, but no boats had survived. It is my most painful memory of the war that we had to shout encouragement, knowing well that it was unlikely that they would ever be picked up.
>
> It was an appalling decision to have to make, to stop or go on: but by leaving her place in the search, the ship would leave a gap through which more attacks could be made and more men drowned. We had to go on. After a search plan had been completed I sent back the *Pink* to look for survivors but she failed to find them and after four hours' search I had to recall her to her station. . . .
>
> I could not stop thinking of the men in the water astern and only after the report of the next attack had come in was I able to achieve proper concentration again.

Meanwhile the temporary U-boat vacuum in the North Atlantic was being rapidly filled by a stream of fresh U-boats from Germany and from the Biscay bases. No less than 98 sailed during the month. Dönitz could no longer complain that his forces were being diverted from the main target. But their lack of success was a warning of what was to come.

Gathering round HX233, escorted by the mixed American and British group led by Commander Paul Heinemann, USN, in the Coastguard Cutter *Spencer*, they succeeded in torpedoing only one ship, while *U176* was destroyed by the *Spencer*'s depth-charges in return. This convoy had taken a route more southerly than usual and operations took place in calm, blue weather. Dönitz ascribed the lack of success to these conditions. The U-boat Command War Diary for 18 April 1943 commented, 'Meagre success, achieved generally, at the cost of heavy losses, renders operations in these areas inadvisable.' There was more to it than that, however. His boats, moved north and stationed athwart the route of the slow outward-bound convoys ONS3 and ONS4, found themselves unable to build up any concentration against them. ONS4 was supported by HMS *Biter*, the first British escort carrier to operate on the trans-Atlantic routes. The close escort, one of the most experienced British groups, led by the destroyer *Hesperus*, shepherded the convoy unharmed through the first patrol line encountered, sinking *U191*, the boat which made contact. The second patrol line was similarly thrust through. The boat which made contact was pin-pointed by H/F D/F from the close escort, attacked and driven down by aircraft from the *Biter* and then destroyed by the *Pathfinder*, one of the carrier's screen. The convoy sailed on, more in peril from the swarm of icebergs through which it was routed than from the frustrated enemy.

The last week in April, indeed, constituted the first real signs that the tide of victory had set in the Allies' favour in the Battle of the Atlantic, five U-boats being destroyed round the convoys for almost negligible loss of merchant ships. Before defeat could be turned into rout, however, one final destructive clash had to be experienced. It took place around convoy ONS5 escorted by Peter Gretton's group. It was a small convoy of about 40 ships, mostly elderly tramps of uncertain reliability and speeds—for every ship which floated was being pressed into Atlantic service at this time, to replace the heavy losses of the last 12 months and to speed the build-up in England of vast quantities of munitions and equipment being gathered for the great enterprise of Normandy. The ocean escort, which formed up round the convoy as it passed through the North Channel on 22 April 1943, comprised Gretton's own ship, the destroyer *Duncan*, the frigate *Tay*, one of a new class of escorts, and four corvettes, *Sunflower*, *Loosestrife*, *Snowflake* and *Pink*. Another destroyer, the *Vidette*, had gone ahead to Iceland to escort three ships to join the convoy. ONS5 went through almost every experience possible for an Atlantic convoy. In the course of them it progressed through harsh tribulation to eventual triumph. Its story is worth telling for that reason as well as because it has been judged the turning-point in the Battle of the Atlantic.

The northerly route the convoy had been given, which would take it up into the region of almost constant gales, as well as the venerable appearance and light loading of many of its ships, gave warning to the escort commander of difficulties ahead. Heavy weather would reduce the sluggish pace to a crawl. Some ships would be brought to a standstill, others would fall out of control. It was not long before forebodings became fact. As the convoy plugged its way north-westward, the corvettes were kept busy shepherding stray sheep back into the fold and escorting stragglers who were trying to catch up the main body. During one wild night of tempest, two ships collided and one of them was so damaged that she had to be detached to Iceland for repairs. The convoy commodore, Captain J. Brooks, RNR, could at one time count no less than eight of his ships showing the 'two red lights vertical' of a ship not under control.

Nevertheless, by the 27th, when the gale at last took off somewhat, only the damaged ship and one other which had been detached as too slow were missing. The improvement in the weather also eased Gretton's mind for the time being with regard to that constant anxiety of a sea commander, fuel for his destroyers. The *Duncan* had not been modified like other old destroyers, including the *Vidette*, to carry extra oil fuel by the removal of one boiler. Her endurance was very inadequate for long convoy voyages. Unless she could replenish from time to time from the specially fitted tanker she would be unable to remain with the convoy much beyond the longitude of Iceland. Now, however, both the *Duncan* and the *Vidette*, which had joined with the Iceland contingent the day before, were able to refill their oil tanks.

It was none too soon. Early on 28 April the most northerly of a U-boat group, widely spread on a patrol line running north and south across the convoy routes, caught sight of the convoy. A report was at once on the air to U-boat Command, whence orders sending the whole U-boat pack in pursuit were sent out. Picked up by the H/F D/F operators in the escorts it also served to warn them that the convoy was being shadowed. The brief easement of the weather had passed. Low cloud scudding across a stormy sea prevented any air escort operating. The surface escorts could steam at only moderate speeds which reduced their ability to break up or scare away the gathering pack. However, shortly before dark, taking *Duncan* and *Tay* out in the direction in which a transmission had been detected, Gretton sighted the cloud of spray thrown up by a U-boat travelling on the surface. In the prevailing conditions the asdic failed to make contact with the submarine after it had dived, but *Tay* was left to keep it down until dark.

The threat to the convoy had been quickly appreciated at Western Approaches Headquarters. RAF Coastal Command were called upon for help. Catalina flying-boats from Iceland were despatched. South of the convoy they caught three U-boats heading northwards on the surface. Swooping to the attack they forced them to dive, putting them out of the chase and seriously damaging one of them. Nevertheless, the night which followed was one of repeated efforts by several other U-boats to insinuate their way through the screen of escorts. Six times radar contact was made with them, by the *Duncan* on four separate occasions and once each by *Sunflower* and *Snowflake*. On each occasion the submarine was chased and forced to dive, but in the rising gale and heavy seas, with the ships rolling gunwales under, decks awash and spray flying mast-high, the encounters were inconclusive.

The attempted attacks were foiled. Dawn revealed an undepleted convoy thrusting slowly westwards into steep seas under a lowering grey sky. The wolf-pack, discouraged by the night's events, had given up the chase for the time being and, on orders from U-boat Command, had set off south-westwards to join another group lying in wait far ahead on the convoy's expected route—all except one submarine. This one had attained a good position ahead and, lying submerged, was waiting for his targets to approach. In spite of the difficult weather and the tumbled sea, her commander succeeded in delivering an attack, torpedoing one ship. The escorts at once carried out the pre-arranged search plan for such an occasion but without success. The loss was a mortifying experience after the effective defence put up during the night. However, it was the only one to result from this first encounter with the wolf-pack. For the next five days it was the weather which constituted the enemy to be faced as the wind rose steadily. By the evening of 30 April it was blowing a full gale from the south-west. The 'merry month of May' opened for the convoy in winds of hurricane force and mountainous seas whose crests were whipped off in a solid sheet of spray, reducing visibility to a few hundred yards. The low-powered, lightly loaded tramp steamers of the convoy, riding high out of the water, forced to heave to, could concentrate only on their own safety, while the convoy began to disintegrate. Two ships ran for shelter to Iceland. The remainder became widely scattered. Not until 2 May did the wind take off sufficiently for the escorts, aided by a Liberator aircraft which had come out from Iceland, to set about gathering their flock together again. It was none too soon. For ahead, stretching across the route, was the edge of a great field of icebergs which come drifting south from the Arctic at this time of year. The merchantmen were concentrated into three groups: 20 ships with the commodore forming the main body, ten more being brought to join it under escort of the *Tay*, while some 50 miles astern were six more ships with the *Pink*.

An equally serious aspect of the tumultuous weather conditions and, in the event, of greater consequence, was the impossibility of refuelling destroyers. The *Oribi*, of the 3rd Support Group, had joined the escort three days earlier and, in a brief easement of the weather on 30 April, had been able to top up her tanks. But before others of the escort could do the same the gale had descended again. By 3 May, the *Duncan* was critically short of fuel and in the afternoon of that day had to leave the convoy and make directly for St John's, Newfoundland, where she arrived with tanks almost empty. The duty of Senior Officer of the Escort devolved upon the captain of the *Tay*, Lieutenant-Commander R. E. Sherwood, RNR. His detached group of merchantmen had by this time joined the main body, increasing its number to 30. *Pink* and her stragglers were still far behind.

Meanwhile the convoy was heading for the heavy concentration of U-boats spread across the route. The Admiralty's U-boat tracking organization had made the C-in-C, Western Approaches well aware of the impending threat. A diversion to avoid it was impossible. Reinforcement for the escort in the shape of four more destroyers of the 3rd Support Group, *Offa, Penn, Panther* and *Impulsive*, had joined during 2 May. But by 4 May *Penn, Panther* and *Impulsive* had also reached the end of their endurance and were forced to seek harbour to refuel. Hardly had they gone, leaving the escort of the main body consisting of three destroyers and four corvettes, when the first indications of the enemy's approach were received by the H/F D/F operators. From every direction the wolves were gathering. First blood was to be to the defence, however. The convoy was by now within range of air cover from Newfoundland. Though fog over the air bases reduced the air effort to a few sorties only, a Canso aircraft of the Royal Canadian Air Force surprised *U630* on the surface that evening and despatched it with a well-placed 'stick' of depth-charges.

During the day, with the weather at last calming down, the U-boats, more than 30 of them, gathered round. As night fell, they moved in to the attack. The first to suffer was a straggler, six miles astern of the main body. For the next 24 hours attack after attack succeeded in getting through, and, by the evening of 5 May, 11 ships of the convoy had been sent to the bottom. Though the escorts had again and again detected and driven off attackers, the defence was swamped by sheer numbers. The situation by the evening of the 5th seemed indeed desperate. The senior officer of the 3rd Support Group can be excused for recording at the time that 'the convoy seemed doomed to certain annihilation'. But in fact the dogged, unwearying defence was about to turn the tables. It was aided by the descent of the fog which so often follows an Atlantic storm. Already two U-boats had been sunk. The first had been *U630* as recorded above. Then, during the forenoon of the 5th, the corvette *Pink*, commanded by Lieutenant Robert Atkinson, RNR, still shepherding her little group of stragglers, gained asdic contact with a U-boat shaping up for an attack. The *Pink*'s depth-charges pounded the submarine, later identified as *U192*, to destruction.

The U-boat losses were already such as to make the result so far no better for the enemy than a drawn battle. As the fog settled down the escorts' advantage by reason of their excellent radar became paramount. They took full advantage of it. As Lieutenant-Commander Sherwood reported later, 'All ships showed dash and initiative. No ship required to be told what to do and signals were distinguished both by their brevity and wit.' These were the marks of the well-trained escort group. No less than 24 attempts to penetrate the defensive screen during the night of 5-6 May were defeated. In the course of these encounters, *U638*, caught on the surface by the corvette *Loosestrife*, Lieutenant Stonehouse, RNR, was blown up by a pattern of depth-charges as she was diving. The *Vidette*, commanded by Lieutenant Raymond Hart, detecting a submerged submarine, delivered an attack with her Hedgehog. It was later established that the explosions which followed marked the destruction of *U125*. Two more submarines were to follow her before dawn. Lieutenant-Commander J. C. A. Ingram of the *Oribi*, surprising *U531* in the fog, rammed and cut her down. Finally, Commander Godfrey Brewer of the *Pelican*, bringing his 1st Support Group to reinforce the convoy escort, depth-charged *U438* to destruction.

With daylight on 6 May the battle round ONS5 came to an end as the shaken and demoralized survivors of the U-boat pack withdrew. As many as 60 U-boats in all had been directed to join the attack. Twelve merchant ships had been sunk at the cost to the enemy of six of their number destroyed by surface and air escorts. Two others, running through the night in chase, had collided and gone down. A number of others had narrowly escaped destruction and been badly damaged. Such an exchange, as Admiral Dönitz has recorded, constituted a defeat for the U-boats. As the losses became known and the stories of survivors, surprised on the surface again and again and barely escaping destruction, spread through the U-boat Command, morale plunged. Re-directed to the homeward-bound convoys HX237 and SC129, the U-boats displayed a marked reluctance to move in to attack.

HX237 was strongly escorted, having the inestimable benefit of continuous air escort by aircraft from *Biter* as well as of shore-based aircraft. Three ships were lost from the convoy but at the cost of three U-boats. SC129, on the other hand, was beset by a strong group of submarines, losing two merchant ships at the outset. Thereafter, however, the surface escort of two destroyers and four corvettes had no difficulty in keeping the attackers at bay, *U186* being sunk by the destroyer *Hesperus* and several others being severely damaged. Commenting on this action, Dönitz quotes from his War Diary:

No less than 11 of the boats in contact with the convoy were detected and driven off while it was still light. This is a very high percentage. It is obvious that the enemy must have detected all the boats in contact with astonishing certainty.... Since detection on this scale and with such promptitude has hitherto been unknown, the possibility that the enemy is using a new and efficient type of locating device cannot be ruled out.

It was true, of course, that the existence of an efficient, ship-borne H/F D/F was not known to the Germans. The submarines consequently had no inhibitions about use of radio and each transmission was apt to result in the appearance from over the horizon of an aircraft or a surface escort accurately directed on to the transmitter. On the other hand when, as in the case of SC129, it was usually only a 'Flower'-class corvette which could be spared for the purpose, the U-boats with their higher turn of speed had little to fear. In days gone by they would have treated it with contempt. But now the empty gesture of defiance by the escorts was enough to induce the enemy to 'throw in the sponge'. The moral superiority achieved by the escorts was unmistakable. The Monthly Anti-Submarine Report for April, compiled in the Admiralty, contained the prophetic pronouncement:

> Historians of this war are likely to single out the months of April and May 1943 as the critical period during which strength began to ebb away from the German U-boat offensive, not because of the low figure of shipping sunk, not because of the satisfactorily high number of U-boats destroyed, but because for the first time U-boats failed to press home attacks on convoys when favourably placed to do so.

The next homeward convoy to encounter the U-boat packs, SC130, made the picture even clearer. The escort was again Commander Gretton's group. Flushed with their previous triumph, they went gaily and confidently into action. Not a ship of the convoy was sunk while no less than five U-boats were destroyed, two by surface escorts and three by escorting aircraft. In one of them died Dönitz's son. The final discomfiture of the U-boat packs took place round convoy HX239 where aircraft from the United States carrier *Bogue* and from HMS *Archer* drove off the submarines and sent two of them to the bottom on 23 May 1943. Though the fiercely fought battle round ONS5, previously described, has come to be recognized as the final turning-point in the Battle of the Atlantic, it was the almost total failure of the U-boats against the convoys immediately following which marked their decisive defeat. As Dönitz has written, 'The overwhelming superiority achieved by the enemy defence was finally proved beyond dispute in the operations against convoys SC130 and HX239.'

U-boat losses had indeed become a massacre. In the first 22 days of May no less than 31 had been destroyed. For it was not only round the convoys that they were now being sunk. Aircraft fitted with 10-centimetre radar had at last been allocated to the anti-submarine role in something approaching the numbers demanded by the Admiralty. For the first time the 'Bay Offensive' against submarines on passage to and from their bases on the French Atlantic coast had begun to show a reasonable return for the effort involved, six being sunk during May.

The reversal of fortune in the interval since the gloomy forebodings of the Admiralty in March was as complete as it was sudden. By the end of May, 41 U-boats had been sunk during the month. Of these, 14 had fallen to the convoy surface escorts, 11 to air escorts. By 24 May, Karl Dönitz had accepted defeat. His U-boats were withdrawn from the North Atlantic convoy routes.

From June 1943 onwards, merchant ships were being built in Allied

shipyards at a rate much in excess of the losses from all causes, while
U-boats led a harried and haunted existence wherever they operated.
Support Groups of escort ships and 'Hunter-Killer' Groups, mostly
American, each comprising an aircraft carrier and a screen of destroyers
and operating in support of convoys, took such a toll that it became rare
for a U-boat to survive more than two patrols.

Contemplating the failure of his hopes, Dönitz says,

> Again and again we debated most earnestly whether a continuation of
> the U-boat campaign was justified in the face of these heavy losses, or
> whether recourse would have to be made to some other means. But in
> view of the vast enemy forces which our U-boats were tying down, we
> came again and again to the same conclusion: 'The U-boat campaign
> must be continued with the forces available. Losses, which bear no
> relation to the success achieved, must be accepted, bitter though they
> are.'

Though German submarines were to carry on the war against Allied
shipping to the last day and hour of the war in other parts of the oceans,
never again were they seriously to threaten the vital life-line between
Europe and America. Armed with the acoustic homing torpedo they were
to return briefly to the North Atlantic, only to be soundly beaten once
again. Fitted with the 'schnorkel' breathing tube which enabled them to
recharge their batteries while remaining submerged, they tried to regain in
inshore waters the initiative they had lost in the ocean spaces. They
failed.

May 24 1943, therefore, marks the day on which the Battle of the
Atlantic was won, a complete and decisive victory. To quote from
Captain Roskill's Official History: 'After 45 months of unceasing battle
of a more exacting and arduous nature than posterity may easily realize,
our convoy escorts had won the triumph they so richly merited.'

15 *The Convoy Route Secured*

As the summer of 1943 wore on and the newly-won immunity of the trans-Atlantic convoys made the reinforcement of the Western Approaches no longer necessary, the Home Fleet flotillas began to return to Scapa and the berths in Gutta Sound were once again filled. By the beginning of autumn sufficient destroyers had asembled to resume the Kola Run. But the new C-in-C, Sir Bruce Fraser, who had relieved Admiral Tovey in May, was no more inclined than his predecessor to expose the Arctic convoys to the threat of the three German capital ships still lying in Altenfiord.

This threat was about to be drastically reduced, however. Efforts to eliminate that of the *Tirpitz* had been made at intervals ever since January 1942 when RAF bombers had made their first attack on her where she lay in a fiord near Trondheim. They had achieved nothing; nor did subsequent and heavier attacks in March and April of that year.

After her summer sojourn in the far North during which her presence had resulted in such disastrous consequences for convoy PQ17, she had returned to Trondheim for repairs to the numerous defects from which she was suffering. There, a gallant attempt on her had been made by Leif Larsen, the famous Norwegian resistance leader, who chugged into Trondheimfiord in the wholly innocent-seeming 55-foot Norwegian fishing boat *Arthur*, under the bottom of which were lashed two 'human torpedoes' or 'chariots'. Neither they nor the four men of their crews hidden behind a false bulkhead were detected by the German patrols which examined the *Arthur*. Only five miles remained to be covered to reach the *Tirpitz* when disaster struck. A squall swept down the fiord raising a steep short sea in which the *Arthur* rose and fell in jerky motion. The nose rings by which the chariots were secured snapped: both broke away and sank.

In March 1943 the *Tirpitz* had returned to the north, anchoring together with the *Scharnhorst* and *Lützow* in Kaafiord, the steep, narrow landward stretch of Altenfiord, near the North Cape. There she had lain idle throughout the summer. In September, no doubt to restore their crews' morale, *Tirpitz* and *Scharnhorst* were sent on a raid to Spitzbergen, their 15-inch and 11-inch guns being turned on the insignificant target represented by the huts of the Norwegian weather reporting station there. This was the last occasion when the *Tirpitz* put to sea in fighting trim. Even as she was expending her fury on the bleak landscape of Spitzbergen, a little force was assembling which was to put her out of action for the first time. It comprised the six midget submarines, *X5, 6, 7, 8, 9* and *10*. They were to be towed across the North Sea by six conventional submarines, and released off the Norwegian coast to make their way some 50 miles up the fiords to where the *Tirpitz* and, it was thought, *Scharnhorst* and *Lützow* lay in Kaafiord, the steep, narrow landward end of Altenfiord. Their weapons were two-ton charges of high explosive, one on each side, with delay-action fuses; three charges were intended to be released under the hull of the target ship.

In the event *Scharnhorst* and *Lützow* were found to have left. The *Tirpitz* was alone. Of the *X*-craft, two broke adrift on passage and were lost. A third developed a series of defects and, though she penetrated to within a few miles of the *Tirpitz*, was forced to give up the attempt when both compass and periscope retraction failed. After eight days of adventurous wandering she was recovered.

The three remaining boats pressed on to complete what Admiral Sir Max Horton, Britain's most renowned submariner, called 'this magnificent feat of arms'. With the handicap of an only partially effective periscope, *X6*, under the command of Lieutenant Donald Cameron, made its perilous way up Kaafiord in the half-light of early morning. Narrowly avoiding collisions, even passing between a destroyer and its mooring buoy on one occasion, she passed through the boat entrance of the net defences behind a picket-boat, and saw the gate hauled shut behind.

Now *X6*'s luck showed signs of running out. Grounding on the north shore of the netted enclosure she was forced to break surface for a brief moment, during which she was sighted from the *Tirpitz*. But she was not confidently identified, and it was not until she struck a submerged rock 80 yards from the battleship and was thrust fully to the surface that the alarm was given. By this time she was so close that none of the battleship's guns could depress enough to fire at her. Putting his little craft down again, Cameron went on, only to be caught again in an obstruction. On surfacing he found that he was close under the port bow of the *Tirpitz*. Amidst a hail of small-arms fire and hand-grenades he dropped *X6* astern until she was abreast the rearmost of the battleship's two forward turrets. There he released his two charges, set his craft to sink and gave the order to 'Bail out'.

X6's crew were picked up by a German picket-boat and taken on board the *Tirpitz*. Meanwhile *X7*, commanded by Lieutenant Place, had tried to dive under the defensive nets, but had been entangled in them at a depth of 75 feet. For the next 20 minutes Place was in and out of nets, frantically manoeuvring but getting ever closer to his objective till at 0730, a quarter of an hour after *X6*, *X7* ran against the *Tirtpitz*'s side. Dropping one charge roughly where Cameron had laid his, he then dropped back, placed his other under the after turrets and turned to escape.

Eight tons of explosive were now laid, waiting for the timing device to run out before detonating. Cameron and his crew, given coffee and schnapps and blankets to warm them, knew only of the four tons for which they were responsible. Taken for interrogation, they were unable to resist furtive looks at their watches; but there was little the Germans could do in spite of the warning this inevitably gave them. By working cable the captain was able to slew the ship a few yards so that it was no longer directly over the spot where *X6* had sunk but even so when at 0812 two heavy, almost simultaneous explosions took place, the great ship leapt bodily, tossing men into the air; all lights went out and her twisted hull settled back with a list to port with fuel pouring from her amidships.

Panic spread amongst the German crew, guns being fired wildly in every direction as well as at *X7* which had been blown to the surface by the explosion and clear of the net in which she had been entangled. In the confusion the German gunners opened fire on their own tankers and picket-boats. One machine-gun firing at random wiped out a gun's crew on board their own ship. Besides one killed and 40 injured by the explosion, some 60 more were killed or wounded by this undisciplined stampede.

In the brief view he had before taking his boat down and out of the fire being directed at him, Place was disappointed to see that the *Tirpitz* was still afloat. But in fact she had received heavy damage from which she never fully recovered, and which kept her completely immobilized for seven months.

Meanwhile *X7*, her compasses and depth-gauges damaged by the explosion, kept surfacing as Place struggled to extricate her from the maze of defensive netting. On each occasion she was smothered by gun-fire and suffered hull damage. The time came to abandon ship. Fortunately she came to the surface alongside a target raft, on to which Place was able to step out. Before the other three members of his crew could extricate themselves from the narrow, constricted spaces they occupied, the craft sank again. Two and a half hours later Sub-Lieutenant Aitken came to the surface with the aid of his escape apparatus, but the two other members of the crew had died when the oxygen gave out after the boat had filled with fumes.

X5, the third boat to get within sight of the *Tirpitz*, arrived later than the other two and after the explosion. When she broke surface at the outer net defence, she found a fully alerted defence. A blast of fire put her down and depth-charges finished her destruction and that of her gallant crew.

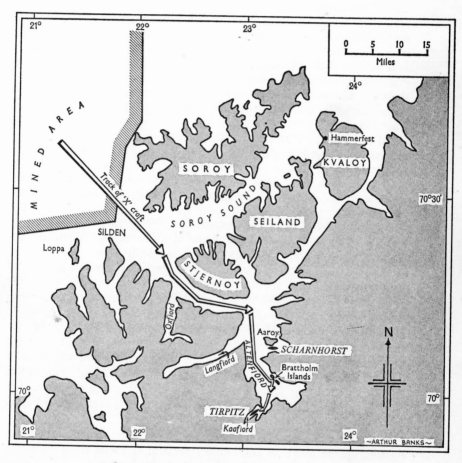

Midget submarines attack *Tirpitz*, September 1943

The *Tirpitz* had been eliminated for the time being. The *Lützow* had already returned to Germany for refit; so now only *Scharnhorst* and six destroyers were left effective in the north. The Admiralty decided at once to resume Arctic convoys.

The first and most urgent need was to fetch back the empty ships, the unfortunate crews of which had been lying idle in North Russia since the spring. A force of eight fleet destroyers, one Western Approaches destroyer-escort, two minesweepers and a corvette was assembled to form their escort under the command of Captain Ian Campbell of the *Milne*.

It was decided to take advantage of this force to convoy five Russian minesweepers and six Russian motor submarine chasers which were on their way to Polyarnoe, the fleet destroyers to act as a covering force, the remainder under the command of Captain Jay of the *Harrier* to be their close escort.

All arrived safely at Kola on 28 October and for the first time the escorts were berthed alongside the jetties in Polyarnoe naval base, Admiral Archer, head of our naval Mission, having at last persuaded the Russians to offer this small hospitality. Encouraged by this, Campbell made a brave effort to establish normal friendly relations with their fleet.

Besides the usual official calls, visits were exchanged between his ships and the Russians. The C-in-C, Admiral Golovko and Campbell exchanged dinners and presents. But it was uphill work. The language difficulty could have been overcome with good-will, but all gaiety and light-hearted talk was smothered by the attitude of the dour, unsmiling political commissars who attended every occasion, their mean, suspicious eyes flickering like those of cornered animals.

The return convoy of 13 ships suffered no interference from the enemy. Indeed it would have been something of a miracle if the Germans had found it at all in the combination of fog, snow and winter gales through which it made its blind, storm-tossed way. The only moment of interest in the voyage was the sighting in a brief clearance of the weather on 6 November of the legendary Bear Island, so often referred to but so very seldom seen by travellers on the Kola Run.

Pale winter sunshine, almost the last it would see for two months, lighting up the hump of land solidly encased in virgin snow gave it a forlorn beauty of its own. But it did not invite closer acquaintance, though a wag amongst the escort captains made a signal to the escort commander, 'Request permission to land libertymen!'

Bear Island was one of those sinister, solitary outcrops of land in the ocean which the seaman views with a shiver of distaste. Another is Haalsbakur or the Whale's Back off the coast of Iceland, a smooth expanse of glistening grey rock lying awash and quite unmarked. In calm weather a long uneasy swell laps it, spreads smoothly over to smother it with barely a hint of warning foam so that it seems to lie waiting in malevolent ambush for the unwary mariner.

The Kola Run had become a very different affair now that Dönitz had accepted the unwisdom of pitting his wolf-packs against well-escorted convoys. Through November and early December of 1943 they ran unmolested.

In his flagship *Duke of York*, the C-in-C, Admiral Fraser, pondered this strange immunity. For he knew that the powerful battle-cruiser *Scharnhorst* and her attendant destroyers were still lying in brooding menace in Altenfiord, whence a short run would bring them to the convoy route. He could only conclude that the Germans had not woken up to what was going on. So that when convoy JW55A, which had left Loch Ewe on 12 December was sighted and shadowed by an aircraft, he felt sure it would rouse the German fleet to some activity.

He therefore decided that the time had come to give close battleship cover to the convoys even inside the Barents Sea. While JW55A was making its passage, therefore, he took the *Duke of York* through to Kola and berthed her in Vaenga Bay for a few days.

The C-in-C was quite right in his belief but for the wrong reasons. The German Naval War Staff had known at once when the Arctic convoys were resumed. But to do something about it was quite another matter. Dönitz was unwilling to accept the losses in U-boats which attack on convoys now entailed. Improved, fast, Type XXI boats and others fitted with the schnorkel, the breathing tube which enabled them to stay submerged indefinitely, would be coming to sea soon, but until then the convoys were to be left alone.

On the other hand Dönitz's staff and the Group Command, North, had been greatly impressed by the evidence that had accumulated on the British radar equipment—radar using the centimetric wave band which gave greatly improved surface warning performance. The German ships had nothing like it. To risk the *Scharnhorst*, the last of Germany's big ships fit for battle, in the winter darkness and snow under such a handicap would be foolish. Such was the view of the German Naval High Command.

But Dönitz, who had achieved his Grand Admiral's baton by his assurance to Hitler that victory at sea could be won by his U-boats on their own, was now forced to eat his words or admit himself impotent to interfere with Allied sea traffic a bare 200 miles from German-held territory. Thus he found himself seeking Hitler's permission to send *Scharnhorst* out against the next convoy.

The Fuehrer's intuition was as unreliable in naval matters as ever. Now, when the opportunity to strike at the Arctic convoys with impunity had gone with the steady attrition his fleet had suffered, Hitler took courage to give Dönitz his head.

Two Arctic convoys were at sea in the latter half of December. JW55B, with a big escort under the command of Captain James McCoy in the *Onslow*, had left Loch Ewe on the 20th. A homeward convoy RA55A left two days later from Kola, its escort under Captain Campbell in the *Milne*. This latter convoy slipped out of harbour and away into the dark and fog to the north undetected and by Christmas Day had passed Bear Island in safety.

JW55B, however, was located as early as 22 December. At once preparations were put in hand at Altenfiord. Minesweepers were set to sweep the exit channel and *Scharnhorst* and her five destroyers were prepared for sea. There they lay, ready to pounce as soon as air reconnaissance or U-boats reported the convoy well into the Barents Sea.

As Christmas approached that year of 1943, it was the crews of the German ships who were best able to enjoy the traditional celebrations up there in the bleak northern latitudes. Snug in harbour they sang their nostalgic Christmas songs; the strains of *Heilige Nacht* echoed from the steep sides of the fiord. Only a bustling of staff officers round the Admiral's cabin in the *Scharnhorst*, a coming and going of signalmen, an increase in the frequency of gun drills, gave an indication that the interminable wait, the ships moored securely inside anti-torpedo nets, was about to come to an end.

But for the Allied ships of the two convoys and the British had Canadian ships of their escorts there was nothing but the date to tell them that it was Christmas. In wild, tempestuous weather they were rolling and plunging their way. There was no turkey or plum pudding for them—more likely a sandwich and a mug of cocoa from a swamped galley.

In the British fleet there was a strong feeling, based on no real evidence, that great events were impending. Both James McCoy, commanding JW55B's escort, and Bruce Fraser, one an Irishman, the other a Highlander, had strong premonitions. The latter so much so that as early as the 24th, when *Scharnhorst* was still mewed up in harbour, he gave orders for JW55B to reverse its course for three hours, calculating that this would prevent the enemy from making contact with it before dark on that day, though in fact German surface forces had never operated so far west.

By Christmas Day the homeward convoy, RA55A, was past Bear Island and reasonably safe, while JW55B was approaching the danger area. Still convinced that something was up, the C-in-C, at sea in the *Duke of York* with the cruiser *Jamaica* and four destroyers, ordered Captain Campbell, escorting RA55A, to send four of his destroyers to reinforce James McCoy. Accordingly Commander Fisher of the *Musketeer* was sent with *Matchless*, *Opportune* and *Virago*.

Meanwhile in Altenfiord, the *Scharnhorst* and five destroyers were raising steam. A Rear-Admiral's flag flew at the battle-cruiser's mast-head, for Vice-Admiral Kummetz was on leave. In his place was Rear-Admiral Bey, a destroyer man through and through, senior surviving officer of the destroyer squadron annihilated in the battles of Narvik and lately commodore of destroyers.

Since the 22nd, when JW55B was first located, his staff had watched the situation developing. The Luftwaffe was entrusted with the duty of maintaining contact and of reconnoitring the whole area for 300 miles round the convoy to bring warning of any covering force. For Bey's orders were precise that though there were to be no half measures in taking *Scharnhorst* in to smash the convoy with her big guns if contact were made, on no account was he to stand and fight if heavy units were met.

The German airmen kept contact with the convoy for the next two days but failed to locate either the *Duke of York* and her squadron to the west or Vice-Admiral Burnett's force of cruisers, *Belfast*, *Norfolk* and *Sheffield*, to the eastward. As darkness fell on Christmas Eve the weather was deteriorating and by the following day was too bad for air reconnaissance. U-boats were in touch, however, and continued to keep Bey informed as to the position and progress of the convoy.

By the evening of Christmas Day it was calculated that by daylight the next morning the convoy would be nicely placed for an attack on it. As dark was falling, Rear-Admiral Bey led his force to sea. The plan which he had communicated to his destroyer captains was for interception to be made shortly before dawn, when three of the destroyers would shadow until there was sufficient light for the battle-cruiser to bring her big guns into play. Then *Scharnhorst* would move in and, with point blank, devastating salvoes, annihilate the convoy. If any heavy ships should appear the action was to be broken off immediately by the *Scharnhorst* while the destroyers would fight a delaying action to cover her retreat.

The plan entirely ignored the greatly superior radar in the British ships or assumed that the escorts would stand idly by while the Germans waited for daylight to begin the action. In any case the Germans would have had to show a great deal more daring than in the past to carry it out in face of the torpedo threat from the British and Canadian destroyers of the escort. But it was never to be put to the test.

Hardly had the German squadron put to sea than Bey began to have doubts. In the heavy seas running, the fighting efficiency of the German destroyers would be much reduced. The heavy guns with which they were armed made them bad sea-boats compared to their British counterparts. Bey asked the shore command for instructions whether the operation should proceed.

The matter was referred to Dönitz himself. There can be little doubt by now the politician in him was overriding the seaman. His reputation with the Führer was at stake. In spite of his sea commander's obvious misgivings, he ordered the operation to proceed. What is more, Bey was told that the *Scharnhorst* might carry on alone at his discretion.

So the die was cast. The great ship rolled on northwards through the rough cold night. Bey's signal picked up by Allied direction-finding stations told the Admiralty that the *Scharnhorst* was out. When the C-in-C, Home Fleets received this news early on the 26th, he knew the time was past for finesse. All that mattered now was to draw the *Scharnhorst* as far north as possible and to get Burnett's force in the convoy's vicinity where they could hold the battle-cruiser in play long enough for the *Duke of York* to come pounding eastward to gain a position between *Scharnhorst* and her base.

To do this, the exact positions of the various units must be known to each other. Wireless silence was broken to order McCoy to divert his course to the north-east to delay the enemy's interception and lure him northward, to order McCoy and Admiral Burnett to report their positions and the latter to close the convoy.

By 0730 that morning these moves were in train. While the German squadron held to its northerly course, closing it rapidly from the eastward were Burnett's cruisers. Then at 0800 a signal reached Bey from one of the U-boats which made it appear that he had crossed ahead of the convoy and was now too far to the north. He at once swung round to a south-westerly course and, reducing to 12 knots, spread his destroyers five miles apart across his front to search.

The British wireless signals if intercepted by direction-finding stations would have given the enemy a rough picture of the disposition of the forces they were liable to meet. But for some reason no advantage seems to have been taken by the Germans of the information thus handed to them, and Bey knew nothing of the near presence of Burnett's squadron nor of the more distant force under the C-in-C.

Similarly in the British cruisers there was as yet no sure knowledge of the enemy's position. But it was known that *Scharnhorst* was somewhere at sea and Burnett was following sound principles in heading north-west to join the convoy, the prize which must surely lure the *Scharnhorst* to it also. He was thus closing the *Scharnhorst* on a course roughly at right-angles to the enemy's when at 0840 radar in the *Belfast* reported a contact at $17\frac{1}{2}$ miles range, west-north-west.

The range decreased rapidly but it was still night, clear and cold but rough and very dark, so that it was not until nearly 0930 that, from the *Sheffield*, the dim bulk of the great battle-cruiser could be made out. At the same moment the *Belfast* opened fire with starshells.

In the *Scharnhorst*, in spite of two presumably serviceable radar sets, there was no forewarning. The first thing that her commander, Captain Hintze, knew was the sudden blossoming overhead of the brilliant yellow flare of a starshell, lighting up the whole length of the ship and exposing her to a hidden enemy. Immediately afterwards the first tall columns from the splash of eight-inch shells rose out of the water alongside.

Surprise was complete and became consternation as an 8-inch shell from the *Norfolk* burst against the *Scharnhorst*'s fore-top, causing many casualties and wrecking her forward radar set. A second shell burst on her forecastle immediately afterwards.

Unable to see the enemy who had taken him thus unawares, Hintze called for full speed and swung his ship round to the south and then south-east. Shells continued to fall around her but there were no further hits and, as speed worked up, her smaller opponents were shaken off. Burnett's cruisers were unable to match the *Scharnhorst*'s 30 knots in the heavy seas that were running, but they struggled along in chase for a time.

As the ranges passed down from the radar steadily increased, Burnett appreciated that he was unable to hold contact with his speedier enemy. All would be thrown into doubt again as the *Scharnhorst* ran out of radar range. But before this took place the British admiral realized that the enemy was edging gradually round to a course of east and then north-east, circling round the cruisers for a new thrust at the convoy. By turning back to his north-westerly course, Burnett could again get between the *Scharnhorst* and the convoy. This he did, confident that it would bring about the further contact which was so vital.

But in the *Duke of York*, still nearly 200 miles away to the westward and pressing forward at her best speed with the south-westerly gale behind her to get between *Scharnhorst* and her base, Sir Bruce Fraser could not be so sanguine. If Bey had turned at once for home, the *Duke of York* would be too late and the *Scharnhorst* would have slipped out of the net. Meanwhile contact had been lost and all was agonized guesswork.

But it was not only on the British side that the brief action had brought uncertainty and anxiety. Communications between the German admiral and his destroyers had been disrupted and while the *Scharnhorst* swerved away to the north-eastward, the flotilla continued on their south-westerly search all unaware that the battle-cruiser had been in action.

By 1000 communications were restored and when Bey found that his destroyers were still searching in the wrong direction he ordered them to turn back to the north-east at high speed. But they were by then too far separated and, as we shall see, were never in fact able to rejoin their flagship.

So for the next two hours, while the Arctic winter daylight grew towards a twilit noon, the two German units and three British went their separate ways. The convoy was steering away to the north-eastwards on orders from the C-in-C, who had also told McCoy to send four of his destroyers to join Admiral Burnett. Accordingly Commander Fisher's division of four ships was despatched and shortly before 1100

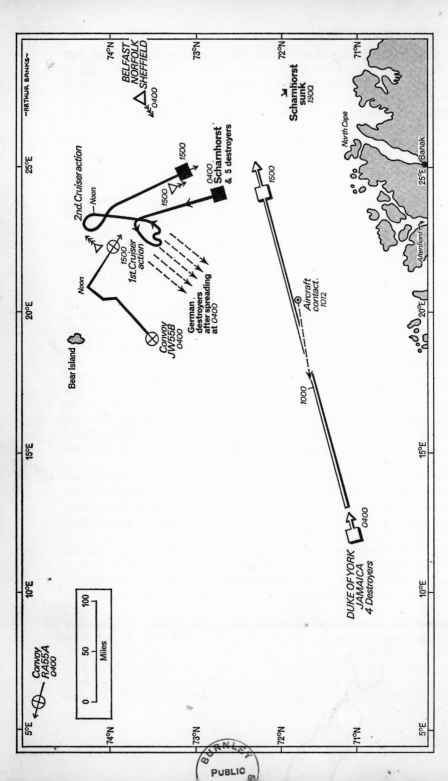

Destruction of the *Scharnhorst*, 26 December 1943

joined the cruisers. Burnett now disposed his ships to await the thrust at the convoy he was sure the *Scharnhorst* would make. While his cruisers zigzagged across the convoy's front and ten miles ahead of it, *Musketeer*'s division was thrown forward four miles as a screen.

Meanwhile a German reconnaissance aircraft had at last located Admiral Fraser's force and had reported its position as 150 miles to the westward of *Scharnhorst* and coming east. The signal as it reached Bey omitted to say, however, that amongst the force was a battleship. Confident in the strength of his splendid ship, designed to withstand as many as 14 torpedo hits, and urged on by a signal from Dönitz exhorting him to 'strike a blow for the gallant troops on the eastern front by destroying the convoy', the Rear-Admiral had discounted this new threat and pressed on for the convoy.

As time wore on without further development, McCoy had decided to resume the convoy's course to the south-east as he had been given discretion to do. The resultant protracted manoeuvre by the unwieldy convoy was still in progress when, at 1205, the *Belfast*'s radar picked up the *Scharnhorst* approaching from the east and Burnett knew that his hunch had been right. Fifteen minutes later she hove in sight.

The cruisers' guns at once roared out and Fisher's destroyers were ordered to attack with torpedoes. But Bey, exasperated to find his late antagonists still barring his way to the convoy, at once turned away to the south-east. Though Fisher took his destroyers in chase and added the fire of his guns to that of the cruisers, there was no possibility of getting into torpedo-firing position.

With daylight, *Scharnhorst* gave a better account of herself in this second action. Revenge was taken on the *Norfolk* who was twice hit. One 11-inch shell plunged through the barbette of a turret putting it out of action. Another hit amidships did much damage and started a serious fire. One officer and six ratings were killed and five others seriously wounded. But *Norfolk* remained in the line, her speed not affected.

From the British angle, though it was thought at the time that *Scharnhorst* was again hit, she did not in fact suffer further damage then. But Bey had had enough and was now heading for home. However, shortly before this encounter he had given his flotilla the convoy's position as reported by a U-boat and had ordered them to attack it.

The U-boat's signal had been greatly delayed in reaching him and the position was too far to the westward. As the German destroyers turned to obey they were, had they but known it, a bare eight miles to the southward of the convoy. Another ten minutes on their previous course and they would have run slap against it as it steered south-east.

It is fascinating to speculate what might have occurred. The five powerful German ships would have been facing seven less well-armed British and Canadian destroyers, and three older destroyer-escorts. The British force, however, would have been caught widely scattered round the perimeter of the convoy, and before they could have concentrated individual ships might have been overwhelmed. On the other hand, the lack of seaworthiness of the German ships might have cancelled out their advantage in the heavy weather prevailing.

It is impossible to guess what might have happened, and the encounter was not to be. Running off to the westward the German destroyers passed off the scene and an hour and a quarter later were ordered to break off operations and return to harbour.

For Bey had given up all hope of carrying out his mission after his second brush with Burnett and was anxious only to get back safely to harbour himself. But *Scharnhorst*'s fate was already sealed. The time spent in chasing northwards after the convoy had, as Admiral Fraser had hoped, destroyed any chance of escaping the doom hurrying towards her. For all the while, Fraser's squadron, in spite of the heavy following seas which threatened his destroyers with the danger of broaching-to, was racing on at 24 knots.

As Bey now set off for home at high speed, the range opened out. The cruisers ceased fire and settled down to shadow from astern, their excellent radar keeping them informed of every move made by the battle-cruiser, the information being passed on to the C-in-C.

Burnett was well content with the situation. For, all unknown to the Germans, interception by the *Duke of York* was now certain. Already Admiral Fraser had divided his destroyer force into two sub-divisions and stationed them one on each bow, whence, when the time was ripe, they would be able to press on to take the *Scharnhorst* under torpedo fire from two sides.

Time crept by with agonizing slowness in the British force as the two great ships drew near, their courses at right angles to one another, while the short Arctic day faded. Radar operators' eyes in the *Duke of York* almost left their sockets as they strained towards their scans to get the first signs of a contact. Captain Guy Russell paced the bridge in feverish impatience. The C-in-C's burly form stood rigid with anticipation in his operations room as he waited for the word which would tell him that the enemy was delivered into his hands. Excitement through the ship was intense. The weary months of oft-repeated sweeps without ever catching a glimpse of the enemy were now to be rewarded.

Then, at last, at 1615, there was a sudden stir. The 'blip' was there on the scan. Contact at 23 miles.

Almost Bruce Fraser could feel he had the *Scharnhorst* in the hollow of his hand. But the German battle-cruiser still had the legs of any big ship in the British force. Unless her speed could be somehow reduced, she might slip out of the trap yet. How well Guy Russell had trained his ship to shoot would be the ultimate arbiter of the coming action.

For another 35 minutes the *Duke of York* pounded on, the range coming steadily down. At 1650 the *Scharnhorst* was within hitting range and once again, all unaware of her danger, she was suddenly illuminated by a starshell from the *Belfast* as Burnett delivered her into the hands of his C-in-C.

As the great silver-grey length of the *Scharnhorst* sprang into view, the 14-inch guns of the *Duke of York* erupted into action. Out of the very first salvo, a shell hit the German on her starboard bow, abreast the foremost turret which was put out of action at once. A minute later another wreaked heavy damage on the quarter-deck As a demonstration of accurate gunnery it was superb.

Surprise was again complete. The huge pillars of water showing that they were large shells falling round were Bey's first indication that a battleship had come on the scene. Turning to flee, Captain Hintze swung his ship round to the north. But there he found *Belfast* and *Norfolk* waiting for him. Only to the eastward was there temporary safety and, piling on his utmost speed, Hintze headed in that direction.

Running now directly away from the *Duke of York*, the *Scharnhorst*'s range began to increase again. As the battle-cruiser swerved with each salvo so as to bring all her guns to bear, the gunnery problem for the *Duke of York* became more difficult. No more hits were scored for more than an hour, while the *Scharnhorst*'s gunnery, once she had recovered from her initial surprise, steadily improved. The *Duke of York*, pressing on in chase, moved through leaping shell splashes and had both her masts shot through though the shells did not explode.

At 1715, Fraser's two pairs of destroyers had been sent on at their best speed to try to get into position to fire torpedoes. Careering wildly along in the following sea, they were more than ever in imminent danger of broaching-to. Sweating coxswains in their wheelhouses wrestled with the wheel as each successive wave gathered under the stern and threatened to spin their ships round and over on their beam ends. Fuel was low in all of them and such a happening might have meant capsizing. But the hunt was up, the quarry in view. The destroyers' torpedoes might be the deciding factor in bringing the *Scharnhorst* to book. On they drove at full speed.

They were gaining but slowly, however. Commander Meyrick in the *Savage* was leading the *Saumarez*, aiming to get out on the enemy's port side, while Lieutenant-Commander Clouston in *Scorpion* and the Norwegian *Stord* were slanting southwards to take the enemy on her other flank. Commander Fisher's four destroyers, also sent off to the attack, were creeping forward on a course parallel to the enemy's and some miles to the northward, hoping to be in a position to synchronize their attacks with the others when the time came.

But it was only with agonizing slowness that the range in the destroyers was coming down. The *Duke of York* was dropping back, unable to match the battle-cruiser's speed. If the enemy kept on her easterly course it was likely that the *Scharnhorst* would yet escape. By 1820 the destroyers were still six miles astern of the fleeing battle-cruiser. Then, suddenly, the whole picture changed. A shell from the *Duke of York* landed square on the *Scharnhorst* causing underwater damage. Her speed rapidly fell away from 30 knots to 20. The exultant destroyer captains found themselves overhauling their target hand over fist.

By 1840 the range from the *Savage* was down to 10,000 yards and rapidly decreasing. As the *Scharnhorst* turned her secondary armament on to them, the destroyers also opened fire. In the *Scharnhorst* there was great confusion in the gunnery control. Her fire was wild and ineffective and the two destroyers pressed on undamaged, while from the other side of the battle-cruiser, *Scorpion* and *Stord* were coming in unseen.

At 1849, in the light of starshells from *Savage* and *Saumarez*, the enemy was seen to be swinging round to a southerly course, turning at bay. This put *Scorpion* and *Stord* at last in a good position for torpedo fire and they at once turned to starboard to bring their tubes to bear, each firing eight torpedoes at a range of a mile. The *Scharnhorst* swung to comb the tracks so that only *Scorpion* was able to claim one hit. At the same time the battle-cruiser's secondary armament came belatedly into action, firing wildly and without effect while the destroyers' 4.7-inch guns slammed shells into the superstructure of their huge target.

Continuing her circle to starboard until she was on a south-westerly course, the *Scharnhorst*, continuously illuminated by starshell flares hanging like a chandelier in the sky over her, now offered herself a target for *Savage* and *Saumarez*. Turning in to the attack at 1855, they drew heavy fire on themselves, particularly the nearer of the two, the *Saumarez*. Hit several times and her decks swept by a storm of splinters which killed one officer and ten ratings and wounded 11 more, *Saumarez* yet managed to get four torpedoes away at a range of 1,800 yards while *Savage* launched her full outfit of eight from a longer range. As they withdrew to the northwards, three distinct concussions were felt as torpedoes got home.

In the *Scharnhorst* there was great confusion by this time. Bey had for some time realized that her end was in sight and had made his last signal to the shore announcing that 'they would fight to the last shell'. And now the *Duke of York* and *Jamaica*, who had ceased firing while the destroyers were so close to their target, re-engaged at a range on 10,400 yards, a killing range for their guns. The great battle-cruiser was smothered with shell hits, fires blazing up and ammunition round the guns exploding. Her main armament was partially out of action and firing only intermittently. Her speed was falling away until it was barely 5 knots.

At 1915 the *Belfast* also joined in from the northward. The death struggles of the dying giant were a fearful sight. Built to be virtually unsinkable by gunfire, her end when it came was bound to be prolonged and agonizing. The C-in-C ordered the *Duke of York* to cease fire and the

Belfast and *Jamaica* to go in and finish the enemy off with torpedoes. Closing in with guns blazing, the cruisers each fired three torpedoes but, misjudging the speed of the *Scharnhorst*, hidden as she was in a pall of smoke, none hit.

A last wild burst of gunfire from the German's secondary armament achieved nothing. By the time the *Jamaica* had turned to fire three more torpedoes, two of which hit, the *Scharnhorst*'s guns were finally silent.

The *Belfast* was similarly manoeuvring to repeat her attack when she found the target masked by the arrival of Commander Fisher's four destroyers bent on being in at the death. *Scharnhorst*'s turn to the southward had left them toiling astern and only now had they been able to reach the scene of action. The oily wake left by the dying battle-cruiser led them to their quarry. Dividing into two sub-divisions, they came, punching into heavy seas, to the attack, *Opportune* and *Virago* from starboard, *Musketeer* and *Matchless* from port. From *Opportune* eight torpedoes sped away, of which two were claimed as hits. From *Virago*, out of seven fired, two were seen to find the target. Then *Musketeer* got four torpedoes away and saw at least two of them hit. Only *Matchless*, the training gear of her torpedo tubes damaged by a heavy sea which had swept her decks, and the bridge swamped by another, was unable to fire.

But it was enough. A dense cloud of smoke, a dull glow at its heart, was all that could now be seen of *Scharnhorst*'s death throes. At 1945, after a heavy underwater explosion, the glow vanished. Nearly 2,000 men and a once splendid ship had met their end. Thirteen hits by 14-inch shells and a dozen more by 8-inch, besides numerous smaller hits by the destroyers' guns, had battered the *Scharnhorst* to a wreck. But it had taken 11 torpedoes to send her to the bottom.

Nothing remained but to rescue as many survivors as possible. But out of 1,903 officers and men and 40 cadets, only 36, all ratings, could be found by *Scorpion* and *Matchless* as they searched amongst the debris. The bitter cold and high seas had claimed most of those who had survived the savage hammering their ship had suffered before its end.

Now, gathering together his scattered forces, Sir Bruce Fraser, well satisfied, steered for Kola where all arrived on the next day to be followed shortly by the convoy, from which nothing of the great fight in its defence had been seen or heard.

Well might the Admiralty reply to the C-in-C's signal of success with, 'Grand. Well done.' For the sinking of the *Scharnhorst* marked the last effort of Germany's surface fleet to challenge British sea power. Henceforth the convoys to Russia would have only Dönitz's U-boats to face and a minor threat from the demoralized Luftwaffe, to meet which the escorts were now fully equipped and trained. The Kola Run had another 17 months of life ahead of it but never again would the convoys have to accept the heavy odds which had always been potentially there if

M

the Germans had been prepared to use their powerful surface fleet with confidence and vigour.

For the time being the threat of attack by the heavy ships of the German fleet on the Arctic convoys which forced the Admiralty to retain so many ships with the Home Fleet, urgently needed elsewhere, had been eliminated. For the *Tirpitz* was still being laboriously repaired in the Norwegian fiord where the midget submarines had crippled her in the previous September.

For the remaining winter months the convoys had only the U-boats to contend with, a form of attack against which the defence had by this time been perfected. In spite of the long-awaited new secret weapon, the acoustic-homing torpedo ('Gnat'), with which the U-boats had now been armed, escorts in larger numbers, including a high proportion of fast destroyers, deployed in double screens to give defence in depth, operating in concert with Swordfish aircraft from escort carriers provided an effective defence.

Out of four Russia-bound convoys, totalling 128 ships, which made the 'Kola Run' before the summer brought them temporarily to a halt, only three ships were lost, though 'Gnats' accounted for two escorts. From the corresponding homeward-bound convoys, totalling 149 ships, only one was sunk.

In March 1944, however, information was received that the *Tirpitz* had completed the repairs made necessary by the midget submarine attack of the previous September and was about to go to sea from Altenfiord for trials. Her return to service would once again make the Arctic convoys a gamble against apparent odds, though, in fact, Hitler's continued restrictions on her being risked unless the Home Fleet's carriers had been eliminated, greatly reduced the threat she posed.

Nevertheless it was decided that the great battleship must again be put out of action. And now the Royal Navy had a weapon for the purpose in her Fleet Air Arm, at last emerging from the long eclipse suffered through its divorce between 1918 and 1937 from Admiralty control and administration. The lumbering Swordfish and Albacore biplanes had been replaced as the Navy's strike aircraft by the Fairey Barracuda, an aircraft of none too good a performance and far less than popular with naval pilots; but it filled the dual purpose of torpedo plane and dive-bomber—the first of the latter provided since the relegation of the Skua in 1940; and dive-bombing was essential to get at the target as she lay in the steep-sided fiords.

American carrier fighter planes—Grumman Wildcats and Hellcats and Vought Corsairs—had come to replace the outclassed Fulmars, Sea Hurricanes and, for the most part, the short-range and fragile Seafires, and had been embarked in escort carriers no longer required with the convoys.

With these new planes the Barracudas could be given fighter cover and the *Tirpitz* strafed to distract her anti-aircraft gun crews.

A carrier force was therefore assembled, comprising the fleet carriers *Victorious* and the veteran *Furious* from which two striking forces of 21 Barracudas each were to be launched, while 40 fighter escorts for each strike would come from the escort carriers *Emperor*, *Searcher*, *Fencer* and *Pursuer* as well as some from the fleet carriers.

Preliminary practices and rehearsals were carried out in a Scottish fiord, Loch Eriboll, on the north coast; and at dawn on 3 April 1944 the first swarm of planes took off in clear blue weather and headed for the target 120 miles away. The Barracudas were armed either with 1,600-pound armour-piercing bombs, 500-pound semi armour-piercing bombs, anti-submarine bombs with which it was hoped to cause underwater damage by near misses, or fragmentation bombs to cause personnel casualties.

To avoid detection by radar the whole formation skimmed low over the wave tops until, 50 miles from the shore, they climbed to 8,000 feet, the Corsairs soaring higher into the blue to give top cover. As the water of the fiord came into view, with the *Tirpitz* already weighing anchor before manoeuvring clear of her net obstructions, smoke from the screen generators was streaming across her; but it was still only partly covering her—not enough to hide her from the Hellcats and Wildcats as they swooped with their machine cannons clattering, or from the Barracudas as they dived steeply down to score a number of hits, wounding the *Tirpitz*'s captain and causing great confusion, at the cost of one Barracuda shot down.

The second strike found the smoke screen in full operation when they arrived, but this seemed to blind the flak batteries rather than the attacking planes which again scored repeated hits for the loss of only one Barracuda. As the roar of planes and the boom of gunfire ceased to echo round the hills and cliffs, the *Tirpitz* lay damaged by 14 bomb hits. From this she never recovered sufficiently to become fully operational. She was eventually moored at Tromsö where her big guns were given a coastal defence role. And there, at last, the RAF's expert blockbuster squadron succeeded in hitting her with 12,000-pound bombs causing her to capsize.

Like the monstrous Japanese battleships *Yamato* and *Musashi*, the *Tirpitz* went to the bottom sunk by air attack without ever having fired her guns at an enemy warship. Her presence alone, however, poised in the Norwegian fiords, and posing a threat both of a break-out on to the Atlantic convoy routes or against the Arctic convoys, had for two years tied up a large portion of the Royal Navy in the Home Fleet. With her final elimination the Royal Navy was freed to play its full part at last in the fight against Japan in the Pacific.

Before the convoys to Russia were resumed in August 1944, the biggest convoy operation as well as the biggest amphibious assault ever mounted had taken place in the English Channel. Before we conclude this volume with the very brief account of that final and decisive application of sea power we should, perhaps, see how the grim contest in Arctic waters went on without let-up until the very end of the war.

The first convoy of the season demonstrated the ascendancy the air and surface escorts had by this time established over the U-boats in the open ocean. Though the frigate *Kite* was torpedoed and sunk with the grievous loss of life inevitable in those icy waters, all efforts of the submarines to get at the convoy were beaten off and one of their number was destroyed. When the same pattern was repeated with subsequent convoys, though without the satisfaction of being able to hit back at the escorts successfully, the Germans decided to take advantage of their latest device, the 'schnorkel' breathing tube which enabled them to stay submerged indefinitely, to operate where the convoys were most vulnerable—in the approaches to Murmansk.

When the support groups attached to convoy JW61, which arrived there unopposed in October, 1944, went ahead to sweep the approaches to the Kola Inlet, they found the waters alive with U-boats. By dint of feverish activity, the frigates kept the submarines too occupied with their own preservation to hinder the safe arrival of the merchantmen and the carriers. But try as they would the asdic operators could wring no information out of the seemingly sound-proof Arctic waters, and no U-boats were sunk.

The combination of poor asdic conditions, schnorkels and Gnats had swung the advantage heavily on to the side of the Germans. Had their U-boat commanders been of the same calibre as those who had decimated the convoys in the early years of the war the situation would have been serious indeed. But the rapid expansion of the U-boat arm and its earlier heavy losses had inevitably led to a great many boats being sent to sea with inexperienced and scantily trained crews. Furthermore, though morale was to remain high in some submarines to the end, the clear indications of approaching defeat must have robbed others of the incentive to take any risks.

On the British side improved anti-submarine weapons were helping to redress the balance, in particular one known as the 'Squid'. This was fitted in many of the escort frigates and consisted of a four-barrelled mortar which could simultaneously hurl four depth-charge projectiles some hundreds of yards ahead of the ship. With the aid of an improved asdic set which would give an estimation of the target's depth, a submerged submarine could now be bombarded with considerable accuracy from a distance. The necessity to run over the target to deliver an attack as with depth-charges—and so lose contact at the crucial moment—was eliminated. It was a deadly weapon once contact with a U-boat was established.

But even so, so long as water conditions deadened the asdic's sound beam, the advantage still lay with the submarine. By flooding the sea area off the Kola Inlet with escorts at the appropriate moment it was at least possible to ensure the safe passage of the merchant ships in and out. Throughout the mid-winter months not one was lost; but casualties amongst the escorts were numerous and narrow escapes legion.

The first to suffer was the frigate *Mounsey*, damaged by a Gnat as the off-shore waters of Kola were being swept for the passage of RA61. She was able to struggle back to harbour on her own. But when the destroyer *Cassandra* was torpedoed while performing the same service for RA62, she was only saved by a notable feat of seamanship and endurance.

It might be thought, as the area where these torpedoings were taking place comprised the home waters of the Russian Northern Fleet at Polyarnoe, the Russians themselves would bestir themselves to drive off the U-boats. Submarine chasers built in America for them had been delivered in considerable numbers but they did little but rush about ineffectively. From Russian airfields near by, air patrols could have made life unbearable for the U-boats, but these were impossible, protested the Russians, because there were so many fishing boats off the coast which might be confused with U-boats.

Rear-Admiral Roderick McGrigor, who commanded many of the escorts of the convoys at this time, never missed an opportunity to chide the Russians on their lack of offensive spirit, but in vain. It was an inescapable fact that the Russians lacked all flair for naval warfare at that time, whatever they may have developed since. The success of the Arctic convoys owed almost nothing to the efforts of those for whose benefit they were run.

However, at the turn of the year, the Royal Navy could look with a good deal of satisfaction, if not complacency, at results so far. The vicious weather was still the enemy foremost in the minds of escorts and merchantmen alike. Eighty-knot gales with great rollers 45 feet in height charging down the wind, their crests streaming away before them in flying spume till the black darkness of the almost continuous Arctic night was as thick with it as fog, were the usual conditions they had to suffer. Even the high flight decks of the escort carriers were swept with green seas.

With increasing daylight in February, the Luftwaffe made a last effort to stage a come-back. Formations of 12 and 24 Ju.88s tried to attack the outward JW64; but fighters from the carriers made them pay heavily and they failed to score any success. It was still in Russian waters that the real danger lay. The last ship of this convoy was torpedoed as she shaped up to enter Kola Inlet and was only saved from total loss by being beached.

When escorts swept the approaches prior to the sailing of the next

homeward-bound convoy, the frigates *Lark* and *Alnwick Castle* found
and destroyed one of the lurking U-boats; but one of the convoy was sunk
and the corvette *Bluebell*, engaged in the Battle of the Atlantic from the
earliest days, blew up as a torpedo exploded in her magazine. Then more
than 20 torpedo-carrying Ju.88s made a spirited attack on the convoy
only to be foiled by smart manoeuvring of the merchantmen in the heavy
seas running at the time. A solitary straggler, however, was set upon and
sunk by another large formation.

It was off the Kola Inlet that the last losses of the Arctic convoys
occurred in the spring of 1945, two freighters and the frigates *Lapwing*
and *Goodall*. The long story ended with the arrival of convoy RA67 in
the Clyde on 31 April 1945.

It has been said not least often by the Russians, that the supplies
transported to Murmansk and Archangel at such cost and in such
hardships were but a drop in the ocean compared to the Russian needs.
The enemy did not think so, however.

Vice-Admiral Ruge, a distinguished German writer on naval affairs
has said,

> Between August 1944 and April 1945, the 250 plus ships on the Arctic
> run carried over 1,000,000 tons of war material. The weapons
> equipment and vehicles allowed the Russians to equip a further 60
> motorized divisions which gave them not only numerical but material
> superiority at focal points of the battles. Thus the Anglo-American sea
> power also exerted a decisive influence on the land operations in
> Eastern Europe.

It was fortunate for the Allies that such appreciation of the situation
was not made earlier in the war by the Germans. More than double this
number of ships had reached North Russia before the period reviewed by
Ruge. They had brought aid to the Russians at a time when they were
fighting with their backs to the wall, the rumble of enemy gunfire shaking
the windows of Moscow itself.

So the Arctic Ocean reverted to its immemorial, empty waste of wild
waters. Bear Island and Jan Mayen have become once again simply
names on maps and charts. The great icebergs drift southwards to their
dissolution all unseen. The mighty gales waste their demoniac forces on
thin air and shipless seas.

Long may it remain so.

16 Return to Europe:
The Final Triumph of Sea Power

Since those catastrophic days in 1940 when sea power had had to undertake its defensive role to extricate the defeated armies of Britain and her Allies from overrun France, there had never been a moment when Great Britain's ultimate aim had not been to return with whatever allies she could attract to her side and to resume the fight on the continent. Tentative plans looking as much as three years ahead were made, based on hopes of the decay of German military strength and of the re-establishment of sea and air domination of the surrounding waters.

When the United States ranged themselves alongside Britain in December 1941, the latter had ready to offer an outline plan—'Roundup' —for such a landing in the 'final phase of the war' which was hopefully foretold for 1943. With the prospect of American aid this was expanded to 'Sledgehammer'. But neither Russian demands for the opening of a Second Front, nor American euphoria, which led to wild underestimation of the magnitude and complexity of the task, could disguise the fact that such an operation could not be mounted before 1943.

Nevertheless it was only after President Roosevelt had been asked for a ruling that the American Chiefs of Staff had agreed to striking first in the Mediterranean and to launch Operation 'Torch'. Further British arguments at the Casablanca Conference had persuaded their ally that the invasion of Sicily and the elimination of Italy must be the next step and that not until 1944 could sufficient trained troops, landing craft and the multifarious other shipping that a Channel landing would require, be accumulated.

Some idea of the magnitude of these requirements had emerged from the deliberations of the Combined Allied Staff which, under Lieutenant-General F. E. Morgan, had been planning an invasion of France since the end of 1942. This plan, which envisaged an assault landing on the 30 miles of Normandy coast between the Rivers Orne and Vire, the widest front possible for the force of three assaulting divisions which had been allocated by the Chiefs of Staff, was approved at the Quebec Conference in August 1943.

In December 1943 General Eisenhower was apppoined Supreme Commander; he soon decided that the plan for Operation 'Overlord', as it was code-named, provided far too weak an assault on too narrow a front. General Sir Bernard Montgomery, appointed in the same month to command the military assault forces, and Mr Churchill both backed this view. Two extra divisions were to be allocated and the assault front increased to 50 miles by the addition of a further stretch of coast on the Cotentin Peninsula. To provide the extra divisions and shipping, the planned simultaneous Operation 'Anvil' on the south coast of France was put off and 'Overlord' was postponed from May to June.

Operation 'Overlord' as it finally emerged, with its subsidiary naval element 'Neptune', was the most grandiose and most intricate combined operation ever contemplated. This was on account not so much of the size of the military force committed as of the vastness and the immense variety of the supporting elements by sea and air made necessary by the almost impregnable coastal defences, by the lack of any port facilities in the assault area, and by the necessity to maintain a sea supply route for many weeks after the assault and to build up the strength of the assault forces at least as rapidly as the enemy could bring forward reinforcements.

From the fact that the orders for 'Neptune' alone comprised a book of 700 pages; that 1,213 warships and 4,126 landing ships and craft of 23 different types took part in it, it will be appreciated that only an outline is possible within the scope of this book.

The end-product of 'Neptune' was to be the delivery at the selected D-day and H-hour of two British and one Canadian division at beaches off Ouistreham (sword), Courseulles (Juno) and Asnelles (Gold) and of two American divisions at beaches off St Laurent (Omaha) and Varreville on the Contentin Peninsula (Utah). On the second tide of D-day the first follow-up troops would be landed; more on D+1 and then a steady build-up at the rate of one and a third divisions a day. Two Naval Task Forces were formed to achieve this; the Western (American) under Rear-Admiral A. G. Kirk, USN was responsible for landing the US First Army on Omaha and Utah beaches; the Eastern (British), commanded by Rear-Admiral Sir Philip Vian was to land the British Second Army on Gold, Juno and Sword.

Meanwhile, to secure the flanks of the beach-head, the 6th British Airborne Division were to be parachuted to the east of Caen during the night before D-day, while a similar American force was to be dropped at the foot of the Cotentin Peninsula.

To make the landings possible, various conjunct operations were necessary. The coastal defences, for instance, were of several kinds, each calling for special treatment. Off-shore were defensive minefields through which ten channels were to be swept and marked with light buoys by minesweepers steaming ahead of the assault convoys. Other sweepers would clear the anchorage area for the Landing Ships. Special clearance parties to deal with the obstacles thickly spread between high and low water marks would be among the first to disembark. Meanwhile in other channels specially swept for them, the three American and two British battleships, the 21 cruisers (14 British, 2 US, 2 Dutch, 2 French and 1 Polish) and 58 destroyers (33 British, 17 US, 3 Norwegian, 2 Polish, 2 Canadian and 1 French) of the bombardment forces were to engage the numerous enemy batteries of guns of various calibres, with the aid of air spotting by pilots of Spitfires each flying in company with an escort.

These batteries, most of them in heavy concrete casemates, perhaps the most daunting of the defences to be faced, would have been heavily attacked from the air in the period before D-day as part of a massive offensive widespread enough to prevent any indication of the selected assault area. But on the night before D-day heavy bombers would concentrate on the principal coast defences and shortly after daylight medium bombers would deal with other selected batteries; and finally the beaches were to be smothered in a 45-minute hail of bombs during which some 4,200 tons would be dropped.

While the assault convoys were approaching, the bombardment forces, by this time in their allotted positions, would simultaneously open their tremendous two-hour cannonade. Leading the assault would come the support landing craft mounting quick-firing artillery or with banks of rocket projectors capable of launching devastating flights of missiles. Only then would the first wave of assault troops, supported by amphibious tanks and other types equipped with whirling flails to explode ground mines, wade ashore to face the long-prepared defences of 'Fortress Europe'.

Such was the spearhead that was to be hurled by Operation 'Neptune'. It had then to be supported and its momentum maintained by a build-up of forces and a massive flow of supplies of all sorts for the disembarkation of which no port facilities existed. In substitution for these, a scheme as ingenious as it was bold had been devised—the construction of two artificial harbours or 'Mulberries' out of concrete caissons, 200 feet in length, and blockships, towed or steamed from various English ports and sunk in position.

Each 'Mulberry' was to comprise an outer breakwater about three and a half miles long composed of these caissons sunk end to end about a mile off-shore and parallel to it, with a 300-yard break to provide an entrance. From the end of this line, separated from it by gaps to provide two more entrances, two arms were to stretch shorewards. The area thus enclosed would provide a sheltered anchorage for seven deep-draught ships, more than 400 coasters, tugs and auxiliary vessels and 1,000 small craft.

Running out from the shore inside this area would be two floating roadways terminating at a long jetty, which could also move up and down

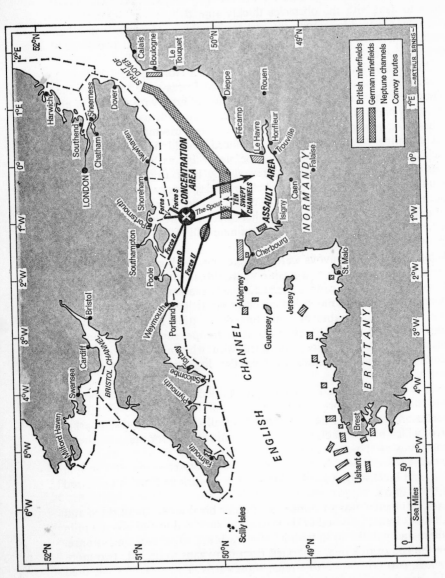

Operation 'Neptune', 5–6 June 1944

with the tide, where coasters could unload straight into trucks. A smaller pier would accommodate barges bringing supplies unloading from the big ships; another, the LST pier, was designed to take vehicles from landing ships. Half a mile outside this inner harbour, a line of floating steel structures known as 'Bombardons' was to be moored to provide some shelter for a deep-water anchorage.

The blockships—55 old merchant ships and four obsolete warships—were to be sunk, some alongside the main 'Mulberry' breakwaters to reinforce the caissons, the remainder to form three shelters (Gooseberries) for small craft close inshore, off Varreville in the American sector and off Courseulles and Ouistreham.

The construction, assembly and towage of the many unwieldy structures forming the 'Mulberries' was but one of the subsidiary operations which went to make up Operation 'Neptune'. There were many others, some of which will appear as they take their place in the narrative of events.

In the weeks preceding D-day which, on 8 May 1944 had been provisionally fixed for 5 June, the southern counties of England began to fill up with the troops and vehicles of the five assault forces which were to embark in numerous ports between Plymouth and Newhaven, the follow-up troops from the Thames, from Plymouth, Falmouth and Harwich, and those for the build-up from the Bristol Channel and the Thames. Naval covering forces assembled at other ports. No less than 286 escort vessels, mostly British and American but including Dutch, French, Polish and Norwegian ships, were moving to their start positions. The Solent and Spithead became jammed with shipping. The vital necessity to keep information of all this activity from the enemy offered one of many reasons why the cross-Channel invasion could not have been mounted earlier. An absolute command of the air so that not a single German reconnaissance plane was able to overfly the Channel coast was essential and had been achieved. To provide fighter cover for the 'Neptune' convoys and over the beach-head, 171 squadrons of Allied fighters had been allocated.

From his headquarters at Southwick House, near Portsmouth, Admiral Ramsay, on 28 May, promulgated to his forces that D-day was to be 5 June; the vast, complex series of movements called for by Operation 'Neptune' began with the unobtrusive departure in tow of two trawlers, of the midget submarines *X20* and *X23* on the evening of 2 June. They were to be slipped in mid-Channel before daylight on the 3rd and proceed to take up positions as mark-boats for Juno and Sword beaches. Soon afterwards the main British bombardment force composed of the battle-ships *Warspite* and *Ramillies*, the monitor *Roberts*, five cruisers and 15 destroyers sailed from the Clyde.

From then on, over the next 36 hours, from other ports round the coast, convoys of various compositions got under way at the times calculated to fit them into the intricate pattern which would bring them in their proper order to the assembly area south-east of the Isle of Wight, and thence by their allotted swept channel to the Normandy beaches. But during the night of the 3rd, the ruthless arbiter of all naval operations took a hand to show that even in mid-summer it could not be ignored: the wind rose out of the west to drive heavy seas up the Channel, making conditions on the beaches impossible.

The forecast for the 5th offered no hope of an improvement. At Southwick House, General Eisenhower was forced to postpone D-day for 24 hours. Convoys had to reverse course and anchor; unhappy soldiers, many miserably seasick, faced an extra day afloat. Worse—unless prospects for the 6th proved better, it would be necessary to postpone the operation for two weeks with all the complications and risks of loss of secrecy and surprise that that would entail.

The tense situation at Southwick as Eisenhower waited for the advice of his meteorologists has often been described. On the strength of a forecast of some improvement on the 6th, while the storm still raged, the decision was taken. The vast machinery of 'Neptune' was set again in motion and all through 5 June the convoys of assault craft were arriving on time at the assembly area, in spite of the rough seas, and turning south into their allotted routes down the 'Spout' already swept and marked by the minesweepers.

That such a vast armada could achieve complete surprise, even with the help of the various deceptions, diversions and ruses employed, was hardly to be hoped for. But in fact, owing to a combination of damage to some German radar stations by bombing raids and jamming of others, the enemy had been electronically blinded. The paratroop landings soon after midnight, of course, raised the alarm, but little action could be initiated and certainly no appreciation of an approaching invasion on a massive scale was made by the German defenders as they cowered for the next five hours under the hail of 5,000 tons of high explosive dropped by British bombers on the coastal batteries and on communications in their rear, followed by the bomb-loads of 1,630 American bombers. Not until the ships of the bombardment force loomed out of the twilight and at 0530 began their cannonade with guns of all sizes from 15-inch to 4-inch did realization of what faced them come to the Germans. Even then there was little they could do about it as the waves of fighter bombers and medium bombers concentrated on the beach defences while the first landing craft were making their approach, the rocket-fitted LCTs loosing their dense showers of vicious missiles.

The time for the touch-down of the first assault craft (H-hour) depended upon the state of the tide, the chief consideration being the beach obstacles which the Germans had strewn with a lavish hand. It was important that these should be uncovered at H-hour to permit the clearance teams to get to work and the landing craft to beach short of them. Thus H-hour in the American sector was at 0630, one hour earlier than in the Eastern Sector.

Each of the two Naval Task Forces had worked out their own time-table for the assault and ordered the method of execution. There were important differences. In the Western Sector the Lowering Position for the assault craft was established 11 miles off-shore as compared to seven miles in the Eastern Sector. The time ordered for opening the bombardment of the defences at Utah and Omaha was fixed for 0550, only 40 minutes before the assault craft were to touch down. At Gold, Juno and Sword the cannonade which opened at 0530 had two hours for the same purpose.

Neither of these factors seriously affected the landings on Utah partly owing to the comparatively smooth water in the lee of the Cotentin Peninsula which prevented confusion amongst the landing craft in spite of casualties and breakdowns of guide craft. The fact that the landings were made a mile farther down the coast than planned proved to be an advantage as they encountered less opposition than would otherwise have been the case. The longer run-in, which was to be so disastrous for the 'swimming' (DD) tanks at Omaha was avoided by the initiative of the LCT captains who took them in to 3,000 yards before launching them; they reached shore safely to give splendid support to the infantry. H-hour had been accurately assessed and difficulties in clearing the obstacles, experienced elsewhere, were avoided. Finally, the American paratroops had played their part efficiently and were already in control of the causeways leading inland from the beaches. So the landing at Utah was a splendid success. Against light opposition the assault troops pressed inland; behind them the follow-up progressed so rapidly that, by 1800 on D-day 21,328 men, 1,742 vehicles and 1,695 tons of stores had been landed.

To their left, across the River Vire, however, a far less happy situation had developed in the assault on Omaha. In the less sheltered offing a steep sea was running. During their three-hour run-in from the lowering position a number of assault craft foundered including many of those equipped to clear the obstacles. As the survivors reached them, some were wrecked as they tried to force a way through; but the majority brought up short and, manoeuvring sluggishly in the awkward sea, trying to find a gap, soon lost cohesion and became a disorganized mass. Soon the rising tide covered the obstacles; clearance would have to wait until the waters ebbed again; meanwhile the landing craft had to retire seawards to find room to re-form.

Such troops as had got ashore were met by heavy fire from the well-sited German batteries which neither the air bombardment nor the 40-minute cannonade by warships had been able to neutralize. Tank support, too, was less than planned owing to the launching of the DD tanks on the left too far out, leaving them three miles of breaking seas to cover. Only five of the 32 launched reached the shore. Fortunately on the right senior officers of the LCTs carrying the DDs had the good judgment to take their right craft into shallow water where the tanks grounded at once and successfully climbed out on to the beach.

Nevertheless the leading assault troops were pinned down on the beach throughout the forenoon under fire from artillery, mortars and machine guns. And even after the German beach defences were overcome and the American troops were able to advance, the follow-up troops were met by accurate artillery salvoes as their landing craft beached. Much of this galling fire came from the battery on Pointe de Hoc on the right wing of the assault where US Rangers had been given the task of scaling the cliffs and storming the position. Arriving late, 35 minutes after the bombardment by the 14-inch guns of the *Texas* had ceased at H-hour in accordance with the plan, they were met by heavy opposition from German troops who had thus been able to leave their shelters and man the cliff-top. Although, with the support of gunfire from two destroyers which closed to within 2,000 yards, they eventually reached the cliff-tops, they were pinned down there and cut off for the next 48 hours. Fortunately the six 6.2-inch guns of the battery, which had survived the bombardment through having been shifted from their casemates to a position about a mile away, were overrun and captured before the end of D-day.

Omaha was the one black spot of the whole, huge operation. As at Utah, the landings at Sword, Juno and Gold were splendidly successful even though tidal conditions, affected by the storm, were not as expected and the obstacles were under water. Casualties to landing craft were numerous as they beached amongst them. But though the beaches were soon littered with stranded craft, disembarkation and unloading were carried on in dauntless style. The long and heavy preliminary bombardment backed by further supporting fire from destroyers, from self-propelled guns in landing craft and the missiles of rocket craft during the landings, reduced the artillery opposition to a light scale. An exception was the western end of Gold, where batteries in the villages of Le Hamel and La Rivière had been missed by the air attacks aimed at them and were so sited as to be safe from low trajectory naval gunfire. The enfilading fire from these positions was not silenced until a combined attack by destroyers, support landing craft and a battalion of infantry led to their capture in the afternoon.

By the end of D-day a beach-head had been established along the whole 50-mile stretch of coast assaulted. In all 132,715 Allied soldiers had been put ashore; the leading troops were pushing inland; behind them reinforcements and supplies were pouring in; the 'impregnable' defences of Hitler's 'Fortress Europe' had been breached at the astonishingly low cost of some 4,300 British and 6,000 American casualties.

Space does not permit any account of the further progress of this gigantic combined operation; not even those purely maritime aspects of it, the establishment of the 'Mulberries' and 'Gooseberries', nor the havoc caused to the former and amongst the great concourse of shipping by the great gale of 19–22 June; the resultant critical hold-up of supplies to the Allied armies and the emergency steps which restored the situation.

The enemy's efforts to attack the anchorage and the many convoys of supplies that thronged the Channel from D-day onwards must, however, be touched on. So far as attack from the air is concerned, it is perhaps sufficient to say that the absolute ascendancy which had been established by the Allied Air Forces reduced it to negligible proportions by a combination of devastating bomb attacks to neutralize the Luftwaffe's air bases and a continuous fighter umbrella over the Channel. Thus were gathered the fruits of the years of fighting for air supremacy, fruits which would not have been ripe had 'Overlord' been mounted in the previous year as desired by Britain's allies.

The same can be said of the situation at sea. There the most serious opposition to be faced was that by the German U-boat fleet. This was still numerically large; many of the boats had by this time been equipped with the schnorkel breathing tube which enabled them to operate with some chance of success even in such narrow, easily air-dominated waters as the Channel. All were armed with improved torpedoes, including the acoustic homing type.

But their defeat in the Battle of the Atlantic in the previous year and the improved training and equipment and huge expansion of the British escort forces, surface and air, had give the latter an ascendancy as great as that of the Allied Air Forces over the Luftwaffe. Nevertheless the U-boat could still be a most elusive antagonist and no efforts were spared by the Admiralty to combat the desperate attempts they must surely make to get at the great concentration of shipping in the Channel.

Besides the escorts allocated to the many convoys which carried the assault, follow-up and build-up forces, ten anti-submarine support groups, including three escort carriers were deployed in the Western Approaches to the Channel. At the same time Coastal Command of the RAF was reinforced so that 21 squadrons were available to patrol the same area with such an intensity that any one position would be under observation every half-hour by night and day.

The odds against the U-boats were thus overwhelming. The results were to bear this out. By the end of June 12 U-boats had been sunk in the Bay of Biscay and the Channel area while in return two British frigates and an American LST had been sunk. During July and August the U-boats were little more successful, though in the latter month they succeeded in getting eight boats up Channel who, between them, sank six merchantmen, the Canadian corvette *Regina*, a LCT and a minesweeper. But during the two months they lost 11 in the Channel and the same number in the Bay of Biscay.

The threat from above and from below to the invasion force was thus successfully countered. The surface threat came primarily from German motor torpedo boats based chiefly at Le Havre and Boulogne and three of these from the former had come into action as early as the dawn of D-day when they attacked the bombardment ships of Sword force. The Norwegian destroyer *Svenner* was torpedoed and sunk but the other torpedoes were avoided.

These craft were essentially designed for night attacks. They attempted, with only minor success, to get at the convoys making for the invasion anchorage and, in their turn, were harried by Beaufighters of Coastal Command, which sank several of them. When air reconnaissance reported a growing number of them concentrated at Le Havre, a heavy raid by 325 Lancaster bombers destroyed 14 of them and sank about 40 other small craft. When Boulogne was similarly devastated the following day, the threat was eliminated until the arrival of fresh forces in July. Then the convoy escorts and British light forces again found themselves involved in confused night mêlées amidst streams of tracer bullets, the tracks of racing torpedoes and even collisions between opposing units. Though the German boats had no success on the cross-Channel route to and from the beaches, they succeeded in some attacks on convoys off the English coast. It was once again Bomber Command aircraft which put an end to their successes by attacking them in Le Havre.

The final effort by the Germans to disrupt the vital flow of supplies to the Normandy beach-head took the form of attacks by swarms of one-man torpedoes (Marders) and radio-controlled explosive motor boats (Linsen) on a number of occasions in July and August. They were ingenious and they were operated with a desperate gallantry; but they achieved little and nearly all were destroyed with their crews by the defensive screen of coastal and landing craft guarding the eastern flank of the assault area.

In the middle of August came the break-out by the Allies from the Normandy beachhead. Striking eastwards along the coast the British Second Army captured Dieppe on 1 September and Le Havre, which had been by-passed, on the 12th. The closure of the last of the Normandy supply beaches on 7 September marked the successful end of the greatest invasion operation in history and, it can be said, the greatest single, clear result of the five-year struggle to secure and maintain unchallenged sea power by sea and air.

Between 24 June and 12 September 1944, over a stretch of sea which had, since the summer of 1940, been largely denied to the shipping of both sides in the war, 1,410,600 tons of stores, 152,000 vehicles and 352,570 men had been safely carried.

The war in Europe had a further eight months to run. It was mainly fought on and over the land, however, though the Allied naval forces had still to launch an invasion in the south of France and to ensure the supply of the armies advancing towards Germany. The latter involved the clearance of the mouth of the Schelde, including a costly combined operation to capture the island of Walcheren. And as we have seen, support of the Russian ally by means of the Arctic convoys continued to the end.

But the naval task had been largely completed when the break-out from the Normandy beachhead took place. The Royal Navy could now turn to deploy its main strength alongside the US Navy in the Pacific to complete the defeat of Japan.

Wars cannot be won by maritime operations or sea power alone. In the end it is the soldiers who must, by their physical presence on the enemy's soil, force on the enemy the acceptance of defeat and the victor's terms. Nevertheless, in global war, sea power—the ability to use the seas freely for one's own purposes and prevent the enemy from doing so—is essential for victory.

In the 'Hitler War', as it is hoped this book has shown, control of sea routes by a combination of underwater, surface and air forces played a decisive part at every stage and in every theatre. Loss of sea power through inadequate air strength allowed the Germans to conquer Norway. Had the German U-boats succeeded in their attempt to control the North Atlantic, Great Britain's industry and war effort must have ground to a halt and her people must have been starved into surrender.

Winston Churchill was to write: 'Battles might be won or lost, territories might be gained or quitted, but dominating all our power to carry on the war, or even to keep ourselves alive, lay our mastery of the ocean routes and the free approach and entry to our ports. . . . The only thing that ever really frightened me during the war was the U-boat peril.'

Defeat of the U-boat also permitted the vast overseas expeditions to North Africa and Italy which inflicted defeat and crippling losses on the Axis and the elimination of Italy. In the Mediterranean, the inability of the Axis to control the oversea supply routes of their armies in Cyrenaica against sea and air attack defeated the potentially mortal Axis thrust into the Middle East and beyond.

Finally, only under conditions of complete supremacy at sea could the vast, complex operation to land Allied armies in France—a vital step towards the defeat of Germany—have been prepared, mounted and successfully launched.

The last word may well be left to Francis Bacon who, more than 300 years earlier, in his Essay 'Of the True Greatness of Kingdoms', had written:

Thus much is certain; that he who commands the sea is at great liberty, and, may take as much and as little of the war as he will.

Bibliography

GENERAL

Bernotti, Romeo, *La Guerra Sui Mari Nel Conflitto Mondiale*, Societa Editrice Tirrena, 1948

Bragadin, Commander, *The Italian Navy in World War II*, US Naval Institute, Annapolis, Md.

Cunningham, Admiral of the Fleet Viscount, *A Sailor's Odyssey*, Hutchinson, 1951

Dönitz, Admiral Karl, *Memoirs*, Weidenfeld and Nicolson, 1959

Morison, Professor S. E., *History of the US Navy in World War II*, Little, Brown & Co.; Oxford University Press

Raeder, Grand Admiral Erich, *The Struggle for the Sea*, Kimber, 1959

Roskill, Captain S. W., *The War at Sea*, 4 vols, HMSO London, 1954

Ruge, Vice-Admiral Friedrich, *Sea Warfare. A German Concept*, Cassell, 1957

RIVER PLATE

Pope, Dudley, *The Battle of the River Plate*, Kimber, 1956

NARVIK

Macintyre, Captain Donald, *Narvik*, Evans Bros., 1959

DUNKIRK

Divine, David, *The Nine Days of Dunkirk*, Faber, 1959

THE ATLANTIC

Frank, Wolfgang, *The Sea Wolves*, Weidenfeld and Nicolson, 1955

Gretton, Vice-Admiral Sir Peter, *Convoy Escort Commander*, Cassell, 1964

Macintyre, Captain Donald, *The Battle of the Atlantic*, Batsford, 1961

Seth, Ronald, *The Fiercest Battle, The Story of Convoy ONS 5*, Hutchinson, 1961.

THE 'BISMARCK'
Berthold, Will, *The Sinking of the 'Bismarck'*, Longman, 1958
Forester, C. S., *Hunting the 'Bismarck'*, Michael Joseph 1959
Grenfell, Captain Russell, *The 'Bismarck' Episode*, Faber, 1948

THE MEDITERRANEAN
Cameron, Ian, *Red Duster, White Ensign*, Muller, 1959
Clark, Alan, *The Fall of Crete*, Blond, 1962
Horsley, David, *Operation Pedestal*, Digit Bles, 1957
Iachino, Angelo, *Gaudo e Matapan*, Arnaldo Mondadori, Milan
Liddell Hart, Captain B. H., (Ed), *The Rommel Papers*, Collins, 1951
Macintyre, Captain Donald, *The Battle for the Mediterranean*, Batsford, 1964
Newton, Don, and Hampshire, A. Cecil, *Taranto*, Kimber, 1959
Pack, S. W. C., *The Battle of Matapan*, Batsford, 1961
Seth, Ronald, *Two Fleets Surprised*, Bles, 1960
Shankland, Peter, Hunter, Anthony, *Malta Convoy*, Collins, 1962.

THE ARCTIC
Campbell, Vice-Admiral Sir Ian, and Macintyre, Captain Donald, *The Kola
    Run*, Muller
Ludlam, Harry, and Lund, Paul, *PQ 17, Convoy to Hell*, Foulsham, 1968
Ogden, Lieutenant Michael, *The Battle of North Cape*, Kimber, 1962
Pope, Dudley, *73 North, The Battle of the Barents Sea*, Weidenfeld and
    Nicolson, 1958
Schofield, Vice-Admiral B., *The Russian Convoys*, Batsford, 1964
Tuleja, Thaddeus V., *The Eclipse of the German Navy*, Dent, 1959
Woodward, David, *The 'Tirpitz'*, Kimber, 1953

THE CHANNEL
Busch, Fritz-Otto, *The Drama of the 'Scharnhorst'*, Hale, 1956
Busch, Fritz-Otto, *The Story of the 'Prinz Eugen'*, Hale, 1960
Robertson, Terence, *Channel Dash*, Evans, 1958
Potter, John Deane, *Fiasco: Breakout of the German Battleships*, Heinemann,
    1970

NORMANDY LANDING
Edwards, Commander Kenneth, *Operation Neptune*, Collins, 1946
Michie, Alan A., *The Invasion of Europe, The Story Behind D-Day*, Allen &
    Unwin, 1963
Ryan, Cornelius, *The Longest Day*, Gollancz, 1960

Index